Toward Sustainability Through Digital Technologies and Practices in the Eurasian Region

Gainiya Tazhina
University of International Business, Kazakhstan

Judith Parker
Teachers College, Columbia University, USA

A volume in the Practice, Progress, and Proficiency in Sustainability (PPPS) Book Series

IGI Global
DISSEMINATOR OF KNOWLEDGE

Published in the United States of America by
IGI Global
Information Science Reference (an imprint of IGI Global)
701 E. Chocolate Avenue
Hershey PA, USA 17033
Tel: 717-533-8845
Fax: 717-533-8661
E-mail: cust@igi-global.com
Web site: http://www.igi-global.com

Library of Congress Cataloging-in-Publication Data

Names: Tazhina, Gainiya, 1956- editor. | Parker, Judith, 1943- editor.
Title: Toward sustainability through digital technologies and practices in the Eurasian region / Gainiya Tazhina and Judith Parker, editors.
Description: Hershey, PA : Information Science Reference, an imprint of IGI Global, [2020] | Includes bibliographical references and index. | Summary: "This book provides research on the implementation of digital initiatives within Eurasian countries and their social and economic principles. While highlighting topics such as educational technologies, mobile applications, and sustainable business, this publication explores the cultural aspects and social interaction of digital applications within this region of the world"-- Provided by publisher.
Identifiers: LCCN 2019042257 (print) | LCCN 2019042258 (ebook) | ISBN 9781799825517 (hardcover) | ISBN 9781799825524 (paperback) | ISBN 9781799825531 (ebook)
Subjects: LCSH: Computer networks--Social aspects--Eurasia. | Sustainable development--Eurasia.
Classification: LCC HM851 .T675 2020 (print) | LCC HM851 (ebook) | DDC 302.30285095--dc23
LC record available at https://lccn.loc.gov/2019042257
LC ebook record available at https://lccn.loc.gov/2019042258

This book is published in the IGI Global book series Practice, Progress, and Proficiency in Sustainability (PPPS) (ISSN: 2330-3271; eISSN: 2330-328X)

British Cataloguing in Publication Data
A Cataloguing in Publication record for this book is available from the British Library.

For electronic access to this publication, please contact: eresources@igi-global.com.

Practice, Progress, and Proficiency in Sustainability (PPPS) Book Series

Ayman Batisha
International Sustainability Institute, Egypt

ISSN:2330-3271
EISSN:2330-328X

Mission

In a world where traditional business practices are reconsidered and economic activity is performed in a global context, new areas of economic developments are recognized as the key enablers of wealth and income production. This knowledge of information technologies provides infrastructures, systems, and services towards sustainable development.

The **Practices, Progress, and Proficiency in Sustainability (PPPS) Book Series** focuses on the local and global challenges, business opportunities, and societal needs surrounding international collaboration and sustainable development of technology. This series brings together academics, researchers, entrepreneurs, policy makers and government officers aiming to contribute to the progress and proficiency in sustainability.

Coverage

- Intellectual Capital
- Knowledge clusters
- Socio-Economic
- Environmental informatics
- Green Technology
- Eco-Innovation
- Sustainable Development
- E-Development
- ICT and knowledge for development
- Global Content and Knowledge Repositories

IGI Global is currently accepting manuscripts for publication within this series. To submit a proposal for a volume in this series, please contact our Acquisition Editors at Acquisitions@igi-global.com or visit: http://www.igi-global.com/publish/.

The Practice, Progress, and Proficiency in Sustainability (PPPS) Book Series (ISSN 2330-3271) is published by IGI Global, 701 E. Chocolate Avenue, Hershey, PA 17033-1240, USA, www.igi-global.com. This series is composed of titles available for purchase individually; each title is edited to be contextually exclusive from any other title within the series. For pricing and ordering information please visit http://www.igi-global.com/book-series/practice-progress-proficiency-sustainability/73810. Postmaster: Send all address changes to above address.

Titles in this Series

For a list of additional titles in this series, please visit:
https://www.igi-global.com/book-series/practice-progress-proficiency-sustainability/73810

Examining the Environmental Impacts of Materials and Buildings
Blaine Erickson Brownell (University of Minnesota, USA)
Engineering Science Reference • © 2020 • 358pp • H/C (ISBN: 9781799824268) • US $245.00

Cross-Border Cooperation (CBC) Strategies for Sustainable Development
Rui Alexandre Castanho (University of Dą browa Górnicza, Portugal)
Engineering Science Reference • © 2020 • 348pp • H/C (ISBN: 9781799825135) • US $225.00

Membrane Technology for Water and Wastewater Treatment in Rural Regions
Rosalam Sarbatly (Universiti Malaysia Sabah, Malaysia)
Engineering Science Reference • © 2020 • 354pp • H/C (ISBN: 9781799826453) • US $205.00

Smart Materials for Environmental and Industrial Applications
Khaled Salah Abou-El-Sherbini (National Research Centre, Egypt) Nasrallah Mohamed Deraz (National Research Centre, Egypt) and Alia Hosni Salama (National Research Center, Egypt)
Engineering Science Reference • © 2020 • 300pp • H/C (ISBN: 9781799829317) • US $215.00

Handbook of Research on Health and Environmental Benefits of Camel Products
Omar Amin Alhaj (University of Petra, Jordan) Bernard Faye (Independent Researcher, France) and Rajendra Prasad Agrawal (Independent Researcher, India)
Medical Information Science Reference • © 2020 • 480pp • H/C (ISBN: 9781799816041) • US $285.00

Interdisciplinary Approaches to Public Policy and Sustainability
Rituparna Das (Adamas University, India) and Nivedita Mandal (Adamas University, India)
Information Science Reference • © 2020 • 320pp • H/C (ISBN: 9781799803157) • US $195.00

African Perspectives on Reshaping Rural Development
Mavhungu Abel Mafukata (Department of Development Studies, University of South Africa, South Africa) and Khathutshelo Alfred Tshikolomo (Limpopo Department of Agriculture and Rural Development, South Africa)
Information Science Reference • © 2020 • 403pp • H/C (ISBN: 9781799823063) • US $195.00

IGI Global
DISSEMINATOR OF KNOWLEDGE

701 East Chocolate Avenue, Hershey, PA 17033, USA
Tel: 717-533-8845 x100 • Fax: 717-533-8661
E-Mail: cust@igi-global.com • www.igi-global.com

Editorial Advisory Board

Table of Contents

Detailed Table of Contents

Section 1
Digital Economics

The idea of digital transformation permeates economies and regions. The digitization of the economy has many advantages and information technologies are actively introduced in all sectors. At the same time, the impact of technology and change is more visible in the government and the financial sector. In the subsequent chapters of this book, you will find practices of the digital economy in the Eurasian region. The studies examine digital technologies in government interactions with the public through the concept of e-democracy and the possibility of partnerships between government bodies, businesses, and research institutions within the economic system framework. The reader is also invited to review the implementation of digital technologies, such as remote sensing and geodata for the sustainable development of agriculture lands. For a digital economy to grow, investment and entrepreneurial activity must be stimulated. Another chapter shows that in developing countries, such as Tajikistan, financial resources, bank loans for enterprises are needed to improve sustainable employment. Today, the economic aspect of international relations is having an ever-increasing impact on world politics and is promoting the interests of transnational corporations around the world. You will see an example of a multinational corporation's diplomatic resources in China, Russia, and Kazakhstan for a sustainable economy. Finally, digital agropolis is a very interesting, colorful and promising-inspiring model for sustainable development of rural areas in Eurasia. The authors are confident, and we believe that the model can be reproduced with modifications in the Eurasian region since it meets the general strategic goals of sustainable digital development of mankind

The concepts of e-democracy and e-government in Kazakhstan have been introduced as innovative technologies for the interaction of state power with civil society institutions. Digital technologies are considered in the light of implementing the principles of cooperation, conscientious fulfillment of the state, and population obligations.

Promoting such issues increases public services, helps to create new conditions for ensuring transparency and honesty of the state system, strengthens trust between the parties, promotes further societal democratization, and raises the main aspects of national security. Discussing/sharing experiences, we appeal to scholars in political sciences and state officials, to contribute to the background for justification/implementation of new technologies and ways of cooperation between state authorities and the population. The chapter outlines effective ways of state development to be a competitive subject of international relations able adequately to meet the contemporary challenges, keeping up with the times and puts the interests of the population first.

In this article public-private partnership issues are considered. The purpose is to offer a partnership trio model for the Republic of Kazakhstan. This is possible taking into account international experience, as well as by exploring the possibilities of partnership among government agencies, business entities and scientific organizations within the national economic system. A model of forming a trio partnership, which is one of the most developed forms of public-private partnership, has been proposed. This is important from the point of view of the development of the state as a whole. The article also discusses the forms of contribution of each of the participants of the partnership to achieve the goal of improving efficiency. The research methodology is based on the developments of scientists in the field of partnership between science and business, institutional economics, the use of an integrated approach and the principles of dialectics to identify the essential characteristics of partnerships, as well as the conditions for their successful application in the national economy.

Enterprises have traditionally played a vital role in providing sustainable employment, thus contributing to overall social and economic growth of countries. However, many developing countries such as Tajikistan face unemployment because enterprises are not fully functioning there. Evidence from this study shows that enterprises, especially SMEs, could help improve sustainable employment if not faced with obstacles to flourish. The main challenges causing enterprises in developing countries to fail include lack of skills, access to bank credits, access to markets, high tax burdens, insufficient state support, inability to compete, etc. This study looks at the role enterprises, especially SMEs, could play in improving sustainable employment through increasing their access to financial resources in Tajikistan.

Foreword

Digital Technologies have played a critical part in sustainability practices globally in the past decades, particularly in regions such as Eurasia, where countries such as Kazakhstan, Tajikistan and Russia are not yet close to achieving the ideals of the "digital economy". Citizens in these countries possess excellent skills for the elaboration, mastering, and application of these technologies in their home countries. Their governments proclaim support for digital initiatives in support of their economies' high adaptability, renewability, dynamics, and efficiency. The uniqueness of this book is not that the people who wrote it explore some issues and recipes for "digital practice". The nature and core of the extremely mobile, rapidly changing, unimaginably wide scope of "digital technologies" attract authors as a means of "sustainable development" in intersections of social sciences, humanities, economics, and technologies. This experience of Eurasian Region is especially thought-provoking. It is unique, but also intersects with similar issues for countries in the region and globally.

The book combines the results of sectorial and interdisciplinary research of a group of social scientists in the realities of globalization. The principles of such an association have become a modern experience of the Eurasian Region in the implementation of worldwide digital initiatives. These are only a few of the issues explored by the authors. Of considerable interest are studies on the social, cultural, and spiritual aspects of the implementation of the Digital Idea. The new "digital age" is changing the mentality of people, the practice of their social interaction, and communication. It alters the landscape of social management. This "digital age" presents a new perception of space and time that will transform the approach of those who are immersed in historical, social, cultural, and philosophical research. New models and expanded paradigms as well as a comparative analysis of existing scientific concepts, recommendations and best practices in the Eurasian context are presented in this book.

This book will be useful for researchers and practitioners alike in the Social Sciences, Humanities, Economics, Information Technologies, Education and International and Intercultural Studies. The contributions represent the thinking and studies of professionals across the Eurasian region. One may find enough in this volume to deal with sustainability practices: Section 1, "Digital Economics"; Section 2, "Education: Realities and Perspectives." This is a "must-read" book for anyone wishing to help our world move forward through digital initiatives.

Victor Wang
Liberty University, USA

Preface

This time is portrayed by a breakthrough expansion of digital technologies, and an acceleration of the globalized economies. Information is a key resource in social and economic processes and the penetration of digital technology into life is becoming a feature of the future world. Today, the transition to the rails in digital format is one of the main priorities for the development of the world community. Researchers and professionals believe that the digital segment of a modern company is extremely significant. Research and practice show the introduction of information and communication technologies is a natural and universal process, and therefore inevitable. The basic reason for expanding the digitization of the economy is the growth of the transaction sector such as public administration, information services, consulting, finance, services.

The opportunities provided by digital technologies for transforming the economy of the Eurasian region are exceptional. The Implementation of digital technologies erodes geographical and physical boundaries and opens up new prospects for the economic, social and cultural development of the region, as well as for the growth of regional and global competitiveness (McKinsey Global Institute Report, 2016).

The dynamics of economic development in the digital age are not only ensured by new technology companies and enterprises: more than 75% of the added value comes from traditional industries due to increased productivity with the Internet (European Commission report, 2018).

OPPORTUNITIES

As world experience shows, the digital economy is the driving force for accelerating global economic progress, increasing production yield, creating new markets and industries. It also opens new opportunities for inclusive and sustainable growth (G20 Digital Economy Development and Cooperation Initiative, 2016). However, the acceleration of economic development is sought by those countries and economic associations that are systematically building the foundations and mechanisms of leadership in the digital economy. As it is indicated in a recent study of The World Bank (Reaping Digital Dividends: Leveraging the Internet for Development in Europe and Central Asia, 2017), not all benefit equally from the spread of the Internet, i.e. there is an increase in inequality between countries and population groups within countries. It entirely depends on the right choice of mechanisms for implementing digital transformation in the general context for creating the necessary conditions of significant social transformations.

Within the framework of the digital transformation in the Eurasian region, great opportunities are opening up for the change of a number of economic activity areas. The contribution to the economic growth of the global digital economy is in the stage of active growth, rapid innovations' development, as well as the widespread use of digital technologies in all sectors. Given the unique geographical location of the Eurasian region, it can become an important node according to the Europe's Digital Progress Report (European Commission, 2017).

The development of the digital economy inevitably leads to a significant transformation of the labor market. This transformation is complex and takes place gradually as more and more traditional sectors of the economy become involved in the digital economy. Moreover, this transformation affects jobs in different directions. However, according to global studies, the main effect of the development of the digital economy in terms of jobs will be positive (McKinsey Global Institute report, 2016).

The practice of leading countries shows that digital technologies help to improve public services for the population and business. Innovatively oriented governments make it easier for citizens to access public services and move from simply administering services to regularly empowering citizens to participate in developing and delivering services (McKinsey Global Institute report, 2013). This helps not only to expand the choice of services, but also to increase the productivity of government bodies, increases the efficiency of public administration, and increases the level of public confidence in the government. Significant opportunities and dividends promise the initiation of the concept of an open government. The Europe's Digital Progress Report (European Commission, 2017) considers such services as entrepreneurship support, street services, call management, publication of acts, joint budgeting, joint decision making. It is important to consider that for the formation of open government services, a sufficient database of open data is needed, accessible to the public and business.

The Eurasian region is on the edge of a historic transition to a new digital world, where digital technology plays a key role in transforming all societal areas and economic activities. To ensure an effective and holistic transition requires involvement, knowledge, and experience of many stakeholders. This contributes to the creation of an information highway linking Asia, Eurasia, and Europe.

The research results presented in this book can be used to assemble programs and strategies for the growth of the digital economy and sustainable regional socioeconomic progress.

BACKGROUND

Much of the work on this book has been accomplished throughout 2019 so it seems fitting to begin by remembering an event that ushered in 2019 and will change the course of our ideas of who we are as individuals inhabiting regions of the planet earth in our solar system and beyond. On January, 2019 an American spacecraft, New Horizons, that had been traveling through space for 13 years discovered Ultima Thule, the farthest object – four billion miles from Earth. Launched on January 19, 2006 from Cape Canaveral Air Force Station, Florida, USA, its flyby of Pluto on July 14, 2015 was observed by many who remember the image of the heart shaped feature on this dwarf planet that New Horizons photographed and sent to earth. After that, information about the spacecraft disappeared from media attention until January 1, 2019 when Ultima Thule, an object far beyond Pluto, was the farthest object to be discovered in our solar system.

With that reappearance, came a new connection to modern day earth. In late 2018, the American movie Bohemian Rhapsody was nominated for numerous awards. The film about the rock group Queen included one member, Brian May, an astrophysicist who was a member of the New Horizons NASA team. To celebrate the January 2019 discovery by New Horizons, Brian wrote and played his new musical tribute to his team's success. Viewers had enjoyed listening to his tribute on YouTube. But this significant discovery in January 2019 was the amazing integration of art and science, of feeling and discovery, and of the passion that transcends the artificial boundary between them.

This volume, *Toward Sustainability Through Digital Technologies and Practices in the Eurasian Region*, is evidence of disappearing boundaries: disappearing geographical, political, and philosophical boundaries and the new horizons for the Eurasian Region. Over the past almost 30 years, political changes have paralleled technological changes in the region and globally. These countries have engaged in a search for sustainable growth. They have searched for the ideal of a digital economy. Throughout history, education and economics have been at the core of any forward moving initiative whether individual or organizational and no matter how large or small the organization.

The countries of the Eurasian Region are not yet close to the ideals of the "digital economy" proclaimed by their governments, with those economies' high adaptability, renewability, dynamics, and efficiency. That is, the problem has long passed from the field of "theory" and "understanding" to the area called "practice." But the main "intrigue" of the book is not at all that the people who wrote it explore some issues and recipes of the "digital practice". Remarkably, the nature and core of the extremely mobile, rapidly changing, unimaginably wide scope of "digital technologies" are attracted by authors as a means of "sustainable development" in intersections of social sciences, humanities, economics and technologies. This experience of Eurasian Region is thought-provoking. It is unique, but also intersects with similar issues for countries in the region.

This book combines the results of sectorial and interdisciplinary research of a group of social scientists in the realities of globalization. The principles of such an association have become a modern experience of the Eurasian Region in the implementation of worldwide digital initiatives. This is only part of the issues explored by authors. Of considerable interest are studies on the social, cultural, and spiritual aspects of the implementation of the Digital Idea. The new "digital age" is changing the mentality of people, the practice of their social interaction, and communication. It changes the "landscape" to social management. The "digital age" allows us to perceive space and time, to intensively approach those who are immersed in historical, social, cultural and philosophical research. New models, a comparative analysis of existing scientific concepts, recommendations and best practices in the Eurasian context are presented in this book. This book is organized into two sections: Section 1: "Digital Economics" (Chapters 1-6) and Section 2: "Education: Realities and Perspectives" (Chapters 7-14).

ORGANIZATION OF THE BOOK

Section 1: Digital Economics (Chapters 1-6)

The idea of digital transformation permeates economies and regions. The digitization of the economy has many advantages and information technologies are actively introduced in all sectors. At the same time, the impact of technology and change is more visible in the government and the financial sector. In the subsequent chapters of this book, you will find practices of the digital economy in the Eurasian region. The studies examine digital technologies in government interactions with the public through the concept of e-democracy and the possibility of partnerships between government bodies, businesses, and research institutions within the economic system framework. The reader is also invited to review the implementation of digital technologies, such as remote sensing and geodata for the sustainable development of agriculture lands. For a digital economy to grow, investment and entrepreneurial activity must be stimulated. Another chapter shows that in developing countries, such as Tajikistan, financial resources, bank loans for enterprises are needed to improve sustainable employment. Today, the economic aspect of international relations is having an ever-increasing impact on world politics and is promoting the interests of transnational corporations around the world. You will see an example of a multinational corporation's diplomatic resources in China, Russia, and Kazakhstan for a sustainable economy. Finally, a digital agropolis is a very interesting, colorful and promising-inspiring model for sustainable development of rural areas in Eurasia. The authors are confident, and we believe that the model can be reproduced with modifications in the Eurasian region since it meets the general strategic goals of sustainable digital development of mankind.

Chapter 1 introduces the e-government in Kazakhstan and the concept of e-democracy for the state-public interaction.
Chapter 2 presents the evolution of business-government interaction models and their use and management in Kazakhstan.
Chapter 3 examines a case study of the improvement of sustainable employment through increasing access of enterprises to financial resources in Tajikistan.
Chapter 4 develops the Digital Agropolis as a model of sustainable development in rural areas of the Eurasia Region.
Chapter 5 explores the sustainability of agricultural areas in Southern Kazakhstan using remote sensing and geodata for mapping landscapes and soils.
Chapter 6 reviews McDonald's in Russia, China, and Kazakhstan as the nexus of geopolitics and economic sustainability.

Section 2: Education – Realities and Perspectives (Chapters 7-14)

The massive spread of digital technology in education is a sustainable development trend and is seen as a guarantee of the competitiveness of states in the new global economy. This section brings together articles on new horizons for adult learning and similar practices in the countries of the Eurasian area, including the possibilities of creating a network of partner universities and regional resource centers, the prospects of the University 4.0 Models for the knowledge society. Innovative teaching methods are discussed in the chapters on the use of mobile devices and social media in training and the learning achievements of students while implementing flipped classrooms. However, all the problems discussed above can only be solved by improving the ESL competence of students and faculty. Overcoming the language barrier is the factor affecting all areas of the internationalization in the university's educational and scientific activities, as well as its entry to a higher world level. The last chapters address the challenges of learning English in non-English native countries, including Kazakhstan and the Netherlands. Particularly, that book chapters testify the professionally-oriented English-speaking competences of Eurasian scholars for their business and professional partnerships, and their communication with the worldwide academic community.

Chapter 7 suggests that new horizons for sustainable growth in Eurasia can be powered by technology infused adult learning.
Chapter 8 examines University 4.0 and academic communication as models of educational approaches and strategies in the knowledge society in Kazakhstan.

Chapter 9 presents the regional universities' partnership for sustainable development in the age of digital technologies.
Chapter 10 identifies the impact of the flipped classroom on students' academic achievement in secondary schools.
Chapter 11 addresses how social media usage influences the students' learning outcomes.
Chapter 12 explores mobile devices in education.
Chapter 13 reviews the implementation of multilingual education for sustainable development in the Netherlands and Kazakhstan.
Chapter 14 examines English as a medium of instruction on the road to sustainability and internationalization in non-English speaking countries.

This book addresses the many issues that are connected to sustainable growth and how this ideal can become practice through exploration of the theories and practices of learning and economics infused with technology. While the details and examples are specific to the Eurasian Region, the underlying ideas are applicable to many other regions around the globe and will be useful in global interactions. As Moe (2000) looked to the new millennium in his publication "The Knowledge Web", he saw that while historically "nations have developed based on their access to physical resources or their ability to surmount physical barriers" (p. 33), today's knowledge based economy in which the use of the Internet and electronic delivery of information relies on the "resources of brainpower and the ability to acquire, deliver and process information effectively" (p. 33). He notes widespread optimism surrounding the twenty-first century with "futurists predicting a period of rapid growth at the magnitude of the industrial revolution, if not greater, with the advent of the knowledge-based economy" (p. 33). Now, nearly twenty years into that new millennium, this book attempts to provide insights into the various aspects of that future and how the Eurasia Region might leverage its expertise in economics and education to maximize its sustainable growth.

Gainiya Tazhina
University of International Business, Kazakhstan

Judith Parker
Teachers College, Columbia University, USA

REFERENCES

G20 Digital Economy Development and Cooperation Initiative. (2016). Retrieved from http://www.eurasiancommission.org/ru/act/dmi/Pages/digital_agenda.aspx

EAEU digital agenda 2025: prospects and recommendations. (n.d.). European Commission.

European Commission. (2017). *Europe's Digital Progress Report*. Retrieved from https://ec.europa.eu/digital-single-market/en/european-digital-progress-report

European Commission. (2018). *Digital transformation*. Retrieved from https://ec.europa.eu/growth/industry/policy/digital-transformation_en

McKinsey & Co. (2013). *Government by design: Four principles for a better public sector*. Retrieved from http://www.mckinsey.com/industries/public-sector/our-insights/government-by-design-four-principles-for-a-better-public-sector

McKinsey Global Institute. (2016). Digital globalization: The new era of global flows. Retrieved from http://www.mckinsey.com/business-functions/digital-mckinsey/our-insights/digital-globalization-the-new-era-of-global-flows

Moe, M. (2000). *The knowledge web*. Beverly Hills, CA: Knowledge Enterprises Group.

The World Bank. (2017). Reaping Digital Dividends: Leveraging the Internet for Development in Europe and Central Asia. Retrieved from http://www.worldbank.org/en/region/eca/ publication/digital-dividends-in-eca

Acknowledgment

The editors would like to acknowledge the help of all the people involved in this project and, more specifically, to the authors and reviewers that took part in the review process. Without their support, this book would not have become a reality.

First, the editors would like to thank each one of the authors for their contributions. Our sincere gratitude goes to the chapter's authors who contributed their time and expertise to this book.

Second, the editors wish to acknowledge the valuable contributions of the reviewers regarding the improvement of quality, coherence, and content presentation of chapters. Most of the authors also served as referees; we highly appreciate their double duty.

Gainiya Tazhina
University of International Business, Kazakhstan

Judith Parker
Teachers College, Columbia University, USA

Section 1
Digital Economics

The idea of digital transformation permeates economies and regions. The digitization of the economy has many advantages and information technologies are actively introduced in all sectors. At the same time, the impact of technology and change is more visible in the government and the financial sector. In the subsequent chapters of this book, you will find practices of the digital economy in the Eurasian region. The studies examine digital technologies in government interactions with the public through the concept of e-democracy and the possibility of partnerships between government bodies, businesses, and research institutions within the economic system framework. The reader is also invited to review the implementation of digital technologies, such as remote sensing and geodata for the sustainable development of agriculture lands. For a digital economy to grow, investment and entrepreneurial activity must be stimulated. Another chapter shows that in developing countries, such as Tajikistan, financial resources, bank loans for enterprises are needed to improve sustainable employment. Today, the economic aspect of international relations is having an ever-increasing impact on world politics and is promoting the interests of transnational corporations around the world. You will see an example of a multinational corporation's diplomatic resources in China, Russia, and Kazakhstan for a sustainable economy. Finally, digital agropolis is a very interesting, colorful and promising-inspiring model for sustainable development of rural areas in Eurasia. The authors are confident, and we believe that the model can be reproduced with modifications in the Eurasian region since it meets the general strategic goals of sustainable digital development of mankind.

Chapter 1
Introducing E-Government in Kazakhstan:
The Concept of E-Democracy for the State-Public Interaction

Aida Kuatova
University of Interntional Business, Kazakhstan

Togzhan Bekbasarova
University of International Business, Kazakhstan

Ruslan Abdrashev
University of International Business, Kazakhstan

ABSTRACT

The concepts of e-democracy and e-government in Kazakhstan have been introduced as innovative technologies for the interaction of state power with civil society institutions. Digital technologies are considered in the light of implementing the principles of cooperation, conscientious fulfillment of the state, and population obligations. Promoting such issues increases public services, helps to create new conditions for ensuring transparency and honesty of the state system, strengthens trust between the parties, promotes further societal democratization, and raises the main aspects of national security. Discussing/sharing experiences, we appeal to scholars in political sciences and state officials, to contribute to the background for justification/implementation of new technologies and ways of cooperation between state authorities and the population. The chapter outlines effective ways of state development to be a competitive subject of international relations able adequately to meet the contemporary challenges, keeping up with the times and puts the interests of the population first.

DOI: 10.4018/978-1-7998-2551-7.ch001

INTRODUCTION

The current Constitution of the Republic of Kazakhstan embodying universal democratic values has opened up wide scope for building a modern legal, socially oriented and open state. The basic law of the state ensures the stability of organization and activities of the state apparatus, stability of law enforcement practice fixing the fundamental foundations of Kazakhstani statehood.

Over the past few years significant changes had taken place in the legal regulation of the informational sphere of Kazakhstan. Informational legislation is developing dynamically along with active development of e-government, which is one of the priority areas of the Government of the Republic of Kazakhstan. The main goal of creating electronic government in the Republic of Kazakhstan is formation of the mechanism for interaction between the functioning of the government and local authorities, which will be focused on providing services to citizens and organizations through information technology.

The purpose of the given research is to study the features of building a democratic society through the improvement and further development of e-government and the transition to the format of e-democracy.

From a consumer's point of view introduction of e-government technologies is aimed at simplifying access to information for citizens, obtaining public services in an electronic format increasing transparency and control of state power on the part of society reducing the influence of the human factor in the activities of the executive apparatus and attracting wide layers of citizens to governance.

At present, quite a lot has been done to form E-government in Kazakhstan. State programs aimed at eliminating information inequality are being actively introduced. They are aimed at introducing information and communication technologies, raising the educational level, lowering tariffs for Internet users, computerizing governmental agencies and educational institutions as the part of the program to reduce informational inequality in the Republic of Kazakhstan.

The 21st century was marked by introduction of innovative digital technologies in all spheres of society. The most promising is the process of using Internet technologies to expand further the capabilities of the existing system of representative democracy and development of the processes of so-called "e-democracy".

E-democracy ("e-democracy", "virtual democracy") is a form of democracy characterized by use of information and communication technologies (ICT) as the main means for collective thinking (crowdsourcing) and administrative processes (informing, making joint decisions while electronic voting, controlling execution of decisions etc.) at all levels that is from the level of local governance to the international one (Ibraeva, 2018).

E-democracy is use of modern digital technologies for organization and implementation of civil initiatives, active use in the election campaign and other mass campaigns.

The concept of e-government should be distinguished from e-democracy ideas. E-government is simplification of citizens' access to state bodies from anywhere in the world. That is no more than a change in the interface in relationships of managers and managed without a radical change of the system. E-democracy means not just ability of citizens to use public services, but to influence actively on governmental decisions.

THEORETICAL FRAMEWORK

So, the introduction of the "e-democracy" system allows:

- To ensure quality of electronic information services, which generally affects improvement of the quality of all other public services;
- E-services can reduce corruption, increase transparency of state bodies and equalize the opportunities of citizens at the stage of obtaining information about public services;
- At the stage of transition of the country from state centralized governance to local decentralized governance, provision of services to the population through websites will reduce negative consequences of transfer of the competence from one body to another one (Arkhipova, 2016).

A key element of e-democracy is e-government, which is formed through transformation of functions of providing governance services to the population. Legitimacy of e-government is ensured by real increase in efficiency of public administration, improvement in quality of services provided by the state and a strong social policy.

E-government covers processes both inside and outside the public sector, for example, between governmental agencies and the public, economy, non-governmental organizations. It uses the Internet, electronic databases, e-mail and exchanges electronic information. E-government is combination of the following components: information, democracy, communications, forms, transactions (commerce and services), work processes, payments etc. (Styrin, 2013).

Modern ICT using the Internet ensure transparency of decisions made, financial transactions, personal responsibility for each decision.

On the portals of websites of state and local authorities it is possible to organize a dialogue and interaction with civil society institutions for joint participation in implementation of administrative and economic reforms. Informational transparency with the help of the Internet makes the activities of the executive, legislative and judicial authorities, local governments much more efficient. Introduction of e-government is undoubtedly another step towards development of the process of full observance and realization of human rights.

Based on the analysis of special literature and modern practice one can come to the conclusion that there are two understandings of electronic technologies: in a narrow sense, as providing a certain set of information and other services to the population (e-government) and in a broader sense, as a form of realization of constitutional rights and freedoms by citizens (Styrin, 2013).

Such a widespread approach is based on experience of emergence of e-government ideas. For the first time, development and practical implementation of e-government was started in the USA in 1991 (Soros, 1997). The actual start was implemented by creation of the White House website in 1993, which presented information on the work of governmental agencies and the possibility of paying taxes by the Internet. Currently, in the United States the main law governing e-government is the Law "On e-government" adopted in 2002, which includes later amendments on statistical efficiency of public administration and on protection of confidential information of citizens and the special unit of the Presidential administration manages and develops e-government called "Management of e-government." A feature of development of e-government in the United States is creation of information superhighways allowing to provide universal service to citizens and provide information on the problems of public administration (Smirnov, 2005).

The foundation for development of e-government in European countries was the "Informational Society Forum" established in 1995, its goal was to create social and democratic values in a "virtual society", as well as sustainable development of technologies and infrastructures. In 2000 the countries of the European Union adopted the E-Europe 2002 Action Plan, in connection with its implementation e-governments were created in European countries in 2005.

"The concept of e-government" as one of the manifestations of e-democracy being actively implemented in Russia. The idea of effectiveness of e-democracy is based on both theoretical studies (information theory of democracy) and experimental data obtained in the course of research. Thus, according to the sociological survey conducted by the manufacturer of SAP software in Russia the authorities attempt to make governance of a country more transparent and open through e-government systems and e-democracy is perceived in a positive way. The given survey showed that the majority of respondents do not use all the opportunities provided by these resources (Chetvernin, 2003).

FINDINGS AND DISCUSSION

In Kazakhstan by the initiative of the First President of the country N.A. Nazarbaev over the past ten years much work has been done for implementation of the "electronic government". The Resolution of the Government of the Republic of Kazakhstan dated by 30 November, 2007 #1155-1 approved the Development Program of the "e-government" of the Republic of Kazakhstan for 2008–2010, which was later included in the Action Plan of the Government for implementation of the State program on accelerated industrial-innovative development of Kazakhstan for 2010–2014. It replaced the State Program for Formation of the "Electronic Government" in the Republic of Kazakhstan for 2005–2007 (approved by the Decree of the President of Kazakhstan dated by 10 November, 2004 #1471) adopted in continuation of the implemented State program of formation and development of the national informational infrastructure of the Republic of Kazakhstan (approved by the Decree of the President of Kazakhstan dated by 16 March, 2001# 5731). Currently in Kazakhstan a specific legal framework for the formation of an open interactive state has been created. The Parliament of the Republic adopted the Law of the Republic of Kazakhstan "On electronic document and electronic digital signature" dated by 7 January, 2003, the Law of the Republic of Kazakhstan "On National Registers of Identification Numbers" dated by 12 January, 2007, the Law of the Republic of Kazakhstan "On access to information" dated by 16 November, 2015; the Law of the Republic of Kazakhstan "On Informatization" dated by 24 November, 2015. An important role in creating the informational society in Kazakhstan is played by the Decree of the President of the Republic of Kazakhstan "On the Concept of Informational Security of the Republic of Kazakhstan until 2016" dated by 14 November, 2011 #174, as well as a number of resolutions of the Government of the Republic of Kazakhstan.

In accordance with the national legislation a lot of work is being done in Kazakhstan in the area of forming an "open Government". So, over the past five years alone through the blogging platform of the heads of state bodies of the Republic about 290 thousand requests from citizens have been received, which is about 4 thousand requests per a month. Currently, Kazakhstan has a single portal of "open data", which contains 180 data sets on the areas of health care, education, transport and communications, social security, as well as a single platform for discussing draft laws of public service standards of other regulatory legal acts (Zhvirblis, 2015).

In addition, as a part of the implementation of five institutional reforms it is planned to create a state corporation, so called Government for Citizens, which will become a single provider of public services by the model of Canada Service in Canada and Centrelink in Australia. The state corporation will integrate all public service centers into a single system: citizens will receive all public services in one place. It is also envisaged to ensure the online accessibility of statistical databases of central state bodies. All budget and consolidated financial statements, the results of an external financial audit, the results of evaluating the effectiveness of public policy, the results of a public assessment of the quality of public services, a report on implementation of the republican and local budgets will be published.

In order to form further the "open Government" the Law of the Republic of Kazakhstan "On Informatization" was adopted on 24 November 2015, which clearly outlines all necessary legal norms on formation of the "open Government" and "open data". The latest models on the "open budget" and "open petitions" are regulated and reflected (Kazi & Chalgimbaeva, 2016).

As a part of implementation of five institutional reforms on implementation of the Open Government system, the Law of the Republic of Kazakhstan "On Access to Information" was adopted on 16 November 2015. It made it possible to make any information belonged to state bodies, except for those classified as state secrets and other information, protected by law.

In this regard, with the necessity to strengthen the feedback of state bodies with the population, in order to create legislative guarantees of the right of citizens to have an access to official information of state bodies, it seems to accelerate the adoption of the draft law "On access to public information" by the Parliament of the Republic of Kazakhstan together with the Institute of Parliamentarism and prepared by the legal council under support of "Nur Otan", the political party. The bill contains the rules requiring public information owners regularly to update it on their websites (at least once a week). The chapter of the bill is of a particular interest, it is dedicated to the issues of public access to meetings of collegial bodies establishing the procedure for consideration of requests, citizens' requirements and their terms. So, to participate in collegial meetings, information holders monthly publish a meeting plan indicating their agenda, time and place. There should be special places for visitors in the meeting room or broadcasting by television monitors located outside the meeting room should be provided (www.egov.kz, 2019).

As you can see the bill is not only about the simple access of citizens to public information, but also the creation of a legal framework for establishing feedback and interaction between state bodies and the public based on information available to citizens.

At the same time, it should be noted that the effectiveness of the activities of state bodies also largely depends on the ability of society to adequately perceive and evaluate the changes that have occurred in the functioning of the state mechanism. The fact is that the genesis of state institutions and their development in modern conditions are closely related to the development of society itself. Therefore, issues of increasing the legal and moral culture of officials in the context of a simultaneous increase in the legal culture of the population are becoming increasingly important for the activities of state bodies. Meanwhile, the legal culture of the population and its legal consciousness are not sufficient for the ongoing democratic transformations.

Thus, it seems that taking into account the latest trends in the development of Kazakhstan as an open and interactive information state, in the course of a phased constitutional reform it will be possible to raise an issue of creating a system of public authorities that can significantly increase the efficiency, interactivity and openness of public administration and, as a result, the protection and realization of the rights of citizens of the Republic of Kazakhstan.

Since 2004 phased introduction of e-government has begun, in particular, the information, interactive and transactional stages. In 2014 according to the UN report on the e-government development index, the Republic of Kazakhstan ranked as the 38th (in 2010 it was the 46th place), according to the report of the World Economic Forum on the Network Readiness Index, 55th place (in 2010 it was the 67th place). According to the index of electronic participation, which determines the possibility of citizens' treatment of the government, Kazakhstan ranked the second place along with Singapore.

Introduction of "e-government" in Kazakhstan is aimed at improving the quality and reducing the time frame for state bodies to provide services to citizens and organizations, providing access to information bases for activities of governmental agencies and in the long term taking into account improvement of the administrative system creating an effective and optimal membership of the state apparatus.

The main priorities for creating the "e-government" are providing access to Internet communications, increasing the level of education in the field of information and communication technologies, as well as modernizing the public administration system. The introduction of "e-government" will allow us to improve constantly the system of state governance, first of all, the executive bodies, since formation of electronic public services provides for reengineering of administrative processes (www.akorda.kz, 2018).

Creation of the "electronic government" in Eurasian Region taking into account analysis of world experience, has a long-term perspective and is being implemented in three stages. The first stage is creation of e-government infrastructure, it is aimed at creating such basic components as the portal and e-government gateway, "payment gateway" for interaction with the banking system, the national identification system, the unified transport environment of state bodies, creation and development of interdepartmental and model systems of central and local executive bodies, as well as carrying out activities to ensure access to electronic services, organizing work on elimination of information inequality and improving education in the field of information and communication technologies.

The second stage is development of e-government services is aimed at development of a variety of services covering all spheres of life of citizens and functioning of state bodies, as well as conducting a full-scale reengineering of administrative processes.

The third stage is construction of the informational society, which provides for transformation of the activities of state bodies and organizations, construction of the information society including implementation of such projects as e-medicine, e-education, e-culture, e-democracy and others (Chernysheva, 2018).

Kazakhstan at the present stage of its development has taken a course on development of democracy, the fight against corruption and a new level of relations between citizens and the government, namely, to ensure open access to information for every citizen of the country in order to enable him to participate actively in all democratic transformations taking place today in the state both at the national and local levels.

Kazakhstan has introduced the system for evaluating the effectiveness of state agencies, where use of information technology is an evaluation criterion, which makes it possible to track the rating of the work of the state apparatus. Also 219 transactional and interactive services are provided to individuals and legal entities.

Global trends aimed at reducing barriers to information interaction between authorities and public organizations, as well as creating democratic principles for managing society the Republic of Kazakhstan has gained some experience in introducing "e-democracy" as an innovative technology for participation of people in the state governance process. The key element of e-democracy is e-government. However, in order to create conditions for effective use of e-government opportunities, in our opinion, it is necessary:

- To develop the regulatory framework governing the functioning of e-government and its users.
- To provide a comprehensive and systematic study of the problem of forming e-democracy by political scientists, sociologists and lawyers with the subsequent development of relevant proposals for implementation through e-government.
- Because of the complexity of the very subject of the e-government institute, it seems appropriate to develop the special Law;
- To provide appropriate implementation of the principle of reciprocal liability of state and society.

THE CONCEPT OF BUILDING A CIVIL SOCIETY AND AN OPEN STATE THROUGH THE EXERCISE OF CITIZENS' RIGHTS TO INFORMATION

In modern conditions of gradual democratic transformations in Kazakhstan, the importance of the formation of an open state is significantly increasing. The efforts of many state bodies form a new way of thinking in relation to the problems of building an open democratic statehood. Achieving a balance of interests of the state and citizens through the openness of state bodies is also relevant in the context of increasing global changes in socio-political processes and economic development in Kazakhstan and in the world.

The urgent task is to ensure favorable conditions for the development of an open state through the creation of platforms for open state bodies (Parliament, Government, ministries, departments, etc.). An open state is a system of principled approaches to the organization of state power, which is based on the involvement of citizens, public associations, political parties in adoption, development and application of decisions on governmental issues (www.akorda.kz, 2018). The purpose of such public participation is to strengthen civilian influence on decisions taken by state bodies and achieve a balance of interests in governmental events. Expert assessments of the effectiveness of the mechanisms of openness of state bodies allow taking into account certain criteria for working with citizens and their associations in order to strengthen democratic processes in the country.

"An open state is primarily a social state, where emphasis is placed on the responsibility of the state to society for ensuring social justice and social security in the country and thereby political stability. In an open state and representative democracy, labor productivity, competitiveness and the growth rate of the national economy are ensured including strengthening the market regulation mechanisms and reducing the state bureaucracy and state budget (Chetvernin, 2003).

Currently, Kazakhstan has developed an Open Government Program, which is a fundamental platform for civil-state interaction in public administration and construction of further democratic processes. On the basis of such a significant platform all interested political parties, public associations including citizens, legal entities can hold open discussions on all issues of legislative support for state policies and discussion of draft laws adopted by the Parliament. Advancement to an open state in Kazakhstan, first of all, is based on the introduction of "electronic Government", which has become an exclusively fundamental step in the process of informatization and ensuring civic participation in government.

Deepening the development process of an open state is aimed at strengthening the process of bringing the state closer to civil society and strengthening state influence on political processes in society through interaction and mutual participation of state institutions and civil society (Akopov, 2013).

The features of the development of the rule of law in Kazakhstan are the following factors:

- The rule of law in the Republic of Kazakhstan was born on the basis of the former socialist system and learned to create a legal development space using the methods of the democratic mechanism.
- The birth of democratic foundations of a legal society took place in Kazakhstan, when the base and basic institutions of democracy were already created in other European countries.
- Any legal state positions with constitutional foundations aimed at strengthening the freedoms of all members of society.
- The state becomes the main institution for implementation of the constitutional system and has the ability to transform with the proper direction of its influence.
- The transition from a totalitarian state system to a democratic one was manifested in the application of new development tools such as freedom of conscience, observance of the principles of a secular state and approximation of state bodies to citizens.

Therefore, the formation and development of the rule of law in Kazakhstan influenced the formation of the constitutional foundations of the state and stimulated the state to apply the principles of openness in civil society. Civil society found its development using the methods of developed democracy and strengthening the rights of citizens of the country. Civil society is becoming a powerful tool in enhancing the rights of ordinary citizens and striving to improve people's lives at the economic and social level. Many studies of legal scholars indicate a high level of development of the constitutional level of the state when using the methods of developed democracy and interaction of the state with the civil society. This state of society is dictated by the fact that the processes of political transformation of society are aimed at creating an open state position.

The very development of a legal society consists in deepening the processes of the constitutional system, which carry the ideas of freedoms and equality of all people before the law, the application of the rule of law in practical life, changing the format of public administration aimed not at supporting the bureaucracy, but at strengthening the constitutional foundations of a democratic state (Baranov, 2011).

All these factors made it possible to carry out administrative reform in Kazakhstan, to create conditions and incentives for the development of e-government, which allows for a gradual transition to an open state.

The principles of e-government were laid in the creation of a system of open dialogue between governmental bodies and the population, implementation of the national program for informatization of society, creation of conditions for citizens to access the information resources of state authorities and approximation to effective public administration in society.

The gradual development of e-government will allow realizing the goals of the strategic development of an open state. The attributes of such a state include:

- Openness in the dialogue between the state and citizens;
- Strengthening and improving civil society;
- Involvement of citizens into governance.

On this basis, the Kazakhstan population informatization program was developed, an electronic government was created with the ability to use information technology in providing the necessary information to citizens of Kazakhstan via the Internet, the foundations for development of the "Open Government" on the basis of improving the electronic government platform were developed.

This event was organized to promote a more open dialogue between citizens and the Government and to attract them to participate in the creation and development of legislative projects in various areas of economic and public activity.

Developing the state concept of openness and participation in the "Accountable State" reform, the following is important:

- Effective interaction of all programs and goals between ministries and agencies by type of reporting,
- More effective implementation of openness methods in the modernization of public administration,
- Assessment of information in order to monitor the effectiveness of governmental bodies;
- Analysis of the costs of financing the programs to stimulate citizens' participation in implementation of the concept of openness,
- A comparative analysis of the experience of other countries and their achievements in the field of creating an open state.

The study allows identifying certain parameters of the rule of law:

- The norms of the objective law defining the limits of freedom of each and limiting the interests of all members of society.
- Protection of subjective rights in dissemination of personal freedom.
- The rule of law for state bodies, determination of their powers.
- Separation of the executive from the legislative, participation of public elements of the legal process (Sidorenko, Bartsits, 2019).

Such a definition makes it possible to develop democratic principles in solving the tasks of public administration and create an environment for a developed civil society, where activation of citizens will not be connected with social tension, but with systematic participation in civil-state activities. The postulate of state monopoly should be a thing of the past and the modern face of a progressive state should be built on the constitutional rights of all citizens.

The constitutional foundations of the rule of law reflect the following principles:

- The Constitution is a legal act of legal force, a public document approved by the people.
- Recognition of the rule of law. The law is the regulator of main aspects of state and public life.
- The law acts as primary organization of all state institutions.
- The rule of law recognizes the priority of human rights and legitimate interests and considers them effective.
- Orientation of state institutions to ensure the rights and freedoms of citizens, a functional characteristic of activities of all organizations.
- The state is such a device of power that guarantees fair decisions and actions.

Then implementation of the principles of the rule of law can lead to further deepening of the processes of democratic advancement and progress that creates the conditions for harmonious development of socio-economic processes (Arkhipova, 2016).

An open government (open state) is a doctrine of public administration that supports the right of citizens to access documents and actions of the state with the goal of the possibility of effective public control over state regulation. In its broadest statement, it opposes attempts to legitimize the expansion of secrecy and non-public activities of state structures. Arguments in favor of an open government date back to the time of the European Renaissance: to debate about the proper arrangement of the then civil society (Lopatova, 2019).

State transparency is often associated with accountability. Transparency often allows citizens of democratic countries to control their state and reduce corruption, bribes and other official crimes.

The modern doctrine of openness of the state finds strong support among non-profit organizations engaged in opposing what they see as a continuous tendency of the state to go into secrecy, wherever possible. They support the application of openness and transparency throughout the world and convince them of the need for such standards for prosperity and development of democratic societies (Kholodnaya, 2018).

World practice in the field of openness of the state is very broad and includes many topics and directions that the governments of the countries choose as priority. At the same time, a number of areas are presented everywhere and considered inalienable to ensure publicity of the state. These areas include:

- Freedom of information.
- Freedom of access to state information for citizens.
- Open data. Open governmental data. Free use of governmental data by developers and employees of NGOs.
- Open dialogue. An open dialogue between citizens and the state. The ability of citizens to influence government structures.
- Open budget. Openness of governmental spending including state and municipal budgets, government procurement, government contracts, grants and subsidies.
- Open parliament. The openness of representative authorities, including freedom of access to parliamentary information, availability of parliamentary information in a structured and open format, clarity and publicity of the adoption of laws and involvement of citizens in development of draft laws (Afanasyeva, 2012).

These areas are partially represented in Kazakhstan in the form of non-systematized state and public initiatives.

One of the significant problems of communication between state representatives and citizens is the problem of incomprehensibility of state information for ordinary people. This problem is widespread throughout the world and in all developed countries it is now being addressed through an approach called "open data". Open data is a special way of publishing information in formats suitable for subsequent processing and analysis. They are also called open machine-readable data. This approach allows widespread reuse of public governmental databases by business, media and civil society.

The difficulties in developing an open state are that the state has 80% of material resources in the country's GDP and is the main owner of all enterprises in the country. Therefore, the implementation of many programs is associated with its dominant role in the economy. Creating incentives for development of civil society requires decisions that operate from below. Civil society should influence the state and not vice versa, create opportunities for participation in public administration and raise issues of discussion of regulatory documents with it.

An assessment of the constitutional foundations of the rule of law indicates its elements:

- Consider a person, his rights as the highest value, which is important in the relationship between the state and an individual. Recognition of this right and protection is the duty of the state.
- The people are the bearers of power, therefore the principle of democracy is that the people exercise their power through a referendum, free elections.
- Separation of powers characterizes Kazakhstan as a democratic state, which creates conditions in order to avoid arbitrariness of state authorities and separation of powers.
- Sovereignty appears in the political and legal form to express the sovereignty of people and the sovereign will of nations and nationalities.

Full compliance with constitutional rights should characterize the rule of law as an effective mechanism for exercising state power aimed at fulfilling the will of people. In this regard, an open state is the most complete expressed structure of interaction between the state and citizens and finds its expression in the realization of rights of constitutional pluralism.

Important tools for implementing the concept of an open society are information support tools like e-government. It is effective for:

- Stimulation of interaction between citizens, governmental organizations including the processes of public administration;
- Technologies (in particular, the Internet) that transform the process of public administration;
- The electronic vertical (changing the relationship between different levels of government) and electronic democracy (increasing the degree of civic participation, online voting, ethics, security and privacy issues increasing transparency);
- Actions of the environment for development of legislation and public policy: political initiatives of the government; regulatory environment; implementation of initiatives such as legalization of electronic digital signatures; a large degree of civic participation in the development of public policy (Afanasyeva, 2010).

The experience of developing and applying legislation on citizens' access to information has also revealed some shortcomings of this legislation. So, the legislation guarantees access exclusively to information of state bodies leaving outside the regulation of information of representative and judicial bodies, documents of political parties. Legislation regulates access to decisions made, but does not provide for the right of citizens to access draft decisions of executive authorities.

The process of creating an open interactive state was preceded by a series of political actions by the leadership of the countries that introduced and successfully use the openness system to create the informational society. It is necessary to clearly define the political goal of state programs that is to make governmental bodies more open and accessible for all segments of the population.

The international openness of the Republic of Kazakhstan entails a difficult competitive entry into the global economic, informational and political space, which should be based on reciprocity and equality.

Communication in the messenger, online payments, electronic services, all this is becoming part of the daily affairs of a modern person. Digitalization, which has intensively entered the life of Kazakhstanis with the adoption of the state program "Digital Kazakhstan", creates a new model of the economy, in which not only basic industries and business are digitized, but also the whole life of society.

For example, the eGov.kz e-government portal works to ensure that citizens have quick access to public services. These are services such as filing applications, obtaining certificates, licenses, registration and other operations. Governmental agencies, as well as many other organizations, such as banks and mail, also translate their work into electronic format, getting rid of paper workflow. But the problem is that not all citizens know how to use new technologies. To solve it, it is necessary to educate the population in a new way to use the usual services.

In the field of retraining of the personnel, local executive bodies on ongoing basis conduct training and retraining of the population in demand for digital skills. Also. this event covered representatives of small and medium-sized businesses (www.egov.kz, 2019).

In 2018 in each region of Kazakhstan (in district centers, villages and towns) the courses were held to train the population in basic digital literacy skills. Training courses were provided free of charge for everyone who wanted to increase their competence in one or four skills:

- "Basic digital skills". They include the confident use of a personal computer and laptop, mobile devices, the Internet and also cover topics of security and data protection.
- "E-government and e-government services". The topic covers the skills of working with the e-government portal, which includes obtaining the necessary electronic public services online without leaving home.
- "Open Government". Training on this topic includes skills in using four components of an open governmental portal: open data, open regulations, open dialogue and budgets.
- "Electronic commerce". The training unit includes the skills of acquiring, selling and promoting goods and services online.

The training took place on the basis of schools, colleges and libraries. Throughout Kazakhstan, 2,729 institutions were involved in the courses.

All four competencies of digital literacy can be studied in one or two days depending on the schedule and academic performance of the group. Many people learn one skill and after a while another one. In the first week of digital literacy more than 140 thousand Kazakhstanis studied. Among them there were many pensioners and teachers of those schools, where the courses were held. Digital literacy training courses have been successfully launched in all regions of Kazakhstan. As part of the state program "Digital Kazakhstan" it is planned to gradually increase the level of digital literacy of the population to 83% by 2022.

One of the real achievements of Kazakhstan in this area can also be noted. It is event happened on 14 June, 2019 in the capital of Kazakhstan, Nur-Sultan the ceremony of signing a technical agreement on cooperation in the field of information and communication technologies between National Infocommunication Holding Zerde JSC, National Information Technologies JSC and Electronic Project Management Center Government and the digital economy under the National Agency for Project Management under the President of the Republic of Uzbekistan". The aim of the Agreement is to develop mutually beneficial cooperation on the principles of equality, joint development, mutual understanding, respect and trust between the Parties in e-government. Also, the Agreement will serve as the basis for the interaction of the Parties in the development of recommendations, exchange of knowledge, experience and innovative solutions. On 25 October 2018 a memorandum of cooperation was signed between National Information Technologies JSC and Electronic Government System Development Center of the Republic of Uzbekistan. On 10 January 2019 by decree of the President of the Republic of Uzbekistan the new State Unitary Enterprise "Center for Project Management of Electronic Government and Digital Economy under the National Project Management Agency under the President of the Republic of Uzbekistan" was established (Pivovarov, 2013).

CONCLUSION

During the research the following problems and issues were put forward that need to be further investigated and resolved as their settlement gives an opportunity for development prospects:

1. Large units of governance should be built using digital methods and capabilities that will help to establish the real system of checks and balances. Without such a mechanism as public and state control over the activities of the branches of power it will be ineffective.
2. Departmental barriers are an obstacle in the way of constructing an open state. Society needs transparency, openness, transparency in the activities of the political leadership and state apparatus. These values should be embedded in the programs of political parties and public consciousness.
3. It is necessary to make an analysis of the openness of state structures and institutions.
4. A serious problem is the inability or unwillingness of the state authorities to use the possibilities of creating an open state, which are represented by the Constitution of the Republic of Kazakhstan. This also applies to the activities of political leaders, elites, parties, social movements. A negative factor is also the low political and legal culture of citizens.
5. The Law of the Republic of Kazakhstan dated by 23 November 2015 # 416-V "On the Public Service of the Republic of Kazakhstan" and a number of other regulatory legal acts affecting openness, transparency, feedback in the activities of public and state authorities need to be revised.
6. The openness and transparency of state bodies is also hindered by conflicts in society itself, especially at different levels of government and administration.
7. The Internet, electronic media, e-government, modern computer and information technologies open up new opportunities for citizens to participate in lawmaking, in governance, in election campaigns, for monitoring and controlling representatives of society over the activities of state bodies.
8. For a democratic, open state, the lack of censorship is not enough; it should provide a platform for the media, all the legal political forces of the country. True publicity and transparency in the activities of the state and the media implies the absence of black PR and the observance of ethical codes by both state officials and journalists.
9. An important role is played by the interaction of religion, state and society. Especially for the Central Asian region, where representatives of all world religions and faiths peacefully coexist. Through digitalization the clergy can become more involved in civil society.

Thus, we can conclude that today Kazakhstan has enough experience and practice in introducing electronic services and has the opportunity to share this experience with neighboring countries to achieve successful sustainable development of the region. At the same time there is also something to improve and develop due to certain features of the development of democracy in the Central Asian region.

RECOMMENDATIONS

The authors have investigated the practice of forming e-democracy on the example of Kazakhstan. The conclusion is made about the necessity for an integrated approach when introducing new formats for the provision of public services and data management. The necessity for a significant research of the regulatory framework governing the formation of the data market and access to them has been substantiated. The main goal of e-democracy has been formulated as the following: the use of information and communication technologies to improve democratic governance. It is noted that the driving force of e-democracy is meeting the requirements of democracy, not technology. The authors analyzed the impact of information and communication technologies on the processes of electronic democratization in the country. The potential of new information technologies can be used both for the good and for the bad of democracy. The results of the research make it possible to say that in each particular country democratic and human values, as well as ethical considerations are inseparable parts of the technological aspects of e-democracy. Nowadays in the world along with the existence of legal states we can see the rapid process of building electronic states. In the Republic of Kazakhstan all available opportunities have been taken to implement the work of e-government, however it is also necessary to take steps to ensure their accurate, uniform implementation and execution for the normal functioning of the state apparatus and interaction with society. An integrated approach is necessary while introducing new formats for the provision of public services and data management. There is a necessity for a substantial research of the regulatory legal framework governing the formation of the data market.

FUTURE RESEARCH AREAS

The goals in the future are to investigate and determine the significance of the digital transformation of government as a strategic vector of public administration reform. Also the goals include research of the mechanisms for improving the quality and efficiency of the public sector, defining the essence of the state and "public administration" at the market environment, research of the necessity for the developed regional policy and structure of local authorities, improving the quality and efficiency of the public sector, participation of civil society in governance.

REFERENCES

Afanasyeva O.V. (2010). Access to information: Russian and international legislation. Social sciences and modernity.

Afanasyeva O.V. (2012). Postmodernity as a crisis. Toward a new understanding of social openness. The policy.

AkopovA.K. (2013). Модель глобального электронного правительства.

Aldoshenko, E. V. (2014). Electronic government as a stage of formation of electronic democracy. Retrieved from www.cyberleninka.ru

Arkhipova, Z. V. (2016). Transformation of E-Government into Digital Government. Retrieved from: https://cyberleninka.ru/

Baranov, A. V. (2011). On the problems of formation of "Electronic state."

Chernysheva, T. K. (2018). Implementation of the E-Government concept in the context of the transition to a digital economy in the Russian Federation. Retrieved from: https://cyberleninka.ru/

Chetvernin, V. A. (2003). *Introduction to the course of the general theory of state and law*. Moscow: Institute of State and Law, Russian Academy of Sciences.

Ibraeva, A. (2018). How is the e-government portal of Kazakhstan developing? Retrieved from https://kursiv.kz/

Kazi, A., & Chalgimbaeva, S. (2016). Formation and development of "Electronic government. Retrieved from https://zerde.gov.kz/

Kholodnaya, E. V. (2018). On some prospects for the development of electronic governance in the conditions of digital transformation. Retrieved from www.cyberleninka.ru

Kudaykulova, H. S. (2007). Electronic government in the Republic of Kazakhstan. Retrieved from https://cyberleninka.ru/

Lavrik, N.V. (2017). E-democracy: world experience. Retrieved from: https://cyberleninka.ru/

Lopatova, N. (2019). *International experience in the formation of digital government*. Moscow: Economics and Law.

Message from the Head of the State Kassym-Zhomart Tokayev to the people of Kazakhstan. (2019). Retrieved from http://www.akorda.kz/en/addresses/addresses_of_president/poslanie-glavy-gosudarstva-kasym-zhomarta-tokaeva-narodu-kazahstana

Pavlyutenkova, M. Y. (2016). Electronic government as a vector of innovative state transformations. Retrieved from www.cyberleninka.ru

Pivovarov, Y. S. (2013). *Russian political tradition and modernity*. Brewers Y.S. Moscow. INION RAS.

Sidorenko, E. L., & Bartsits, I. N. (2019). The effectiveness of digital public administration: theoretical and applied aspects.

Smirnov, V. V. (2005). *An open state: ways to achieve it*.

Smotritskaya, I. I., & Chernykh, S. I. (2018). Modern Trends in the Digital Transformation of Public Administration. Retrieved from: https://cyberleninka.ru/

Soros J. (1997). A new look at open society. Moscow. Master.

Styrin, E. M. (2013). *The movement towards open government: global experience*. Moscow: Publishing House of the Higher School of Economics.

Styrin, E. M. (2013). *On some prospects for the development of e-government in the context of digital transformation*. Moscow: Pravo.

The portal eGov.kz. (2018). Retrieved from https://egov.kz/cms/kk US Open Government Directive

Vladimir, S. (2018). *Business & Economics, International Journal of Business and Economic Sciences Applied Research*. IJBESAR.

Zhvirblis, A. (2015). Elektronnaya demokratiya. Retrieved from https://www.opendemocracy.net/en/elektronnaya-demokratiya

Chapter 2
Evolution of Business-Government Interaction Models:
Their Use and Management

Sofiya Zhaleleva
https://orcid.org/0000-0002-5669-0018
University of International Business, Kazakhstan

Raziya Zhaleleva
https://orcid.org/0000-0002-5669-0018
Institute of Economics, Committee of Science, The Ministry of Education and Science, Kazakhstan

Alexandr Pasternak
https://orcid.org/0000-0002-5669-0018
University of International Business, Kazakhstan

ABSTRACT

In this article public-private partnership issues are considered. The purpose is to offer a partnership trio model for the Republic of Kazakhstan. This is possible taking into account international experience, as well as by exploring the possibilities of partnership among government agencies, business entities and scientific organizations within the national economic system. A model of forming a trio partnership, which is one of the most developed forms of public-private partnership, has been proposed. This is important from the point of view of the development of the state as a whole. The article also discusses the forms of contribution of each of the participants of the partnership to achieve the goal of improving efficiency. The research methodology is based on the developments of scientists in the field of partnership between science and business, institutional economics, the use of an integrated approach and the principles of dialectics to identify the essential characteristics of partnerships, as well as the conditions for their successful application in the national economy.

DOI: 10.4018/978-1-7998-2551-7.ch002

INTRODUCTION

Recently, proactive management approaches have been used in partnerships that change the innovative and industrial level of the national economy. The mechanism operates through a public-private partnership, which is widely used in various sectors of the economy, in the areas of economic and social infrastructure in industrialized, and in developing countries. The framework of the Nation's Plan "One Hundred Concrete Steps", the Law of the Republic of Kazakhstan "On Public-Private Partnership" has recently been adopted in Kazakhstan.

In this context, the overwhelming majority of the principles and forms of the economic interaction of business, scientific community and government are not yet adequately covered in domestic economic literature. It is rather a consideration not of two, but of three partners, because there are goals to achieve a high level of innovative industrialization in the country. Without scientific institutions as a part of partnership this goal cannot be achieved. Such a direction of increasing certain innovativeness level can be considered as a multistage program of industrial-innovative development of Kazakhstan. The issue is discussed in a Draft programme of industrial-innovative development of Kazakhstan for 2020-2025 presented in Nur-Sultan (2019). First of all it is required to create relationships between the state and business as a basis for trio partnership. This can be achieved by: government contracting, establishing a mixed public-private entrepreneurship, what is mainly viewed from the position of state regulation of a market economy; rent, concession, state property trust – from the point of view of market forms of state property management; leasing – as a form of small business support; investment - a component of the government's economic policy. In the context of this chapter, they are considered as forms and methods of economic interaction between business and government structures. This chapter considers an obtaining of new knowledge in the area of improving the management of partnerships among business, science and the state. The dynamic formation and development of the social economy in the republic depends on the efficiency and effectiveness of the improving process.

In general, the global and domestic experience of creating and operating a public-private partnership model deserves great attention and application in the republic. This should take into account not only the positive results achieved in the world practice, but also the negative consequences, possible risks, as well as the specifics of the national economy so as not to worsen the current situation, but to build own model leading the state to achieve high goals of economic growth and improving the welfare of citizens (Zhaleleva, 2016). Nowadays there is one-directed interaction in Kazakhstan: government creates conditions for business entities, infrastructure of entrepreneurship, guarantees implementation of legal and tax regulation. One of the examples can be found in analyzing of Doing Business ranking. According to the ranking Kazakhstan is working in direction to make better conditions for entrepreneurship. In recent years the position of the country has significantly increased from 77th in 2015 to 25th in 2019 (Ease of Doing Business rankings, 2019; Doing Business 2015. Going Beyond Efficiency, 2014). But the main problem is not in doing business easier even if great results are achieved. It is more important to find qualitative changes in the structure of Kazakhstani economy that is hard to do without increasing its innovative level. Also, it is assumed to realize principles of digitalization of economy, overall use of informational technologies.

The peculiarities of partnership relations between business community and state structures with the inclusion of the scientific environment into this process are very important and effective for Kazakhstan, when major changes are taking place in the national economy. The latter is aimed at significant changes in the level of innovation economy, increasing its competitiveness (R. Zhaleleva, Gabdullin, & Zavalishina, 2013).

The mechanism of public-private partnership with its wider implementation in economic processes allows obtaining such advantages as reducing costs and achieving efficiency. Even Western countries are not all fully covered by such a mechanism. For example, in the US, only 25 states have public-private partnership legislation. Other states, such as Ohio and Hawaii, are only studying such laws. There are those who are just beginning to assess the need to use the mechanism of public-private partnership. The growing interest in such projects is due to the fact that the public-private partnership mechanism is most applicable to complex, expensive, and long-term projects. American experience also shows that the success of a public-private partnership is achieved through a combination of two parameters – using the best opportunities of the government and the core value of the private sector, i.e. its effectiveness. The advantages include the fact that various forms of interaction are distinguished by reliability, transparency, timeliness of execution, reduction of the duration of implementation of infrastructure projects, etc., which is caused by duplication or inconsistency of the functions of various administrative bodies (Public-private partnerships in the US: The state of the market and the road ahead, 2016; Zhaleleva, 2010b).

BACKGROUND

Various aspects of the essence of public-private partnerships, as well as the processes of its formation and the technology of its functioning are rather deeply studied by foreign researchers, among which works of (Kim & Oh, 2010) and Osborne (2010) are distinguished.

Studies of Russian scientists are devoted to studying the interaction of business and government in various sectors of economy: Glazyev (2012); Jacovec (2004); Zudin (1996), Shamkhalov (2002), and others.

Features of public-private partnership as a phenomenon and a concept are considered in the works of Varnavskiy (2005); Zhaleleva (2016); Serikov (2013); Spanov and Zhaleleva (2017); Khalitova (2010), and others.

Various researchers of the problems of public-private partnerships, among which not only economists, but also lawyers, political scientists, etc., distinguish its most diverse models and forms in their works. It is noted that there are certain difficulties in classifying the latter, and their list is not exhaustive, since the choice of a specific form of public-private partnership depends on the economic efficiency of the implementation of each individual project. For example, Varnavskiy (2005) attributes a variety of contracts that the state provides to private companies to the forms of public-private partnership: for performance of work and provision of public services; for management; for supply of products for state needs; technical assistance contracts; rental (leasing) relations arising in connection with the transfer by the state in rent to the private sector of its property: buildings, facilities, production equipment; production sharing agreements; public-private enterprises; concessions.

However, despite all the diversity of modern publications on the issues of partnerships and management that regulate the state's influence on creating favorable conditions for the functioning of entrepreneurship, including monographs, textbooks, various articles in compilations and journals and other publications, problem of effective interaction of discussed parties is still unsolved. In particular, wider coverage of the problems associated with the implementation of partnerships in a situation of global instability is required. In this regard relations of public-private partnership are considered as an effective measure. In such relationships effective mechanisms of interaction among business structures, government institutions, the scientific and innovation community are aimed at improving the quality and competitiveness of Kazakhstan-made products, including goods and services, are accumulated. These imply the formation of conditions for the innovative industrialization of the national economy.

Methodology

The methodological basis of the work consists of an integrated approach and dialectical principles that allow revealing the essential characteristics of partnerships, forms of manifestation of this process and determine the trends of their development. The work also relies on the methodology of modern institutional-evolutionary theory, the theory of transition economies, the neoclassical school, as well as fundamental concepts. The basis for studying systemic changes in the institutional and organizational sphere of interaction between business, science and state was a combination of generally accepted assumptions in economic theory about the objective conditionality of the formation of new institutions that ensure the harmonization of public interests, tools for redistributing the income of large companies and small businesses, and others.

Main Focus of the Chapter

The current stage of development is tuned to new qualitative transformations of the economic system, which, as authors believe, cannot be achieved using only the levers of market self-regulation or relying solely on government regulation. All this requires an in-depth study of a possible set of methodological approaches known to the practice of economic activity and explains the renewing and cyclical revision of the existing and used levers of economic functioning. Each subsequent economic transformation is associated with the revision of mechanisms and the reform of the entire economic system.

The economic environment of the business is determined by the framework of the national economic system. Therefore, for successful business performance, government support and participation is an indispensable condition, which implies work of management apparatus. In this regard, it is quite appropriate to consider the interaction of state bodies of government and business in a broad and narrow sense. The first seems to be legitimate for the economic functioning within the national economy, regardless of whether it belongs to state or private property. Both those and others not only act on a common space, but also interact in various combinations as subjects and objects of the economy. Thus, state bodies manage state objects. In addition, they are subject to regulation of non-state property. The interaction of the state and business in a broad sense is reduced to the formation of conditions for a successful environment for economic activity carried out by business.

An important component of the modernization program should be the improvement of the national economy management system, which takes into account the need for synchronized transformation of controlling and controlled subsystems that meets strategic objectives of the competitive and safe development of the Republic of Kazakhstan. Synchronized modernization allows for the solution of a set of problems, with the implementation of which the model of the economy of Kazakhstan acquires an adapted development perspective even in the conditions of global instability, and in the conditions of steady growth receives an accelerated impulse. It is the last argument that makes it necessary to clarify the "rules of the game", since the wrong direction of movement and the force of inertia may not lead to the result expected to be achieved (Zhaleleva, 2013).

FINDINGS AND DISCUSSION

In Kazakhstan in connection with the reform of economic system two decades ago, it was decided to build a socially-oriented system. This decision was due to the existing experience of managing the national economy in the framework of two systems, namely command-administrative and market. It should also be noted that at the end of the last century, when moving from one system to another, our republic gained some experience of market self-regulation. Although, of course, that in a transitional economy, the role of state bodies and government is undoubtedly increasing, and especially during the period of growing crisis. Instead, in Kazakhstan, there was some loosening of government and, conversely, an increase in self-government, since the principle that the market would place the necessary accents was generally adopted.

In modern conditions, there is a change in a quality of business environment, which is given an increasingly stimulating character, especially in the sphere of innovations, which makes it necessary to form a new approach to the interaction of state bodies and business structures. All of this is impossible without the "rules of the game" of such interaction, which are established by the governance. In addition, in modern conditions, when special emphasis is placed on increasing the level of provision of a new round of technical and technological development of the production-economic and social environment, which is observed throughout the world economic space. A widespread innovative transformation of unused potential is assumed as a partnership mechanism as one of the untapped resources based on the alliance of government and business. A new level of innovation achievements is associated with the active participation of science and the entire scientific community.

In the last decade, there has been an active interaction of government and business through the mechanisms of public-private partnership in various sectors of the economy, the spheres of economic and social infrastructure. There are many examples in the economic literature, including systems with high, medium and low levels of economic development (Table 1).

In a crisis, overcoming it, stabilizing and resuming the growth of the national economy, this interaction can provide a synergistic effect, which gives an enhanced impact, and therefore takes on particular significance. In such critical periods, the state may be faced with the need to solve a set of social and economic problems. For example, this may be due to the need to help the areas affected by the crisis successfully confront general economic downturn and protect the most vulnerable categories of the population. Solving such problems requires investments of considerable public funds, and in fact in such years the society suffers from a lack of funds limited by general tax and budget revenues and the possibilities of internal and external borrowing. As well as during the crisis, and in a post-crisis period, there is a need for austerity and mobilization of efforts of all subjects of the national economy – the government, entrepreneurs, and financial structures involved in general socio-economic processes of functioning.

It is appropriate to focus on the interpretations of public-private partnerships used in the world practice. Today, there is a lively discussion in the economic literature and so far there is no consensus on how to correctly interpret a public-private partnership. The term has different usages even abroad. For example, in European countries and in developed Asian countries the abbreviation PPP is used (Public-Private Partnership), in USA and Canada – P3 or P-P Partnerships, in the UK the term "Private Finance Initiative" is generally accepted (PFI), in France the term "concession" is used. Naturally, such a variety in the designation of the concept of public-private partnership did not arise by chance, it was formed over many years. According to some sources, a public-private partnership first emerged in France in the form of a so-called concession, which arose in creating the infrastructure necessary for economic

Table 1: Various definitions of public-private partnerships

Authors and organizations applying different interpretations of the public-private partnership concept	Definition of public-private partnership
H. Van Ham, Y. Kopenyan	Long-term public-private partnerships, in which they jointly develop a product or service, share the risks, costs, and resources associated with these products or services.
G. Hodge, K. Greve	Institutional agreement between the public and private sectors for the purpose of cooperation, which is implemented through the creation of a new organizational unit.
V.G. Varnavskiy (2005)	Strategic, institutional and organizational alliance between government and business in order to implement socially significant projects in a wide range of activities – from basic industries and research and development to the provision of public services.
UN Practical Guide	Public-private partnership is based in the field of infrastructure to provide funding, planning, execution and operation of facilities, production and provision of public sector services.
OECD Science and Technology Policy Committee	Public-private partnership in the scientific, technical and innovation spheres – any legal and equal contractual relationship for a fixed or indefinite period of time among legal entities of the public and private sectors.
Commission on UK PPPs	Risk sharing relationships based on a concerted desire between public and private sectors to achieve the desired public policy.
Canadian Council for PPPs	Joint activities between public and private sectors, based on the expertise of each partner, which best satisfies clear public needs through an appropriate distribution of resources, risks and rewards.
HMT, Infrastructure Procurement: Delivering Long-Term Value,	Schemes characterized by joint activities of public and private sectors.
March 2008	Types of public-private cooperation and interaction, as well as the distribution of risks in the implementation of strategies, provision of services and construction of infrastructure.
Law of the Republic of Kazakhstan "On Public-Private Partnership"	Form of cooperation between a public partner and a private partner, corresponding to the characteristics defined by this Law

Source: (Reznichenko, 2010; Kholodnaya, 2009; Kazantsev & Rubvalter, 2010; Limonov & Oding, 2015; Law of the Republic of Kazakhstan "On Public-Private Partnership", 2015)

development in the 17th century. Then models of public-private partnerships were further spread and developed in Europe in the nineteenth century (there were projects related to transport infrastructure). In the 20th century, during the Great Depression, when the role of public administration in the economy became noticeably stronger, the importance of all types of partnership weakened. By the end of the same century, the intensification of processes of interaction between the state and business was again observed. Today, national economies of many countries have already come to understand that this mechanism is necessary for the full functioning of large economic systems, such as regional, national and global (Reznichenko, 2010).

In modern conditions, the accumulated experience in the use of public-private partnership is very interesting and extremely useful for Kazakhstan and can provide a noticeable economic result that contributes to improving the competitiveness of the national economy in the world market place. SWOT-analysis of public-private mechanism application in Kazakhstan can describe opportunities of it. Thus, there are next strengths: balanced distribution of risks, responsibilities and rights between the public and private sectors; reducing the burden on the state budget; transfer of use and ownership of state property to the private sector; increasing the transparency of government spending on the maintenance of the PPP object; more rapid introduction of new technologies; clearer orientation of services to consumer needs;

stimulating the development of the stock market and the banking sector; attraction of private internal and external investments; development of small and medium business; a variety of forms of long-term contracts concluded by the private sector with state and local authorities. In using the mechanism of public-private partnerships the following weaknesses were identified: longer planning procedures compared to budget investments; difficulty of forecasting for a long period of time due to changes in the market conditions; restrictions in some sectors (tariffs, licensing and others); difficulties in attracting investors to large projects; imperfection of the legal framework in the field of PPP. The SWOT analysis revealed the following opportunities for the functioning of the public-private partnership mechanism: political support; support from international organizations; improving the regulatory framework in the field of PPP; implementation of long-term development programs of the country; experience in the use of concessions in energy and transport sectors; emergence of new forms of interaction with the private sector; obtaining and disseminating knowledge and experience in the field of PPP; creation of new jobs; development of "near project" infrastructure; providing quality services at an affordable price; implementation of international standards, models, techniques and others. There are threats to use of public-private partnerships in Kazakhstan: worsening of the country's financial performance due to dependence on mineral prices and rising inflation; lack of knowledge in the field of PPP; lack of qualified personnel when using new technologies; incompatibility of standards.

It is obvious that there are many strengths and opportunities of the functioning of public-private partnership mechanism in our republic in comparison to weaknesses and threats when implementing public-private partnership projects. All of the above provisions testify in favor of introducing and improving partnership mechanisms of various economic entities in the national economy.

Based on the study of world experience in the use of mechanisms of interaction between state and business, as well as its various definitions, the authors' definition of a public-private partnership is considered as cooperation between government bodies, scientific organizations, business structures, and scientific and business associations in order to obtain a positive economic, social and environmental effect, acting within the framework of established common rules.

In the economic literature, there are at least two models of public-private partnership, operating in real economic practice (Varnavskiy, 2005; Kholodnaya, 2009; Kondratiev, 2002; Ignatyuk, 2006; Molchanova & Livshin, 2009; Gladov, 2008). One of them is a cooperation model, and another one is a contractual model. Within these models, there are various forms. Thus, according to the model of cooperation, state ownership is transferred to private ownership. Forms of this program are as follows:

- Corporatization of state property
- Transfer of object to private property
- Rent of state property with subsequent redemption

Forms of contractual model are the followings:

- Government procurement contracts
- Contracts involving the operation of the object by partners
- Project management support contracts
- Technical support contracts
- Retail public service contracts
- Contracts of rent and leasing operations

- Agreements under which the division of products is carried out
- Contracts under which the design and construction of facilities are carried out

There are conflicting opinions on the presented forms, which is due to differences in the interpretation of public-private partnerships, but, in authors' opinion, this can be overcome by using the terminology of state-business interaction, which allows resorting to the so-called expansive concept, pushing the formal framework of the approach.

Within the framework of a public-private partnership, a system is being formed that implements certain projects. Apparently, for the successful solution of the tasks put forward in the project, this system should be based on management principles that allow getting closer to the desired result.

A set of rules according to which the public-private partnership mechanism operates is its principles. According to the authors, the most important and key principle that stands out from the general system of management principles is the need for subordination and orientation of the mechanism to fulfill and achieve the goals of the partners. For example, if partnerships are among government agencies, the business community and scientific organizations, then it is natural to assume that all partners are interested in receiving well-defined dividends. In general form, state bodies are aimed at achieving public interests, other partners are also interested in realization of these public interests, since they are included in the public system, but at the same time, they have private interests. The latter can be participants in the creation of an innovative product, interested in making profit, etc.

Another equally important principle that underlies the public-private partnerships mechanism is a union of partners to achieve common interests, which involve mutual resources and efforts of partners in obtaining a final result. For example, state structures form necessary conditions for the implementation of projects. Business structures with modern management and other resources put into practice innovative projects. In turn, the scientific contribution is to bring the necessary knowledge and projects to create an innovative product. Combining into partnerships, these structures form a single mechanism for the implementation of the proposed project.

Next principle, which operates under the conditions of a public-private partnership, is related to the fact that these relations impose on each participant the possible risks and preferences of the project. At the same time, despite the partnership relations between its participants, the interests of the state have the highest priority. Participants of these relations in the implementation of projects are responsible for the work assigned to plan and ensure the overcoming of emerging risks. Also, partners knowingly determine the preferences and benefits obtained as a result of project implementation. In cases where the anticipated preferences of public-private partnership projects for some reason become not feasible in full or in part, the conditions for obtaining them are revised, but this is negotiated by contractual relations. Selected principles form the conditions that ensure the operation of the public-private partnership mechanism. Obviously, the system is not limited by these principles, it can be supplemented by other components.

Foreign experience provides various examples of interaction between government and business. For example, in the US public-private partnership is carried out in two possible directions. Firstly, it is the creation of a separate company implementing a project in a private sector, secondly, the formation of a special joint venture for the implementation of any project.

The successful implementation of projects contributes to the existing Advanced Technology Program (ATP). Within the framework of this program, the granting, conclusion of agreements on joint research and development, and the conclusion of contracts are permitted. Real practice gives preference to the use in this program of the second option of creating a joint venture and including small, medium and large companies. It is assumed that the project implementation period is not more than 5 years. In this case, payments for the project are carried out in the amount of budget funds allocated to the program. Noteworthy for the implementation of projects are similar conditions, according to which project initiators cannot be government organizations, academic institutions or independent research organizations. The exception is made by projects when an independent non-profit research organization establishes a partnership with two organizations aimed at making profit from the project (Kazantsev & Rubvalter, 2010).

The experience of using the mechanism of public-private partnership in Korea is interesting. In this economic system, public-private partnership projects are successful. Its results are presented in the form of competitive with modern analogues of the final product supplied to various markets by the most advanced world representatives. In Korea, partnerships are widely used. Moreover, it is reasonable to talk about the partnership of the state system, the business community and the scientific sphere. This is confirmed by the fact that a large number of technical innovations are produced in Korea: modern computer devices, cars of various classes of comfort, buses, medical equipment, etc. The economic system of this country fully provides its population with consumer goods: food, clothing for all age groups, cosmetics, etc. It is also worth noting the fact that the goods produced in Korea are exported all over the world, including Kazakhstan (Kim, 2013).

The interaction of the state system and business structures through the mechanism of public-private partnership will allow achieving the following:

- Firstly, creation of value added services, their cheaper provision by private entities with result-oriented management, modern planning methods and ability to quickly innovate and improve efficiency;
- Secondly, effective overcoming of joint risks with a private partner due to arising difficulties in current activities;
- Thirdly, obtaining benefits from ongoing projects, as well as from indirect effects associated with the revival of market conditions and growth of investment attractiveness.

The overall project, carried out in the framework of public-private partnership, is carried out by joint efforts of all participants. So, the business provides funds for the project, invests financial resources, professional experience, uses effective management, with flexibility and efficiency in decision-making, as well as the ability to innovate. This set of measures is usually carried out using effective work methods, improving equipment and technologies, applying more effective forms of organizing production, creating new enterprises, possibly with foreign capital, and establishing effective relations with suppliers and customers.

The state creates favorable conditions for implementation of the project in practice, providing tax and other benefits, subsidies and guarantees, as well as material and financial resources. To improve performance in the course of the project, it uses functions of planning, organization, motivation and control. Through direct and indirect influence, the state enhances business activities using various tools, methods and forms of management.

If the state, a business structure, and a scientific organization operate separately, it is difficult to implement any project in the current conditions of project promotion, especially in the period of global uncertainty. The interaction of these structures involves the implementation of joint projects. Thus, interests of all the participants of the partnership are realized, taking into account strategic interests of the country, in order to fully meet the needs of the population in providing with socially important goods and services, including consumer goods, housing and utilities services, medicine and education, infrastructure and transport, and etc. At the same time, the state creates favorable business conditions and capital investments, which guarantee an increase in the competitiveness of products, obtaining high added value and profits.

The government structures interacting with business and scientific organizations can get not only a reduction in the burden on the budget, but also provide a more flexible and efficient system for implementing a joint project. On the other hand, the business acquires a certain set of guarantees and preferences. The advantages of this approach in implementing socially significant projects with the help of commercialization are to reduce the share of expenditures of budgets at different levels to finance projects while achieving the desired economic and social effects. A major obstacle to the involvement of private investors in the implementation of such projects is the coordination of the interests of all project participants, including different levels of the state hierarchy.

When implementing socially significant projects, there is a contradiction associated with the indispensable accompaniment, since this is one of the conditions for business participation. Overcoming this contradiction is achieved by solving optimization problems, when they provide the expected effect with limited material, labor, financial and other resources. In addition, the formation of the investment attractiveness stimulates the participation of investors in socially important projects for the state.

Interaction of the government and business should be viewed as a combination of resources and opportunities for the implementation of socially significant projects and programs in many industries, services, and also in social sphere. Such interaction between the government and business can be the basis for the effective functioning and development of a modern economy. These relations between the state and business are based on the deep interdependence of partnerships in many planes and links of functioning including the scientific sphere.

Among the most important tasks of improving the management system a radical increase in the controllability of the socio-economic development processes at the level of individual regions can be identified. Despite the fact that Kazakhstan is a unitary state, the system of market relations objectively requires the decentralization of functions directly related to the livelihoods of the population and the development of the local economy, taking into account the peculiarities of the natural and socio-economic potential of each region (S. Zhaleleva, 2016).

Modernization of the system is closely related to the problem of its effectiveness. The everyday reality testifies the large role of public administration, which is strengthening in the conditions of complication and intensification of social processes. This is especially noticeable during periods of reforms and crises.

The relevance, characteristics, goals and structure of management systems are determined not only by the increased role in the life of society, but by the totality of its current tendencies and patterns, primarily socio-political, dictating a particular type of social management system and its transformations. Because of this, modernization process of management system must be comprehensive, covering both its constituent parts and organizational forms and functional manifestations of objects being managed and systems of society management.

The ability of state bodies under a democratic system of governance to provide, in conditions of severely limited resources, the satisfaction of the immediate needs of society as a whole and individual citizens serves as a criterion of its effectiveness. Management modernization will be successful while improving its structural and institutional organization and the quality characteristics of the staff of state bodies..

Kazakhstan has got many years of experience in operating a business. The legal basis for entrepreneurship has been defined, conditions for effective activity are created, which brings positive results for both the company and society as a whole.

Structural and functional construction of a public-private partnership can be presented in the form of three blocks:

- Goal-setting, including goals, objectives and principles of public-private partnership (joint participation of state and business in the formation of an innovative environment that ensures achievement of the goal of high performance and competitiveness in the market of goods and services; separation of possible innovative risks in implementation of joint projects of state and business; involvement and use of various channels of state support for innovation; attraction of various levers of public administration, ensuring the implementation of joint projects in practice).
- Organizational elements (government structures regulating public-private partnerships).
- Mechanisms of interaction between government and business, as well as the trio-partnership process.

The interaction of partners is needed for the creation of the competitive goods, services. Achievement of the goal will lead to an increased national competitiveness as well as to the formation of a favorable environment for interaction between economic entities. The organizational elements are designed to ensure the smooth interaction of the three considered partners. The Ministries of Finance, Investments and Development, Education and Science, Energy, Justice, etc., may act as indirect regulators. The direct regulatory body JSC Kazakhstan Center for Public-Private Partnership has originally been established under the Ministry of Economy and Budget Planning. After changing the structure of the government, it has become accountable to the Ministry of the National Economy (S. Zhaleleva, 2010, a).

The final block represents the process of interaction between state bodies, scientific sphere and business structures, which are considered as interaction factors leading to an effective trio-partnership (S. Zhaleleva, 2012). The result of such cooperation should be a new product, which is the achievement of the objectives.

According to some authors, the degree of interdependence of the state and business can be determined by the share of their participation in the partnership. For example, it is demonstrated by different stages of such cooperation (Figure 1).

According to the authors, the form of cooperation among state, science and business is at the highest level of interaction (trio partnership), and this is shown in Figure 1, where the ascent of the forms of partnership is presented. The trio partnership necessarily requires a high level of capacity and responsibility of managerial and other personnel, achievement of a certain indicator of the country's development, and etc. The use of this form of partnership will lead to the achievement of goals and certain results. But today in the Republic of Kazakhstan the partnership between state and business is at the level of a concession, which is an important form in the development of relations between government bodies and business representatives. It means an agreement on the transfer into operation of natural wealth, companies, enterprises and other economic objects belonging to the state or municipalities for individuals and legal entities for a certain period. The concession is also called the enterprise itself, organized on the basis of such a contract. In practice the definition is also used as an agreement that objects of contractual relations (property, certain types of activities) are in the undivided, monopolistic possession of only one of the parties to the agreement, namely the state or other public law institution. Another party to the

Figure 1. Development of partnership forms of state and business
Source: (Kosarlukov, 2012)

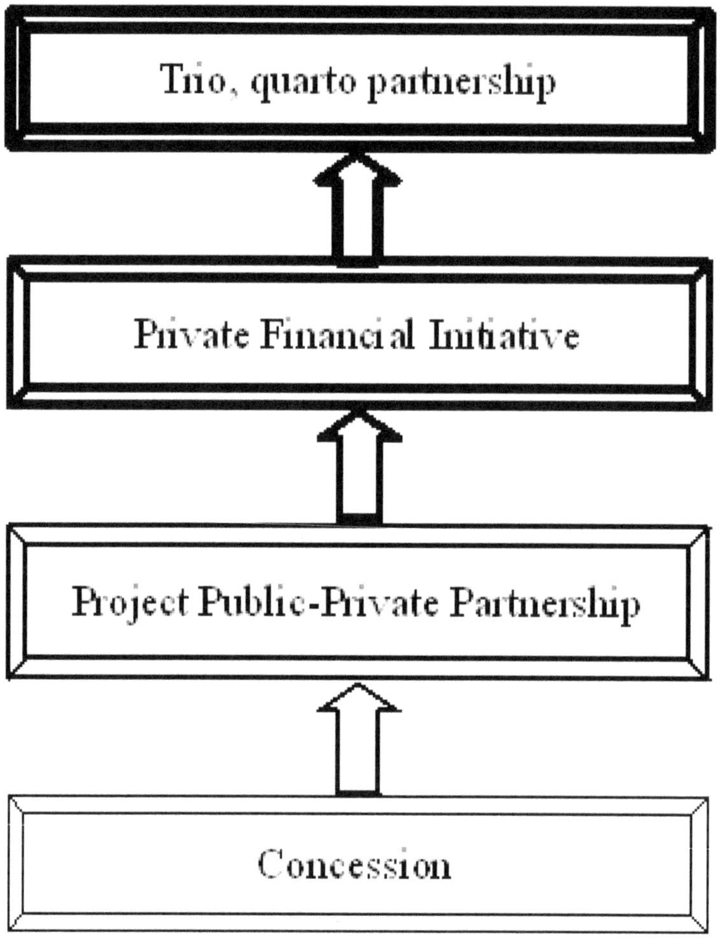

agreement is always an individual who assumes certain obligations in exchange for the rights granted to them. In a broad sense concession means an agreement between state and business, fixing conditions for the use of state-owned business (Sosna, 2003).

These relations can be considered to be at the initial level of formation In Kazakhstan. This process began to be formed relatively recently. Only in 2006 the Law of the Republic of Kazakhstan "On Concessions" was adopted, which contributed to the creation of a legal framework for using the concession mechanism for the purpose of implementing investment projects. This mechanism is widely used in the field of transport and energy. The regulatory framework on this issue is in the process of continuous improvement, it takes into account achievements of international practice (e.g., USA, Korea). For instance, in 2008 and 2010 a number of amendments were made to the legislation on concessions on the procedures for transferring objects to a concession, expanding state support measures and increasing the attractiveness of concession projects, canceling the issuance of infrastructure bonds.

In 2008 to strengthen the institutional system and economic expertise of concession projects, the Government of the Republic of Kazakhstan established a specialized organization for the concession issues – JSC "Kazakhstan Center for Public-Private Partnership". Its main tasks were defined as follows: providing high quality assessment and economic expertise of concession and budget investment projects; development of recommendations for the authorized body and interested state bodies on the improvement of the institutional system in the field of public-private partnership.

The Law "On Public-Private Partnership" was adopted in 2015. The law reflects the basic principles and norms of interaction between government structures and business entities. As a result, some programs of increasing the effectiveness of partnership relationships have been developed.

The modernization of the national economic system is connected to the development of the scientific and innovative sphere. Despite the fact that innovation is considered as the main feature of entrepreneurship, in Kazakhstan the state becomes the initiator of innovative transformations in the conditions of global instability.

Thus, the formation of innovative business in the Republic of Kazakhstan and the improvement of the economic indicators of the regions and the country as a whole is ensured by the use of productive, proactive management. This forms a positive effect of economic activity in the national economy. For the successful development of trio partnerships the Kazakhstan Public-Private Partnership Center has been created. The Center is designed to facilitate partnership projects at the micro level in the implementation of transport, social, automobile, railway public-private partnership projects (Kazakhstan Public-Private Partnership Center, 2016). This justifies the need to use proactive management tools in organizations associated with partnerships.

Thus, business management permeates the entire system including the implementation of specific projects at the micro level, the use of it by local government and self-government bodies. It contributes to the formation of a stable external environment that ensures the smooth functioning of the business, increasing the competitiveness of a region or city; providing opportunities for creating a small business by reducing tax rates, barriers to entry into the market, assisting in conducting marketing research; providing highly qualified assistance to small and medium-sized businesses in those areas that contribute to increasing labor productivity, introducing innovations, developing the enterprise and improving management; combining state, regional, as well as business resources with bases of higher educational institutions in order to meet the needs and requirements of business; protection of business interests through active support and assistance, control over the implementation of norms and laws in this area.

SOLUTIONS AND RECOMMENDATIONS

In general, in a short period of time, a versatile and fairly progressive system of public-private partnership has been created in Kazakhstan. It includes the followings:

- Government support (loans, guarantees, preferences and benefits, financing instruments).
- Contractual instruments (different types of concessions, service contracts).
- Infrastructure tools (free economic zones, industrial zones and technology parks, etc.).
- Corporate tools (state participation in the capital of legal entities - holding companies, national companies, joint-stock companies, development institutions, social-entrepreneurial corporations, venture and investment funds).
- Stock market (infrastructure bonds), etc.

Using the existing legislation, current situation and global experience, it becomes necessary to build and develop own model of public-private partnership. The model should take into account the specifics of the national economy. In this situation, in authors' opinion, an example of a public-private partnership created by Korean government bodies, scientists and businessmen is noteworthy, which is an example of a trio partnership. Authors can schematically suggest the model of Kazakhstan-private partnership (Figure 2).

In this trio, the government influence is carried out through direct and indirect methods that affect economic development, results of scientific activities and implementation of business processes. Direct regulators include legislative and administrative forms of government (laws, orders, decrees, directives, decisions of the authorities), and indirect regulators include economic forms (taxes, prices, tariffs, customs duties, loan interest, depreciation rates, compensation for work in harmful conditions) (Zhaleleva, 2016).

The scientific field, which is under the direct patronage of government, conducts fundamental and applied research and develops innovative projects (Kim & Oh, 2010). It is necessary to allocate scientific divisions and centers related to state institutions as well as private ones. At the same time both of them can carry out research studies using the funds of the state budget or their own investments.

Business process in terms of public-private partnership is based on the conditions generated by the state regulation and uses the achievements of scientific and engineering structures. To give innovativeness to the processes of interaction between public administration and business structures, it is necessary to attract a third partner, namely the scientific community. Moreover, this interaction should not just happen at the level of individual relations such as "state – science", "state – business", "business – science". For such a project to become successful, it is necessary to have an understanding of entrepreneurs about how this kind of cooperation can be successful for business. The benefits received by business structures can be expressed in the increased efficiency and effectiveness of their activities. The cooperation with scientific organizations and the creation of innovative products significantly increase the competitive-

Figure 2. Model of public-private partnership

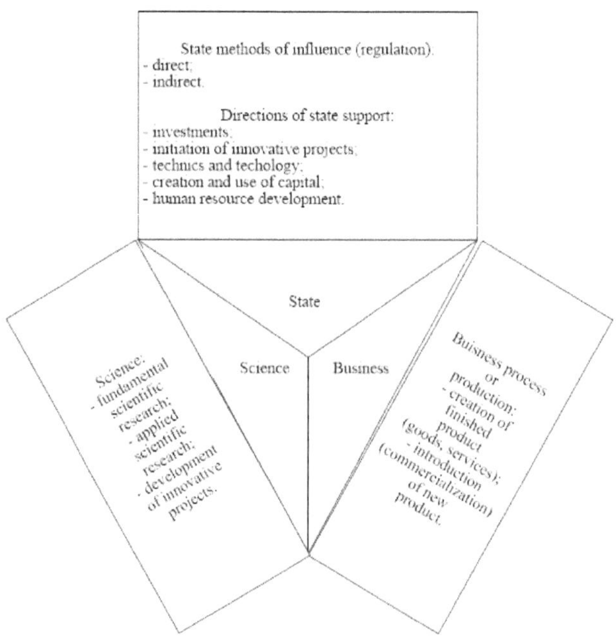

ness of the organization. The cost of production of goods and services is reduced and the opportunity to enter international markets appears, etc.

The state also receives many advantages when participating in trio partnerships. The main one is the increasing of national competitiveness, which is the ultimate goal of many Kazakhstani development programs and plans.

As a result, the scientific community as a partner has advantages of commercialization of new ideas, i.e. their introduction into production and obtaining the greatest benefits.

FUTURE RESEARCH DIRECTIONS

Discussed PPP model is applicable for different countries of Eurasian region, where many of them in face of their governments are trying to implement the best practices to achieve desirable state of social and economic effectiveness. Kazakhstan is active participant of different programs and policies in direction of sustained economic growth, social improvements, strengthening of competitive advantages. One of the examples that in recent years many of Eurasian countries including Kazakhstan are intensively introducing the development programs into governmental strategies according to principles of Organization for Economic Co-operation and Development (OECD). Many of them participate in programs such as OECD Eurasia Competitiveness Programme (ECP), Support for Improvement in Governance and Management (SIGMA), Green Action Program in Eastern Europe, the Caucasus and Central Asia (EaP GREEN), etc. (Supporting Eurasia countries in their reform efforts, 2019).

All the projects can be successfully realized with the use of public-private partnership model in different areas. The participation of the parties (state and business subjects) can add the value, expressed in achieving of expected results. Thus, according to considered interaction model, government will create normal conditions of functioning for business entities. The latter will play a decisive role in implementation of different joint projects with the use of effective managerial approaches. The realization of the principles of partnership between government and business is expected to improve relationships in economic industries of countries. These improvements will result in increased competitiveness at micro and macro levels. It is important to understand that it will be not only economical or financial (commercial), but also social and environmental (ecological) effects. Due to the fact that business entities should answer principles of social responsibility they can easily manage the process. On the basis of these directions a lot of global risks of modern time are considered that should become trends for further development (The Global Risks Report 2019, 2019). It is a basis for introduction of innovations. All of the listed effects will be possible to achieve by means of sharing of best experiences among countries with the active participation of businesses, governments and scientific institutions.

CONCLUSION

The mainstay of modernization transformations in the national economic system is the development of scientific and innovative spheres. Innovation is considered as the main feature characterizing entrepreneurship, in particular small and medium-sized businesses. But the state becomes the initiator of innovative transformations in Kazakhstan in conditions of global instability.

Thus, the formation of innovative business and the improvement of economic indicators in the Republic of Kazakhstan and in its regions are ensured by the use of productive, proactive management. They form a positive effect of economic activity in the national economy. The successful development of trio partnerships in the Republic of Kazakhstan is facilitated by the implementation of projects at the micro level (transport, social, automobile, railway, etc.). This justifies the need for proactive management tools in organizations associated with partnerships.

Thus, business management pervades the entire system. It includes the implementation of specific projects at micro level, the use of it by local authorities and self-government bodies. This contributes to the formation of a stable external environment, ensuring the followings:

- Uninterrupted business operation, increasing the competitiveness of a region or a city;
- Providing opportunities for a small business creation by reducing tax rates, barriers to entry into the market, assisting in conducting marketing research.
- Providing highly qualified assistance to small and medium-sized businesses in areas that contribute to increasing of labor productivity, introducing innovations, developing an enterprise and improving management.
- An association state, regional, and business resources with higher educational institutions in order to meet the needs and requirements of business.
- Protection of business interests through active support and assistance, monitoring the implementation of norms and laws in this field.

REFERENCES

Doing Business. (2014). Annual Report. Retrieved from https://www.doingbusiness.org/content/dam/doingBusiness/media/Annual-Reports/English/DB15-Full-Report.pdf

Draft programme of industrial-innovative development of Kazakhstan for 2020-2025 presented in Nur-Sultan (2019). Atameken. Retrieved from https://atameken.kz/en/news/32482-proekt-gpiir-00-0-prezentovali-na-ploshadke-atamekena

Ease of Doing Business rankings. (2015). Doing Business. Retrieved from https://www.doingbusiness.org/en/rankings

Gladov, A. V., & … . (2008). Foreign experience in the implementation of public-private partnership: General characteristics and organizational and institutional framework. *Bulletin of SamSU*, *7*, 36–55.

Glazyev, S.Y. (2012). Modern theory of long waves in economic development. *Economic science of modern Russia, 2*(57), 8-27.

Ignatyuk, N. A. (2006). Public-private partnership in Russia. *Law and Economics*, *8*, 3–7.

Jacovec, J. V. (2004). *Epochal Innovations of the 21st Century*. Moscow, Russia: Economics.

Kazakhstan Public-Private Partnership Center. (2016). Official Web page. Retrieved from https://kzppp.kz/

Kazantsev, A. K., & Rubvalter, D. A. (2010). *Public-private partnership in science and innovation.* Moscow, Russia: INFRA-M.

Khalitova, M. M. (2010). *Economic interaction of the state and business in the context of strengthening the social orientation of the economy of Kazakhstan: theory, methodology, mechanism* [Doctorial dissertation]. Institute of Economy, Almaty, Kazakhstan.

Kholodnaya, N. D. (2009). Public-private partnership - a new type of relationship in the Russian economy. *State and Municipal Administration Issues*, *2*, 42–49.

Kim, B. (2013). Impacts of S&T Investment as an Innovation Tool in Korea. In *Symposium on Global Perspectives and Issues – Measurement of Economic and Social Impacts of S&T Investments, AAAS 2013 Annual Meeting*. Academic Press.

Kim, B., & Oh, S. H. (2010). *7 Knowledge-Based Elements for Strategic Science and Technology Planning*. Seoul, Korea: Ad Fly.

Kondratiev, N. D. (2002). *Large conjuncture cycles and prediction theories*. Moscow, Russia: Economics.

Kosarlukov, A. V. (2012). Public-private partnership as a form of interaction between the state and business. In *Proceedings of the VIII International Scientific and practical Conference "Science days – 2012"* (pp. 8-11). Prague, Czech Republic: Publishing House.

Law of the Republic of Kazakhstan of October 31, 2015 No. 379-V *"On Public-Private Partnership"* (with changes and amendments as of 04.03.2019). (2019). Retrieved from https://online.zakon.kz/document/?doc_id=37704720

Limonov, L. E., & Oding, N. U. (2015). *Actual problems of the development of PPP projects in the social sphere in the regions of Russia. International Centre for Social and Economic Research "Leontief Centre". The project "PPP in the social sector - the dissemination of the experience of the UK and St. Petersburg*". St. Petersburg, Russia. Retrieved from http://www.leontief-centre.ru/?lang=l2

Molchanova, O. P., & Livshin, A. J. (2009). *Public-private partnership in education.* Moscow, Russia: KDU.

Osborne, S. P. (2010). *Public private partnerships: theory and practice in international perspective.* London: Routledge.

Public-private partnerships in the US: The state of the market and the road ahead. (2016). Price Waterhouse Coopers. Retrieved from pwc.com/us/infrastructure-ppp

Reznichenko, N. V. (2010). Models of public-private partnership. *Bulletin of St. Petersburg University. Management Services*, *4*, 59–83.

Serikov, R. S. (2013). Systematization of the main forms of public-private partnership. *Actual Problems of Economics.*, *9*(147), 492–496.

Shamkhalov, F. I. (2002). *Theory of Public Administration.* Moscow, Russia: Economics.

Sosna, S. A. (2003). Concession agreement - a new type of contract in Russian law. *Journal of Russian Law, 2.* Retrieved from http://uristy.ucoz.ru/publ/12-1-0-616

Spanov, M.U., & Zhaleleva, S.Z. (2017). Mechanisms of public and private partnerships for the effective development of self-employment in Kazakhstan. *Bulletin of Kazakh National University, 4*(122), 208-216.

The Global Risks Report 2019 (14th ed.). (2019). *World Economic Forum.*

The OECD and Eurasia. (2019). Supporting Eurasia countries in their reform efforts. Retrieved from https://www.oecd.org/eurasia/countries/

Varnavskiy, V. G. (2005). *Partnership between the government and the private sector: forms, projects, risks*. Moscow, Russia: Science.

Zhaleleva, R. Z., Gabdullin, R. B., & Zavalishina, A. A. (2013). Factor-targeted approach in the implementation of innovative industrialization of the economy of Kazakhstan. *Actual Problems of Economics, 7*, 323–332.

Zhaleleva, S. Z. (2010 a). Development of public-private partnership in the Republic of Kazakhstan. *KIEM Science Journal, 2*(11), 161–164.

Zhaleleva, S.Z. (2010b). Model of interaction of government and small business in the Republic of Kazakhstan. *Economy: strategy and practice, 2*(14), 82-86.

Zhaleleva, S. Z. (2012). Features of modern transformations of economic systems. In *Proceedings of the VIII International Scientific and practical Conference "Science days – 2012"* (Vol. 21, pp. 32-35). Prague, Czech Republic: Publishing House.

Zhaleleva, S. Z. (2013). Constructing the model for public-private partnership in the Republic of Kazakhstan. *Actual Problems of Economics., 7*(145), 315–322.

Zhaleleva, S.Z. (2016). *Management of Partnership Relations in Kazakhstan.* Almaty, Kazakhstan: Nur-print.

Zudin, A.J. (1996). Russia: business and politics (business and government interaction strategies). *World economy and international relations, 4*, 17-27.

KEY TERMS AND DEFINITIONS

Concession: An initial stage of public-private partnership associated with projects in energy and transport sectors.

Corporatization of State Property: A reorganization of state companies with the aim of their privatization and PPP project organization.

Innovative Industrialization: A process of economy transformation ensuring its innovative reorganization.

Proactive Management: A management activity aimed at preventing negative trends during project implementation.

Public-Private Partnership (PPP): A cooperation between government bodies, scientific organizations, business structures, and scientific and business associations in order to obtain a positive economic, social and environmental effect, acting within the framework of established common rules.

Strategic Management: A long-term management action aimed at achieving the goal with the use the most efficient managerial solutions, for PPP projects can be up to 30 years.

Trio-Partnership: The highest level of interaction in PPP project implementation, where the number of participants is three, namely government, business and science.

Chapter 3
Improvement of Sustainable Employment Through Increasing Access of Enterprises to Financial Resources in Developing Countries:
The Case of Tajikistan

Shokirjon Mahmadov
Russian-Tajik Slavonic University, Tajikistan

ABSTRACT

Enterprises have traditionally played a vital role in providing sustainable employment, thus contributing to overall social and economic growth of countries. However, many developing countries such as Tajikistan face unemployment because enterprises are not fully functioning there. Evidence from this study shows that enterprises, especially SMEs, could help improve sustainable employment if not faced with obstacles to flourish. The main challenges causing enterprises in developing countries to fail include lack of skills, access to bank credits, access to markets, high tax burdens, insufficient state support, inability to compete, etc. This study looks at the role enterprises, especially SMEs, could play in improving sustainable employment through increasing their access to financial resources in Tajikistan.

INTRODUCTION

Enterprises play a crucial role in the development of economy, especially when negative effects of recent economic downturns in many countries around the world cause obstacles to their overall social and economic development. The development of enterprises is becoming important in Tajikistan, a country with growing population, due to the economic recession in Russia that is hosting more than 1 million labor migrants (guest workers) from Tajikistan. There is no doubt that healthy enterprises contribute to the

DOI: 10.4018/978-1-7998-2551-7.ch003

development of economy in the form of new products, new jobs, greater exports and taxation revenues. It is necessary that small, medium and large enterprises enhance their job creation abilities to respond to negative effects of recent economic downturns (Kongolo, 2010). However, Tajikistan enterprises have not yet been able to respond to the needs of the country to tackle unemployment, have more taxation revenues, and help the country overcome the dependence on imported products. Enterprises have historically faced failures in creating sustainable jobs. As a result, thousands of people among whom the majority is youth (aged 18-39) go to Russia or other countries to seek jobs, usually seasonal ones. There are many reasons behind enterprise failures, including, but not limited to, lack of skills of both managers and employees, access to financial resources and credits, access to markets, high tax burdens, insufficient state support, inability to compete, etc.

There is no a doubt that along with enterprises, banks contribute to the social and economic development of the country, especially to the development and expansion of activities of enterprises, thus, increasing of export, creation of jobs, as well as other income generating activities. The role of banks, especially commercial ones, is essential in providing financial resources for enterprises in need of funds to cover their investment activities. However, banks, as financial institutions to accumulate financial resources and direct them to potential clients such as enterprises, among others, have not been sufficiently able to perform their main function.

Although the Government of Tajikistan and its development partners have undertaken necessary measures to address the said barriers, the issue of access of enterprises to both internal and external financial resources remain crucial. Therefore, this study aims to look at the role that enterprises, especially SMEs, could play in improving sustainable employment through increasing their access to financial resources. It will look at factors, especially the lack of access to financial resources, causing enterprise's failure in Tajikistan, thus, failing to ensure sustainable employment. This will help to have a good understanding of stagnate economic development in Tajikistan, including its dependence on remittances, huge migration, budget deficiency, import dependence, social instability, etc. Viable solutions to solve the said problem are necessary. The paper tries to come up with some recommendations that are expected to open up some discussions among both scholars and practitioners.

The main objective of the chapter is to determine main causes of the lack of access of enterprises to financial resources which will help to improve their survival and development. To determine the said causes and to broadly understand the relationship between unemployment and enterprises problems, as well as to see the extent of importance of financial resources issues, the following questions need to be answered:

1. What are the main causes of the failure of enterprises to create jobs in Tajikistan?
2. What are the causes of the lack of access of Tajik enterprises to finance?

In making an attempt to answer the above questions, it is worth mentioning that while the chapter admits that there are several causes of the failure of enterprises, it will look at the lack of enterprises' access to financial resources as the main reason of their failure. In addition, the chapter looks at the reasons of the lack of access to funds, with a special focus on access to bank credit.

The chapter assumes that although a lot of support by development partners (USAID, Asian Development Bank, DFiD, World Bank) and the Government of Tajikistan has been provided to enterprises in the country, the measures to increase their access to finance have been insufficient. Newly established enterprises need financial resources to operate and expand their activities to respond to populations growing needs, however, despite not having enough internal resources, they face lack of access to external funds such as banking loans. Therefore, the assumption is that once, along with other support, access to finance is ensured, Tajik enterprises can survive and develop and, thus, create more jobs and bring other benefits to the economy that will ensure sustainable development. This shows that sustainable employment is an important trigger of sustainable development of the economy.

Making an attempt to provide an overview of the situation of unemployment and enterprises failure to provide sustainable jobs due to their limited access to finance, this chapter is in its essence a brief survey of existing literature and studies on enterprises' access to finance in Tajikistan. It is also based on personal observation of the situation by the author. As such, it does not claim to be a complete research with some concrete examples. The main contribution of the chapter is to open up some issues and problems that could be the subject of further discussion and research by scholars within and beyond Tajikistan.

RESEARCH BACKGROUND

The role of enterprises in the economic development has always been a topic for discussion of both scholars and practitioners. When it comes to Tajikistan, after the demise of the Soviet Union, the country suffered from a harsh civil war (1993-1997) that brought about many economic and human ruins and losses. The economic infrastructure, including plants, factories, etc., were left ruined. As a result, thousands of people lost their jobs. Therefore, economic revitalization seemed logical with a focus on rehabilitation of plants and factories. However, it was not easy for the country to fully restore its economic infrastructure. Therefore, the majority of the population, especially the youth, faced difficulties to find jobs and, thus, started migrating to other countries, mainly Russia and Kazakhstan. Migration has a huge impact not only on the lives of migrants themselves and their families, but on the whole economy too. For instance, in 2013 the remittances from labor migrants made up to 52% of Tajikistan's gross domestic product (Trilling, 2014). Attempts to support enterprises to be able to create jobs have failed due to geographic (poor infrastructure), technological (lack of innovative production, business and managerial skills), financial (unfavorable lending conditions), bureaucratic (complicated procedures to start a business) hurdles, etc.

Because of the reasons mentioned above, the country has not only been unable to provide its growing population with jobs, but has also faced other economic issues like insufficient tax revenues, dependency on import, mass migration of its working population, inflation, etc. These, coupled with the recent economic decline in Russia, have made it necessary to think about the support of enterprises, especially small and medium ones, in the country. Therefore, the Government of Tajikistan has prioritized productive employment in its National Development Strategy for the period up to 2016-2030 along with such priorities as overcoming communication/connectivity deadlock, promotion of energy efficiency, achieving food security and safety, etc. The National Development Strategy for the period up to 2016-2030 emphasizes the importance of financial institutions in the development of the national economy. The Strategy envisions that the financial sector, including the banking system of Tajikistan, will be a competitive and effective sector by 2030. The banking system will contribute to the creation of a conducive environment for sustainable development of the national economy. The Strategy also mentions about the challenges of the financial sector that need to be addressed. These difficulties include the fact that the banking sector does not fulfil its main role – financing the national economy, streamlining the process of domestic production, supporting the economic growth, contributing to the development of key sectors of the economy, etc. It is well known that financial institutions, or banks, are milestone of the economic development. Therefore, financial stability of banks and the development of the national economy are indispensable. The prosperity of banks depends on the development of production sector, while the development of the production sector depends on the effective functioning of the banking system.

To ensure protection and support of enterprises, the Government of Tajikistan has also adopted a Law on the State Protection and Support of Entrepreneurship. The Law is very important in terms of defining the main concepts related to enterprises, as well as singling out the main rules for running a business. The following definitions are taken from the said law for the purposes of this chapter (2017, p.3). The entrepreneurship is defined as "an independent activity by persons (at their own risk and peril) who are registered in accordance with existing laws of the Republic of Tajikistan". As for the enterprises, the Law defines them as "physical and legal entities registered in accordance with the provisions of the legislation of the Republic of Tajikistan". The law also distinguishes between small, medium and large types of business entities. Small enterprises are individual entrepreneurs and legal entities whose gross income is up to 500,000 Tajik Somoni (approximately 50 000 USD) per year. Medium-sized enterprises are legal entities, the annual gross income of which is between 500,000 (five hundred thousand) and 15, 000, 000 Tajik Somoni. Large enterprises include legal entities whose annual gross income is more than 15, 000, 000 Tajik Somoni.

It should be noted that Tajikistan's private sector is mostly represented by individual entrepreneurs making up 89% of total business entities in the country and 11% of legal entities (medium and large enterprises).

Tajikistan government's efforts have also been supported by development partners to improve the doing-business environment. However, the number of enterprises is drastically shrinking. For instance, according to the Ministry of Industry and New Technologies of Tajikistan, 181 enterprises, which employed around 2, 000 people, have closed down in the six months of 2019 (Chorshanbiev, 2019). Being predominantly represented by small enterprises, Tajikistan's private sector is non-dynamic and faces more failures than successes.

The problem of enterprises failure and success in changing environment has been studied both by local, as well as international scholars. It is thoroughly studied in Africa, Middle East, Russia, but Tajikistan's case, especially the financial aspect of the problem with a special focus on increasing access of enterprises to financial resources, has not yet been sufficiently studied. Although the number of international publications, especially publications in English, on the access of enterprises to bank credits/financial resources is limited, there are some scholars and economists studying different aspects of the banking system and its role in the development of the economy. Their publications are available in the Tajik language and are published in local journals.

Theoretical and practical aspects of the banking system in Tajikistan, especially its role in the development of economy as a whole, have been studied by such scholars as Rakhimov, Rakhimov, Safarov, Umarov, Aminov, Yatimov, etc. Research conducted by the said scholars has undoubtedly contributed to the study of the bank loans as the main source of funds for the investment activities of enterprises in Tajikistan. However, the research has focused on bigger issues related to micro- and macroeconomic aspects of the banking system. For instance, a local scientist Rakhimov (2003) emphasizing the important role of credit organizations in the economy, states that the possibilities of economic growth, the development of the real sector of the economy, non-economic relations, the activity of stock exchanges and improving the living standards of the population as a whole are largely determined by the level of development of the banking system. In his opinion, improper management of the banking system and inefficient use of banking resources can lead to the destruction of the national economy. Supporting this position, Safarov (2010) notes the importance of the role of credit organizations in the development of the real sector of the economy. He emphasizes that the credit organizations, as the main and integral elements of the national economy, play a special role in the development of production, the supply of credit, the redistribution of capital, settlements, etc. This chapter also agrees that the credit institutions, with the help of their resource and the provision of other types of services, contribute to increasing the country's economic potential and, as a whole, lead to economic growth. Specifically, the credit institutions can play a vital role in accumulating financial resources and providing necessary loans to enterprises that need capital for the expansion of their investment and other business activities.

A famous Tajik economist Umarov (2005) has also agreed with such point of view. According to him, credit is important to develop various areas of the national economy. In his turn, Aminov (2010) stating that credit organizations are the main factor in the development of the economy, notes that credit organizations can significantly affect the course of development of the country's economy through the provision of credits.

It is clear that bank credits are one of the main sources of financing of investment activities of enterprises, medium and small businesses, and other economic entities. The role of the banking system and its influence on the development of the economy was studied by Yatimov (2004). Agreeing with the opinion of most scholars that credit institutions are an important element of the economy, he writes that the bank is a special institution that plays a significant role in improving the economy of a country, including in the Republic of Tajikistan. He also considers crediting to be one of the main aspects of the activities of banks and their impact on the economy.

A review of papers and articles published by local and foreign economists shows that they consider credit to be a main factor in the development of the national economy. Given credits are important for enterprises to be able to create jobs in a country with huge unemployment rate, like Tajikistan, this chapter supports the point of view above.

In addition to scholarly articles on the importance of credits for the economy as a whole and job creation in particular, access of enterprises to financial resources, there are some studies and reports by financial institutions and international organizations. For example, Organization for Economic Cooperation and Development's "Enhancing excess to finance for SME development in Tajikistan" (2015) delivers practical advice on the implementation of reforms to improve access to finance for small and medium-sized enterprises in Tajikistan. The recommendations build on discussions of public-private working groups. Thus, we can infer that both scholars and practitioners agree on the importance of enterprises for job creation and the role of the bank credit for them to expand their activities.

FOCUS OF THE CHAPTER

After gaining independence, Tajikistan faced many problems and challenges due to the devastating civil war (1993-1993). As many plants and factories stopped providing sustainable jobs for the population, thousands of young people, especially male, left to other countries (Russia, Kazakhstan, etc.). As a result, the country faced nationwide poverty and other social and economic problems. However, the country has recently made continuous progress in reducing poverty and growing its economy. Between 2000 and 2017, the poverty rate fell from 83% to 29.5%, while the economy grew at an average rate of 7 percent per year.

However, job creation has not taken place sufficiently to meet the demands of the growing population, leaving the economy dependent on other countries and vulnerable to external shocks. The private sector's role in the economy remains limited, contributing to only 13% of formal employment and 15% of total investments. It is clear that the lack of employment opportunities in the country is directly connected to the failure of enterprises to create necessary jobs. To better understand the causes of failure of enterprises to create jobs for the growing population, it is crucial to look at the population growth and employment in the country and then provide some overview of the situation with enterprises and their access to financial resources. It is also necessary to look at the banking system of Tajikistan as the main potential source of finance for the activities of enterprises. Despite the civil war in early 1990s that caused more than 150, 000 human deaths and thousands of people's displacement, the Tajikistan population had been dynamically growing and reached 8.9 million people in 2017 compared to 5.3 million in 1990. Moreover, the share of population of 14 years old is huge making up 1/3 of the total population that will undoubtedly become a substantial burden for the labor market in the near future. Coupled with devastated damages of the economic infrastructure, the growing number of the population has made it difficult for the economy to be able to create enough jobs. It is quite normal not to have enough employment opportunities in a situation when there is a big population growth and the number of enterprises is slumping.

Although the portion of unemployed population is huge in the country, the official statistics shows the following rates: 2.5% in 2014, 2.5% in 2015, 2.4% in 2016 and 2,3% in 2017. This is because there is no reliable data on unemployment in Tajikistan and many unemployed citizens do not register their status due to difficulties caused by complicated bureaucratic procedures. The Government of Tajikistan develops a special program aimed at analyzing the current labor situation and foreseeing the trends in coming years. For example, in accordance with the State Employment Promotion Program for 2018-2019 (2017), the number of labor resources is expected to reach 5, 395, 200 in 2018 and 5, 519, 200 in 2019. Compared to the number of labor in 2016, 5,6% increase will occur. Due to the natural increase of the population and labor resources in 2018-2019, the labor force (economically active population) will also increase. The program foresees that during 2018 - 2019, the number of Tajikistan's labor force will reach 2, 584, 700 and 2, 644, 000 people. Compared to 2016, the growth in the labor force during these years will grow approximately by 8.4%. During this period, the employed population will amount to 97.6 percent of the workforce and in 2018 will amount to 2, 522,700 people, and in 2019 2, 580, 500 people. Over the next two years, the number of employed people will increase by 8.2 percent compared to 2016.

Although the Program does not have the real number of unemployed population in the country, it is still clear that due to the natural growth of the population in the country, the labor market will force more supply of labor than it demands (compare growth in increase of labor force by 8.4% with the increase in the number of employed people by 8.2%).

As for the current state of the labor market, according to statistics, the labor force amounted to 2, 301, 400 people in 2017, out of which 2, 247, 400 people (97.7%) were employed and 54, 000 people were officially registered as unemployed (2,3% of the workforce). However, in reality the rate of unemployment is much higher, especially in rural areas (ADB, 2016). The Tajikistan Living Standard Survey conducted in 2009 estimated the unemployment rate at 21% and the youth unemployment rate (aged 15-24) at 37%. Due to further population growth and economic decline in Russia that has forced many migrants to leave Russia and come back to Tajikistan, the unemployment rate is likely to have substantially increased by now. This has revealed Tajikistan economy's high vulnerability to external shocks due to its dependence on migrant remittances that are subject to economic situation of Russia and other countries receiving labor migrants from Tajikistan.

As the real situation with unemployment is different and the country faces a lot of unemployment (evidenced by huge migration), the Government of Tajikistan understands the real problem and undertakes necessary activities to tackle it. For example, the State Employment Promotion Program for 2018-2019 identifies job creation, with focus on jobs for youth and women, as one if its priorities. Therefore, to reduce the dependency on remittances sent back home by labor migrants from Russia and other migrant-receiving countries, development of the private sector and encouraging enterprises to create sufficient sustainable employment is important for Tajikistan. There is no doubt that enterprises are essential for Tajikistan's socio-economic development. They can boost inclusive and sustainable economic growth by increasing employment opportunities throughout the country, from rural areas to big cities, and help reduce mass labor migration and offer returning labor migrants better conditions.

The private sector of Tajikistan is mostly presented by small and medium enterprises (SMEs). However, it should be noted that along with not professionally developed business strategies, poor management, lack of knowledge and know-how, the development of enterprises is mainly hampered by the lack of access to finance. Majority of SMEs are unable to access affordable funding to start, run and grow their businesses. For instance, the World Bank's enterprise surveys (2014) have revealed that 22.7% of Tajikistan's SMEs identify access to finance as a major constraint in their business. Many of enterprises identify access to finance hurdles as much hampering their businesses development than obstacles related to taxation or to external factors, such as geographical isolation or the deteriorating infrastructure. While access to credit from financial institutions is constrained, internal resources are also lacking, as capital is scarce for all enterprises. Only 13.3% of SMEs in Tajikistan have a bank loan compared to an average of 39.1% in the Eastern Europe and Central Asia region (EECA). Only 5.5% of SMEs' investments are financed by banks opposed to 14.8% in the EECA (World Bank, 2014).

Because the banking sector is not sufficiently satisfying credit needs of enterprises, the Government of Tajikistan has supported the establishment of a special fund to support SMEs through subsidized credit lines. The Entrepreneurship Development Fund provides direct credits at preferential terms to SMEs and is administered by the State Committee for Investments and State Property Management. As of October 2017, the Fund has supported around 154 enterprises (200 million Tajik Somoni (about 20 million USD). Similarly, there are funds supported by development partners. For example, the Tajikistan Rural Finance Program financed by KFW and administered by the Ministry of Economic Development and Trade of Tajikistan provides preferential credits through microfinance institutions with the aim of stimulating rural development. While these efforts are very crucial in supporting enterprises in the country, the funds are not still sufficient to meet credit demand in Tajikistan.

If Tajik enterprises have difficulties to access bank credits due to the problems associated with the banking system on the one hand, their access to credits is constrained by their inability to meet requirements of lending organizations, on the other hand. For example, up to January 1, 2017, 69, 5% of created enterprises (28697) closed down in the country. Since the private sector accounts for about 67% of national employment, 68% of GDP and 89% of tax revenues, such business failures are hampering the development of the economy as a whole.

Arguing on the vitality of enterprises for job creation, scholars have identified main reasons of their failures in developing countries. For instance, discussing the access of small and medium enterprises to the capital, Malhorta et al. (2006) have demonstrated that SMEs are more credit constrained because of the following reasons: (i) lack of well-functioning financial market; (ii) lack of know-how on the side of suppliers of credit; (iii) high risks associated with lending to SMEs, etc.

As mentioned above, one of the major challenges faced by Tajik enterprises is a constrained access to affordable finance. However, access to finance is essential for Tajik enterprises to fully employ their potential. According to Akhmedov (2018, pp. 20-21), the main reasons behind failures of many enterprises in Tajikistan include, but not limited to, depreciation of fixed assets, lack of working capital, lack of demand for domestic products and many others. Taken together, these causes create a barrier to sustainable economic development in the country. To solve these problems, enterprises need additional capital to expand their activities by having more investment. In such situation, bank credit is considered one of the main sources of investment activities of enterprises. Consequently, the weak access of enterprises to bank credit remains one of the key factors in the degradation and lag of production and, thus, failure of enterprises to create jobs.

In order to better understand the access of enterprises to credits in Tajikistan, understanding the banking system and the situation around it is essential. The modern banking system of the Republic of Tajikistan is a set of credit organizations that implement their own function aimed at meeting the needs of the population in banking services and products. In accordance with the Law of the Republic of Tajikistan "On Banking Activities" (2009, p. 1), the banking system of the Republic of Tajikistan is a two-layered system consisting of the National Bank of Tajikistan and other credit organizations functioning in the country.

According to the Law of Tajikistan "On Banking Activities" (2009, p. 1), the National Bank of Tajikistan is the main element of the banking system in Tajikistan. The main objectives of the National Bank of Tajikistan set out in article 5 of the Law of the Republic of Tajikistan "On the National Bank of Tajikistan" (2011) are to maintain a long-term internal level of price stability, achieve and maintain stability in the purchasing power of the national currency, develop and strengthen the banking system of the Republic of Tajikistan and contribute to the efficient and smooth functioning of the settlement system. It should be emphasized that the National Bank of Tajikistan is a key institution in the development of the national economy.

According to the National Bank of Tajikistan, as of September 30, 2019, the second layer of the banking system of Tajikistan is represented by 75 credit organizations, including 17 banks, 21 microcredit deposit organizations, 6 microcredit organizations and 31 microcredit funds.

Discussing on the importance of banking sector's contribution to the national economy, Gayurov (2019) has divided the influence of banks on the economy into direct and indirect. The direct influence of banks on the economy are credits as one of the main financial sources of investment in the economy. Indirect influence of banking sector is demonstrated through two areas – monetary policy and infrastructure. In Tajikistan, banks have a substantial influence on the economy mainly through their credits (direct influence). Therefore, it is crucial for Tajikistan banks to identify sound ways to manage their credits effectively. However, due to lack of effective management of credits, the sector is facing many difficulties and challenges.

Hence, one can surely say that there are many problems associated with crediting of investment activities of enterprises in Tajikistan. Substantial amount of credits provided by Tajik banks have too short maturity level – up to a year. The volume of long-term credits is 6-7% (Gayurov, 2019). However, enterprises usually need long-term credits, especially if these are needed for their investment activities. The reason Tajikistan banks cannot provide long-term credits is the lack of financial resources in the banks. Banks themselves need capital as, on the one hand, their own capital is not sufficient, on the other – they have difficulties to attract external resources such as deposits by the enterprises and population.

Moreover, interest rate is very high and makes it difficult for the majority of enterprises to afford it. The average interest rate in the banking system of Tajikistan has recently decreased from 36% to 28, 18%. Compared to other countries, the interest rate in Tajikistan is too high (Gayurov, 2019).

Because of the factors mentioned above, the volume of bad loans has been drastically increasing recently. This indicator increased in the analyzed period by 7.1%. The total amount of bad loans in 2017 amounted to 1,655 billion Tajik Somoni, thereby making up 17.1% of the loan portfolio of credit institutions. This indicates that the financial condition of credit organizations is deteriorating in the country adversely affecting the overall situation with the provision of credits for enterprises. To solve such problems, an evidence-based strategy and tactics of credit management is necessary. Otherwise, the number of credit organizations will continue to shrink.

As a result, the number of credit organizations is decreasing in the country. If in 2012 the total number of credit organizations was 143, it shrank down to be 85 in 2017 (Gayurov, 2019). If the number of credit organizations continues to decrease, Tajikistan economy will encounter huge challenges in providing enterprises with necessary financial resources. As a result, the employment opportunities will further decrease.

Taking into account the above mentioned, one can conclude that there are a number of factors causing limited access to financial resources, mainly bank credits. The reasons can be grouped as follows:

1. The financial sector is limited and lacks competition. The banking sector is insufficient and dominated by four local banks (Agroinvest Bank, Oriyonbank, Amonatbank, Tojiksodirotbank). Competition, including from foreign banks, is very limited. As mentioned above, there are 75 credit organizations, including 17 banks, 21 microcredit deposit organizations, 6 microcredit organizations and 31 microcredit funds, as well as 327 branches of financial institutions throughout Tajikistan.
2. Deposits remain low. Due to a lack of deposits, especially long-term deposits, the financial institutions have difficulties in providing credits, especially long term-credits. It is explained by the fact that either the population, as well as enterprises, does not have sufficient money to deposit in financial institutions, or there is low confidence in banking system due to its fragility. According to the National Bank of Tajikistan, although there is a growing need in credits by both the population and enterprises, the volume of deposits has remained at almost the same level as shown in the Table 1 below:
3. Interest rates for credit from financial institutions are very high and collateral requirements difficult to meet. According the National Bank of Tajikistan (NBT), as of August, 2019, the weighted average rate on credits in local currency is 24.49% (NBT, 2019). In addition, some studies of the interest rates of different banks in Tajikistan reveal still higher rates of interest: up to 35%.
4. Maturity of credit is very short. SMEs are also constrained due to the usually very short maturity of credit – most loans are due after a period of six months to one year.
5. Moreover, many enterprises face difficulties regarding the amount of credit they obtain which does not fulfil their credit needs.

Table 1. The volume of deposits

Year	Deposits, total (thousand Tajik Somoni)
2015	93 512 504
2016	113 415 765
2017	109 539 026
2018	113 016 087

Source: National Bank of Tajikistan (https://nbt.tj/ru/banking_system/overview_banking_system.php)

The problems mentioned above are of system character and cover state (creation of conducive environment for the development of financial sector), banks (development of sound lending strategies meeting the requirement of enterprises), as well as population and other businesses (deposits). Here, it becomes clear that a system approach to solving the problem of access to finance is necessary. The author tries to provide some solutions below that are expected to open up some discussion among scholars and practitioners for further in-depth study and elaboration.

SOLUTIONS AND RECOMMENDATIONS

Given important role of enterprises to improvement of sustainable employment and, hence, the as a whole economy, activities to support, promote and enhance their access to finance are justified. Because the banking sector is insufficiently developed in Tajikistan and the lack of enterprises' access to finance remains one of the main barriers to doing business, it is recommended to take some actions to further develop enterprises by providing them with necessary financial support through improving access to finance.

While efforts have been undertaken by the government and development partners to improve the situation, it is necessary to fully support the sector to increase banks' competitiveness, to attract foreign banks to the market, to promote banks attractiveness for deposits, etc. At the same time, it is important to promote enterprises financial literacy, business strategy, especially a credit strategy so that they could develop a viable business and be able to return lent money timely. In a short-run, the government should be actively engaged in developing enterprises through providing finance on favorable terms given the commercial banks are not sufficiently providing enterprises with necessary funds.

As Tajikistan faces mass migration due to its inability to provide the growing population with sustainable jobs, the amount of remittances is substantial being the main income source for majority of households in Tajikistan. However, remittances are rarely put in banks as they are received cash and kept at home and are mostly used for consumption. By undertaking some sound activities, like motivating labor migrants to use their money in the economy, remittances could make a substantial contribution to finance the local businesses and, thus, improve sustainable employment. Overall, the following three ways are proposed:

- To improve the state support of financial institutions, including through provision of subsidized credits to commercial banks;

- To improve the knowledge and skills of commercial banks in providing "friendly" credits, including close cooperation with enterprises in developing their business, a well as credit strategies;
- To seek to change the mindset of businesses and the population to deposit their money into banks, including increasing their confidence through enhancing banks' reliability.

These measures require a set of activities to be conducted, including reforms by the government, trainings for state and bank officials, awareness raising campaigns for the population and businesses, etc.

FUTURE RESEARCH DIRECTIONS

Having studied the situation with the role of enterprises in improving sustainable employment through increasing their access to finance, with a particular focus on banking credits, as well as hurdles causing them to fail, this study does not claim to be a complete research with some concrete examples, as well as clear focus on certain types of industries or regions. Therefore, after having provided an overview of the situation of unemployment and enterprises failure to provide sustainable jobs due to their limited access to financial resources in Tajikistan, as well as making an attempt to open up some issues and problems that could be the subject of further discussion and research, it is worth mentioning that the topic of the financing sources of investment activities of enterprises, particularly of the banking credit as such, has been studied by international and domestic scholars. However, despite the fact that the access of enterprises to bank credits and other sources of financing is important for the private sector to develop and prosper, in Tajikistan it remains one of the main causes of enterprises' failure.

Therefore, further research to assess the financial situation of enterprises at the regional and national levels and banks' investment activities with specific examples of providing credits to enterprises, solvency assessment of enterprises, risk analysis, as well as the ways and approaches to attracting and effectively using bank credits and other related, is necessary. Although the study has revealed some causes of enterprises' failure, further study is necessary to study the link of each cause to such a failure. It is crucial to look at the role microfinance intuitions play in lending money to enterprises. In addition, it could also be useful to research the role and importance of remittances in improving the access of enterprises to finance so that to ensure sustainable employment in the country. Lastly, some comparative studies of a similar situation could be conducted to reveal lessons learned in other countries and draw some necessary conclusions and recommendations to improve the situation in Tajikistan and other developing countries.

With regard to the three ways to solve the issue of access of enterprises to finance, it is proposed to deeply study the following:

- The current situation around state policy to support banks, their competitiveness, as well as challenges and opportunities. It could also be beneficial to study experiences of other countries in supporting banks through subsidized state loans so that banks could provide low-interest, long-period maturity credit;
- Find out knowledge and skills gaps of banks' staff, including in strategic planning, credit provision and management, etc. This can help develop some models, including based on similar experiences of other countries;
- Thinking and common financial practices of the population to find out justified ways to attract them to deposit their money. This could focus especially on migrants, as they are sending big

amount of remittance that, if appropriately streamlined, could improve not only attracted resources of commercial banks, but also livelihoods of migrants, thus contributing to socio-economic development of the country.

CONCLUSION

From the above, it is obvious that the development of enterprises is essential in providing sustainable employment in developing countries, like Tajikistan. The role of enterprises in providing sustainable jobs is crucial as the country's population is growing and the economy is not able to adequately respond to employment needs. Therefore, many people, especially males are seeking jobs in other countries such as Russia and Kazakhstan, etc. Although there are many factors hampering the enterprises to sufficiently function, the access to finance remains one of the biggest hurdles causing a higher failure rate of enterprises in Tajikistan.

The following problems in accessing credit have been identified:

1. The financial sector is limited and lacks competition;
2. Deposits remain low;
3. Interest rates for credit from credit organizations are very high and collateral requirements are difficult to meet;
4. Maturity of credit is very short;
5. Amount of credits is not sufficient to satisfy credit needs of organizations.

The results of the study reveal that access to finance is hampered by unfavorable terms and conditions such as high interest rate, short repayment periods, long consideration of applications, etc. Many enterprises face these obstacles in getting loans which is necessary for them to expand their activities through investment. Thus, failure of enterprises adversely effects the ability of enterprises to contribute to sustainable employment. Facing many obstacles, both internal and external, enterprises need state support in making their business successful. The current chapter has shown that enterprises could create sufficient employment should they have access to enough financial resources. A sufficient banking system backed by sound government interventions is necessary for the prosperity of the economy. This demonstrates that there is an urgent need to develop and carry out a set of activities aimed at creating a better banking environment with enterprises having better business strategies and vision to effectively and efficiently run credit policies. The government-run Entrepreneurship fund could have more positive impacts should it increase interaction with local banks both in improving access to credits and conducting educational campaigns on better business management. The chapter has also reveled that due to the lack of a special and in-depth study on the essence and role of the credit as the source of financing of enterprises' investment activities, solvency assessment of enterprises, risk analysis, as well as the ways and approaches to attracting and effectively using bank credits and other related further research by both scholars and practitioners is important is crucial to assess the financial situation of enterprises at the regional and national levels and banks' investment activities with specific examples of providing credits to enterprises, solvency assessment of enterprises, bank credit risk analysis, etc.

REFERENCES

Akhmedov, M. Z. (2018). *Improvement of the mechanism for interaction of banking sector and the real sector in Tajikistan (the case of bank loans) (PhD dissertation).* Khujand State University named after Gaforov, Khujand, Tajikistan.

Aminov, Kh. I. (2010). *Modelling and information technology of the assessment of the credit risk of the commercial bank in the Republic of Tajikistan.* Dushanbe, Tajikistan: Monographiya.

Asian Development Bank. (2016). *Tajikistan Promoting Export Diversification and Growth.* Philippines: Asian Development Bank.

Chorshanbiev, P. (2019, June 30). Predpriyatie v Tadzhikistane bol'she zakrivayut, chem otkrivayut (in Tajikistan, enterprises are more closed down than established). The Asia Plus.

Gayurov, G. H. (2019). *Organizational and economic aspects of the use of banking potential in the Republic of Tajikistan] (PhD dissertation).* Tajik National University, Dushanbe, Tajikistan.

Kongolo, M. (2010). Job creation versus job shedding and the role of SMEs in economic development. *African Journal of Business Management, 4*(11), 2288–2295. Retrieved from http://www.academic-journals.org/AJBM

Law of the Republic of Tajikistan on the State Protection and Support of Entrepreneurship (2017). Republic of Tajikistan.

Malhorta, M., Chen, Y., Criscuolo, A., Qimiao, F., Illieva, I., & Savchenko, Y. (2006). *Expanding access to finance: Good practices and policies for micro, small and medium enterprises.* Washington, DC: World Bank.

OECD. (2015). Enhancing excess to finance for SME development in Tajikistan.

Rakhimov, Z. (2003). *The development of the banking system of Tajikistan in a transitional economy* [doctoral dissertation]. Russian Economic Academy, Moscow, Russia.

Safarov, E. R. (2010). *Banking and real sectors of economy of Tajikistan* [PhD dissertation].

The law of the Republic of Tajikistan "On banking activities." (2009). Government of Tajikistan.

The law of the Republic of Tajikistan "On microfinance organizations." (2012). Government of Tajikistan. Retrieved from https://nbt.tj/tj/laws/

The law of the Republic of Tajikistan "On the National Bank of Tajikistan." (2011). Government of Tajikistan.

The State Program for Promotion of Employment in the Republic of Tajikistan for 2018-2019] (2017), No 499, Dushanbe, Tajikistan. Available at http://www.adlia.tj/show_doc.fwx?rgn=130357

Trilling, D. (2014, April 15). Tajikistan: Migrant remittances now exceed half of GDP. *Eurasia Net.* Retrieved from http://www.eurasianet.org/node/68272

Umarov, K., & Zarifiva, Z. (2005). *Monetary and credit problems of development of the national economy*. Dushanbe, Tajikistan: Irfon.

World Bank. (2014). *Doing Business: Going Beyond Efficiency*. Washington, DC: World Bank Group.

Yatimov, Kh. M. (2004). Development of banking services of the national economy (the case of Tajikistan). Unpublished PhD dissertation, Tajik State University of Commerce, Dushanbe, Tajikistan.

KEY TERMS AND DEFINITIONS

Bank: A credit organization the main purpose of which is to make profit, has its equity registered capital established by the National bank of Tajikistan, as well as a right to fulfill at least three of the following operations: attracting deposits, issuing credits, opening and managing bank accounts (Law on Banking Activities, 2009).

Banking System of the Republic of Tajikistan: The National bank of Tajikistan and credit organizations functioning on the territory of Tajikistan (Law on Banking Activities, 2009).

Credit Organizations: Legal persons (banks, non-bank credit organizations and microfinance organizations) carrying out all or some of the banking activities after obtaining the license issued by the National bank of Tajikistan (Law on Banking Activities, 2009).

Entrepreneurship Development Fund: A fund established by the Government of Tajikistan to support entrepreneurs mainly through providing start-up funds.

Microcredit Deposit Organization: A legal entity created in order to attract deposits, savings and the provision of microcredits in accordance with the Law of the Republic of Tajikistan on microfinance organizations (2012).

Microcredit Fund: A non-profit legal entity created in accordance with the Law of the Republic of Tajikistan on microfinance organizations (2012) to provide microcredits.

Microcredit Organization: A legal entity created in order to provide microcredits in accordance with the Law of the Republic of Tajikistan on microfinance organizations (2012).

Sustainable Employment: Created jobs throughout an extended period.

Tajikistan National Development Strategy (2016-2030): A strategic document of the Government of Tajikistan reflecting its development vision, mission and goals up to 2030.

Tajik Somoni: Tajikistan's national currency.

Chapter 4
Digital Agropolis as a Model of Sustainable Development in Rural Areas of Eurasia Region

Galym Issabayev
Kazakh Leading Academy of Architecture and Civil Engineering, Kazakhstan

Alma Issabayeva
University of International Business, Kazakhstan

ABSTRACT

The concept of digital agropolis was proposed to ensure food security through the creation sustainable rural eco-settlements in the Eurasian region to produce environmentally friendly products through modern agricultural and digital technologies which cause minimal damage to nature. The digital agropolis model was developed in the form of a detailed description of the distinguishing features of structural systems, functions, and features that leverage green and digital technologies throughout all its components. The model can be replicated with modifications in the Eurasian countries, since it meets common strategic objectives, such as the sustainable development of rural territories; the export-oriented production/processing of organic agricultural products; the sustainable development of rural areas based on the green economy, smart agriculture, and the operations/logistics digitalization; and development of new technologies for organic farming and livestock.

INTRODUCTION

The agro-industrial sector in the countries of Eurasia faces the problems such as the need to increase food production and create employment opportunities for the population in the rural area. In addition, global factors and rapid technological changes are affecting the agricultural sector. Thus, it is vitally necessary to create a model of sustainable rural development in the region.

DOI: 10.4018/978-1-7998-2551-7.ch004

Food security is critical to the economies of developing countries - according to the global report on food security in 2018, 113 million people from 53 countries experienced hunger (Global Report on Food Crises, 2019). Earlier, the authors proposed a new definition - "Bio-food security" (Issabayev & Issabayeva, 2013; Issabayeva & Issabayev, 2013) in global, regional and national contexts, given the high importance of the combination of terms - "food security" and "food safety."

The main objective of this study is the theoretical and practical justification of the feasibility of creating a Digital Agropolis as an innovative form of using rural resources in the aspect of a sustainable development strategy in the direction of ensuring bio-food security using digital technologies in the Eurasian region.

The starting point is a confidence that the organic agriculture (Sugden, 2001; ScienceDaily, 2017; Raja & Masresha, 2015) can be an effective way to improve the global economy by ensuring bio-food security and promoting the health of future generations. Global conversion to the organic farming can contribute to a deeply sustainable food system combined with further measures, in particular, one-third of animal products in the human diet, less concentrated feed and less food waste. At the same time, this type of food system has extremely positive environmental consequences, a significant reduction in chemical fertilizers and pesticides and a reduction in greenhouse gas emissions, and does not lead to increased land use, despite lower agricultural yields (ScienceDaily, 2017, November 15). In 2007, EU Regulation (EC) 834/2007 introduced principles and criteria for the processing of organic food. Several scientific publications and research project reports have analyzed and discussed these rules. In recent years, these principles and criteria determine the quality of organic food, after testing and adaptation of its processing (Kahl et al., 2014).

Agricultural production in Eurasia can bring profit to millions of rural residents. It should be noted that the foothill regions in the countries of the region have great potential for the development of organic farming. However, the industry has so far failed to diversify its exports, which would allow it to play a more significant role, for instance, in the economies of Central Asian countries (Voices on Central Asia, 2018, October 11) – the part of the Eurasian region. Based on the ideas of bio-food security, the concept of a Digital Agropolis proposed to create sustainable rural eco-settlements in the Eurasian region that produce environmentally friendly products using modern agricultural and digital technologies with minimal damage to nature.

The fertile piedmont zones of Zailiysky Alatau in Kazakhstan, the Kyrgyz Alatau in the Kyrgyz Republic, and the Kuraminsky ridge in Uzbekistan (Fig.1) were selected because they are favorable for the development of organic agriculture. These regions have little exposure to chemical fertilizers, and are optimal for the use of green energy sources - wind flows, solar radiation, and biomass energy. Water from several rivers, as well as from the groundwater sources, supplies these fertile soils and irrigated lands.

The abovementioned factors create good basic conditions for the production of organic crops. These areas are also ecological zones with traditional livestock breeding (Issabayev & Issabayeva, 2013) and they are ideal conditions to create a full cycle of bio-production within the framework of the Digital Agropolis concept.

The map retrieved from http://www.asia-atlas.com/central-asia.htm

The Digital Agropolis model provides a detailed description of the distinctive features of structural systems, functions and capabilities compared to other forms of organization of the agro-industrial cluster. It proposes to create a complex for the production and processing of organic agricultural products, research services and housing using green and digital technologies in all its components. It is possible

Figure 1. Location of Digital Agropolises identified by the authors

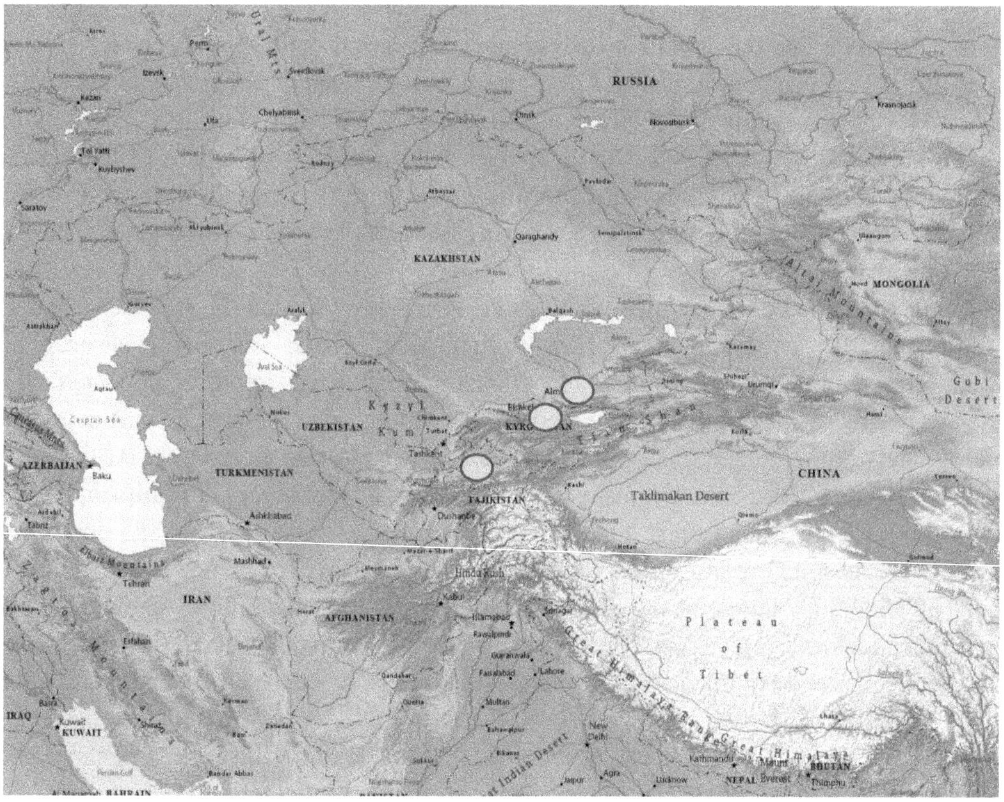

to replicate the model with various modifications in any country of the Eurasian region with similar environmental conditions.

BACKGROUND

The study includes the analysis of data collected in the course of literature reviews and cartographic studies, with a critical assessment of existing opinions and specific geographical, geological and climatic conditions in the foothills of Eurasian countries. This allowed developing a model of sustainable agro-settlement for organic farming using innovative technologies, renewable energy sources, and a modern digital management system.

As a part of the research method, the authors developed graphic materials, layouts of master plans, as well as diagrams. The presented model also incorporates smart-control center with sensor systems for monitoring soil moisture, plant growth, applying organic fertilizers, as well as digital monitoring of processes: work of agricultural machinery in the fields, processing of agricultural products and logistics, etc.

This chapter is organized as follows: a) describes climatic conditions of the selected zones; b) presents outlines of the model of Digital Agropolis; c) describes principles of territorial planning of a Digital Agropolis, and shows master plan layouts for Kazakhstan, Kyryzstan, and Uzbekistan; and d) concludes the chapter.

MAIN FOCUS OF THE CHAPTER

Climatic Conditions of the Three Considered Zones

The Zailiysky Alatau ridge, like all internal mountain systems, has a climate associated with the vertical zoning, latitude and longitude of localization, and considerable distance from the seas and oceans. Localization in the middle of the Eurasian continent and the southern location focused on increasing the amount of heat, reducing humidity, and the sharp continental climate.

Due to the increase in the relative height above the sea level in the foothills and, accordingly, the increase in humidity, not very hot weather in summer is established here, and the winters are milder. At the beginning of the vast foothill plain, from the Ili River and the Kapchagai artificial reservoir to the glacial peaks, the climate changes quite significantly over a hundred kilometers - from the hot, dry, and sharply continental climate to the humid and very cold on one of the branches of the Silk Road. ("Climate of Zailiysky Alatau", 2019). The above climatic characteristics of this steppe piedmont zone are analyzed by the weather stations located in such points as Almaty city (observatory area, at the altitude of 848 m above the sea level), Talgar (1015 m above the sea level), and the Kamensky plateau (1350 m above the sea level).

In general, the foothill zone has not very hot and humid climate. The average temperature throughout the year ranges from 7.7°C to 8.7°C. The average temperature in July has a plus of 19.3°C - 22.4°C, and in January within - minus 3.7°C-7.4°C. In the summer months, the air temperature exceeds 20°C. The average annual rainfall is 559 mm. In total, positive atmospheric temperatures range from 2510 to 3140', SCC 0.7 - 1.0, and the number of the frost-free days with nights is 174 - 181 days.

The main precipitation occurs in the spring-summer period, with a maximum in springtime. Autumn has mainly dry and warm conditions. In such months as August, September, October, the amount of average monthly rainfall is in the range of 10 - 30 mm. In the zone under consideration, relative humidity is optimal and approaches on average 55–60%. In the hottest months, the relative humidity occasionally has the indicator below 50%. The usual duration of the winter period having a snow cover reaches 101 - 104 days.

Snow cover in winter reaches a height of 25-30 cm. Depending on humidity these average data may have deviations in different years. The Almaty region has up to 924 mm of rain in the wet years and up to 293 mm in more arid years. Therefore, irrigation is required for normal conditions of plant growth, mainly at the end of summer and autumn.

While the colder regions of the country have a large amount of precipitation which causes significant moisture or even flooding of soils, this foothill zone has no excessive moisture: the evaporation is so significant that the humidity approaches 1500 mm.

Dry years in this area are also not critical. During the significant heat and dry weather, the intensity of glacial melting increases, and as a result of this, the water flows in mountain rivers for irrigation increase. During this period, crops show a significant yield on irrigated soils.

The experts of the Kazakh Research Hydro-Meteorological Institute analyzed the amount of precipitation, temperature differences, fairly mild and relatively dry winter periods, and with a certain degree of conventionality, attribute the climate of the foothill zone of Almaty and Almaty region to as close to the Mediterranean, favorable for human habitation, animal breeding and growth plants ("Climate of Zailiysky Alatau," 2019; Bolch, 2007).

The climatic conditions in the foothills of the ridge of Kyrgyz Alatoo are very similar to the foothill zone of the Zailiysky Alatau. Thus, according to the main climatic parameters, it can be considered equivalent and optimal for the development of organic farming.

The distinguishing climatic features of Uzbekistan are the aridity and large amount of heat and light. Moreover, the region's climate is continental, manifested in inter-annual and inter-specific variability of climatic characteristics. The territory of the northern part of the Republic of Uzbekistan can be attributed in terms of the climate characteristic as moderate extreme, and the southern part - as subtropical. At the same time, geographic localization, the intensity of solar radiation, local conditions of atmospheric circulation, and the characteristics of the terrain affect the climate indicators within the region.

The territory of the country is located in the middle of the Eurasian continent, as well as the previous two regions, far from the seas and oceans. In the region under consideration, there are a significant amount of sunny days, large daily and annual temperature fluctuations, and insignificant amount of precipitation. In the summer, the sun in Uzbekistan reaches a considerable height above the horizon. On June 22, the sun in the northern part of the country is above the horizon at an angle of 68°, in the southern part at an angle of 76°. On the flat parts of the country - in the deserts and steppes of Kyzylkum, Mirzachul and Karshi, the indicator of solar radiation reaches 137-160 kcal during the year.

The period of time for the fall of solar radiation extends longer than in the Mediterranean and California (USA), which are located at the same latitude (Kļaviņš, Azizov, & Zaļoksnis, 2014). At the same time, the average temperature in the atmosphere in January can reach 0° C and sometimes lower. For example, at the Ustyurt plateau - as low as -10°C, in the oasis city of Tashkent up to -1°C, in the city of Termez - up to + 2.8°C. In the summertime, warm air currents localize in the valleys. The atmosphere becomes dry and hot, filled with the fine dispersed dust. The average atmospheric temperature in July is between 32-33.5°C in the north on Ustyurt and 36-37.5°C in the south - in Termez. The mountain systems situated in the eastern part of the country trap southwestern humid atmospheric masses. This leads to significant precipitation in the mountain and foothill zones.

Outlines of the Model of Digital Agropolis

The Digital Agropolis concept is innovative because it represents the territorial-planning decisions of agricultural territories in the selected foothill zones – the ranges of Zailiysky Alatau, Kazakhstan and Kyrgyz Alatau, Kyrgyzstan, and the Kuraminsky ridge in Uzbekistan. These spatial planning solutions are adapted to local climatic conditions, for modern production and processing of organic agricultural products using digitalization, and the energy supply from green renewable energy sources. The Digital Agropolises should become the driver of the socio-economic development of the areas due to creation of a system of smart agriculture, application of biotechnologies, digital management and control, energy self-sufficiency, and comfortable living conditions.

Smart Agriculture in the Digital Agropolis

The Digital Agropolis model foresees usage of principles and technologies of the Smart Farming (SF). The agricultural sector is undergoing a new revolution and transformation based on Internet of Things (IoT), sensor technology, Big Data (BD), and cloud computing. This digital revolution in agriculture looks like an irreversible process, ready to revolutionize agriculture and the entire food production sector (Himesh, 2018). However, agriculture does not utilize the potential of information technologies (IT) in full (Milovanović, 2014). Intelligent agriculture includes the implementation of information and communication technologies in machinery, equipment and sensors for use in agricultural production systems.

The key advantages for the food production and logistics in Smart Farming are real-time transparency in delivery of the diverse groups of agricultural products from suppliers to consumers, autonomous monitoring, and control systems. Logistic processes should have more opportunities to maximize compliance with the industry 4.0 requirements, in terms of both applying the latest technologies and increasing vertical and horizontal interaction between industrial partners throughout the supply chain (Kayikci, 2018). At the same time, integration between various systems available on the market has been identified as one of the main factors limiting the development of SF. Another limiting factor is the education, ability and skills of farmers to understand and use SF tools (Pivoto et al., 2018). To overcome the latter, it proposed that the Research and Development Center in the Digital Agropolis would provide training courses for farmers and other relevant staff.

Out of the high technologies used in the agricultural sector in recent years, the space monitoring of cultivated lands becomes very relevant. For example, the aridity of agricultural land is one of the main threats in the agricultural sector, which can lead to significant crop losses even in the foothill areas. In this case, for flexible response to the situation, the space monitoring of agricultural territories can provide substantial assistance. For example, data from the European Space Agency (ESA) on surface temperature was used to control drought in agricultural land (Hu et al., 2019).

Thus, the space and aerial photography of regional land resources and mapping them to assess soil and crop conditions allows modeling processes associated with regional activities, predicting crop yields, livestock numbers and product prices (Markelov, Golovin, & Brumshteyn, 2019). There is an interesting fact in Kazakhstan - a startup by young researcher Zhandos Kerimkulov helps the Kazakhstani farmers to forecast field yields by snow cover height, soil moisture, and nitrogen content in the soil. What is very important, this startup is financially affordable to any Kazakh farmer. The author of this startup automatically digitized the space data on the sown areas of Kazakhstan using satellite imagery in the public domain and developed software. As a result, the farmers have the opportunity to load their agricultural plots on a cadastral number and obtain information on vegetation, soil moisture, nitrogen content, chlorophyll levels, etc. Based on these data, farmers can re-sow fields or direct irrigation to the desired part of agricultural land and thus minimize risks in harvesting (Forbes Kazakhstan, 2019).

Recently, the research and development were done on the use of computer vision in precision agriculture through the use of graphic processors and artificial intelligence systems (Patrício & Rieder, 2018). The computer vision is a technology for creating machines and mechanisms that track and classify objects and receive information from their images. Computer vision can track both the growth of crops in the fields, and, importantly, the sorting of agricultural products in the process of harvesting and processing. So in one of the studies it was justified the use of computer vision for sorting tomatoes, which consists of two stages - the development of hardware and development of software. The hardware is involved in capturing the images of fruits, and moving them to the appropriate boxes. The software ensures the functioning of the analysis of fruits' images checking defects and their maturity. This method for sorting fruits provides high accuracy in assessing their quality - 96.47% (Arakeri, & Lakshmana, 2016).

In the above context, the Digital Agropolis may become a spot for application of innovations towards full-pledged Smart Agriculture.

Production and Processing of Organic Food in the Digital Agropolis

The Digital Agropolise concept proposes to use an environmental technology of minimal impact on the soil when growing crops - "no-till", for gentle tillage with no erosion and leaching (Vincent-Caboud, Peigné, Casagrande, & Silva, 2017). In this technology, the soil is not processed, but covered with mulch, a surface layer of both organic materials e.g. hay, straw, leaves, bark, etc., and inorganic e.g. geotextiles, polymer films, etc. The mulch preserves the looseness of the soil, its moisture, prevents spread of weeds, overheating in summer, and freezing in winter. The mountain rivers, that flow from the gorges and wells, water the fertile lands in the selected areas using drip irrigation with smart control. Drip irrigation provides an efficient and optimal consumption of water and organic fertilizers. There can be introduced a recently proposed system optimally watering agricultural crops based on a wireless sensor network - a control system using node sensors with data management via smartphone and a web application (Jirapond et al., 2019).

The greenhouse facilities with lightweight large-span structures made of recycled wood and metal occupy large areas of the Digital Agropolises for year-round agricultural production. Multi-level racks are planned to be installed in the greenhouses, to grow vegetables and other produce using hydroponics technology – the groundless technology with supply of nutrient solutions on a special substrate (Palande, Zaheer, & George, 2018). Hydroponics make it possible to cultivate agricultural products in an automatic mode with IT controlling system, with no exposure to pests - insects, fungi and diseases in the soil crop production.

The processing of organic food products is an important component in the concept of Digital Agropolis, and it is mainly focused on modern technology of the so-called freeze-drying. The meaning of the technology lies in the fact that any agricultural products consist of more than 70-80% of water. At the time of processing, the products are dehydrated and lose weight of the mass of contained water. Moreover, due to sublimation, more than 90 percent of vitamins and minerals are preserved in the agricultural products. The storage of such processed products does not require refrigeration units, and the transportation costs are much less due to the lower weight and volume of processed products. Therefore, today sublimation is one of the advanced technologies among other processes of conservation of agricultural products. Further restoration and readiness for use of sublimated products is carried out by adding drinking water at the temperature necessary for the consumer (Tarafdar, Shahi, Singh, & Sirohi, 2017; Ciurzyńska & Lenart, 2011).

The Digital Agropolis will have a modern production and logistics complex for freeze-drying with smart control and installation of photovoltaic panels on flat roofs, including manufacturing, technological, storage buildings, as well as administrative, residential and recreation spaces for staff (Issabayev G.A., 2019). The production and logistics complex is shown in the Figure 2.

Research and Development Center for Biotechnologies in the Digital Agropolis

The organic crop production and related traditional animal husbandry in the selected areas can be further considered as a kind of ecological zone for creating a full cycle of bio-food production including processing and certification (Veldstra, Alexander, & Marshall, 2014).

The proposed model also suggests the use of environmentally friendly biotechnologies to protect plants from harmful effects (insects, diseases, etc.) with the acceleration of their metabolism for optimal growth. The Research and Development Center for Biotechnologies (R&D Centre) in the eco-settlement

Figure 2. Production and logistics complex for agricultural products processing, the sketch developed by G. Issabayev

will do just that with the necessary laboratories and technical facilities (Fig. 3). The R&D Centre will also control the entire process of production and processing in compliance with certification standards for organic products (Issabayev, 2019).

In the foreground of Figure 3, there is the Research and Development Centre for Biotechnologies, behind the Centre the administrative complex is located, surrounded by townhouses and cottages for scientific and technical personnel; to the right there are sport facilities (with green roofs). Thus, the people would have very comfortable conditions for work and leisure at the Digital Agropolis.

Utilization of Green Energy Sources in the Digital Agropolis

In the recent years, a pressing issue in the development of many countries of the world is the introduction of the concept of a green economy for sustainable growth. Understanding sustainability issues becomes a key foundation of the global world order. The recent scientific studies show how the environment is damaged and the climate is also changing, and, consequently, it is clear that the existing model of economic growth needs to be changed (Bhamra, 2018).

The Digital Agropolis concept conveys an important message of the use of renewable energy sources for functioning the planned agro-industrial complexes, buildings, and residences. The use of green renewable energy sources seems to be the best approach for both autonomy and access to energy, as well as to the energy security, reduction of impact on the environment, and creating separate ecological niches, systems and territories aimed at the production of certified organic agricultural products.

Figure 3. Research and development centre for biotechnologies, the sketch developed by Issabayev

In the Digital Agropolis it is also important to use the Smart Grid (SG) system in energy consumption from the renewable sources. This allows the energy users to optimize its consumption, with minimal damage to the environment and minimal carbon emissions. For the proper functioning of this system, the cost of electricity in the actually used period of time, the demand for electricity, and the parameters of green renewable energy are to be taken into consideration. In addition, it is important to use the genetic algorithm (GA) in managing and planning workloads in the middle and peak periods (Asgher, 2018).

The concept of a Digital Agropolis involves the use of three "green" energy sources for its activities – wind, solar, and organic waste.

The main renewable energy producing source of the Digital Agropolis is the vertical-axis wind generator (Patil, Chake, Helonde, & Gupta, 2015; Stout et al., 2017; Rezaeiha, Montazeri, & Blocken, 2018; Möllerström, Gipe, Beurskens, & Ottermo, 2019), that work on not strong but constant wind flows of mountain-valley circulation along mountain gorges. The most optimal arrangement of wind generator farms is their location in the valleys, directly at the "exit" from the mountain gorges. The most effective period for the use of vertical-axis wind generators is the time from evening to early night, when the katabatic flow of cooled air from the mountain slopes is concentrated in the gorges and goes to the valley.

Near the wind generators, immediately before the raise to mountainous terrain, there is an optimal location for the farms of the photovoltaic panels. Photovoltaic panels are also one of the leading generating sources of green energy (Inganäs & Sundström, 2016), in conditions a large amount of solar radiation in the foothill zones under consideration.

Another significant green source of energy in the Digital Agropolis is biogas, as a sustainable solution to manage organic waste from both agricultural and livestock farms. The concept foresees complexes of biogas plants using a large amount of organic agricultural waste, as well as (after passing through sedimentation tanks) utilizing sewage drains. The biogas production through anaerobic digestion of organic waste and residues provides a range of environmental and socio-economic benefits, which help to monitor the complex relationships between human health and the environment (Voicu1, Dincă, Paraschiv, & Moiceanu, 2015).

The biogas plants (Prasad, Rathore, & Singh, 2017; Sárvári Horváth, Tabatabaei, Karimi, & Kumar, 2016) play a key role in the Digital Agropolis concept, since in addition to its function to generate the electric and thermal energy, the plants utilize the agricultural waste, and, even most importantly, produce organic fertilizers, which are to be used for organic food production. Currently, to expand the capabilities of biogas plants, new substrates and technological innovations are needed, in particular membrane technologies for fermentation without air access (Sárvári Horváth, Tabatabaei, Karimi, & Kumar, 2016).

Organic fertilizers from biogas plants called biogas suspension can be considered as high-quality organic fertilizer for sustainable agriculture. A biogas suspension provides tremendous nutritional potential for vegetative and reproductive growth of field crops with long-term resistance (Kumar, Malav, Malav, & Khan, 2015; Tarafdar, Shahi, Singh, & Sirohi, 2017). Studies show that organic fertilizers lead to better absorption of nutrients than chemicals (Li et al., 2017). Moreover, the organic fertilizers proved to ensure higher crop yields without the use of harmful chemicals (Jannoura, Joergensen, & Bruns, 2014). In addition, organic fertilizers can contribute to the soil bioremediation - the method of cleaning soil and other areas of the environment such as water, atmosphere, etc., using the metabolic potential of biological objects (Chew, Chia, Yen, Nomanbhay, Ho, & Show, 2019).

Using green energy from three energy-producing sources: wind generators, photovoltaic panels, and biogas plants, would provide a synergistic effect (Benedek, Sebestyén, & Bartók, 2018) in the functioning of the Digital Agropolis. During daylight hours, there is a maximum energy production from photovoltaic panels. The most efficient energy generation from wind generators occurs at the time of mountain-valley evening and day breezes. Biogas plants have the ability to generate energy around the clock. Using these three sources of energy and their accumulation in modern batteries (Francesco, Petrozzi, & Montesarchio, 2014), as well as distribution through the smart energy management system (Wen & Mu, 2015) of a Digital Agropolis, it is possible to obtain optimal parameters for the most efficient use of green energy generation.

Residential Area of the Digital Agropolis

For the proper functioning of the Digital Agropolis' structures, it is necessary to create comfortable living conditions for the scientific and technical personnel and their families. The residence area is showed on Figure 4. All buildings and premises will be built in modern architectural style with the use of environmentally friendly materials and technologies.

Buildings for the staff residences will be built with traditional inexpensive materials: (1) clay blocks, with plastering the surfaces of the walls, and (2) earthquake-resistant frame, made of recycled wood or metal. Utilization of these materials would create an eco-friendly housing that is optimal in terms of hygienic characteristics and price - in the range of USD150-250 per 1 sq. m., that is very important for the rural territories in Eurasian countries.

Inclined roofs of houses with photovoltaic panels will collect rainwater into special tanks. Rainwater is to be reused both for utilization in residences for technical needs and for irrigation in the fields.

The residential buildings also have the heat recycling systems that would save the thermal energy in the range of 50-70% due to the fresh air recovery in heat exchangers.

Figure 4. Residential area of Digital Agropolis, the sketch developed by Issabayev G.

Interconnections of IT Centers for Process Management and Control

Modeling the agro-industrial complex management processes makes it possible to undertake justified, well-grounded decisions in a complicated system of its functioning - from production of products (not always in the most productive seasons), its processing, storage, delivery, sales, etc. Agricultural researchers examine the latest generation models to achieve optimal management results (Jones et al., 2017; Antle, Jones, & Rosenzweig, 2017).

The Figure 5 shows the relationship between the various centers of the process smart-control in the Digital Agropolises. The following blocks are highlighted here: 1, 1A – IT center for the production of organic crop and livestock; 2 – IT management for the production and logistics center for processing agricultural products; 3 – IT center for the Research and Development Centre for Biotechnology; 4 - IT center for land resources, aerial photography and mapping monitoring of soil conditions; 5 – IT center for control and optimization of energy consumption from the renewable energy sources, 6 - the Main Smart Center, and 7 – IT center for modeling the management processes and production planning.

The IT centers for management of organic crop production (1) and livestock (1A) through the necessary system of sensors and analysis systems interact directly with the IT center for land resources, aerial photography, mapping, and soil monitoring (4), as well as with the Research and Development Center for Biotechnologies (3). In turn, the above-mentioned IT centers (1, 1A, 4, and 3) are interconnected with the Main Smart Center (6), which carries out a general monitoring of all the IT centers of the Digital Agropolis. The IT center for management of production and logistics complex of processing of agricultural products (2) also interacts with the Main Smart Center, while monitoring the entire chain of processing, storage and supply of produced organic agricultural products. IT Center for Optimization and Management of renewable energy (5), interconnected with all IT centers (1, 1A, 2, 3, 4, 7) and the

Figure 5. Smart-control system of digital agropolises, developed by the authors

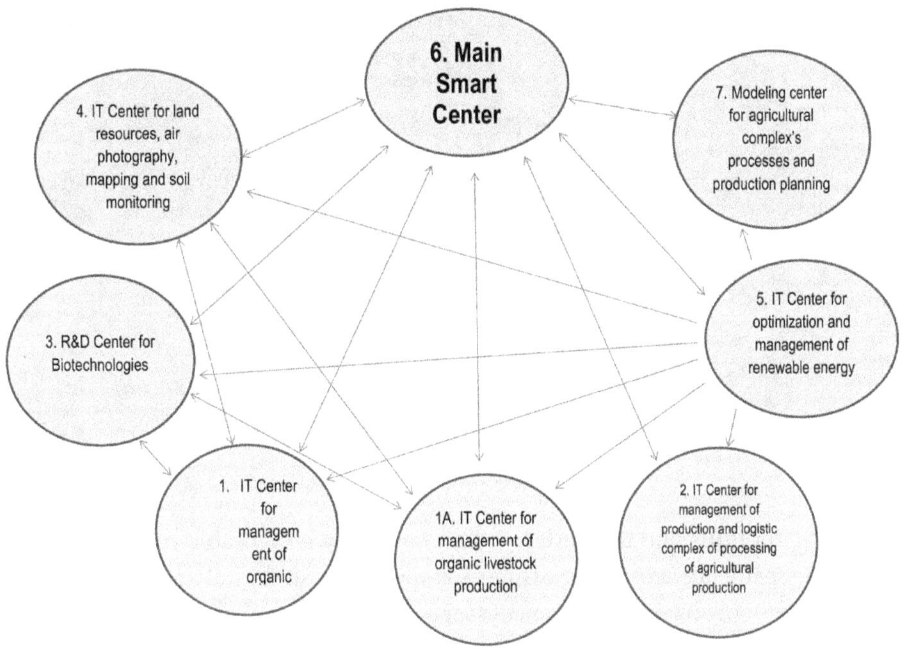

Main Smart Center (6), performs an important function of energy supply to all systems and facilities of the Digital Agropolis. The IT center for modeling the management processes and production planning (7) being the most important subsystem of the Main Smart Center (6) analyzes achievement of both tactical and strategic goals and objectives of Digital Agropolis development.

Territorial Planning of the Digital Agropolis

The most optimal place for the innovative settlements with the location of residential and public zones with smart management centers for agro-industrial processes and the scientific and biological center for the growth and bio-protection of crop and livestock products is at the junction of valleys and foothills, as it is the most comfortable zone for living

For optimal spatial planning of agricultural cities, vertical zoning is of great importance, as shown in the Figure 6.

The vertical spatial zoning of agropolises is largely similar in natural and climatic conditions of the foothill zones in the Zailiysky, Kyrgyz Alatau, and Kuraminsky ranges. On the right side of the diagram, there are foothills in the form of hills (so-called mountain "counters") and a gorge with a mountain river formed inside the foothill system. Directly on the border of the foothills and to the left of the vast valley, there is a farm of vertically axial wind generators working due to the mountain-valley breezes. The most effective place to capture the evening "katabatic" runoff of chilled air masses is the "exit" from the foothill gorge to the valley. The fertile valley, flat in relief and having drip irrigation, is the most optimal for locating fields for growing organic crop production and localizing the livestock complex.

Figure 6. Vertical zoning of territories of digital agropolises, developed by the authors

At the border of the foothills and the valley, which has its own favorable microclimate, there is an eco-settlement with the residence and smart offices for specialists in digital agriculture, biotechnology, food-processing, logistics, etc., as well as the necessary social facilities.

Near the eco-village, on the foothills, not-occupying the flat terrain fields, there is also a farm of photovoltaic panels. Below the farm (in the diagram to the left of the fields and the livestock complex), there is the production and logistics complex for processing agricultural products located near to the latitudinal regional highways. There should be also located a greenhouse complex and a farm of biogas plants working 24/7 all year round and utilizing the agricultural and organic waste.

The master plans' layouts of Digital Agropolises for three countries in Eurasia are given below.

Digital Agropolis' Master Plan Layout for Kazakhstan

The Digital Agropolis's location is in the foothills of Zailiysky Alatau in Kazakhstan (Fig. 7). The following structure of localization of production, logistics, energy, and residential areas is proposed: farms of vertical-axis wind generators (1) are located at the place of exit of nightly and daily mountain-valley wind flows from the foothill gorge, the farms of photovoltaic panels (2) are located next to the vertical-axis wind generators, creating the "upper" energy-generating zone of the Agropolis.

To the north, directly at the beginning of the valley with a flat, not crossed relief, the territory of the residential village (3) is located for engineering and technical staff, research personnel, and administration. In the residential village, there are also the smart center for the digital management of agricultural production processes and logistics, the research and development center for biotechnology, administration offices, a shopping and entertainment center, sports facilities, etc.

Not far from the residential village, to the east, a car and tractor station is located; all the machines work on biogas from the biogas plant, with no emission. The production and logistics center (4) is located 4 km to the north from the residential village, adjacent directly to the agricultural field zone with organic crop products, and also located in the convenient transport localization - at the intersection of the local and regional highways. Nearby, to the west from the production and logistics center, there are

Figure 7. Master plan layout of Digital Agropolis for Kazakhstan, developed by the authors. The map retrievedfrom https://www.google.com/maps/d/viewer?ie=UTF8&t=h&oe=UTF8&msa=0&mid=1DayHk74XQHB1StkXz5_yeCdlzeo&ll=43.16062798408715%2C76.22127571113867&z=13

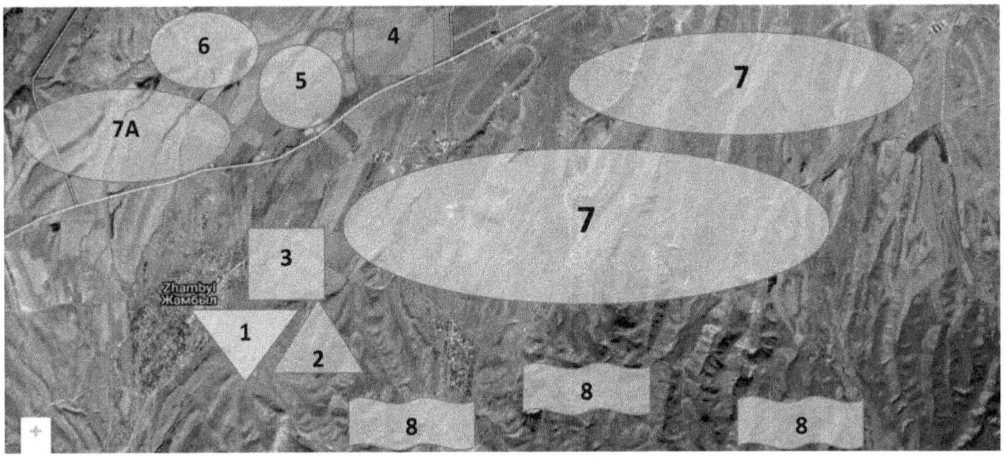

zones of biogas plants and greenhouses (5, 6). The biogas plants produce the necessary heat in the cold season for the round-the-clock functioning of greenhouses.

There are fields for growing organic crop (7) in between the residential village and the production and logistics center in the latitudinal direction. To the west from the agricultural fields, there is the livestock complex zone (7a). Directly on the foothill "counters", there are spots of garden crops (8).

Digital Agropolis' Master Plan Layout for Kyrgyz Republic

The layout of the master plan of the Digital Agropolis in the foothills of the Kyrgyz Alatau ridge in Kyrgyz Republic (Fig.8) also shows the location of territories and zones that are optimally located in the similar climatic conditions to the previous scheme. Here, at the exit from the gorges to the valley, there are farms of wind generators (1) and photovoltaic panels (2), on the same belt with which there is a residential eco-village (3) with the centers of smart management, biotechnology, etc. In a flat relief terrain with fertile irrigated, the large fields are located with the soils for growth of organic farming crops (7). On one latitudinal belt with fields, there is a livestock complex (7a). The production and logistics center for processing and storage of agricultural products (4) is also located below the fields, next to the highway. Here, there is the zone of biogas plants (5) and greenhouses (6). On the mountain shelves, on a rather rough terrain, a favorable territory for the cultivation of garden crops (8) is located.

Digital Agropolis' Master Plan Layout of for Uzbekistan

In contrast to the above two schemes of master plans in many respects similar in climatic parameters, the one in the valleys of Uzbekistan - the foothills of the Kuramin ridge (Fig. 9), should take into account the larger solar radiation and, correspondingly, higher average annual summer temperatures, at the same time with cool enough winters. Thus, the Digital Agropolis in Uzbekistan may produce more heat-loving crops in the summer period.

Figure 8. Master plan layout of Digital Agropolis for Kyryzstan, developed by the authors

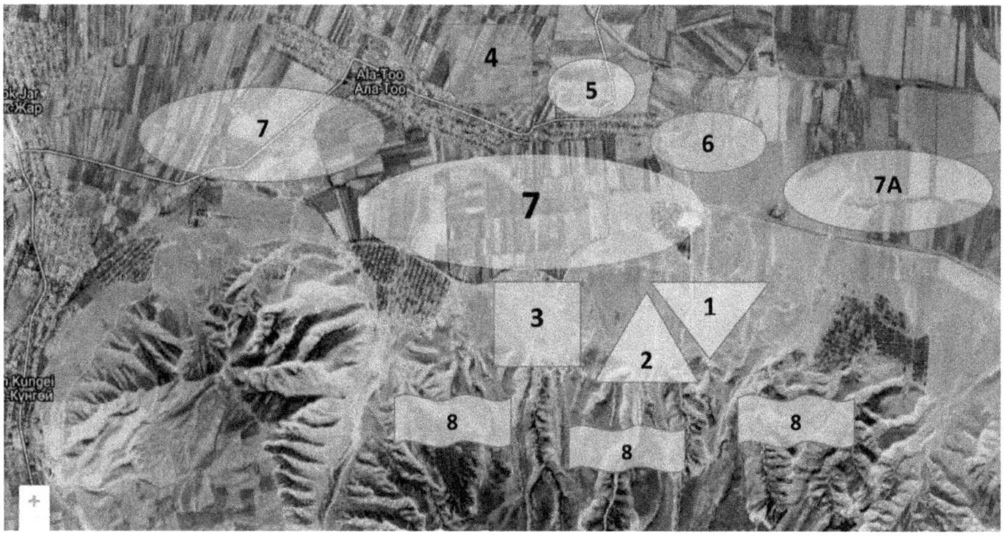

Figure 9. Master plan layout of digital Agropolis for Uzbekistan, developed by the authors

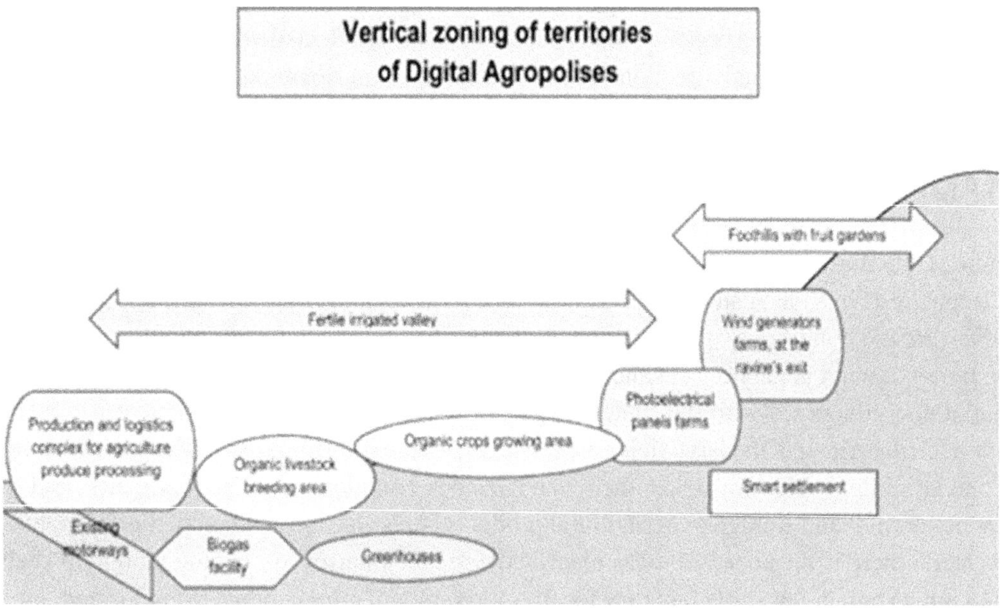

The zone of fertile irrigated fields for the growth of organic agricultural products (7) is narrower here in width and practically sandwiched between one ridge in the south and the river with a second ridge in the north. The wind generators zone (1) is also located directly at the exit of the mountain gorge into the valley. Near to the east and to the west, there are farms of photovoltaic panels (2) and residential eco-villages (3). The zones of greenhouses (6) and biogas plants (5), due to the narrowness of the valley and the lowering relief, are located directly to the north of the residential village. Further to the south from the biogas plants zone, near the intersection of local and regional roads, there is a production and logistics center (4) for processing and storage of agricultural products. Livestock complexes (7A) are located to the east of the production and logistics center. The zones of garden crops are located (8) in the foothill "counters", similar to the other two layouts.

FUTURE RESEARCH DIRECTIONS

Further development of the concept would allow to elaborate a project feasibility study tied to a specific territory, local legislation, and investment opportunities. Decision-taking on such a project would require involvement of the society and government of a country/region, and private companies. The Public-Private Partnership seems the best option for the project financing.

Digital Agropolises will (1) meet strict environmental requirements, (2) develop and use biotechnologies for crop production, (3) generate and use green renewable energy, (4) operate with the modern digital management and monitoring systems, (5) create additional job places for the rural population in the region, and (6) create favorable conditions for business and leisure for farmers and scientists by building eco-villages from local materials.

Thus, the formation of a network of Digital Agropolises as innovative eco-territories with the production and processing of environmentally friendly agricultural products should become a driving force for socio-economic development in the foothills of the Eurasian region.

CONCLUSION

The Eurasian region needs a systematic and integrated review of its important role in ensuring food security in a global context. The countries of the Eurasian region have good chances to focus on organic crop and livestock farming as well as the deep processing of organic products.

As mentioned above, the production of organic products in ecologically clean areas that have not yet been treated with chemical fertilizers, with the predominant use of bio-stimulants and green renewable energy sources that do not negatively affect the air basin and ecology in general, is becoming one of the leading trends in many modern agricultural zones. It can be precisely attributed to the territories of the above three Digital Agropolises in the foothill zones of the countries of Eurasia.

The presented concept meets the strategic development directions common to the Eurasian countries, such as (1) sustainable rural development (Velten, Leventon, Jager, & Newig, 2015); (2) export-oriented production/processing of organic agricultural products (Kahl et al., 2014); (3) sustainable rural development based on a green economy (Kamble & Ovhal, 2016) and digitalization of production and logistics operations (Kayikci, 2018); and (4) the development of new technologies for organic farming and animal husbandry (Pivoto et al., 2018).

The Digital Agropolis concept proposes an advanced agro-urban model for the production and processing of environmentally friendly agricultural products for the sustainable development of rural areas. Although the Digital Agropolis model has been developed for the foothills territories, it can serve as a basis for developing such a model for other climatic and geographic locations in the Eurasian region.

REFERENCES

Agriculture in Central Asia Unlocking the Potential (Interview with Irna Hofman, Leiden University). (2018, October 11). *Voices on Central Asia*. Retrieved from https://voicesoncentralasia.org/agriculture-in-central-asia-unlocking-the-potential-interview-with-irna-hofman

Alpen-Adria-Universität Klagenfurt. (2017, November 15). Organic farming can make an important contribution to world nutrition, research shows. *ScienceDaily*. Retrieved from www.sciencedaily.com/releases/2017/11/171115092144.htm

Antle, J. M., Jones, J. W., & Rosenzweig, C. E. (2017). Next generation agricultural system data, models and knowledge products: Introduction. *Agricultural Systems*, *155*, 186–190. doi:10.1016/j.agsy.2016.09.003 PMID:28701811

Arakeri, M., & Lakshmana. (2016). Computer Vision Based Fruit Grading System for Quality Evaluation of Tomato in Agriculture industry. *Procedia Computer Science*, *79*, 426–433. doi:10.1016/j.procs.2016.03.055

Asgher, U., Babar Rasheed, M., Al-Sumaiti, A. S., Ur-Rahman, A., Ali, I., Alzaidi, A., & Alamri, A. (2018). Smart Energy Optimization Using Heuristic Algorithm in Smart Grid with Integration of Solar Energy Sources. *Energies*, *11*(12), 3494. doi:10.3390/en11123494

Benedek, J., Sebestyén, T.-T., & Bartók, B. (2018). Evaluation of renewable energy sources in peripheral areas and renewable energy-based rural development. *Renewable & Sustainable Energy Reviews*, *90*, 516–535. doi:10.1016/j.rser.2018.03.020

Bhamra, A. (2018). *India Green Economy Barometer 2018*. Green Economy Coalition. Retrieved from https://www.greeneconomycoalition.org/assets/reports/Barometers-2018/India-Barometer-2018-Full-November-Draft.pdf

Bolch, T. (2007). Climate change and glacier retreat in northern Tien Shan (Kazakhstan/Kyrgyzstan) using remote sensing data. *Global and Planetary Change*, *56*(1–2), 1–12. doi:10.1016/j.gloplacha.2006.07.009

Camargo, L., & Stoeglehner, G. (2018). Spatiotemporal modelling for integrated spatial and energy planning. *Energy, Sustainability and Society*, *8*(1), 32. doi:10.118613705-018-0174-z

Chew, K. W., Chia, S. R., Yen, H.-W., Nomanbhay, S., Ho, Y.-C., & Show, P. L. (2019). Transformation of Biomass Waste into Sustainable Organic Fertilizers. *Sustainability*, *11*(8), 2266. doi:10.3390u11082266

Ciurzyńska, A., & Lenart, A. (2011). Freeze-Drying – Application in Food Processing and Biotechnology – A Review. *Polish Journal of Food and Nutrition Sciences*, *61*(3), 165–171. doi:10.2478/v10222-011-0017-5

Francesco, S., Petrozzi, A., & Montesarchio, V. (2014). An Integrated System for the Energy Production and Accumulation from Renewable Sources: A Rural Tower Prototype. *Energy Procedia*, *59*, 205–212. doi:10.1016/j.egypro.2014.10.368

Global Report on Food Crises 2019. (2019). FSIN Platform. Retrieved from http://www.fsinplatform.org/sites/default/files/resources/files/GRFC%202019_Full%20Report.pdf

Himesh, S. (2018). Digital revolution and Big Data: A new revolution in agriculture. *Perspectives in Agriculture, Veterinary Science, Nutrition and Natural Resources*, *13*(021). doi:10.1079/PAVSNNR201813021

Hu, X., Ren, H., Tansey, K., Zheng, Y., Ghent, D., Liu, X., & Yan, L. (2019). Agricultural drought monitoring using European Space Agency Sentinel 3A land surface temperature and normalized difference vegetation index imageries. *Agricultural and Forest Meteorology*, *279*, 107707. doi:10.1016/j.agrformet.2019.107707

Inganäs, O., & Sundström, V. (2016). Solar energy for electricity and fuels. *Ambio*, *45*(1), 15–23. doi:10.100713280-015-0729-6 PMID:26667056

Issabayev, G., & Issabayeva, A. (2013). Emerging Countries for the World: Bio-Food Security through Technologies. *Proceedings of International Conference on Business Management & IS, 1*(1). Retrieved from http://ojs.ijacp.org/index.php/ICBMIS/article/view/59

Issabayev, G. A. (2019). *Sovremennyi urbanizm: osnovnyie innovacii i perspectivy razvitiya* [Contemporary urbanism: major innovations and development prospects]. Almaty: Lantar Trade.

Issabayeva, A., & Issabayev, G. (2013). Bio-Food Security for Future Generations. *Proceedings QUAESTI, 1*(1), 55-57. Retrieved from https://www.quaesti.com/archive/?vid=1&aid=1&kid=160101

Jannoura, R., Joergensen, R., & Bruns, C. (2014). Organic fertilizer effects on growth, crop yield, and soil microbial biomass indices in sole and intercropped peas and oats under organic farming conditions. *European Journal of Agronomy, 52*(B), 259-270. doi:10.1016/j.eja.2013.09.001

Jones, J. W., Antle, J. M., Basso, B., Boote, K. J., Conant, R. T., Foster, I., ... Wheeler, T. R. (2017). Brief history of agricultural systems modeling. *Agricultural Systems*, *155*, 240–254. doi:10.1016/j.agsy.2016.05.014 PMID:28701816

Kahl, J., Alborzi, F., Beck, A., Bügel, S. G., Busscher, N., Geier, U. A., ... Załęcka, A. (2014). Organic food processing: A framework for concept, starting definitions and evaluation. *Journal of the Science of Food and Agriculture*, *94*(13), 82–94. doi:10.1002/jsfa.6542 PMID:24375441

Kamble, P. S., & Ovhal, V. V. (2016). Analysis of green economy of India. *North Asian International Research Journal of Social Science & Humanities, 2*(8), 41-66. Retrieved from http://www.nairjc.com/?re=paper&value=social-science-humanities&month=08&val=NAIRJC&year=2016

Kayikci, Y. (2018). Sustainability impact of digitization in logistics. *Procedia Manufacturing*, *21*, 782–789. doi:10.1016/j.promfg.2018.02.184

Kļaviņš, M., Azizov, A., & Zaļoksnis, J. (2014). Environment, pollution, development: The case of Uzbekistan. Riga: UL Press. Retrieved from https://uzwater.ktu.lt/index.php/download-files/compendia-and-textbooks/module-a-environmental-science/129-environment-pollution-development/file

Klimat Zailiyskogo Alatau [Climate of Zailiyskiy Alatau]. (2019). *Silk Road Adventures.* Retrieved from https://silkadv.com/ru/node/6153

Kumar, S., Malav, L., Malav, M., & Khan, Sh. (2015). Biogas Slurry: Source of Nutrients for Eco-friendly Agriculture. *International Journal of Extension Research*, *2*, 42–46. Retrieved from http://www.journalijer.com

Li, S., Li, J., Zhang, B., Li, D., Li, G., & Li, Y. (2017). Effect of different organic fertilizers application on growth and environmental risk of nitrate under a vegetable field. *Scientific Reports*, *7*(1), 17020. doi:10.103841598-017-17219-y PMID:29209063

Markelov, K., Golovin, V., & Brumshteyn, Yu. (2019). Informatization of Astrakhan agriculture under conditions of Caspian states international relations development In *Proceedings of the International Scientific and Practical Conference "Digital agriculture - development strategy" (ISPC 2019)*. Academic Press. 10.2991/ispc-19.2019.51

Milovanović, S. (2014). The role and potential of information technology in agricultural improvement. *Economics of Agriculture*, *61*(2), 471–485. doi:10.5937/ekoPolj1402471M

Möllerström, E., Gipe, P., Beurskens, J., & Ottermo, F. (2019). A historical review of vertical axis wind turbines rated 100 kW and above. *Renewable & Sustainable Energy Reviews*, *105*, 1–13. doi:10.1016/j.rser.2018.12.022

Muangprathub, J., Boonnam, N., Kajornkasirat, S., Lekbangpong, N., Wanichsombat, A., & Nillaor, P. (2019). IoT and agriculture data analysis for smart farm. *Computers and Electronics in Agriculture*, *156*, 467–474. doi:10.1016/j.compag.2018.12.011

Nastyukova, O. (2019, April 02) Prosto kosmos: Kazakhstanec otkryl startup dlya fermerov, ispolzuya dannye NASA. [Just space: a Kazakhstani opened a startup for farmers using NASA data]. *Forbes Kazakhstan*. Retrieved from https://forbes.kz/made_in_kz/prosto_kosmos_kazahstanets_otkryil_starap_dlya_fermerov_ispolzuya_dannyie_nasa/

Palande, V., Zaheer, Z., & George, K. (2018). Fully Automated Hydroponic System for Indoor Plant Growth. *Procedia Computer Science*, *129*, 482–488. doi:10.1016/j.procs.2018.03.028

Patil, A., Chake, A., Helonde, M., & Gupta, P. (2015). Vertical Axis Wind Turbine with Maglev Technology. *International Journal for Scientific Research & Development*, *2*(12). Retrieved from http://www.ijsrd.com/articles/IJSRDV2I12180.pdf

Patrício, D. I., & Rieder, R. (2018). Computer vision and artificial intelligence in precision agriculture for grain crops: A systematic review. *Computers and Electronics in Agriculture*, *153*, 69–81. doi:10.1016/j.compag.2018.08.001

Pivoto, D., Waquil, P. D., Talamini, E., Finocchio, C., Corte, V., & Mores, G. (2018). Scientific development of smart farming technologies and their application in Brazil. *Information Processing in Agriculture*, *5*(1), 21–32. doi:10.1016/j.inpa.2017.12.002

Prasad, S. B., Rathore, D., & Singh, A. K. (2017). Recent Advances in Biogas Production. *Chemical Engineering & Process Techniques, 3*(2): 1038. Retrieved from https://www.semanticscholar.org/paper/Recent-Advances-in-Biogas-Production-Prasad-Rathore/b080344c36fd6a08041c92a5b6ac1b64fc943bae

Raja, N., & Masresha, G. (2015). Plant Based Biopesticides: Safer Alternative for Organic Food Production. *Journal of Fertilizers and Pesticides*, *6*(02), e128. doi:10.4172/2471-2728.1000e128

Rezaeiha, A., Montazeri, H., & Blocken B. (2018). Towards optimal aerodynamic design of vertical axis wind turbines: Impact of solidity and number of blades. *Energy, 165*(B), 1129-1148. Doi:10.1016/j.energy.2018.09.192

Sárvári Horváth, I., Tabatabaei, M., Karimi, K., & Kumar, R. (2016). Recent updates on biogas production - a review. *Biofuel Research Journal, 3*(2), 394–402. doi:10.18331/BRJ2016.3.2.4

Stout, C., Islam, Sh., White, A., Arnott, S., Kollovozi, E., Shaw, M., ... Bird, B. (2017). Efficiency Improvement of Vertical Axis Wind Turbines with an Upstream Deflector. *Energy Procedia, 118*, 141–148. doi:10.1016/j.egypro.2017.07.032

Sugden, A. (2001). Organic farming. *Science, 293*(5527), 17. doi:10.1126cience.293.5527.17a PMID:11995386

Tarafdar, A., Shahi, N., Singh, A., & Sirohi, R. (2017). Optimization of Freeze-Drying Process Parameters for Qualitative Evaluation of Button Mushroom (Agaricus bisporus) Using Response. *Journal of Food Quality*. doi:10.1155/2017/5043612

Tarafdar, A., Shahi, N. C., Singh, A., & Sirohi, R. (2017). Optimization of freeze-drying process parameters for qualitative evaluation of button mushroom (Agaricus bisporus) using response surface methodology. *Journal of Food Quality*. doi:10.1155/2017/5043612

University of British Columbia. (2017, March 10). Organic is only one ingredient in recipe for sustainable food future: Many shades of gray: The context-dependent performance of organic agriculture. *ScienceDaily*. Retrieved from www.sciencedaily.com/releases/2017/03/170310142337.htm

Veldstra, M., Alexander, C., & Marshall, M. (2014). To certify or not to certify? Separating the organic production and certification decisions. *Food Policy, 49*(2), 429–436. doi:10.1016/j.foodpol.2014.05.010

Velten, S., Leventon, J., Jager, N., & Newig, J. (2015). What Is Sustainable Agriculture? A Systematic Review. *Sustainability, 7*(6), 7833–7865. doi:10.3390u7067833

Vincent-Caboud, L., Peigné, J., Casagrande, M., & Silva, E. M. (2017). Overview of Organic Cover Crop-Based No-Tillage Technique in Europe: Farmers' Practices and Research Challenges. *Agriculture, 7*(5), 42–58. doi:10.3390/agriculture7050042

Voicu, G., Dincă, M., Paraschiv, G., & Moiceanu, G. (2015). A Review Regarding the Biogas Production Through Anaerobic Digestion of Organic Waste. *Advanced Engineering Forum, 13*, 185-193. doi:10.4028/www.scientific.net/AEF.13.185

Wen, C., & Mu, Y. (2015). Power and Performance Management in Nonlinear Virtualized Computing Systems via Predictive Control. *PLoS One, 10*(7), e0134017. doi:10.1371/journal.pone.0134017 PMID:26225769

KEY TERMS AND DEFINITIONS

Biomass Energy: One of the renewable energy sources, based on the processing of plant/animal waste or biomass.

Digital IT System: A digital data analysis system that uses information technologies

Intelligent Agriculture (SF): Agricultural production systems associated with the use of information and communication technologies in machinery, equipment, and sensors.

Organic Farming: The production of agricultural products associated with the use of exclusively biological methods of plant protection and organic fertilizers.

Piedmont Zones: The territories of valleys adjacent directly to hilly and mountain ranges.

Smart Irrigation: A system of automatically started/interrupted irrigation associated with the use of soil moisture sensors.

Synergistic Effect: Joint complementary action of various processes and actions – in the context of this chapter: the complementary generation of green energy from photovoltaic panels, wind generators, and biogas plants.

Vertical-axis Wind Generator: A device that generates clean electric energy from the weak wind flows, due to the magnetic "cushion" between the rotor - movable part of the wind generator with blades, and the stator - immovable base of the wind generator.

Chapter 5
Sustainability of Agriculture Territories in South Kazakhstan:
Remote Sensing and Geodata for Design of Landscape and Soil Maps

Aizhan Assylbekova
Al-Farabi Kazakh National University, Kazakhstan

Natalya Tsychuyeva
Al-Farabi Kazakh National University, Kazakhstan

ABSTRACT

The increasing anthropogenic impact on the soil and vegetation cover, insufficient effective land management, and climatic changes, the degradation process of soils and agrolandscapes is accelerated, and as a result, lands have low productivity, and agrolandscapes have poor environmental sustainability. In this regard, on the basis of modern digital technologies of remote sensing and geoinformation systems (GIS), an initial study in Karasai district of Almaty region in Kazakhstan was conducted, which is aimed at the timely identification areas of degradation agrolandscapes for the adoption of preventive measures. Based on spatial analysis of remote sensing data and field data, a soil-geomorphological map and landscape map of the region was compiled on a scale of 1:100000, which covers several taxonomic units: classes, subclasses, and types of landscapes. The territory of the Karasai region is a complex biogeosystem, as the analyzed territory consists of 52 types of landscape. This data allows a modern analysis of the agrolandscapes of the region.

INTRODUCTION

The objectives of rational nature management are one of the main aspects of sustainable development and environmental stability of Central Asian states and entire Eurasia. At the same time, agriculture remains one of the main sectors of the national economies of the countries of the continent. New environmental challenges of our time forced to use adaptive systems of organization and farming. One of these methods,

DOI: 10.4018/978-1-7998-2551-7.ch005

based on the transition from zonal farming systems to landscape farming, is the adaptive-landscape farming method (Kiryushin, 1996). This approach takes into account both the needs of society in agricultural products and the agroecological requirements of crops.

The mentioned method of adaptive landscape farming systems requires a preliminary study of the territory, the creation of a landscape and soil maps of the area, and recommendations on the use of the territory. In this regard, for any territory on which this method of farming will be applied, a detailed landscape and soil maps is needed. The creation of such maps using digital technologies of remote sensing and GIS is demonstrated in this chapter.

Landscape maps are used to describe types of geographic pattern and their distribution and the geo-complexes and their spatial structure in an integrative way. A detailed landscape map in a scale of 1:10000 and larger includes landscape topological landscape units on the generalized large-scale and medium scale (scale 1:10000-1:1000000) maps landscape mezo units and areas on small-scale (smaller than 1:1000000) mainly landscapes, although in some cases can be shown (in a highly generalized form) landscape geotopes and landscape meso units (Knizhnikov, 2003).

For purposes of adaptive landscape farming systems landscape maps focused on large-and medium-scale. Such maps should be based on field survey and on the interpretation of high-resolution remote sensing data (Räsänen et al., 2019, Forkuor et al., 2017). Depending on the purpose of landscape maps the legends varying in detail. They from a brief reference to the main components of indicators of geographical complexes (relief, vegetation) to a detailed differentiation of indicators (e.g. by including elements of climate, moisture conditions, soil, etc.) (Isachenko, 1991).

A landscape science possesses the basic research by the development of specific recommendations and proposals for the implementation and the improvement of the production systems in the agricultural sector. Recently a significant decrease of the yields per ha have been observed here (Kenenbaev, 2009). If there are a high natural resource potential on a site for arable production with fertile land and a high content of humus in the soil the average yields of the main food crop wheat can be more than three times higher (Geldyeva, 1992) than the average yield in Kazakhstan. A comparable success in several countries of the world when using farming systems for the site differentiation with regard to the agro-ecological conditions and by the awareness of the obvious need for adaptation of agricultural technologies can not be observed in Central Asia at moment. Such site adaptive agriculture should also include a site specific intensification of the production, the economic structures and the markets for agricultural products.

Consequently, there is an urgent need for a new agro technological policy based on the design and development of environmentally sound landscape-adaptive farming systems (Kiryushin, 2005). These adapted systems should integrate agricultures on a local and regional scale level. This is a new approach compared to the foundation of agriculture and crop production when traditionally recommending sets of separate and sometimes not interconnected activities sometimes influencing negatively each other. In this regard, we studied the scientific and methodological sources and used the overall trends in the legislation to solve the environmental and agristructural problems of the former kolkhoz system. The most important methodological principles of integrated landscape analysis are the recognition of its objective nature and the principle of complexity. Regulations on the leading role of the principle of complexity expressed Gvozdetsky (1963), Nefedova (1990).

Most researchers are of the opinion that the landscape map is the basic foundation for the formation of geoinformation systems for various purposes (Trofimov, Panasyuk, 1984, Linnik, 1990, Vinokourov, and others, 2000, Snytko et al, 2002). Commonly used options of landscape maps for the various tasks of landscape and interpretive mapping, industrial design, etc. This gives rise to special problems of formalization of database landscape maps (Shibkikh, 2002), comparing them with maps of state variables, to determine the sensitivity, value, stability and other characteristics of landscapes, database integration of component maps based on a network of landscape units. Spatial analysis, based on landscape maps that lets you find all sorts of economic, environmental and other indicators in the context of various landscape types.

*Remote sensi*ng (RS) technologies are providing for the geosciences new methodological opportunities to study the surface of the Earth. Recently a significant increase of data availability in terms of volume, variety and the quality of remote sensing data is observed. RS is an indirect method by which information is gathered about the object without direct contact with him. GIS technology is usable for the integration of layers of remote sensing information and to spatialise databases, procedures and methods of mathematical analysis of image-mapping (Labutina, 2004, Bartalev et al., 2016). Such spatialised information is often critical for socio-economic development, planning, and territory management. Other modern methods such as: adaptation of the classical methods of vegetation mapping to GIS and RS technology (Kariyeva & van Leeuwen, 2011); field studies using modern devices for remote diagnostics of plants (Schmidtlein et al. 2013) also can be used for more detailed research of landscapes.

GIS and RS are recognized as a suitable information technology to clarify the variety of regional geo-ecological problems in Eurasia. These objects are demanding a territorial and geographical analysis to design landscape-adaptive farming systems, which consists of several stages of implementation (Kenenbaev et al., 2009). Landscape type mapping starts with the territorial and geographical analysis (see also figure 1). This step is followed by the assessment of the ecological status and the development of agricultural activities the landscape. Thus, the steppe chernozem zone of Eurasia, a plain or slightly hilly landscape, is well suitable for the cultivation of crops and for the development of a site specific agricultural technology. Within this zone a variety of landscapes exists is calculated from a few thousand natural landscape systems.

GIS technology usage in this chapter for landscape type mapping is combined with the RS. It is applied specifically for the initial phase of the spatial differentiation of landscape types by the aim of designing site adaptive landscape farming system. The results of these studies, the actual inventories of performances of natural resources and the processes occurring in the studied region. They are: fourteen languorous monographs on "The soil of Kazakhstan (by area)", study the problem of anthropogenic landscape professor Dzhanaleeva and others. On the basis of these materials released "The concept of development of agricultural technologies in the adaptive landscape, south-east of Kazakhstan till 2010" (Kenenbaev and others, 2006) and conduct comprehensive research to create of adaptive landscape farming system a scale in Republic.

Consequence the above sources, this chapter focused on creation a number of large-scale maps (1:100000) to develop methodological applications of GIS and RS technology in the territorial and geographical analysis to create adaptive-landscape system of agriculture in Karasai district of Almaty region in South Kazakhstan: map of the hydrological network, soil map and landscape map. A landscape-indicator method is applied to differentiate landscapes using remote sensing data to determine the specific boundaries of environmental systems.

STUDY AREA AND METHODS

Study area

The study area of this investigation is the territory of Karasai district in the Almaty province, which has an area of 2100 km2. Of these, suitable for agricultural land use are 512.3 thousand hectares by including 49.3 thousand hectares of arable land, 22.1 thousand hectares of pasture and 1.4 thousand hectares of grasslands. 13.2 thousand hectares are forest (Climate…, 2004).

The south and south-eastern part of the study area is occupied by mountain ranges of the Trans-Ili Alatau. The central part of the study area is a very complex watershed differentiated into plains in the lower parts and foothills and piedmont plain. The general slope is orientated to the north. The highest point in the district is located near the spring of the River Aksay, starting near the peak Aydatau (4029 m), which is always covered with ice. The peak is located near the border with Kyrgyzstan. At an altitude of 800-1000 m, there is some Karasai district with high population density, which is mastered in terms of agriculture. The climate of the study area is continental, the winter is not very cold and the summer is warm. The average temperature in January varies between -6° and -9° C, the average temperature in July between +22° and +24° C. The annual precipitation in the foothill plains is 300 - 500 mm and in the mountains with up to 1000 mm. The main rivers in the district are Kaskelen, Shamalgan (Kaskasu), Uzynkargaly, Aksai, Big Almatinka Rivers.

The soil types depending on the geography and the altitudinal zones of this part of the Trans-Ili Alatau. From mountain to plains the soils are differentiated by mountain meadow and mountain forest soils, to mountain chernozem, to chestnut soils and gray soils in the plain.

The population in the district is 159.1 thousand people (2006), which mainly live in the plains area. The average population density is 65.3 inhabitants per km2. This is elevens times higher compared to the Kazakh average. Main parts of the district are used by agriculture, which formed at present more than 500 of small and medium-sized agricultural units (Kenenbaev, 2006).

Data

The analysis of satellite images and the interpretation of the images was performed with the the programmes ArcGIS 9.3 and ENVI 4.7. The combination of different approaches of geography, pedology, geobotany and mapping was applied. Starting with the study of the landscape system, several data sets have been stored, recalculated and integrated by the use of GIS. During the map production process used methods of analysis of various library materials belonging to the Karasai district. Main data sets used are:

- The topographic map of Kazakhstan of Almaty region. Scale 1:100000. (Publisher RSCE "Cartography"; Almaty, 2002).
- The soil map of Almaty region. Scale 1:300000. (Publisher: Institute of Soil Science, Academy of Sciences Kazakh SSR, Alma-Ata, 1951, by IA Assing et al).
- The map of pastures of the Kaskelen District, Alma - Ata, Kazakh SSR region. Scale 1:100 000. (Publisher: Institute Kazgiprozem Gosagroprom Kaz SSR" Alma - Ata, 1989, by Kontserova).
- The Land use map Karasai district of Almaty region of Kazakhstan. Scale 1:75000. (Publisher: Almaty "SPC earth" 2005).

- The publication: Landscapes of the Asian steppes. Moscow State University Press, Moscow, 1999, by Nikolaev).
- Satellite images for the study area: Landsat 7 ETM (http://eros.usgs.gov/#/Find_Data/Products_and_Data_Available/ETM)

Collection and analysis of data. The topographic map contains the objective information about topography and hydrography. It is the source of information about the qualitative characteristics. Direct information (absolute elevation) and morphometric information (angles, depth and density of the subdivision) are taken from this map. The topographic map is the basis for the systematization of relief elements and forms and used for the morphological analysis of the territory (Kiryushin, 2005).

Satellite images are of advantage when reflecting the heterogeneity of soil cover because of the lack of information about soil in topographic maps. Satellite image from IRS (which was kindly presented from Institute of Space Researches in Almaty) with resolution of 5.6 m for summer season, was used as high-resolution basses for vectorization and correction of landscapes borders. Satellite images of Landsat 7 ETM are used to produce maps were obtained from the site of the Geological Survey of USA (http://eros.usgs.gov/#/Find_Data/Products_and_Data_Available/ETM). Installed on the satellite Landsat-7 survey equipment ETM + (Enhanced Thematic Mapper Plus - Enhanced Thematic Mapper), provides images of the Earth surface in the six channels with a resolution of 30 m, one IR channel with a resolution of 60 m and simultaneously in the panchromatic mode with a resolution of 15 m. The width of coverage of a survey scene for all the channels about 185 km.

METHOD FOR LANDSCAPE MAPPING

The methods development for the usage in site adapted agriculture bases on the two main steps of landscape analysis and mapping. The results of these methods are landscape differentiations of the study area. These allows further analysis e.g. of the human modification of natural systems, the evaluation of the structure and dynamics of geosystems which was transformed by the interaction of environment and agricultural production.

Landscape examines the origin, structure and dynamics of landscapes, the laws of their development and deployment and transformation in the economic activity of the human society. One of the objectives of the landscape the study of parts of the landscape: geosystems lowest level (district, delineated areas of landscape, landscape facies), their mutual arrangement, interaction, types of which they form spatial structures and their changes over time (morphology of the landscape) (Isachenko, 1965).

In calculation of the landscape map is performed by the following steps: map of surface waters with remote sensing, three-dimensional image terrain study area for geomorphology, for soil and vegetation maps were made NDVI areas, outline all segments have been established to each other using GIS technology to create a landscape map (Terekhov, et al., 2007, Tsychuyeva, 2010). This is schematically shown in the Figure1 (Assylbekova, 2010).

The methodological basis of the following investigations are the scientific-theoretical concepts and methodologies described by Kiryushin (2005) and Kenenbaev (2006).

Kiryushin (2005) offers an application of GIS for agro-ecological land evaluation that allows the transferring a new quality based solution to a problem. The method is especially usable for the design of intensive farming systems and agricultural technologies, by formulating adaptive-landscape systems

Figure 1. Methodological steps for the calculation of the landscape type map

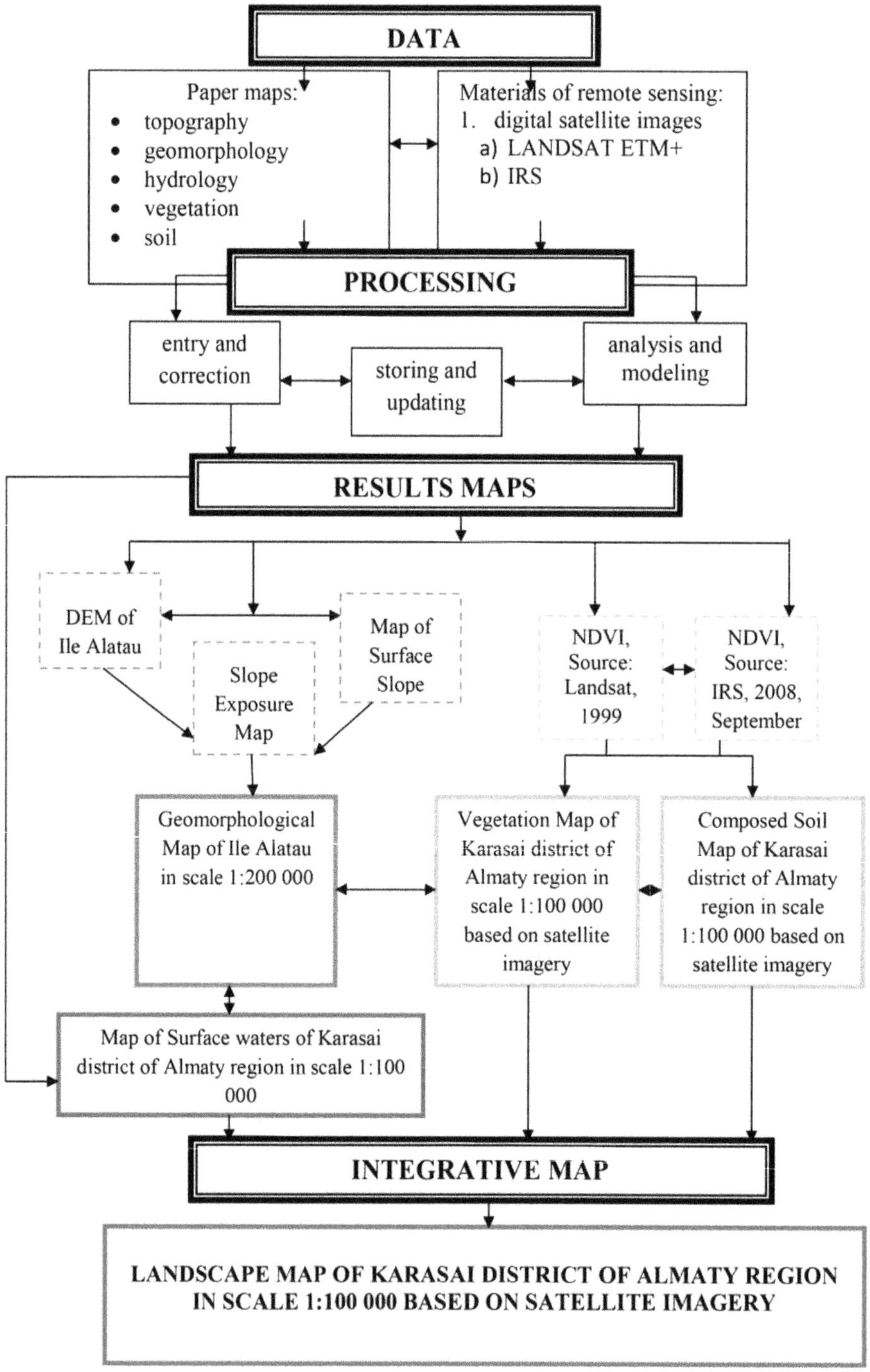

of agriculture of high site specific accuracy. The method includes tools for land evaluation systems, precision farming and is almost impossible to apply without GIS technology (Kiryushin, 2005).

Kenenbaev (2006) developed an adaptive-landscape systems by using primarily a system of agro-ecological land evaluation. It is, as noted above, differs significantly from traditional evaluation applied previously and not having an environmental targeting, characterized by a weak reflection of the structure of the soil cover, topography, lithological conditions, that it was a significant disadvantage, providing little opportunity for differentiation and depth adaptation of the zonal farming systems that is, bringing them to the adaptive-landscape systems (Kenenbaev, 2006).

Hydrological network

In connection with the development of remote sensing technique of thematic decoding images quickly filled with new content. The engine of this progress is the practical need for a substantial broadening of the studied natural history of problems (resource, dynamic, forward-looking and other areas), as well as the introduction of automated processing systems. Remote sensing information, which requires more attention of geographical patterns and relationships between the components of the environment. But due to the complex structure of the natural landscape, which depends on many physical and geographical factors, a strict analogue of this standard do not always find, even within a limited area - geotop, mezzo units or area. Water surface in the passive mode of the remote location is almost completely absorbs the light flux, so the images received in panchromatic material in the visible region of the spectrum (0,4-0,8 mm), it is generally dark and smooth. However, the return of the incident water flow energy, reflecting the way, the bone surface of the water depends on many factors: the angle of 'tilt sunlight, the depth of the water body, the nature of the soil and aquatic vegetation, solid runoff (river turbidity), etc. Therefore, the black-and-white photographs automatic tone changes, varying within very wide limits. Denser tone image (to black) has a deep and clear water, a lighter (to white), shallow and polluted.

More classes were visually checked and the class of relevant hydrographic network. Snapshot cameras ETM + has been processed using unsupervised classification. The method of ISODATA identified 8 classes. Rivers: the full-flowing, medium, small, and drying. Channels, dams, bridges and lakes. River with about 10 m. deciphered about 2/3 of the total number of cases, they attributed to the "middle of the river, they deciphered strongly depends on the location relative to the direction of shooting and hide the objects on the shore: trees, buildings, and the height of the banks. The rivers 20-30 m wide on interpretable images be recognized fairly confident they are a group of "big river".

Soil

Creation of a soil map was carried out in several stages. First of all, the data of historical soil maps, cited above, were digitized. Soils are the geographical objects which are not quickly changed, that is why it is possible to use historical information from previous 20 years, as a base. The next step, according to space imagery, the NDVI vegetation indices for different vegetation seasons, were calculated and classified. Finally, according to the high-resolution image, the boundaries of soil taxonomic groups were specified.

Soil line is a hypothetical line in spectral space, which describes the variation of the spectrum of open ground in the picture. The line can be defined through the definition of two or more standards of bare soil on the image having different reflection and identifying the most appropriate lines in the spectral space. Good soil line cannot get if you work in very rich vegetation. Because of this, the best is to use the spectral vegetation index NDVI, because it works best in areas with abundant vegetation (Gopp, N.V et al, 2017).

For the contours and the description of soil need to fund the study area map. The next stage of automated processing is to classify images. Unambiguous universal principles of classification did not exist. The study tested algorithms uncontrolled, controlled, and expert classification. As a rule, satisfactory results are obtained when using hyper parallelepiped method of supervised classification (decision rule of classification is determined by the method of maximum likelihood). Many opportunities also have an expert classification. In this case it is a well-designed decision tree, integrating into his interpretation of the same features as the criteria and rules (Scherbenko, 1990).

Making a systematic list of soils carried out according to accepted methods is the goal in this part of the investigation. Dedicated in previous surveys (Kravtcova, 2005), soil are differentiated in the zonal sequences. Each type of soil is characterized by weather conditions, the processes of soil formation, the morphological structure of the profile, characteristics, diagnostic signs of the genetic horizons, the indices adopted to represent them and the finer classification unit in the sub-types, genera, species (according to the existing soil classification) with the corresponding morphological features and variety and discharges.

Vegetation

Vegetation cover is one of the most informative indicator of the landscape. Therefore, determining the boundaries of plant facies and its state is one of the main tasks in creating a landscape map.

According to satellite imagery data for different seasons of the year, the classes of objects of land cover were determined based on the Isodata classification method. Then, NDVI vegetation indices were calculated to determine the state of the land cover within the obtained vegetation classes. High-resolution images were used to clarify the boundaries of vegetation classes. To determine the species composition and the exact name of the classes, literary data and maps of previous years, indicated in the chapter Data, were used.

At present methods for pixel classification is well developed and widely used. We use direct object properties directly manifested in the earth's surface and displayed as a set of characteristics of remote images. Methods of automatic classification with prior training are able to operate as a set of indirect and contextual features, but under strict rules, defined on the stage of training system. Photo interpretation was carried out on the basis of visual images of space allocated to the reference sites. For the available satellite imagery Landsat has been developed algorithm for automatic classification of different types of surfaces. The basis was taken by the method of learning the classification by the method of maximum likelihood (for classification according to the spectral image of objects). The next stage of work focused on the search for discrepancies between what has been from classified file and the source images.

As result a list of vegetation types based on materials of previous soil and geo-botanical surveys, topographic maps, literary sources was developed.

Landscape mapping

The landscape map is a composite product of combining data from soil map, geomorphological map, vegetation map and maps of the region's water resources.

Nikolayev (1999) offers landscaping studies in developing activities for the rational use and optimization of modified human landscape, giving the physical-geographical basis of the recommendations of the territorial organization of land improve agricultural techniques, reclamation, treatment of livestock management, etc.

Thus, the study of landscape differentiation is an important basis for sustainable land management. The natural landscapes of the northern slope of the Ile Alatau have good potential for arable land use.

Detailed analysis basing on landscape maps of Karasai district of Almaty region (from literature) by using remote sensing data used to determine the specific boundaries of environmental systems. A landscape-indicator method is applied to differentiate the landscapes.

One of the main methods of verification of the obtained data was the method of field surveys. Data from field surveys conducted during the spring-summer 2007-2008 in the research region showed an 80% coincidence of the classes of maps received.

FINDINGS AND DISCUSSION

On the basis of the above methods and materials used, as well as research expeditions we compiled the following map of irrigation systems Karasai district of Almaty region of Kazakhstan. Scale 1:100000, Map of vegetation Karasai district of Almaty region of Kazakhstan. Scale 1:100000, Map of soil Karasai district of Almaty region of Kazakhstan. Scale 1:100000, Map of landscape type Karasai district of Almaty region of Kazakhstan. Scale 1:100000. The maps and descriptions can be found below.

1. Map of irrigation systems Karasai district of Almaty region of Kazakhstan. Scale 1:100000.

It should be noted that the territorial analysis of Karasai district became necessary to separately allocate the river valleys and plains in the lower division level or zones. Almost all of the existing facility in the study from the source to the end of the flow through all the high-rise waist Ile Alatau. Therefore, we have to create, "Map of surface water and irrigation systems Karasai district, scale 1:100000, based on which defined the class" river valleys and the lower plains (Figure 2). This area of landscape indications were divided into two types: a) grassland and floodplain meadow saline loamy soils with loamy meadow-boggy b) meadow gray soil saline soils, sometimes with a salt-marsh meadow.

2. Soil-geomorphic map of the territory Karasai district of Almaty region of Kazakhstan. Scale 1:100 000 (Figure 3).

(*Nival 2500-3600m asl:* - alpine meadow alpine soils with mountain incompletely developed and bedrock outcrops, ski-alpine grassland soils with bedrock outcrops, Alpine meadow, Alpine incompletely developed loamy soil, mountain forest soils with dark-colored mountain meadow and mountain meadow-steppe loamy soils of the forest zone, rock outcrops, cliffs, moraines snow, ice; *Medium and low mountains 1000-2500 m asl:* mountain forest soils with dark-colored mountain meadow and mountain meadow-steppe loamy soils of the forest zone, mountain dark brown loamy soils; *Foothill plains:* dark brown loamy soils with meadow and meadow brown loamy, light brown loam soils, sometimes with meadow brown loam, serozems light, serozems ordinary loamy, sometimes with a meadow-gray desert soils, salt flats common with ordinary sierozems and meadow-gray desert soils; *River valleys, lower plains:* meadow and riparian meadow saline loamy soils with loamy meadow-marshy, meadow-gray desert saline soils, sometimes with a salt-marsh).

Figure 2. Map of irrigation systems Karasai district of Almaty region of Kazakhstan. Scale 1:100000. (Locality; Waterbody: large rivers, middle rivers, small rivers, drying of the rivers, bridges, lakes; Road: road with asphalt coating, road without asphalt coating, dirt roads, railway; Border area)

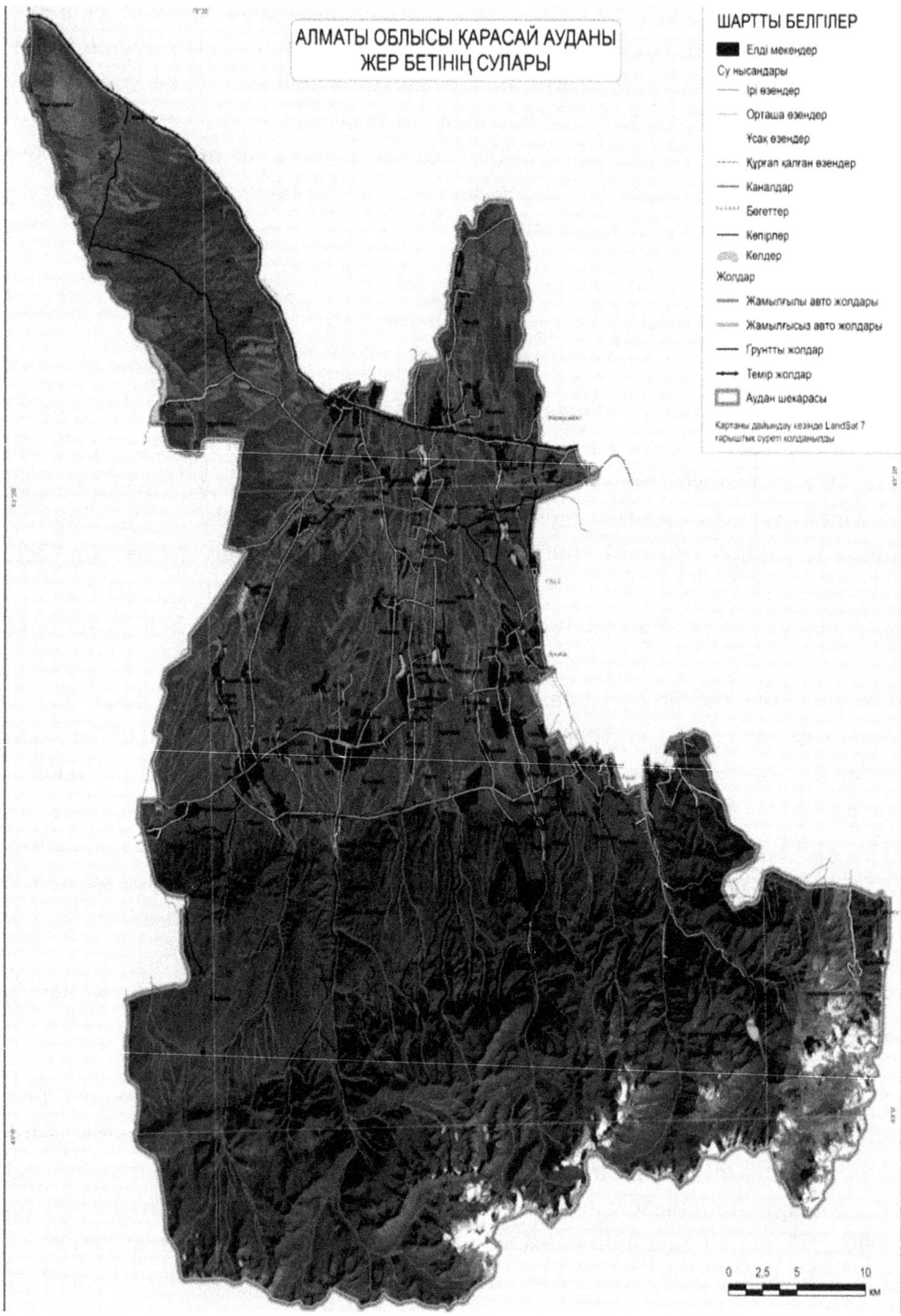

Figure 3. Soil-geomorphic map of the territory Karasai district of Almaty region of Kazakhstan. Scale 1:100 000.

ЗЕРТТЕЛУ АУМАҒЫНЫҢ ТОПЫРАҚ КАРТАСЫ

МАСШТАБ 1:100 000

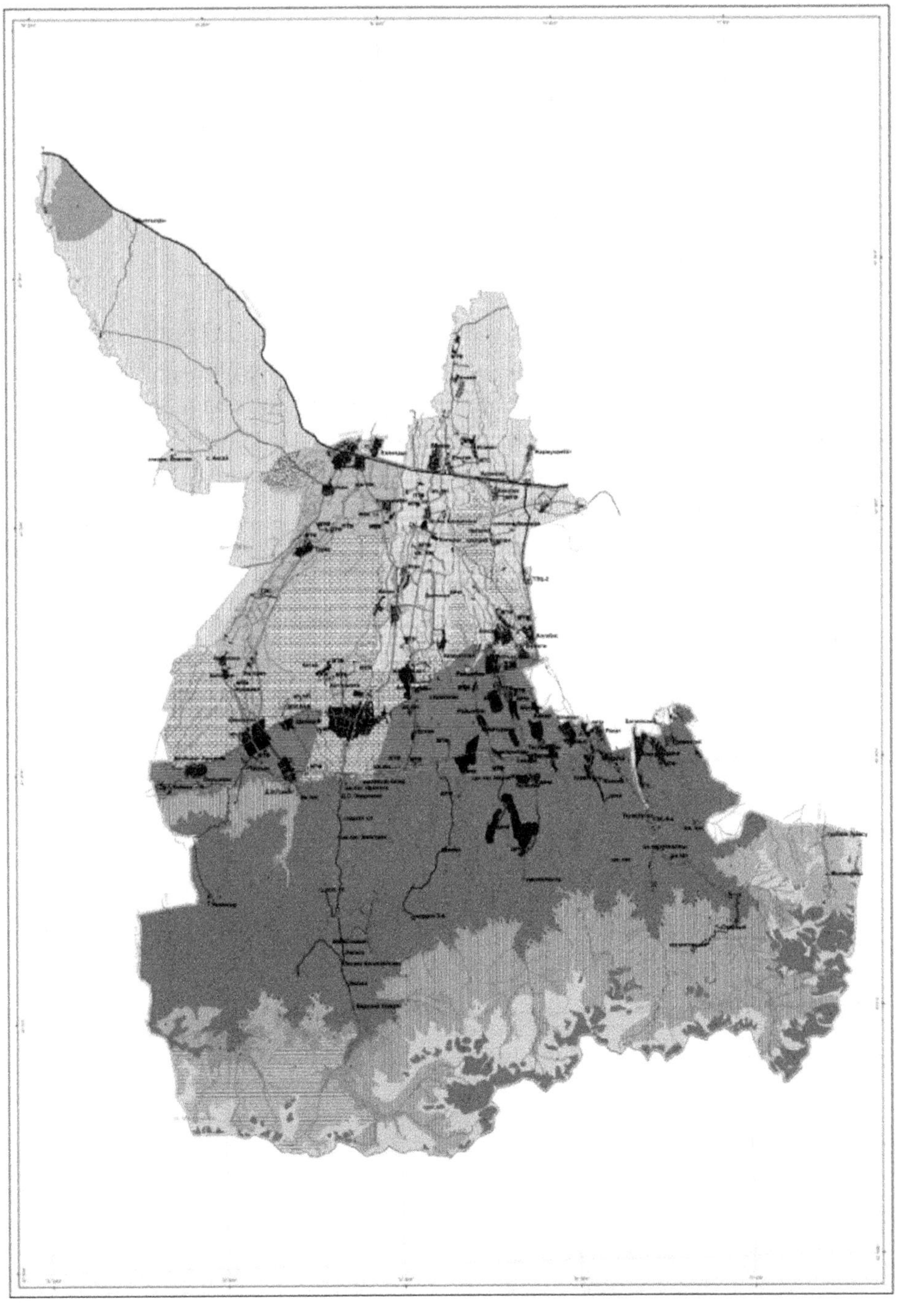

Past geomorphological studies (Digital…, 2012) have shown that the slope agriculture are mainly used in sloping plains at the absolute height of 650-1000 m with distinct forms of micro relief on the general background of meso-and microform holding fairly large areas. Provision has also been a sufficiently large area of the hydrographic network elements: a hollow, hollow, ravine, river valleys, ravines, which indicates a strong degree of horizontal and vertical partition of the territory. A study area was divided into four groups: extreme 2500-3600m asl, medium and low mountains 1000-2500 m asl, foothill plains, river valleys and lower plains.

For the classification of landscapes of the study area the features of the soil were used for basic classification.

3. Landscape map of Karasai district of Almaty region of Kazakhstan.
4. Scale 1:100000 (Figure 4).

From this map, the classification of categories were generated and classified into a hierarchy of natural systems. The hierarchy includes classes, subclasses (zone), types (sub) and subtypes (landscapes) (see table 1). The site investigation identified two classes (mountains and plains). Their characterization implemented here at the level macro relief clarifying the altitude levels of Trans-Ili Alatau, located within the Karasai district. It was found that the mountain area is located within the 1000-3600 m, and the flat part of <100 m above sea level.

The mountainous area (class) is subdivided into three subclasses (zones): The upper mountain range (2500-3600 m above sea level), the medium slopes (1500 - 2500 m above sea level) and the lower mountains (1000 -1500 m asl). The plains include two subclasses: the piedmont area and the lowlands. The boundaries of all the above subclasses (zones) are defined at the level of macrorelief within altitudinal stratification.

The subclasses have been further differentiated into types (and subtypes). As their basic unit the classification used attributes of soil information (see map number-2 explained before), and vegetation information at the level of soil types and classes of plant formations. As a result, the Upper mountain range was differentiated into 4 classes, medium and low mountains - 2, 12 types (by area) and 47 by

*Figure 4. Landscape map of Karasai district of Almaty region of Kazakhstan. Scale 1:100 000. *the legend is described in the Table 1.*

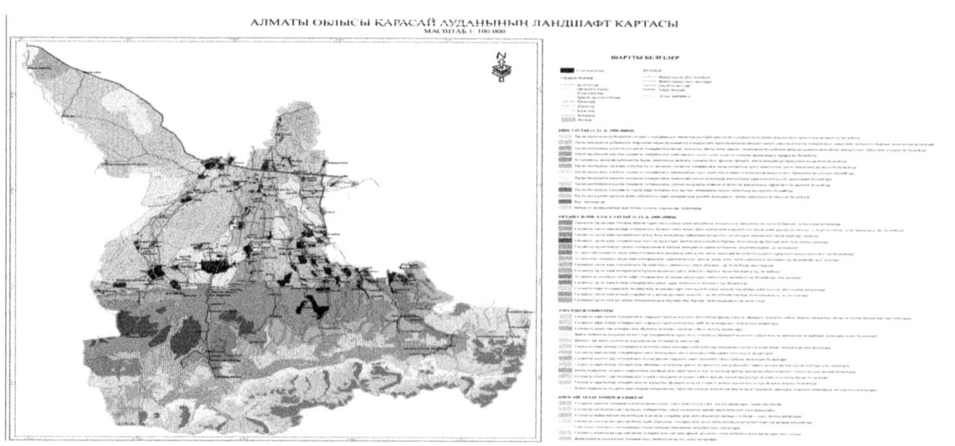

Table 1. The classification categories of landscapes and indication of their details in the Karasai district of Almaty region

Class	Divisions (zones)	Types (by area)	Landscapes
1	2	3	4
		a. Alpine meadow Alpine meadow soils with mountain incompletely developed and bedrock outcrops	i. On the mountain-meadow alpine undeveloped, incomplete development of the loamy soils on the slopes of all exposures and heights in conjunction with kobrezievo-grassland vegetation. ii. On the mountain alpine meadow loamy soils on the northern slopes in combination with kobrezievo-grass vegetation. iii. On the mountain alpine meadow loamy soils on slopes and depressions in conjunction with the sedge-grassland with cobresia vegetation. iv. On the mountain alpine meadow loamy soils on slopes in combination with manzhetkovo different herbal-sedge vegetation. v. On the mountain alpine meadow loam on the slopes in conjunction with zopnikovo-fescue-sedge-grassland vegetation. vi. On the mountain alpine meadow loamy soils on the slopes of the western, northwestern and eastern exposures, coupled with orchovo-sedge-cereal grasses.
	Nival 2500-3600m asl	*b. Alpine meadow subalpine soils with bedrock outcrops*	i. On the mountain-meadow subalpine loamy soils on slopes in combination with manzhetkovo-forb-sedge vegetation. ii. On the mountain-meadow subalpine loamy soils on the northern slopes in conjunction with grass-forb-okonitovoy vegetation.
		c. Alpine meadow subalpine not fully developed loamy soils	i. On the mountain meadow and steppe alpine underdeveloped loamy soils on the slopes, combined with fescue-sedge grasses with grasses. ii. ii. On the mountain-meadow subalpine incompletely developed loamy soils on the slopes of all exposures and peaks in conjunction with the Juniper-sedge-grass grassland vegetation. iii. iii. On the mountain-meadow subalpine underdeveloped loamy soils in combination with Juniper, forb-grass vegetation.
Alpine (1000-3000 m asl.)		*c. Mountain forest soils with dark-colored mountain meadow and mountain meadow-steppe loamy soils of the forest zone*	i. The mountain-meadow alpine and subalpine chernozem soil in combination with coniferous forests. ii. On the mountain meadow soil, mountain black soils in combination with deciduous forests.
	Medium and low mountains 1000-2500 m asl	*d. Alpine loamy black soil with mountain chernozem underdeveloped and mountain meadow loamy soils*	i. On the mountain of loamy black soils on slopes of all exposures in combination with licorice-forb-grass vegetation. ii. On the mountain of loamy black soils on the slopes of the western, eastern exposure, combined with extra vans sagebrush forb-grass vegetation. iii. On the mountain of loamy black soils in the valley, on mountain slopes in combination with grass and grassland, sometimes with buzilnikovoy vegetation iv. On the mountain of loamy black soils on the slopes of all exposures and smooth the tops in conjunction with a different feather-grass and grassland vegetation v. On the mountain chernozem underdeveloped loam on the slopes of the mountains combined with tyrysovo-grass with sagebrush and grassland vegetation. vi. On the mountain of loamy black earth underdeveloped by elephants in the mountains, combined with fescue-grassland, sometimes with sedge grasses and vegetation. vii. On the mountain of loamy black earth underdeveloped on the tops and slopes of the mountains combined with tyrysovo-grass with sagebrush and grassland vegetation. viii. Alpine loamy black soil on the slopes and valleys combined with the shrub-forb-grass vegetation. ix. On the mountain of loamy black soils on the slopes of all exposures in combination with shrub-wormwood-grass vegetation. x. On the mountain chernozem underdeveloped loam on the slopes and the tops of mountains, combined with wormwood-grassy-grassland vegetation
		e. Alpine dark-brown loamy soils	i. On the mountain dark-brown loamy soils on slopes in combination forb-grass vegetation. ii. On the mountain dark-brown loamy soils on mountain slopes of northern and north-eastern, north-western exposures, in combination with shrub-grass and grassland vegetation. iii. On the mountain dark-brown loamy soils on slopes of different exposures in combination with narrow-lobed sagebrush-grass vegetation. iv. Mountain forest dark-colored loam on the slopes and all the exhibits in conjunction with the gardens. v. Mountain forest dark-colored loam on the slopes of all exposures in combination with deciduous forests.
Plains	***Foothill plains***	*f. Dark-brown loamy soils with meadow and meadow-brown loam.*	i. The dark-brown loamy soils on slopes and level terrain, combined with the ephemeral-grassland vegetation. ii. The dark-brown loamy soils on level terrain, combined with various herbal-grass vegetation. iii. The dark-brown, sometimes eroded, loamy soils on slopes, rolling plain with a combination of narrowly lobed wormwood-cereal sometimes with grassland vegetation. iv. The dark-brown loamy soils on the southern and eastern slopes of the hilly-rolling plain with a combination of white land sagebrush ephemeroid vegetation.

continued on following page

Table 1. Continued

Class	Divisions (zones)	Types (by area)	Landscapes
1	2	3	4
		g. Light brown loam soils, sometimes with meadow-brown loam	i. In light chestnut loam soils in south-western slopes and tops of hills and rolling plain with a combination of sedge-ephemeroid, sometimes with tyrsevo-grassland vegetation. ii. In light chestnut loam soils on the tops, northern and western slopes of the hilly-rolling plain with a combination of fescue-grass vegetation. iii. In light chestnut loam soils on slopes and tops of hills and rolling plain with a combination of white land sagebrush-grass vegetation with ephemerals. iv. In light chestnut, sometimes eroded, loamy soils on the hills leveled areas with a combination of autumn sagebrush ephemeroid, sometimes with herbs, vegetation.
		h. Light gray soil	i. At serozems light loam with a combination burntsovo-ephemeral vegetation.
		i. Serozems ordinary loamy, sometimes with a meadow-gray desert soils	i. At serozem ordinary loamy, sometimes eroded, on the tops, ravines and slopes of hills and rolling plain with a combination of different feather grass and sedge = ephemeroid vegetation. ii. At serozem ordinary loam, on the slopes of hills and rolling plain with a combination of Stipa-grass with wormwood. iii. At serozem ordinary loam in the northern and north-western slopes of hills and rolling plain with a combination of the crest can be seen couch-wormwood
	River valleys, lower plains.	*k. Meadow and riparian meadow saline loamy soils with meadow-marshy loam.*	i. In the meadow loamy soils in river valleys, streams, low plains with a combination of licorice-grass-grassland vegetation. ii. On floodplain meadow saline loamy soils in river valleys and streams with a combination of Lasiagrostis splendens-selitrovanny-ephemeroid green. iii. At the salt marsh meadow in depressions, streams dry up with a combination beskilnitsevo-Lebedeva vegetation. iv. On floodplain grassland soils in river valleys with a combination azhrekovoy vegetation.
		l. Meadow-gray desert saline soils, sometimes with salt marshes.	i. In the meadow-serozem loamy saline, loamy soils in river valleys with a combination Lasiagrostis splendens, sometimes with grasses and vegetation. ii. In the meadow-serozem saline, saline loamy soils in depressions and river valleys with a combination Lasiagrostis splendens-shrenkianovo wormwood. iii. In the meadow-serozem saline loamy soils on lower plains, valleys, streams with a combination shrenkianovopolynno-grass, sometimes with saltworts, vegetation

area landscape. It should be noted that during the territorial analysis of the Karasai district it becomes necessary to separate the river valleys and plains in the lower division level or zones (see map xx described upper in this chapter).

Based on the classification criteria of landscapes and indication of their details, the proposed Nikolaev (1999), each type has been differentiated into subtypes or landscapes. Nikolaev developed a method for assessing, proposed to classify the scape farms land types according to their suitability for a particular type of use. In compiling agrolandscape map system should be characterized with several positions:

1. The internal structure of natural systems (relief, parent rocks, soils and vegetation).
2. Features of the environment (climatic resources, adverse weather events, their frequency of occurrence, etc.).
3. Forms of agricultural use (types of crop rotation, grazing cattle.
4. The average long-term productivity of land (for crops used in crop rotation, in pastures and hayfields).
5. Recommended improvements of agriculture.

Executed subject to the above items typological agrolandscape map can be the basis of natural zoning for agriculture.

Indicators of agro-ecological land evaluation takes into consideration the relevant factors (not just soil, but also the geomorphological, lithological, hydrogeological, soil structure) for large-scale surveys of land and show them on maps. In addition, the hierarchical principle allocation of land categories (type, type, group of land) and the corresponding hierarchy of design elements of farming systems makes it necessary to reflect the structure of the landscape and within the landscape types (Kiryushin, 2005).

To accomplish this separation as classification features by Kiryushin proposes to use the level of soil subtypes and subclasses of plant formations, which are the most important functional components of landscape systems. Consequently, adhering to these principles, we have clarified layers of the landscape in region of study. They are described in detail in the table and shown on the "Landscape Map Karasai district of Almaty region of Kazakhstan" on a scale of 1:100000. A total number of 52 landscape types is differentiated.

The presented map allows you to evaluate the current state of the study area and to take timely preventive measures to improve and preserve their fertility.

The methods that allow their use in the field of plant and soil science are applicable to the research institutes of soil science and agrochemistry named after U. Uspanov and the Kazakh Research Institute of Agriculture and Crop Production. The methods are also applicable to all countries of Central Asia and Eastern Europe.

Thus, the work is of great interest for the implementation of the tasks of introducing new agricultural methods from the point of view of rational nature management.

The remote sensing information and the application of GIS methods used in this study relay to modern methods development of landscape interpretation and differentiation. The methods increase the degree of objectivity when using a comparable classification for larger areas. Some characteristics of landscapes and their components, as compared with visual methods. Many of them also reveal the particular of landscapes are not only qualitative but also quantitative level. Digital processing techniques of multispectral images from space, evaluation capabilities which was carried out in this work are needed in the refinement landscape contours, revealing the dynamics and direction of various natural process, the impact of various objects at each other. These data are essential for assessing the effectiveness of agricultural technologies.

The above system of GIS technology with the use of RS is designed specifically for the initial phase of the design adaptive landscape of agriculture.

It is important to note that maps constructed on the basis of quantitative methods that are precisely reproducible and comparable with similar maps are constructed in other territories, or based on surveys performed at different times. However, there are no restrictions on remote information received at various times from various satellite systems.

FUTURE RESEARCH DIRECTIONS

The introduction of new technologies of spatial analysis of geographical objects on the basis of remote sensing data in landscape planning methodology enhances the reliability of the results of mapping and, consequently, increases the value of the materials of landscape planning as databases and knowledge of nature and landscape for binding sectored and territorial planning. Such method could be improved in the future and be applicable to new standards for adaptive and precision farming. This is possible through the use of the latest ultra-high-resolution remote sensing data and web-based GIS technology. This is the done method in this chapter is relevant not only for Kazakhstan, it is also relevant for the Eurasia countries.

CONCLUSION

Agriculture is one of the main sectors of the economy of the developing countries of the Central Asian region. Therefore, the issue of rational use of land resources must be addressed now. The scientific basis for resolving such issues is the landscape map. The construction of landscape maps of individual agricultural areas on a large scale, with regularly updated taxon borders, is possible only with the use of modern digital technologies, such as remote sensing and geographic information technologies.

On the example of a specific agricultural region in southern Kazakhstan, they demonstrated how this is possible using the literary information of previous studies and new data from satellite images.

On the basis outlined above, the following conclusions are stated: the territory of the Karasai district of Almaty region is a very complex biogeosystem including mountains and lowlands; the soil - geomorphological map of a scale of 1:100000 of the investigation area covers/differentiate the taxonomic units of the landscape map into classes; the territory of research consists of 52 varieties of landscape; the maps of surface water and irrigation systems on a scale of 1:100 000 were used for a zoning of river valleys and low plains. It provides an example for further differentiation of landscapes that can be used as an example to highlight the landscape in similar regions of Central Asia.

REFERENCES

Assylbekova, A. (2010). Investigation of landscapes of the northern slope of Alatau Mountains using satellite imagery. Almaty, Kazakhstan: Kazakh Universiteti.

Bartalev, S., Yegorov, V., Jarko, V., Lupyan, E., & Plotnikov, S. (2016). *Satellite mapping of the vegetation cover of Russia*. Moscow, Russia: IKI RAN.

Climate Handbook of Kazakhstan. (2004). *Long-term data*.

Digital soil mapping: theoretical and experimental studies. (2011). Collection of articles. Russia, Moscow: Soil Institute.

Forkuor, G., Hounkpatin, O. K. L., Welp, G., & Thiel, M. (2017). High Resolution Mapping of Soil Properties Using Remote Sensing Variables in South-Western Burkina Faso: A Comparison of Machine Learning and Multiple Linear Regression Models. *PLoS One*, *12*(1). doi:10.1371/journal.pone.0170478 PMID:28114334

Geldyeva, G., & Veselova, L. (1992). *Landscapes of Kazakhstan. Kazakhstan, Alma-Ata*. Nauka.

Gopp, N., Nechaeva, T., & Savenkov, O. (2017) Indicative capacity of NDVI in predictive mapping of the properties of plow horizons of soils on slopes in the south of Western Siberia. *Eurasian Soil*, *50*, 1332-1343. doi:10.1134/S1064229317110060

Gvozdetsky, N. (1963). *On the altitudinal zonation as the basic laws of landscape differentiation of mountainous countries/Questions of the landscapes. Kazakhstan, Alma-Ata*. Nauka.

Isachenko, A. (1965). *Fundamentals of landscape science and physical-geographical zoning*. Moscow, Russia: Higher School.

Isachenko, A. (1991) Landscape and physical-geographical zoning. Moscow, Russia: Higher School.

Kariyeva, J., & Leeuwen, V. (2011). Environmental Drivers of NDVI-Based Vegetation Phenology in Central Asia. *Remote Sensing*, *3*(2), 203–246. doi:10.3390/rs3020203

Kenenbaev, S. (2006). *The concept of Adaptive - landscape systems of agriculture to the south-east of Kazakhstan for the period till 2010*. Almaty: Almalybak.

Kenenbaev, S., Iorgansky, A., & Borangaziev, B. (2009). Improved crop production in agricultural landscapes of the erosion of southeastern Kazakhstan. In *Proceedings of the International Conference on Soil Erosion: Problems and ways to improve crop production* (pp. 10-16). Academic Press.

Kiryushin, V. (1996). *Ecological bases of agriculture*. Moscow, Russia: Kolos.

Kiryushin, V., & Ivanov, A. (2005). *Methodological guiding on agro-ecological assessment of land, design of adaptive landscapes, farming systems and agricultural technology*. Moscow, Russia: FGU Rasinformagroteh.

Knizhnikov, Y. (2003). *Fundamentals of aerospace research methods*. Moscow, Russia: Moscow State University.

Kravtsova, V. (2005). *Space research methods soils: Proc. handbook for university students*. Moscow, Russia: Aspect Press.

Labutina, I. (2004). *Interpretation of satellite pictures*. Moscow, Russia: Aspect Press.

Linnik, V. (1990). *Construction of GIS in physical geography: Proc. Allowance*. Moscow, Russia: Moscow State University. University Press.

Nefedova, T. (1990). Problems of nature: Methodological approaches to studying, mapping, zoning. *Bulletin USSR, Geographical Series*, *6*, 37–38.

Nikolaev, V. (1999). *Landscapes of the Asian steppes*. Moscow: Moscow State University Press.

Räsänen, A., & Virtanen, T. (2019). Data and resolution requirements in mapping vegetation in spatially heterogeneous landscapes. *Remote Sensing of Environment: Elsevier*, *230*, 111207. doi:10.1016/j.rse.2019.05.026

Scherbenko, E., & Asmus, V. (1990). *The method of digital processing of aerospace information for creating soil maps: Study Earth from space*. Moscow, Russia: Nauka.

Schmidtlein, S., Feilhauera, H., Thonfeld, F., Faudec, U., Hed, K., & Rocchinie, D. (2013). Assessing floristic composition with multispectral sensors— A comparison based on monotemporal and multiseasonal field spectra. *International Journal of Applied Earth Observation and Geoinformation*, *21*, 218–229. doi:10.1016/j.jag.2012.09.002

Shibkikh, A. (2002). Landscape mapping of the Altai region using GIS technologies to address environmental problems. In *INTERCARTO8: GIS for sustainable Territorial Development: Proceedings of the international conference*. (pp. 205-207) Russia, St. Petersburg: JSC “Map”.

Snytko, V., Batuev, A., Whale, A., Konovalova, T., Kuznetsova, T., & Shekhovtsov, A. (2002). Using the experience of the system mapping in the development of regional GIS. In *Proceedings of the VII Scientific Conference on thematic cartography: "Ordnance Survey and GIS support management of regional development* (pp. 57-60). Russia, Irkutsk: Institute of Geography SB RAS.

Terekhov, A., Tsychuyeva, N., & Muratova, N. (2007). The principles of agro landscapes zoning of arable lands in steppe zone of Northern Kazakhstan using MODIS and IRS LISS. *Modern problems of remote sensing of the earth from space, 4*(2), 390–397.

Trofimov, A., & Panasyuk, M. (1984). *Geographic information systems and management problems environment*. Kazan, Russia: Kazan University Press.

Tsychuyeva, N. (2010). GIS-technology application for agrolandscape zoning of arable land in Northern Kazakhstan. *Bulletin of Al-Farabi KazNU, Geographic series., 1*(28), 140–144.

Vinokurov, Y., Rotanova, I., Khlebovich, I., & Shibkikh, A. (2000). News to regional health-ecological mapping / GIS sustainable development of territories. In *Proceedings of the International Conference* (Vol. 1, pp. 84-96). Russia, Moscow: Kola Scientific Center.

KEY TERMS AND DEFINITIONS

Adaptive-Landscape System Of Agriculture (ALSA): A system of land use, which makes use of agri-environmental groups focused on the production and the economic and natural due to the quantity and quality in accordance with the public (market) needs, natural and industrial and natural resource, providing sustainable agrolandscape and soil fertility.

Decryption, Interpretation: The process of studying the territories, water areas and the atmosphere based on the relationship between the properties of the decrypted objects and the nature of their reproduction in images from aerial and space images. The content and task of Decryption is to obtain a certain amount of quantitative and qualitative information on remote sensing data on the state, composition, structure, sizes, relationships and dynamics of processes, phenomena and objects using decryption features.

Geographic Information System (GIS): A system designed to capture, store, manipulate, analyze, manage, and present spatial or geographic data.

Image Classification: The process of extracting classes from multichannel bitmap information. The resulting raster from image classification can be used to create thematic maps. Depending on the interaction between the analyst and the computer during classification, there are two types of classification: supervised and unsupervised.

Landscape: The visible features of an area of land, its landforms, and how they integrate with natural or man-made features. A landscape includes the physical elements of geophysical defined landforms such as (ice-capped) mountains, hills, water bodies such as rivers, lakes, ponds and the sea, living elements of land cover including indigenous vegetation, human elements including different forms of land use, buildings, and structures, and transitory elements such as lighting and weather conditions. Combining both their physical origins and the cultural overlay of human presence, often created over millennia, landscapes reflect a living synthesis of people and place that is vital to local and national identity.

Map: A mathematically defined, reduced, generalized image of the surface of the Earth, another celestial body, or outer space, showing the objects located or projected onto them in the adopted system of conventional signs. The map is considered as a figurative and symbolic model with high information content, spatiotemporal similarity with respect to the original, metricity, special visibility and visualization, which makes it the most important means of knowledge in Earth sciences and socio-economic sciences.

Normalized Difference Vegetation Index (NDVI): A standardized index allowing you to generate an image displaying greenness (relative biomass). This index takes advantage of the contrast of the characteristics of two bands from a multispectral raster dataset—the chlorophyll pigment absorptions in the red band and the high reflectivity of plant materials in the near-infrared (NIR) band.

Remote Sensing: The process of detecting and monitoring the physical characteristics of an area by measuring its reflected and emitted radiation at a distance (typically from satellite or aircraft). Special cameras collect remotely sensed images, which help researchers "sense" things about the Earth.

Space Images: The collective name of data obtained using spacecraft (SC) in various ranges of the electromagnetic range, visualized by a specific algorithm.

Chapter 6
Geopolitics and Economic Sustainability Nexus:
McDonald's in Russia, China, and Kazakhstan

Danial Saari
https://orcid.org/0000-0003-3561-8209
Almaty Management University, Kazakhstan

Aigul Adibayeva
KIMEP University, Kazakhstan

ABSTRACT

New trends in market relations require new methods to solve issues towards TNCs and other actors within multilateral diplomacy. The use of economic diplomacy and responsible business is essential for TNCs to achieve the sustainability in global trading system. It is important due to frequent political changes in the modern world, to which TNCs are highly susceptible, and therefore, must be reliably protected by revised international law, clearly enshrined into relevant multilateral agreements. As the legal status of TNCs is somehow blurred, the cases of unstable TNCs performance due to political atrocities may occur. The latter leads to disruptions in their work making them to obey states' interests and further concern of the issue from states and global business entities. The disruption of both agent interests creates an overall economic instability and negatively affects the process of sustainability achieving. The work summarizes some problems TNCs face due to confrontation between states, and the question of the importance of economic diplomacy use and legal support for TNCs.

DOI: 10.4018/978-1-7998-2551-7.ch006

INTRODUCTION

Problem Statement

At present the system of international relations is framed within geopolitical and globalised economic realms. Such a system produced a number of state and non-state actors on the global arena. Among the non-state actors of international relations transnational corporations (hereinafter - TNCs) represent a special case. While functioning domestically and overseas, TNCs eventually became the models of international business standards, reflecting the latest tendencies in management, production, customer service, and other business-related areas. Newest trends in socially responsible business doing, sustainability, environmentalism, digitalization, etc., embraced into a corporate social responsibility concept, are being also implemented by TNCs. The latter is increasing the importance of the TNCs' role in contributing to Sustainable Development Goals (hereinafter – SDGs) through socially oriented projects, policies and latest digital technological developments. From time to time, however, TNCs, becoming the subjects of international politics, face challenges of being dependent on geopolitical peculiarities of inter-state relations and suffer serious operational disruptions.

In this particular research, the case studies of McDonald's in Russia, China and Kazakhstan are taken to illustrate the necessity of sustainable economic diplomacy as a tool to improve comprehensively the TNCs operational performances and make them less dependent on political atrocities which occasionally appear in their work overseas.

Sustainable Economic Diplomacy Within the System of International Relations

As V. Roberts notes, the political orientations of classical diplomacy are typical for the pre-globalization era and should be transformed today into a new mechanism for resolving both legal and economic problems that many multinational corporations face due to the changing political situation in the international arena (Roberts, 1991). For example, the central issue of traditional diplomacy has always been allocating around political concepts and instruments, acting less significantly in other aspects of foreign relations - both in the framework of bilateral and multilateral agreements. As authors mention, the authority does not imply solely the concept of nation-states in its classic possession of sovereignty (Cerny, 2010). Moreover, the current system of international relations assumes non-state actors with a growing amount of instruments and functions to implement.

Meanwhile, the economic aspect of interstate relations has an ever-increasing influence on the world politics and, therefore, should be reflected in all diplomatic procedures, and in promotion of commercial diplomacy for the benefit of all participants in the world economy. Moreover, new challenges in social, human, environmental spheres are of the combined nature and, thus, require an integrated manner of governance (Moomaw et al., 2016). The economic diplomacy, as a facilitating instrument, is distinguished by a combination of different methods used in solving complex economic problems (Naray, 2008), thus becomes an effective tool to address a number of political interactions conducted by states from one hand, and challenges of transnational corporations as subjects of world politics, - from another. The need for the use of this particular diplomatic resource would ultimately emphasize the responsibility of states and blocs of states in ensuring the economic and legal security of transnational corporations.

Sustainable Economic Diplomacy and Transnational Corporations

Today, the sustainable economic diplomacy is increasingly focusing on promoting interests of TNCs around the world. The latter, as international relations participants, are of increasing importance due to global changes and challenges in the modern period, as well as progress of TNCs' operational performance. TNCs no longer represent mere economic entities that are solely oriented to making profits. Nowadays they perform with the growing efforts in the context of socially responsible business doing, accompanying their economic success with ethical, environmental and social activities. The latter has a greater socio-economic effect rather than a simple positive image TNCs create to maintain in the competitive markets. It eventually contributes to the sustainable development goals, where socio-economic, political, human and environmental fields are highly interconnected and interdependent. The efficient legal, political and social responsibility framework in TNCs' performance can be achieved with the wider implementation of sustainable economic diplomacy.

Development of new conceptualizations in understanding the diplomacy phenomenon within the newly appearing sustainable development goals is yet another important dimension. In this context again the classic diplomacy concept is often altered or added by sustainable economic diplomacy concept. For instance, some experts (Moomaw et al., 2016) are challenging the solution of the contemporary issues of social and environmental nature through the classic implementation of diplomacy only. Defined as a tool to regulate the inter-state relations (Hamilton & Langhorne, 2011), it does not fully regulate sustainable development challenges (Moomaw et al., 2016). With the remaining of traditional diplomacy practices to be used, other types of governance are being utilized to advance sustainable development. One of them could be definitely an instrument of sustainable economic diplomacy, which eventually evolves to a reliable tool in reaching sustainable development goals.

In the context of TNCs operations worldwide as recognized non-state actors of international politics and global economy, it is especially important to facilitate and intensively apply the sustainable economic diplomacy in the solution of certain issues and decision-making process around their activities. Such issues arise from various geopolitical processes and interactions among state-actors, greatly affecting the system of international relations. Although, those shifts lay in the sphere of inter-state political relations, they may directly affect the conditions and efficiency of large international corporations operating abroad. This leads to the situation when, apart from social, ethical and environmental dimensions in the TNCs functioning, the corporations face functional difficulties operating overseas. Considering the tendency of frequent geopolitical changes one can observe today a set of mechanisms is required to be developed to minimize the shortcomings TNCs may suffer from. The necessity of such tools is of a greater importance when sustainability goals are at stake.

Corporate Social Responsibility and Sustainable Development

The operational activities of TNCs are currently rather inclusive with social, ethical, human and environmental dimensions exercised. Accumulatively, the performance of such socially responsible business by companies refers to a large Corporate Social Responsibility (hereinafter - CSR) concept. CSR is aiming to minimize the shortcomings of companies' business-related activities onto human, social and environmental standings, eventually complements the achievement of sustainable development goals.

The definition of corporate social responsibility has changed over time. As UNCTAD experts point out, there is still neither universally recognized definition of CSR, nor a consensus on the issues this concept covers. It is generally recognized that CSR is not just charity work or a mere compliance with the law. The common denominator of most definitions is that CSR is a concept, according to which enterprises integrate social and environmental issues into their business policies and activities in order to make their impact on society more preferable.

The Report of the UNCTAD Secretariat (2003) mentions several definitions. Private sector organizations' definition, such as, for example, of Social Responsibility of Business Circles states that CSR "means doing business so that it meets the expectations of society or even surpasses such expectations in the ethical, legal, commercial and civilian aspects." The OECD specialists position CSR as a "corporate responsibility includes the effectiveness of the degree to which relations between commercial enterprises and the society in which they operate are well-established. A key element of corporate responsibility is entrepreneurship itself." Yet, the wording of the World Business Council for Sustainable Development differs significantly, referring CSR as representing "the continued determination of entrepreneurs to demonstrate ethical behavior and contribute to sustainable economic development, while improving the standard of living of workers and their families, as well as local community as a whole." and, thus, emphasizes CSR's link with sustainable economic development goals. Finally, the World Bank continues with the notion of CSR as an "intention of entrepreneurs to contribute to sustainable economic development through collaboration with employees, their families, the local community and society as a whole, in order to improve the quality of life in ways that are beneficial for business and favorable for reaching sustainable development goals."

As well as, in general, in its relation to sustainability concept, CSR and its implementation evolved to a solid research interest and literature. The latest studies include such scopes as businesses social commitments, state policies and public benefit strategies, discourses on companies CSR greenwashing cases (Du, 2015), CSR dimensions (Capelle-Blancard, 2016), content analysis of the CSR literature (Lee, 2016) and others.

One should note that the forms and dimensions of modern CSR, being eventually adopted into corporations' policies, are clustered within four major types of CSR. The first type, usually called as ethical, refers to creation of fair labor and product standards within the corporation. The philanthropic type of CSR provides a variety of charity-like activities devoted to a needy part of the population, essentially performed in the form of donations for a number of need-based purposes, from disaster and poverty-related to human rights contributions. The environmental type of responsibility includes a rich spectrum of companies' activities and projects on planet resources protection from business operations, reducing water and air pollution, and greenhouse effect. The business (economic) responsibilities involve a complex approach in a company's decision-making process that estimates overall impact on environment, society and business itself as a whole.

Meanwhile CSR has evolved within its dimensions to the principle of voluntariness. The latter emphasizes the understanding of the willingness and enthusiastic nature of some actions and believes the corporation holds upon its CSR performance, rather than obligatory character of certain ethical or socially responsible projects (Scilly, 2016). Yet, the voluntariness principle substantially enriches, not weakens the CSR substance and development perspectives, involving new agendas into TNCs' practices and additional approaches in reaching the sustainable development goals.

THEORETICAL FRAMEWORK

Evidently, there are many researchers who possess their distinctive views towards different issues and situations in the entire world. As a rule, economic interests imply a paradigm of realism concepts in international relations (Morgenthau, 1946), since they reflect, to a greater degree, national interests, economic benefits and are based on competition in profits' pursuit and consumerism behavior (Fisher, 2009). "To know that nations are subject to the moral law is one thing, while to pretend to know with certainty what is good and evil in the relations among nations is quite another", Morgenthau H. says (Morgenthau, 1946). Whereas the concept of social responsibility, ethics, morality, charity reflects more altruistic origins being the part of the idealistic deontological school (Kant, 1785), which is aimed at a clear understanding of duty, responsibility and conscience in its absolute sense and is close to neoliberalism positions (Hayek, 1960). In its turn, the ethics of neoliberalism implies the use of traditional ethics to strengthen capitalism ideologically (Bloom, 2017). Sustainable economic diplomacy and corporate social responsibility, in their turn, synthesize these contrasting schools, thus, representing potential and reliable tools in solving relevant issues. For instance, such issues may involve the framework of large international companies' functioning within the global economic market and minimum insurance of public good. Or the case of political relations between states can undergo ups and downs, sustainable economic diplomacy and corporate social responsibility of business can neutralize the severity of shortcomings in the geopolitical games between the leading world countries, ensuring certain level of stability in the economic standpoints.

METHODOLOGY

The case methodology or situational analysis is used to illustrate the real-life situation related to the activities of TNCs in three countries of the Eurasian region, Russia, China and Kazakhstan. The latter is conducted through the literature review and content analysis of media recourses of the cases abovementioned in order to follow up and question on the extent of compliance with sustainable development goals. The case with McDonalds's is based on real-life factual material, processing which made it possible to identify the status of this global corporation in the current geopolitical situation and the factors influencing its operations in Russia, China and Kazakhstan. Through a detailed analysis of political situation over the last five years the authors trace the interconnection between the global political challenges, international legal framework, social corporate responsibility standards in the ultimate performance of the mentioned transnational corporation. The case study methodology allows its best to study the evolution and dynamics of TNCs functioning in the above-mentioned countries because of the fact that overseas activities suppose the high level of vulnerabilities which corporations face due to frequently changing domestic and international political climate.

In the course of studying this case, it was possible to propose recommendations aimed at ensuring greater security in the activities of this corporation abroad in case when politics penetrates into business. This study uses an unstructured case method specifically, since the latter is not intended to find the universally applied solution, but to look at the situation with a synergetic focus combining business, politics, sustainable development and social responsibilities of the enterprise. Due to sufficient amount of information from the published data the authors based the case study on secondary sources. This method was used, to a greater extent, due to insufficient coverage of this case in the scientific literature of the countries of the Eurasian region.

This work attempts to examine economic diplomacy in the context of corporations' dependence on geopolitical patterns while operating in Russian, Chinese and Kazakhstani economies, where political and socio-cultural, rather than economic aspects are often determining factors in the effectiveness of TNCs functioning.

LITERATURE REVIEW

To study the degree of development of this research there was a thorough analysis of the available literature on the topic of the chapter. There was a detected lack of papers devoted to legal, political and ethical issues of TNCs performance in complying with the sustainability goals based on the case study of TNCs operation in Russia, China and Kazakhstan.

Mostly all the works being explored in the study addressed mainly general aspects of the topic or avoiding the situation around sustainable policies in TNCs performance in the Russian Federation, People's Republic of China and the Republic of Kazakhstan. Therefore, the theoretical and practical aspects of TNCs performance in complying with the sustainable economic goals including the direction of its application in the framework of multilateral diplomacy were not fully covered by the previous studies. For the most part they were precisely considered in the work of such scholars as C. Matlack and L. Bannerman, in the work on theory and practice of economic diplomacy in the period of post-modernism; apart from them O. Naray mainly devotes his work to the study of commercial diplomacy in the context of economic globalization at contemporary time; similarly to C. Matlack and L. Bannerman the famous scientist S. Woolcock being one of the founders of a new economic diplomacy together with such scientists such J.M. Waller, A. Jacques, J. Menzel, J. Kurt, J. Peterson and others brought into scientific circulation a completely new notion.

The research on legal, political and ethical problems in the field of multilateral economic diplomacy was reflected in the works of such scholars and practitioners as L Anderson, J. Earley, G. Feketekuty and I. Williamson and others. Their views on the above-mentioned aspects of economic diplomacy were pretty similar. In particular, those aspects were clearly reflected in the work of W. Roberts on economic diplomacy for digital society in the information age on transition from economic stabilization to its gradual growth. This work is helpful for understanding the state of sustainable economic diplomacy in local conditions and to enhance a better consideration of the degree of transnational corporations' influence on economy.

The features of transnational corporations and the future of global corporate responsibility were reflected in the works of S. Kobrin and others, while the case study of the Crimean crisis and the issue of compliance with international law were addressed by J. Losavio.

Problems of improvements of McDonald's socially oriented projects are described in the works of such experts as M. Selezneva, K. Lukovitz and others.

Based on the above-mentioned analysis of previous literature we can conclude insufficient development of theoretical and practical aspects of the topic in literature and it requires further elaboration. It is also necessary to adapt the sustainable development goals concepts to promote transnational corporations as part of the holistic global economic process.

TNCS: FUNCTIONS, IMPORTANCE AND CHALLENGES FACED

Functions of Transnational Corporations

Today transnational corporations perform multiple important functions in the world economy, which correspond to the fundamental goals and principles of sustainable economic development, the set of which is constantly growing. To specify, the main functions are the following ones:

1. Transnational corporations stimulate scientific and technical progress since most researches are carried out within their framework leading to the appearance of new technological developments. Transnational corporations have enough funds to finance research projects as part of their research and development departments;
2. Transnational corporations stimulate the globalization trend of the world economy, contributing to the deepening of international sustainable labor development and involving host countries in international economic relations. They also mobilize labor resources and stimulate labor migration;
3. Transnational corporations stimulate the development of world production. Being the largest world investors, they are constantly increasing their production capacities, creating new types of products and jobs in the host countries, stimulating the development of production in them, and hence the global sustainable economy as a whole;
4. Transnational corporations are constantly stimulating competition on the global labor market. This does not contradict the fact that they have the highest competitiveness.

All four discussed functions are indicating the high level of significance of the TNCs in the context of the global economic system and its sustainability efforts and contribution.

Challenges TNCs Face Operating Overseas: General Features

There are a number of issues the transnational corporations may face while operating in the economies of other countries. Some of them are of political and social nature, while others relate to the factor of economic competitiveness rate among the local and international companies. The latter could potentially cause conflicts between a stronger foreign company and a less competitive company in its country of location. One can note here that the relation of foreign business entities and the government of the hosting state may represent the third cluster of issues, dependent on local legislation framework, as well as social and cultural differences, leading to significant disagreements, reduction of profitability and sometimes even a collapse in cooperation between the parties.

Occasionally large transnational corporations may exert uncontrolled economic pressure on smaller companies in developing or transition economies, which often leads to a feeling of hostility in the host country. For example, some multinational corporations were accused of making too much profit, hiring the best specialists among local residents and sometimes working to the detriment of the social customs of the host country.

Commercial Diplomacy: Assisting Transnational Corporations in Overseas Performance

In order to minimize such negative experiences as well as to increase economic efficiency and security of international companies operating abroad, modern diplomacy, based on the relevant legal foundations, should develop a number of appropriate economic protection mechanisms.

Considering commercial diplomacy and the fact of the appearance and development of the phenomenon itself, it should be remembered that starting from the interwar period (1918-1939), developed countries expanded their fields of activity and went beyond regional borders in global economic diplomacy (Librando, 1959). S. Woolcock, a research fellow for comparative regional integration programs at the United Nations University, proposed definition of economic diplomacy from the end of the World War II to the outbreak of the Cold War as economic and diplomatic relations between countries represented by leading economic powers (Woolcock, 2014).

In this regard, it should be noted that the introduction of the concept of so-called commercial diplomacy into scientific and practical circulation in 1994 is directly related to the former Prime Minister of Italy Silvio Berlusconi. He repeatedly applied to this particular type of diplomacy in 2001-2006, quite successfully promoting the national interests of his country in many areas of international trade (Cassini, 2007). For instance, in 2009, during a working visit as part of the commercial diplomacy to the Gulf countries, he went to Saudi Arabia, the UAE and Qatar (Bannerman, 2009). These visits were of both political and economic importance. Traditionally, diplomacy had a significant political focus, which resulted in the fact that diplomats paid little attention to the real economy and the interests of domestic companies that wanted to work abroad. For decades, small and medium-sized businesses have been forced to look for ways to enter new markets on their own, mainly due to the personal management skills of the owners or their representatives. In the end, Berlusconi played the role of the representative of Italian business interests in the Middle East. Being a strong partner in the region and the largest oil-producing country, Saudi Arabia has a special political influence, manifested in a number of conflict situations. Moderate traditionalist religion and politics, combined with stable relations with the West since 1991, led Saudi Arabia to political alliance with the United States and Europe. Qatar, despite the differences from Saudi Arabia, is no less interesting in terms of a dynamic and rapidly growing economy. It was Berlusconi who conducted active diplomatic negotiations with these countries, which could help Italian companies find a way out of the crisis that shook them on their own markets. He actively established contacts in all directions, which contributed to increasing the international influence and prestige of his country (Bannerman, 2009).

The aforementioned Italian case, does not, surely, always serve as an example, guarantor or basis for commercial diplomacy or a conscious vision of state leaders. In fact, the status quo of states often demonstrates the opposite nature of transnational business behavior. The latter becomes the subject of political and geopolitical configurations and, thus, allows states, governments and alliances to purposefully manipulate international companies.

CASE STUDIES: MCDONALD'S OPERATING IN RUSSIA, CHINA AND KAZAKHSTAN

McDonald's Corporation Background

One of the world's largest fast-food giants - McDonald's corporation serves millions of consumers in more than 120 countries worldwide with annual profit of $ 45 billion, taking 17% of the world's food industry market with quarterly profit of around $ 700 million (History of McDonald's, 2018).

The McDonald brothers, Richard and Maurice followed the meat fast food line concept of 1920s, based on quickly served meat menu paper-wrapped, with coffee, milkshakes, crisps and self-service added latter in 1948. They opened the first "Golden arch" restaurant in April 15, 1955 (Rhys, 2019). While the first food lines of the company operated on the mere idea of the convenient fast food selling format followed by the immediate revenue, in 1960s, the new McDonald's chief director Ray Kroc, established a brand new approach to the company's franchising practices. He approached business running with stressing the socially responsible strategy in serving the customers and establishing fair and transparent relations with McDonald's branches, allowing them to enjoy their revenues earned. This strategy turned into a great success of the company shortly afterwards: in 1965 the company had 731 sets within the USA territory. It continues to exercise its mission of "Being our customers' favorite place and way to eat and drink", adding in 2017 the corporate vision as "to move with velocity to drive profitable growth and become an even better McDonald's serving more customers delicious food each day around the world" (Meyer, 2019).

The history of overseas operations started with opening of the first McDonald's restaurant in Canada in 1967, followed by operation in Europe and Japan, which are reported to have a good starting point as well. The success of the strategy was based on finding a reliable business partner on each country's market, traditional McDonald's menu and strict procedures and policies of the company to be implemented locally, as D. Fujita became McDonald's founder in Japan in 1971 with the number of restaurants increasing to 2300 in 1993. Followed by Germany, Australia, France and England, known as McDonald's "Big six", those countries are reported to generate the largest part of the corporation's revenues overseas (Hill & Jones, 2009).

One should point out here that McDonald's turned out to be a great success in the former socialist countries such as Czech Republic, Hungary, Slovenia, as well as in the Middle East states. A significant success there was due to the company's strategy to respect local traditions and customs, illustrated by the examples of serving beef menu in the restaurants in Islamic countries, absence of pictures and symbols of personalities (McDonald) in the product advertisements due to the Islamic prohibition on idol depiction, absence of dairy products in Israeli restaurants that are closed on Saturdays, and lamb menu in Indian branches.

McDonald's Performance in the Russian Federation

Just as in some post-socialist countries, McDonald's corporation also sought the new markets in the post-Soviet space. In January 1990 McDonald's opened its first branch in Moscow. Some sources note that negotiations between the two parties lasted for about 14 years (Khasbulatov, 2010). The final agreement with the Municipal Food Agency of Moscow was reached in 1988, with the allocation of 14,952 million rubles as a budget, and in 1989 the construction works started (Waston, 2006).

Around 5 thousand people gathered on Pushkin Square in Moscow to witness the opening ceremony and more than 30 thousand customers were served within the first day making a record as the longest working day in McDonald's history (Moscow Truth, 1990). Notably, as C. Weaver suggests, opening of the restaurant coincided with the warming period in the bilateral relations between Washington and Moscow (Weaver, 2014). As of today, McDonald's network reached 693 restaurants operating in a number of cities in the Russian Federation and providing 50,000 working places (McDonald's Russia official site).

In February 2014, as a result of lengthy Ukrainian anti-governmental protest actions known as "Euromaidan", the dismissal of the Ukrainian President V. Yanukovich occurred. The new government had undertaken a range of policies with regard to national policies and the language (Russian) status that eventually activated the Russian population in Crimea. In March 16, 2014, the Russian Federation called on the referendum on joining Crimean peninsula to Russia, announcing the next day the Independent Republic of Crimea, with its immediate joining to the Russian Federation. Western countries, considering the process as illegitimate annexation, imposed in March 2014, a number of sanctions against selected Russian statesmen and companies (Dorosh, 2016). This eventually led to the closing of McDonald's in Crimea in April 2014 by its outlet in Ukraine for "manufacturing reasons" denying any link with political situation (Zinets, 2014).

In this context, the McDonald's case in the Russian Federation in late August 2014 can serve as an example of the insecurity and vulnerability of transnational corporations. In general, the presence of McDonald's in Russia can be considered as the success story of the company, which has been one of the top-10 largest branches of the enterprise in the world (Matlack, 2014). For twenty-nine years of its existence in Russia it received more than 5 billion people serving about 1,5 million customers per day (Kamneva, 2018). Rapidly developing the food market in Russia with 440 restaurants across the country, McDonald's heavily survived the crisis in 2014. As some experts suggest, the company was temporarily unable to carry out its activities in the country to a certain extent due to the confrontation between Russia and the West on the Crimean issue (Weaver, 2014). Immediately after the imposition of sanctions against Russia by the EU and the United States of America, regular checks were organized at McDonald's restaurants, and a moratorium on their operational activities was announced shortly afterwards. The official reason claimed by the RosPotrebNadzor (a state agency checking the food-related companies on the matter of sanitary norms compliance) was incompliance of food quality with the local food safety standards, such as E.coli evidence and excessive amount of calories compared to the officially claimed (Weaver, 2014). Undoubtedly, the reasons for the temporary cessation of McDonald's activities in Russia were not announced as directly related to the sanctions. In fact, Russian government officially labeled the RosPotrebNadzor checks as necessary measures to re-equip the McDonald's enterprises. Moreover, some political and loyal youth activists supported the closing McDonald's restaurants with protests and propaganda claims, while the retaliatory food sanctions from Moscow to ban the EU and USA dairy and meat products were launched.

It took several months to re-start the company's operation after the re-equipment works over its enterprises. Yet, after restarting of its operation in 2014, some McDonald's restaurants continued to experience complications with a number of court cases in the Russian Federation. As C. Weaver reports, 100 lawsuit cases against McDonald's restaurants were heard in Russia against 10 for the previous seven years.

Improvements in the Activities of McDonald's in Russia: Social Projects

Following the closing of McDonald's in Russia the planned re-equipment of 170 McDonald's restaurants was conducted (McDonald's in Russia: 25 Years of Success, 2015). Thereupon the company launched additional services such as food delivery and increased the number of restaurants throughout the country. By 2019 about 700 McDonald's enterprises had operated on the territory of the Russian Federation serving more than 1.5 million customers (Seleznyeva, 2018). Within the menu McDonald's has shifted the assortment toward a healthier food concept by decreasing fats and sugar in their meals.

Being a responsible business McDonald's launched a number of social and charity programs with large budgets allocated for social, physical culture, accommodation and environmental purposes. Within the last decade it conducted:

- Creation of fitness center "Ronald McDonald Center" in Moscow for children with special needs;
- Construction of the free Family Hotel for parents whose children receive long-term medical care;
- Opening of the "Family rooms" for parents whose children undergo long-term treatment;
- Providing practical seminars for specialists working with special needs children in the regions of the Russian Federation;
- Construction of the inclusive playgrounds for children in different cities of the Russian Federation;
- Organization and sponsorship of a number of sports projects, such as launch of children's and family programs and in 2014, McDonald's acted as the official restaurant of the Olympic Games in Sochi (Lukovitz, 2014).

Within the concept of sustainable development McDonald's participated in environmental programs. It has implemented energy and resource conservation programs in its restaurants. Every year, the company sends cardboards and tons of waste fats for recycling. It also improved the landscape area around its restaurants.

Finally, the company supports the programs of the World Wildlife Fund (to save endangered species): Earth Hour, Environmental Overshoot Day (World Wildfire Fund).

McDonald's Performance in China

The outlook on transnational corporations in China has changed considerably since 1978, when the country opened its economy and welcomed foreign direct investments, and global players such as Volkswagen, Coca Cola and McDonald's began to explore the market. During the 1980s, other TNCs, such as Motorola, Philips, and NEC, were received with high appreciation. They used corporate taxes half that of local companies and did not pay import duties on capital goods. In general, both the government and consumers respected them. Even in the 1990s, when China and its people began to better understand transnational corporations, foreign companies were the objects of admiration. At that time, Chinese consumers demonstrated an almost unconditional preference for the products and services of transnational corporations (Park & Vanhonacker, 2007).

However, since 2000, when the country's GDP per capita exceeded $ 1,000.00, and especially since 2001, after China joined the World Trade Organization, the Chinese government and consumers have dramatically changed their perceptions of TNCs.

Notably the issues between a state and transnational companies could occur due to such companies' improper activities. The latter may further have a negative overreaction from the local public and the state.

An illustrative example in this context could be the case of McDonald's company in China. The first McDonald's restaurant in China was opened in 1990, and in 1998 the largest food entity of this corporation was opened in Beijing (Watson, 2006). It is mentioned by experts that McDonald's in China is following a strategy to emphasize its high sanitary standards, while other local food entities do not follow those standards, due to the lack of strict policies related to sanitary regulations. Generally, McDonald's is considered to be a successful corporation doing business in the PRC. However, in 2004, the McDonald's had to cancel its TV commercial in China after viewers found it insulting. The advertisement depicted a Chinese man kneeling in front of an electronics seller asking for a discount. TV viewers stated that in the TV commercial the Chinese man was portrayed as poor and unworthy of dignity. Explaining the reason of the ban by the Chinese government state officials said the advertisement was trying to convey the message in an exaggerated, humorous manner (Li, 2005). Chinese TV viewers clearly thought the opposite: 80% found the advertisement offensive.

McDonald's Performance in Kazakhstan

One of the priority directions of Kazakhstan's economic diplomacy is attracting foreign TNCs to develop contacts for possible investors interests (Ministry of Economic Affairs of the Republic of Kazakhstan, 2014). For this reason Kazakhstan establishes favorable investment conditions with simplified taxation policy, permanently adjusting legislation and business preferences.

It took Kazakhstan 18 years of negotiations that resulted in opening of the first McDonald's restaurant in Nur-Sultan City on March 8, 2016, becoming the 120th anniversary country where the world's famous network operates. A bit later, in May 2016, another restaurant was opened in Almaty. Legally the right to develop the McDonald's brand in Kazakhstan was granted to the ex-head of KazRosGas, currently a businessman Kairat Boranbayev, who owns the Almaly Holding. He acquired the right to develop the franchise in Kazakhstan in 2014, though de facto he began working with McDonald's restaurants much earlier, running a similar business activity in the Republic of Belarus (McDonald's Kazakhstan official site).

In terms of further investments, about 40-42 mln. US dollars are aimed to be invested to develop the restaurant chain in eight largest cities of the Republic of Kazakhstan. To a greater extent, the project is largely financed from the holding's internal funds, yet credit lines were also opened, one of which is provided by the public Damu Fund. Each restaurant is to create about 150-200 job places. Importantly and similarly to Russian experience, McDonald's plans to launch several social programs to support a healthy lifestyle via healthier food menu and the Ronald McDonald House charity foundation as well (Mazorenko, 2016).

Two complications that the company faced in its operational activities in Kazakhstan were the supply of basic ingredients and financial cost cutting caused by the local currency devaluation. Regarding the first issue, Kazakhstani local food suppliers are not yet ready to provide ingredients for McDonald's in the country, 85% of ingredients for all main menu dishes are now delivered from the Russian Federation. Necessary products are first consolidated in the distribution center in Yekaterinburg and then delivered to restaurants in Nur-Sultan and Almaty within three days, and later to other cities of the Republic of Kazakhstan.

The second issue was commented by a managing director of "McDonald's Kazakhstan" Alexey Filippenko, who claimed that McDonald's in Kazakhstan was cutting the financial costs, but those cost decreases were not directly linked to the global economic crisis. The main calculations related to the cost of restaurants and necessary purchases were made before the currency devaluation. But the slowdown in economic growth and even switch of the local currency to a free-floating exchange rate did not cause the company to adjust its strategy, as crisis is a temporary phenomenon when the brand continues to operate. According to Filippenko, "crisis is not considered as a serious risk for payback. Payback issues, of course, can undergo some changes, but concerning the restaurant chain itself, the wider it is, the more effective it is from the sustainable economic management point of view." Moreover, he underlines on priority to develop local suppliers and localize production against dwelling on a limited number of investments.

Due to the evident influence of economic sanctions imposed against Russia, the Kazakhstani affiliate plans to develop a resource base on the territory of the Eurasian Economic Union not to be drastically dependent on external food suppliers. Yet one should mention that overall Kazakhstani foreign political strategy is framed into multi-vector doctrine, allowing Kazakhstan to avoid most of the conflict situations.

DISCUSSION

Political vs. Economic Interests

Undoubtedly, the paradigm of sustainable development defines the interdependence between political and economic interests. Based on the case studies one can assume an obvious connection between these two phenomena (closing McDonald's restaurants in Russia and their further reopening in 2014) as an aftermath of certain political events around sanctions imposed against Russia followed by the Crimean crisis. In its turn, this may definitely indicate the need to use economic diplomacy to prevent such processes.

From 2014 to 2019, one can trace the dynamics of changes in policies and strategies in the activities of TNCs, and in particular, in McDonald's operations in the Russian Federation. After RosPotrebNadzor conducted a series of planned inspections, the Russian government did not recognize the fact that those actions were by any means connected with the Western sanctions. In the same manner, when McDonald's enterprises stopped their activity after the announced re-equipment, no connection with sanctions was mentioned in this case either. It is impossible to leave this question open, and based on decent sources on the Russian economy one can conclude that the above-mentioned issue was ambiguous. In 2012, the growth of the Russian economy was at the level of 3.7 percent, in 2013 it fell to 1.8 percent accordingly, and already in 2014 it reached a critical level of 0.7 percent (World Bank Group, 2015). Despite the fact that in response to Western sanctions, Russia took tough retaliatory measures against international transnational corporations and the import of foreign goods, though, these measures were not taken for a long time. It can be assumed that a certain compromise was found and, as soon as possible, the negative effect of previous actions was leveled. The situation with McDonald's clearly fits into this "scenario" as well.

The illustrated situation of geopolitical canvas around McDonald's performance in Russia could be complemented by the case of the Russian fast-food chain Teremok in the USA. The restaurant appeared on the market after the financial crisis of 1998, when the ruble collapsed and Russia defaulted under its debts. The former resident of Kazakhstan, Mikhail Goncharov, inspired by the success of McDonald's Corporation, started his own fast food chain, which offers customers dishes of Russian cuisine instead of a burger (Johnson & Taylor, 2017). Despite of the fact that two restaurants of Teremok network were opened in New York, the owner is opposed to McDonald's getting big preferences on the Russian market. He criticizes Russian business policies and encourages domestic networks to be supported, rather than bowing to McDonald's (Lavin, 2017). Pointing at deteriorated US-Russian relations since 2014, he notes that McDonald's has managed to open even more restaurants in Russia in recent years, while Teremok is forced to close its business in the United States. Presumably, that was the reason of Goncharov's announcement to open his fast food business in Germany, China and Japan (Russia Today, 2017).

Political complications between the West and Russian Federation negatively affected the overall economic situation. The domino principle, which assumes a chain reaction of an event under the influence of a factor affecting the first element of the chain, becomes the basis of the latest trends in both political and economic technologies. Key players in the system of global economic and political relations constantly use it. As a result of applying the strategy of influence by states and their potential alliances to maneuver and manipulate companies experience during conflicts and ultimately suffer heavy losses. Being at the nexus of national states and international organizations, transnational corporations have a fuzzy legal status in order to be fully protected in case of conflict situations. Due to the unclear legal status, transnational corporations, thus, are perceived as a sort of "satellites" of states and political and economic blocs. Assuming that in the case of McDonald's, which Russia regarded the corporation as an "agent" or representative of Western policy, we believe it would be advisable to raise the question of why transnational corporations should be responsible for the external political actions of their home countries.

Obviously, to prevent such problems, it is necessary to clearly define the legal status and immunity of transnational corporations, which are established by the UN declaration on transnational corporations (Geneva, 2013) and could be further used in economic diplomacy around the world. Ignoring the problem of determining the legal status of TNCs inevitably leads to logical reasoning as to why the population of parties involved in the political confrontation should suffer from a boycott of policies imposed by governments. In addition, the issue of legal status will limit or minimize attempts by governments to use transnational corporations as puppets to advance their own political ambitions.

Apparently, until the legal status of transnational corporations and their immunity are not fully specified, country leaders should, at least, be aware that they bear some responsibility for possible restrictions with regard to the interests of the local population that uses goods and services of transnational corporations. Otherwise, TNCs themselves can suffer substantial financial losses if the relevant external relations of the parties are broken.

The awareness of corporate social responsibility by TNCs is a key to sustainable development of society to prevent the limitations of its internal and external freedoms (Hamilton, 1999). Economic diplomacy can play a significant role here, since it is called upon to comprehensively support the activities of TNCs in their attempt to meet the goals of sustainable development. To somewhat a blurred legal status of modern transnational corporations, which can be especially vulnerable during political cataclysms and crises, as it was evidently demonstrated by the example of McDonald's in 2014 in Russia, can become an obstacle in achieving the sustainable development goals for the benefit of a large number of people in the whole world. In this regard, the will of the leaders of world powers and the main actors of multilateral diplomacy (the UNO, the EU, ASEAN and others) is needed to make attempts to clarify and formalize the legal nuances in relation to the status of TNCs in order to avoid possible political restrictions in the future.

Authors express their concern about the possible shortcomings of both American and Chinese economies may suffer from in the context of trade war between the two superpowers – the US and China

(Murray, 2019). Similar assumptions can be made in case of McDonald's in China in the event of the recently started commercial war.

Legal Conditions for Rules-Based Partnership among Local Governments and TNCs in Kazakhstan

In addition to the above international challenges arising out of the activities of TNCs, it is necessary to pay due attention to the internal conditions that are established by the host countries in the field of state policy in relation to foreign companies. Such policy is a natural extension of commercial diplomacy, within the framework of which favorable conditions should be created for the operating activities of foreign companies. As a rule, these conditions should be reflected in the legislative system of nation-states. In this regard, the legislation should take into account the following issues in the field of cooperation with TNCs:

1) guarantees for the protection and support of long-term investments;
2) simplification of procedures for obtaining entry visas and permits for staying in the host country for a foreign workforce;
3) awareness of foreign business circles about the prospects for investment in the host country.

Considering the issue of legislation regarding the activities of TNCs, we believe that the experience of the Republic of Kazakhstan based on the adopted Convention of the Commonwealth of Independent States on transnational companies can serve as a valid example. The multi-vector nature of Kazakhstan's international policy, as well as the long-standing practice of interacting with foreign capital and legal entities has contributed to legislative changes and the search for new legal instruments in the development of international economic cooperation.

During this time, some positive experience was gained, starting with a clearer expression of national interests in cooperation with TNCs and ending up with the reform of the regulatory framework to attract foreign investors with a low risk for the sovereignty of the country. However, it should be noted that the legislation has to consider the balance between maintaining national interests and conditions of a preferential treatment for foreign companies.

In this regard, the Entrepreneur Code of the Republic of Kazakhstan, which regulates the operating activities of TNCs and other foreign companies in the country, is based on national legislation. In addition to support TNCs operations and enlarge local market for attraction of foreign capital, the Article 25 of the above-mentioned Code is fully devoted to the regulation of investment activities.

These regulatory legal acts are supplemented by the State Program of Industrial and Innovative Development of the Republic of Kazakhstan for 2015-2019, the main purpose of which is to stimulate diversification and increase the competitiveness in the manufacturing industry, where one of the important tools in achieving this goal is to attract investments. Today, the legislation of the Republic of Kazakhstan already proposes the introduction of tax and customs preferences for foreign companies. However, it is still required to revise a number of legal acts, deepening the analysis of the various areas of interaction between the state and transnational corporations and optimization of tax policies for foreign economic entities in local markets.

FUTURE RESEARCH DIRECTIONS

Despite the progress made in understanding the challenges TNCs face abroad using the McDonald's example, there are still many open questions related to political, economic and legal sustainability limitations for their activities within political systems at the transnational level. The influence of the policies of foreign states and their political systems on the activities of TNCs was studied in a relative isolation. However, a more comprehensive approach is needed to shed light on how to decrease the influence of political systems on TNCs behavior. It is needed to develop appropriate models covering the entire spectrum of changes taking place at different levels in international politics and economy.

To decrease the implications of research limitations it is required to undertake the following steps:

- To develop an integrated approach to study the impact of various political systems on international trade, in particular, on the activities of foreign multinationals;
- To develop a research database that links the results in relation to politics, economy, CSR and SDGs, studying the possibilities of using international data sources and exploring the global trends concerning TNCs;
- To attract more experts from multidisciplinary areas within the scope of international politics, economic diplomacy, social and corporate responsibility and sustainable development for further wider research of the topic;
- To study the problem of politics intervening into business at several levels (multilateral, bilateral and national) in order to clarify the affect of politics on TNCs weakening in order to achieve the sustainable development goals;

Such a research will be a valuable tool for improving understanding of foreign businesses in the context of geopolitics and economic sustainability nexus for the experts in the field of international politics, regional studies, international trade and promoters of socially oriented projects in order to achieve the SDGs.

CONCLUSION

Today, TNCs can potentially be in the risk zone caused not only by economic reasons, but also by political circumstances. Based on the foregoing research, we can draw the following conclusions:

- In turn, political challenges lead not only to political pressure, but also, to a greater extent, to economic consequences causing TNCs to suffer serious losses;
- Relatively new practice of economic diplomacy could potentially be both an alternative to resolving complex and even conflict situations, and also a preventive tool if political leaders consider and practice it seriously in resolving international economic problems;
- Economic diplomacy alone cannot exist without a serious legal foundation that determines the status of companies, guarantees and procedures for protecting global business entities. These standards should be continuously developed;
- The standards should not be advisory, but legally binding in nature, providing the guarantees of their implementation. Otherwise, all parties become hostages to the harsh realism, where the

strength and superiority detracts not only ethical standards, but certain achievements of economic globalization, the result of which are TNCs themselves;

- For host countries it is extremely important to protect the interest of both investors and foreign companies with a well-designed program that is framed in a semantically correct legal format;
- States, a priori preserving the protection of their national interests through appropriate legal instruments, should also not lose sight of the possibility of a global context of participation in international economic processes, where TNCs are the key actors, creating optimal legal conditions for mutually beneficial cooperation for the latter;
- CSR being inseparable element of sustainable development is exercised by transnational corporations transforming the latter into actors of both international relations and holders of sustainable development values.

Obviously, McDonald's has been the victim of an escalating Russian-American confrontation over the crisis between Russia and Ukraine, as some of Moscow's ultra-patriotic officials were targeting the American fast food giant, presumably as a White House special agent. This position may provoke an increase in the security risks for foreign business in Russia.

Similar problems may occur in Kazakhstan, which is neighboring Russia as a negative effect of Russian-American rivalry.

The recent Trade wars escalation between China and the US may probably affect the presence of TNCs in the People's Republic of China. McDonald's may become a victim of the deteriorated relations of these two superpowers.

This does not bode well for TNCs recipient countries either, since this situation reduces the level of trust among investors contributing into their economies. First, it might increase the risk of lower prices for local assets. Secondly, it will encourage the local businessmen to move out their own capital from their home countries and make it working abroad. Thirdly, this might possibly prevent the flow of foreign direct investments into their markets. Cancellations of transactions in Russia in 2014 and escalation of trade wars between China and the United States confirm these concerns.

REFERENCES

Alexandros, A., & Paraskevi, D. (2019). Cases on corporate social responsibility and contemporary issues in organizations. Hershey, PA: IGI Global.

Amba-Rao, S. (1993). Multinational corporate social responsibility, ethics, interaction and Third World governments. *Journal of Business Ethics*, *12*(7), 553–572. doi:10.1007/BF00872380

Anderson, L., Earley, J., Feketekuty, G., & Williamson, I. (2004). *Legal analysis in commercial diplomacy analyzing applicable domestic laws and international agreements. ITCD*. San Diego Global University.

Bannerman, L. (2009, August 7). Silvio Berlusconi Ridiculed Over Gas Pipe Diplomacy Claims. *The Times.*

Bayne, N., & Woolcock, S. (2003). *The new economic diplomacy: Decision-making and negotiation in international economic relations.*

Bloom, P. (2017). *The Ethics of Neoliberalism: The Business of Making Capitalism Moral*. Routledge. doi:10.4324/9781315619019

Boyar, L., & Davis-Friday, P. (2019). Assessing a golden opportunity: CEO performance at McDonald's. *The CASE Journal, 15*(5), 397-415.

Bulgakova, A. (2019). *Food security and nationalism: Case of import substitution project in the Russian Federation*. Budapest: Central European University.

Capelle-Blancard, G. (2016). The abrogation of the "Impôt sur les opérations de bourse" did not foster the French stock market. *Finance Research Letters, 17*(C), 257–266. doi:10.1016/j.frl.2016.03.024

Capelle-Blancard, G., & Petit, A. (2012). The Weighting of CSR dimensions: Does one size fit all? *SAGE Journals, 59*(6), 919-943.

Cassini, G. (2007). *Gli anni del declino. La politica estera del governo Berlusconi (2001-2006)* [*The Years of Decline: The Foreign Policy of Berlusconi's Government, 2001-2006*]. Milano: Bruno Mondadori.

Černič, L. (2018). *Corporate responsibility in the framework of socio-economic rights*. Routledge.

Cerny, P. (2010). *Rethinking World Politics: A Theory of Transnational Neopluralism*. New York: Oxford University Press. doi:10.1093/acprof:oso/9780199733699.001.0001

Dorosh, S. (2016, December). Sanctions against Russia: was there any effect? *BBC News –Ukraine*. Retrieved from https://www.bbc.com/ukrainian/features-russian-38265024

Du, S., & Luo, X. (2015). Exploring the relationship between corporate social responsibility and firm innovation. *Marketing Letters, 26*(4), 703–714. doi:10.100711002-014-9302-5

Financial Times. (2015, January 29). McDonald's and its challenges worldwide: a market-by-market look. Retrieved from https://www.ft.com/content/f8ac22fc-a7c1-11e4-8e78-00144feab7de

Fisher, M. (2009). *Capitalist Realism. Is There No Alternative?* (p. 8). Oxford Books.

Francisca, F., Grigore, G., Stancu, A., & McQueen, D. (2019). *Responsible people: The role of the individual in CSR, entrepreneurship and management education*. Springer.

Friedman, T. (2000). *The lexus and the olive tree*. London: HarperCollins.

Griffith, W. (2008). *McDonald's has a big appetite for China*. CNBC News.

Hamilton, K., & Langhorne, P. (2011). *The Practice of Diplomacy*. London: Routledge; doi:10.4324/9780203841891

Hamilton, M. (1999). The Business Charter for Sustainable Development. International Chamber of Commerce. Retrieved from https://iccwbo.org/content/uploads/sites/3/2015/09/ICC-Business-Charter-for-Sustainable-Development-Business-contributions-to-the-UN-Sustainable-Development-Goals.pdf

Hanratty, B., Milton, B., Ashton, M., & Whitehead, M. (2012). McDonalds and KFC, it's never going to happen: The challenges of working with food outlets to tackle the obesogenic environment. *Journal of Public Health, 34*(4), 548–554. doi:10.1093/pubmed/fds036 PMID:22611262

Hansen, K. (2014). When French fries go viral: Mobile media and the transformation of public space in McDonald's Japan. Center for Asian and Pacific Studies. San Diego State University, 14(2).

Hayek, F. (2011). The Constitution of Liberty (Definitive ed.). Chicago: University of Chicago Press.

Hill, C. L., & Jones, G. (2009). *Essentials of Strategic Management* (3rd ed.). South-Western Cengage Learning, Nelson Education LTD.

Joanne, J. W. H. (2012). 'Challenge' or 'collaboration' social interaction and recontextualization: McDonald's CSR report. *Critical Discourse Studies*, *9*(2).

Johnson, H., & Taylor, K. (2017, October). We visited the 'McDonald's of Russia' that's trying to take over America — here's what it was like. *Business Insider*. Retrieved from https://www.businessinsider.com/teremok-menu-price-taste-test-review-2017-10

Jones, D., & Smith, M. (2015, September). Return to reason: Reviving political realism in western foreign policy. *International Affairs*, *91*(5), 933–952. doi:10.1111/1468-2346.12391

Kamneva, K. (2018, September 13). McDonald's in Russia: 30 years of investment in the future. Food familiar to everyone. *Russian newspaper RGRU*, *203*(7666). Retrieved from https://rg.ru/2018/09/13/makdonalds-v-rossii-30-let-investicij-v-budushchee.html

Kant, I. (1785). Fundamental Principles of the Metaphysic of Morals (T.K. Abbott, Ed.). Project Gutenberg.

Khasbulatov, K. (2010, January 26). McDonald's in Russia on the eve of its 20th anniversary. Interview. *Echo of Moscow*.

Kheyfets, B., & Chernova, V. II. (2018). Adaptation of market strategies of TNCs in Russia in the context of import substitution policy. *European Research Studies Journal*, *21*(3), 192–205. doi:10.35808/ersj/1053

Kobrin, S. (2008). *Globalization, Transnational Corporations and the Future of Global Governance. Handbook of Research on Global Corporate Citizenship. Cheltenham, UK and Northampton*. MA: Edward Elgar Publishing.

Lavin, T. (2017, April). A Russian Fast-Food Chain Tries Its Luck in America. *The New Yorker*. Retrieved from https://www.newyorker.com/culture/on-and-off-the-avenue/a-russian-fast-food-chain-tries-its-luck-in-america

Lawrence, M., & Friel, S. (2019). *Healthy and Sustainable Food Systems*. Routledge. doi:10.4324/9781351189033

Lee, J., & Rim, H. (2018). Evolution of Corporate Social Responsibility: A Content Analysis of United States Magazine Advertising, 1980–2009. *Journal of Promotion Management*, *24*(4), 555–577. doi:10.1080/10496491.2017.1380111

Li, T. (2005, June 17). McDonald's new ad depicting customers begging on their knees for discounts offends customers. *Chengdu Commercial Daily*.

Li, T. (2005, June 22). Chinese kneeling for discount in McDonald's ad. *China Daily*. Retrieved from https://sloanreview.mit.edu/article/the-challenge-for-multinational-corporations-in-china-think-local-act-global/

Librando, G. (1959). *Diplomazia commerciale: memorie di carriera* [*Commercial Diplomacy: Memoirs of a Career*]. Roma: G. Pastena.

Liu, J. (2008). McDonald's growing in China. *China Daily.*

Losavio, J. (2014, April 2). Crimean crisis and International Law: What Laws are Broken? *Foreign Policy News Journal.*

Lukovitz, K. (2014, January 21). McDonald's Launches Olympics Social Campaign. *MediaPost* Retrieved from https://www.mediapost.com/publications/article/217783/McDonald's-launches-olympics-social-campaign.html

Matlack, C. (2014, October 21). Putin's Latest Target: More Than 200 Russian McDonald's. *Bloomberg Business for the week.* Retrieved from https://www.bloomberg.com/news/articles/2014-10-20/putins-latest-target-more-than-200-russian-McDonald's

Matlack, C. (2014, August 20). Can McDonald's be the last victim of Russian retaliation? *Bloomberg Business Week.*

Matlack, C. (2014, October). Putin's Latest Target: More than 200 Russian McDonald's. *Bloomberg Businessweek.* Retrieved from https://www.bloomberg.com/news/articles/2014-10-20/putins-latest-target-more-than-200-russian-mcdonalds

Mazorenko, D. (2016, March 11). How will McDonald's work in Kazakhstan? *Internet Journal Vlast.* Retrieved from https://vlast.kz/biznes/16203-kak-budet-rabotat-McDonald's-v-kazahstane.html

McDonald's accused of food violations in China. (2012). *The Wall Street Journal Digital Network.*

McDonald's in Russia 25 Years of Success. (2015). Russian Newspaper Delovaya Moscow Retrieved from http://www.delmoscow.ru/news/?cid=3fe6b80e&nid=e57fdc2a

McDonald's Kazakhstan official site. (n.d.). History. Retrieved from https://McDonald's.kz/about#tab-2

McDonald's Russia official site. (n.d.). Facts and Numbers. Retrieved from https://mcdonalds.ru/page/mcdonalds_in_russia/

Meyer, P. (2019). McDonald's Mission Statement & Vision Statement (An Analysis). Retrieved from http://panmore.com/McDonald's-vision-statement-mission-statement-analysis

Ministry of Economic Affairs of the Republic of Kazakhstan. (2014). Economic Diplomacy of the Republic of Kazakhstan. Retrieved from http://mfa.gov.kz/en/content-view/ekonomicheskaya-diplomatiya

Ministry of Economic Affairs of the Republic of Kazakhstan. (2014). Investment climate of the Republic of Kazakhstan. Retrieved from http://mfa.gov.kz/en/content-view/ob-investitsionnom-klimate-rk

Molch, D., & Verlag, G. (2009). *McDonald's Russia: Managing a crisis. Case Study.*

Moomaw, W., Bhandary, R., & Kuhl, L. (2016). Sustainable Development Diplomacy: Diagnostics for the Negotiation and Implementation of Sustainable Development. *Global Policy.*

Morgenthau, H. (1946). *Scientific Man versus Power Politics.* IL: University of Chicago Press.

Murray, B. (2019). *UN Sees U.S.-China Trade War Hurting Both Nations' Economies.*

Naray, O. (2008). *Commercial Diplomacy: A Conceptual Overview.* 7th World Conference of TPOs. The Hague. The Netherlands.

Nelson, R. (2015). U.S. Sanctions on Russia: Economic implications. *Congressional Research Service.* Retrieved from https://digital.library.unt.edu/ark:/67531/metadc501885/

Park, S., & Vanhonacker, W. (2007, July). The Challenge for Multinational Corporations in China: Think Local, Act Global. Retrieved from https://www.researchgate.net/publication/271199219_The_Challenge_for_Multinational_Corporations_in_China_Think_Global_Act_Local

Pomfret, R. (2006). *The Central Asian Economies.* Oxford University Press.

Prahalad, C., & Doz, Y. (1986). *The Multinational Mission: Balancing Local Demands and Global Vision.* New York: The Free Press.

Report of the UNCTAD Secretariat. (2003, August). Retrieved from https://unctad.org/en/docs/c2isard3.en.pdf

Rhys, L. (2019, April 15). 1955: McDonald's opens its first franchise restaurant in Illinois. Business Times. Retrieved from https://home.bt.com/news/on-this-day/april-15-1955-McDonald's-opens-its-first-franchise-restaurant-in-illinois-11363975590701

Roberts, W. (1991). *Diplomacy in the Information Age. World Today.* Royal Institute of International Relations.

Saner, R., & Yiu, L. (2003, January). International Economic Diplomacy: Mutations in Post-Modern Times. Netherlands Institute of International Relations. Clingendael.

Scilly, M. (2016). Five Dimensions of Corporate Social Responsibility. Retrieved from https://smallbusiness.chron.com/five-dimensions-corporate-social-responsibility-54700.html

Seleznyeva, M. (2018, February 15). Less fat and sugar. McDonald's will make Happy Mil more useful. Retrieved from https://life.ru/t/новости/1089472/mienshie_zhira_i_sakhara_makdonalds_sdielaiet_khieppi_mil_bolieie_polieznym

Shima, M. (2005). Role and influence of transnational corporations in the global shift at the turn of the twentieth-XXI centuries. *Problems of the theory and practice of management, 3.*

RT. (2017, December). Russia shouldn't grovel to 'McDonald's bas***ds' – local restaurateur. Retrieved from https://www.rt.com/business/412957-mcdonalds-russia-unfair-benefits/

Taeho, L. (2016). The status of corporate social responsibility research in public relations: A content analysis of published articles in eleven scholarly journals from 1980 to 2015. *Public Relations Review, 43*(1), 211–218. doi:10.1016/j.pubrev.2016.10.001

The Entrepreneur Code of the Republic of Kazakhstan (as amended and supplemented, as of July 26, 2016). (2016). Retrieved from http://online.zakon.kz/Document/?doc_id = 38259854

The New York Times. (2002, March). McDonald's to settle suits on beef tallow in French fries. Retrieved from www.nytimes.com/2002/03/09/us/mcdonald-s-to-settle-suits-on-beef-tallow-in-french-fries.html

The state program of industrial and innovative development of the Republic of Kazakhstan for 2015–2019. (n.d.). Retrieved from http://www.mid.gov.kz/ru/pages/gosudarstvennaya-programma-industrialno-innovacionnogo-razvitiya-respubliki-kazahstan-na-2015

Theodore, H., & Karl, F. (2000). *International Business Diplomacy. School of Foreign Service*. Washington, D.C.: Georgetown University.

Tony, R. (2000). *Working for McDonald's in Europe: The unequal struggle*. Psychology Press.

Van Eyk, S. (2010). *The OECD Declaration and Decisions Concerning Multinational Enterprises: an Attempt to Tame the Shrew*. Nijmegen: Ars Aequi Libri.

Waston, J. (2006). *Golden Arches East: McDonald's in East Asia*. California: Stanford University Press.

Weaver, C. (2014, August 21). Consumer agency takes McDonald's off Moscow's menu. *Financial Times*. Retrieved from https://www.ft.com/content/bfdfe12c-288a-11e4-8bda-00144feabdc0?siteeditio n=intl#comments-anchor

Wohl, J. (2014, December). Most McDonald's in Russia Reopen. *Chicago Tribune*. Retrieved from https://www.chicagotribune.com/business/ct-mcdonalds-russia-1120-biz-20141119-story.html

Woolcock, S. (2014). Globalization, versatility. In M. Teló (Ed.), Europe on the way to better global governance (pp. 203-214). Academic Press.

Worland, J. (2014, August). McDonald's Objects to Russia Restaurant Closures. *Time*.

World Bank Group. (2015, April). *Report on Russian Economy*. Retrieved from https://www.worldbank.org/content/dam/Worldbank/document/eca/russia/rer33-rus.pdf

World Wildfire Fund. McDonald's. Retrieved from https://wwf.ru/business/partners/McDonald's/

Xu, Y. (2014). Understanding CSR from the perspective of Chinese diners: The case of McDonald's. *International Journal of Contemporary Hospitality Management*, *26*(6), 1002–1020. doi:10.1108/IJCHM-01-2013-0051

Young, A., & Peterson, J. (2011). The EU and the new trade politics. *Journal of European Public Policy*, *13*(6), 795–814. doi:10.1080/13501760600837104

Zhu, L., Anagondahalli, D., & Zhang, A. (2017). Social media and culture in crisis communication: McDonald's and KFC crises management in China. *Public Relations Review*, *43*(3), 487–492. doi:10.1016/j.pubrev.2017.03.006

Zinets, N. (2014). McDonald's Closes Restaurants In Crimea. *Business Insider*. Retrieved from https://www.businessinsider.com/r-mcdonalds-quits-crimea-as-fears-of-trade-clash-grow-2014-04

KEY TERMS AND DEFINITIONS

Commercial Diplomacy: Promotion of business between the two countries to obtain commercial benefits in the form of trade and investments through activities to promote business and entrepreneurship in the host country.

Investments: Investing of money or capital in order to gain profitable returns, as interest, income, or appreciation in value.

Legislation: Consists of laws and mandatory regulations adopted by the government.

Sanctions: An embargo imposed by one or more countries against a target self-governing state, group or individual on a number of political, military and social issues to achieve domestic and international goals.

Socially Oriented Projects: Projects aimed at meeting social needs, mobilizing public, managing private and community resources, as well as implementing the necessary measures.

Sustainable Development Goals (SDGs): A set of 17 global goals aimed at achieving a more sustainable future for all. The SDGs were launched in 2015 by the UN and intended to be achieved by 2030.

Sustainable Economic Diplomacy: Includes the use of economic diplomacy tools to keep up with the rapid changes reflected in the sustainable development growth. It is concerned with economic policy questions, including the work of delegations to conferences sponsored by international trade entities.

Transnational Corporations: Enterprises that are involved with the international production of goods or services, foreign investments, or income and asset management in more than one country.

World Trade: an international trade reflected in the exchange of capital, goods, and services across transnational borders or territories.

Section 2
Education: Realities and Perspectives

The massive spread of digital technology in education is a sustainable development trend and is seen as a guarantee of the competitiveness of states in the new global economy. This section brings together articles on new horizons for adult learning and similar practices in the countries of the Eurasian area, including the possibilities of creating a network of partner universities and regional resource centers, the prospects of the University 4.0 models for the knowledge society. Innovative teaching methods are discussed in the chapters on the use of mobile devices and social media in training and the learning achievements of students while implementing flipped classrooms. However, all the problems discussed above can only be solved by improving the ESL competence of students and faculty. Overcoming the language barrier is the factor affecting all areas of the internationalization in the university's educational and scientific activities, as well as its entry to a higher world level. The last chapters address the challenges of learning English in non-English native countries, including Kazakhstan and the Netherlands. Particularly, that book chapters testify the professionally-oriented English-speaking competences of Eurasian scholars for their business and professional partnerships, and their communication with the worldwide academic community.

Chapter 7

New Horizons for Sustainable Growth in Eurasia Powered by Technology-Infused Adult Learning

Judith Parker
Teachers College, Columbia University, USA

ABSTRACT

On January 1, 2019, an American spacecraft, New Horizons, that had been traveling through space for 13 years discovered Ultima Thule, the farthest object in our Solar System. Technology had expanded the view of our immediate solar system beyond the boundaries of our current exploration and opened a vision for the growth of knowledge and discoveries. This chapter explores the vision of a geographical area that began with disappearing geographical, political, and philosophical boundaries and the emerging new horizons for the Eurasian Region. It explores the role of technology infused adult learning in the achievement of that vision that is sustainable. Over the past almost 30 years, these countries have engaged in a search for sustainable growth and for the ideal of a digital economy. Throughout history, adult learning has been at the core of any forward moving initiative. This chapter will address how this ideal can become reality through exploration of the theories and practices of adult learning infused with technology.

INTRODUCTION

New Horizons ushered in the year 2019 with a discovery that signaled new horizons for the understanding of our Solar System. On January 1, 2019, an American spacecraft, New Horizons, that had been traveling through space for 13 years discovered Ultima Thule, the farthest object in our Solar System. Technology had expanded the view of our immediate Solar System beyond the boundaries of our current exploration and opened a vision for the growth of knowledge and discoveries. This chapter explores the vision of a geographical area that began with disappearing geographical, political, and philosophical boundaries

DOI: 10.4018/978-1-7998-2551-7.ch007

and emerging new horizons for the Eurasian Region. It explores the role of technology infused adult learning in the achievement of that vision that is sustainable. Over the past almost 30 years, political changes have paralleled technological changes in the region and globally. Countries have engaged in a search for sustainable growth and have searched for the ideal of a digital economy. Throughout history, adult learning has been at the core of any forward moving initiative whether individual or organizational and no matter how large or small the organization. This chapter will address how this ideal can become reality through exploration of the theories and practices of adult learning infused with technology.

Facing the challenges and taking advantage of the opportunities within the countries of Eurasia requires new skills and insights which could only be gained through adult learning. One example of this importance of education in the region is the Kazakhstan project "Information Society 2030". This initiative highlights four main aspects of modern education: the process of education, the education system, the result of education, and the value of education.

THEORETICAL FRAMEWORK

The theoretical framework for this chapter will include theories about our physical universe developed by scientists and theories about our educational universe developed by educational researchers. The current theories about our universe were developed in the early 1900's through the discoveries of Edwin Hubble while those in education began with adult educators during a similar period and continued with Knowles and others.

Theoretical Framework for the New Horizon

Hubble's model of the universe transformed the thinking of centuries of astronomers but the discovery of Pluto introduced a dilemma closer to home. Hubble offered a model of an expanding universe whose expansion was accelerating. Before the early 1900's, people believed in an essentially static and unchanging universe. But the discovery of Pluto a few decades later expanded the horizon of our own solar system.

Comins and Kaufmann (2012) note that the beginning of modern cosmology is considered to have begun with Einstein's publication of his theory of general relativity in 1915. His general relativity equations indicated that the universe was not static but was instead either expanding or contracting. These new observations began with the work of the astronomer Henrietta Leavitt who published a paper in 1912 that was key to Hubble's calculations of the distance of the Andromeda Galaxy. The calculations showed that Andromeda was 2.2 million light years beyond the Milky Way Galaxy and therefore was not part of the Milky Way as previously thought. These results showed a model in which the universe was recognized to be larger and populated with far bigger objects than most astronomers had imagined.

This significant finding was only the beginning of an even more profound expansion of the model of the universe. Pais (1982) noted that the announcement by Edwin Powell Hubble in December 1924 "of an experimental result which settled a debate that had been going on for well over a century: the first incontrovertible evidence for the existence of an extragalactic object, Messier 31, the Andromeda nebula. Theoretical studies of cosmological models received even more important stimulus and direction from Hubble's great discovery of 1929 that the universe is expanding: nebulas are receding with a velocity proportional to their distance" (p. 268).

At about the same time in history, astronomers began to focus on a newly discovered planet, Pluto, at the edge of our own solar system. For decades it was considered the last object in our Solar System. Pluto held this distinction since its discovery until in 2005, another planet, Eris, was discovered beyond Pluto. The discovery of Eris triggered the realization that our Solar System was larger than had been accepted; there were new horizons to be explored and, new challenges to be met. This discovery prompted the reclassification of Pluto and the newly discovered object, Eris, into dwarf planets. In future years, additional dwarf planets were discovered.

On January 19, 2006 an American spacecraft, New Horizons, was launched from Cape Canaveral Air Force Station, Florida, USA. Its flyby of Pluto on July 14, 2015 was observed by many who remember the image of the heart shaped feature on this dwarf planet that New Horizons photographed and sent to earth. After that, information about the spacecraft disappeared from media attention until January 1, 2019. After traveling through space for 13 years, the New Horizons spacecraft had discovered Ultima Thule, now the farthest solar system object beyond Pluto – four billion miles from Earth.

Hawking (1988) noted that "in less than half a century, man's view of the universe, formed over millennia has been transformed. Hubble's discovery that the universe was expanding, and the realization of the insignificance of our own planet in the vastness of the universe, were just the starting point. As experimental and theoretical evidence mounted, it became more and more clear that the universe must have had a beginning in time, until in 1970 this was finally proved by Penrose and myself, on the basis of Einstein's general theory of relativity." (pp. 50-51).

But looking to the future, Tyson, Liu and Irion (2000) explain that "the amount of matter in the universe determines whether space will continue to expand forever or collapse back in on itself from the force of gravity (p. 197). A parallel for this transformative thinking and expanding model can be seen in the field of adult education when one considers the infusion of technology.

Theoretical Framework for a Universe of Technology Infused Adult Learning

Just as the early work of the Greeks and scientists of the 1600's laid the foundation for Hubble's scientific breakthroughs, the early educators provided a similar service. Knowles (1989) describes great teachers of ancient China, Rome and Greece as having "perceived learning to be a process of active inquiry, not passive reception of transmitted content and therefore "invented techniques for engaging learners in active inquiry" (p. 61). The early 1900's was a time for new thought in the field of education as well as physics and astronomy. Notable educators such as John Dewey and Edward Thorndike began promoting new ideas in the practice of education. Dewey's idea that practice is superior to theory directly conflicted with the theories of Aristotle and Plato who espoused the superiority of theory. Dewey's pragmatism is evident in his famous quotes such as education is not preparation for life; education is life itself and education is a process of living and not a preparation for future living. Thorndike's behaviorist ideas focused education on performance with an emphasis on the scientific method and experimentation to arrive at truth. His 1928 publication, *Adult Learning,* is considered the first major report of research on learning with adults. It reported that adults could be expected to learn at the same rate as younger students and that the best time to learn was just prior to using the knowledge. He expanded the educational universe beyond the realm of children to include adults and learning outside the K-12 classroom. This breakthrough was the beginning of the practice of adult education that has facilitated sustainable growth within organizations ever since.

Malcolm Knowles, credited with popularizing adult learning theory, introduced the term "andragogy" in the United States in his 1970 text *The Modern Practice of Adult Education* and his 1973 *The Adult Learner: A Neglected Species*. Knowles learned the term from a European colleague who defined it as the "art and science of helping adults learn" (Merriam, Caffarella, & Baumgartner, 2007, p. 84).

Jarvis (2009) notes that "as a psychologist I recognized that all the psychological models of learning were flawed, including Kolb's well-known learning cycle, in as much as they omitted the social and the interaction" (p. 23). However, Merriam, Caffarela, and Baumgarten (2007) note that learning styles inventories have "proved useful in helping learners and instructors alike become aware of their personal learning styles and their strengths and weaknesses as learners and teachers" (p. 409). They note that Kolb's Learning Styles Inventory "classified learning styles into four different categories: accommodators, divergers, convergers, and assimilators" (p. 408). Honey and Mumford (1989) developed a learning styles inventory based on Kolb's learning styles. Their four styles were labeled activist, reflector, theorist and pragmatist. They were motivated by the conviction that "people should be helped to learn effectively rather than be exposed to inappropriate learning experiences, or be given learning experiences without learning how to use their learning strengths" (p. 1).

This holistic view is at the heart of Wheatley's model. Wheatley (1999) notes that the earlier machine imagery was grounded in the seventeenth century by Isaac Newton and Rene Descartes. This imagery contained the belief that studying the parts of a machine was the key to understanding the whole. "Attention is given to relationships within those networks. In this admittedly bizarre view, relationship is the key determiner of everything." (pp. 10-11). Wheatley (1999) notes that "we are beginning to recognize organizations as whole systems, construing them as 'learning organizations' or as 'organic' and noticing that people exhibit self-organizing capacity" (p. 15). This integrated holistic model of learning is also essential to an expanding universe of learning.

Just as several of Hubble and Einstein's theories of the 1920s were not proven until the 1970s, the field of adult learning expanded dramatically in the 1970's. Cyrle Houle's publications, *The Inquiring Mind* and the *Design of Education,* lead to Tough's *Learning Without a Teacher* and *The Adult's Learning Projects* which introduced the concept of self-directed learning and other concepts that influenced Knowles. Knowles, Holton, & Swanson (2005) report that Malcolm Knowles formulated his assumptions about adult learners into his six core andragogical principles: "the learner's need to know, self-directed learning, prior experience of the learner, readiness to learn, orientation to learning and problem solving, and motivation to learn" (p. 183). These assumptions were followed by the contributions of numerous adult educators.

Mezirow, for one, described his transformative learning theory as one in which taken-for-granted frames of reference are transformed by making them more "inclusive, discriminating, open, emotionally capable of change, and reflective" (Merriam, Caffarella, Baumgartner, 2006, p. 253).

Brookfield introduced critical reflection but clarified that "although critical reflection is an ineradicable element of transformative learning, it is not a synonym for it. It is a necessary but not sufficient condition of transformative learning...transformative learning cannot happen without critical reflection but critical reflection can happen without an accompanying transformation in perspective" (Brookfield in Mezirow, 2000, p. 125). Brookfield (1986) defines critical thinking or critical reflection as "reflecting on the assumptions underlying our and others' ideas and actions, and contemplating alternative ways of thinking and living" (p. x). If one accepts this definition of critical thinking, then it becomes obvious that critical reflection is not a process that is accomplished quickly but might take days or weeks. Technology can facilitate this critical reflection over time. For example, a face-to-face discussion relies on participants' instant insights and reactions. In contrast, an asynchronous discussion online affords everyone the opportunity to read others' comments, reflect on them, then return to the discussion at a later time with a thoughtful comment as the result of critical reflection creating a foundation for transformative learning. Brookfield's (2005) focus on critical reflection as an essential component of learning is especially significant for an expanding universe of learning.

Heaney (2000) notes that "individual practitioners do not define the field of adult education, nor do experts. A definition of a field of practice is the social product of many individuals who negotiate the values and meaning of work they come to see as serving a common purpose over time" (p. 561).

The interactions between these individuals that result in that social product have been and will continue to be impacted by information communication technology. This theme is supported by Rhoades, Friedel, and Morgan who define Web 2.0 as that second generation of the World Wide Web that "aims to enhance creativity, information sharing, collaboration and functionality of the web" (p. 25) and by Farmer (2010) who describes Web 2.0 technology as a place where "knowledge is collaboratively built and shared" (p. 272). Or to paraphrase, Web 2.0 technology is a place where theories and models are collaboratively developed and shared.

This online environment of Web 2.0 technologies provides a new sense of space and society White and Bridwell (2004) concur by suggesting that new technology is "significantly altering the social role of learning" and that distance learning is only an intermediate step toward a "telelearning environment" in which distance and location become arbitrary (p. 287). In this new societal paradigm, a new sense of community emerges. "The creation of a learning community supports and encourages knowledge acquisition. It creates a sense of excitement about learning together and renews the passion involved with exploring new realms in education" (Palloff and Pratt, 1999, p. 163). This new realm facilitates sustainable learning and growth.

IMPACT OF NEW HORIZONS OF TECHNOLOGY INFUSED ADULT LEARNING ON SUSTAINABLE GROWTH IN EURASIA

The Role of Technology in New Horizons

New technology has always influenced science, education, daily lives, organizations and political and geographical regions. While today, information technology seems synonymous with computers, technology in many differing forms has influenced learning. For example, in about 1440, Gutenberg's invention of the first printing press with movable type dramatically changed the distribution of knowledge. Lesgold (2000) reminds us that "prior to the 15th century, codified knowledge was extremely rare" and that "direct discussion with a wise person was the primary way of gaining knowledge" (p. 399).

Kelly (2010) continues by noting that mass-produced books changed the way people read and wrote. "We became a people of the book" (pp. 122-123). Knowles (1989) credits Gutenberg's invention with having a great "impact on the advancement of adult education" (p. 62). This was the beginning of the expanding universe of technology infused adult learning which influenced the distribution of information and the way in which curriculum and programs were developed and distributed.

Hewitt (2005) noted that "the sixteenth and twenty-first centuries share a dramatic element in common – the birth of a revolution in communication technology" (p. 147). He explains that being able to publish books inexpensively decentralized the power of knowledge. While he calls it an "invitation to new understanding and human liberty" he also warns that it requires the reader to take on the" new responsibility for critical reflection" (p. 48). This responsibility is increasingly important in the 21st century and in the Eurasia region. Lesgold (2000) offers another comparison between the two centuries by noting that just as the book "removed some of the need for memorization as a force for knowledge distribution, so the computer removes some of the need for over learning of routine information processing procedures, since these can be accomplished by computers" (p. 401).

This 21st century revolution began in the late 1960's with the creation of a nation-wide computer network in the U.S. using phone lines and expanding into a network that became the "province of academic institutions, scientists, and government employees engaged in research and communications" (Shea-Schultz & Fogarty, 2002 p. 7). At this point one is tempted to add the cliché that the rest is history. However, history in this case has become a quickly moving target. Wiki's and blogs have become a part of our everyday vocabulary and Web 2.0 surfaces in discussions as online social networks become more commonplace (Parker, 2009). New capablities and higher speeds keep technology applications moving forward. It becomes ever more important to heed the advice of Kasworm and Londoner (2000) "to accept and embrace the possibilities of technology" (p. 225). Throughout history, technology has played an important part in the development and direction of the field of adult learning whose objective was to develop sustainable growth within organizations and move them foreward.

New Horizons of Information and Communication

The expanding universe of digital technology infused adult learning has been a major influence in every aspect of information development and delivery. Anderson and Wolff (2010) indicate that "the Internet is the real revolution, as important as electricity; what we do with it is still evolving. As it moved from your desktop to your pocket, the nature of the Net changed. The delirious chaos of the open Web was an adolescent phase subsidized by industrial giants groping their way in a new world. Now they're doing what industrialists do best-finding choke points. And by the looks of it, we're loving it" (p. 164).

Access to the vast range of information and resources because of the openness of the web has provided a plethora of opportunities including fueling sustainable growth. Bennett and Bell (2010) put this in a historical perspective by explaining that "the thirst for openness of knowledge in democratic society began during the Enlightenment and is revolutionized through new public knowledge forums found on the Internet" (p. 412).

Kelly (2010) presents data that continues to illustrate the dramatic changes that have occurred as our mechanism for obtaining information has changed. "Today some 4.5 billion digital screens illuminate our lives. Words have migrated from wood pulp to pixels on computers, phones, laptops, game consoles, televisions, billboards and tablets. ....We are now people of the screen. And of course, these newly ubiquitous screens have changed how we read and write" (p. 123). And they have changed how we perceive the right to access information that is available 24/7.

Information technology is used to access information, disseminate information in the classroom and on-line in both the traditional and andragogical tradition. However, Cerf (2010) warns that "we don't know whether the information we find (on the Web) is accurate or not. So we have to teach people how to assess what they've found. That's a skill, a critical-thinking capacity, which is important no matter what the medium." (p. 120).

The emergence of information technology has spawned entirely new departments which have become integral parts of the infrastructure of every institution whether academic, business, non-profit or government. Information technology has changed how data is recorded and analyzed and stored. It has changed how ideas are communicated from formal written messages where vocabulary and style were important to today's instant messaging environment with a cryptic style focused on speed of creation and transmission. As technological advances allowed information technology hardware to become smaller and smaller, this miniaturization and relatively low cost have promoted the quick, instantaneous but abbreviated communication that allows the instructor and the student to share new information with peers and with each other. (Parker, 2012)

Kling and Courtright (2004) delineate two contrasting models of the internet. The "standard model" is described as one that "allows people to engage in many of the activities that they have traditionally performed offline, including conversation, work, commerce, hobbies, meetings, worship, reading, and learning, yet without the usual constraints of space and time" (p. 92). The "socio-technical model" features environments that are "populated by many different kinds of spaces, each structured both socially and technically" (p. 95). These include websites with information and those that support more open communication, online games, electronic forums and sustainable growth within organizations.

Access to this expanding universe of information has led to new vocabulary such as knowledge era and knowledge society. Mazarr (1999) notes that "the knowledge era is an interdisciplinary time" (p. 11) and that the "new sciences of complexity remind us that boundaries between problems and disciplines are less important than the threads that connect them (p. 12). Bennett and Bell (2010) add that "a central and largely implicit premise behind the knowledge society is that open access to information will improve society and quality of life. This premise incorporates both individual adult learning as well as collective learning for the betterment of civil institutions and social structure, and it is consistent with the long held emphasis of social justice in adult and continuing education"(p. 411).

Kelly (2010) continues that "the amount of time people spend reading has almost tripled since 1980. By 2008 more than a trillion pages were added to the World Wide Web, and that total grows by several billion a day" (p. 123). This openness and the tasks ahead will be influenced by future societal trends taking shape. But it will also influence those social trends. Loader (1998) addresses that issue by suggesting that "the emergence of the new information and communications technologies such as the Internet are said to herald the coming of the "information society": a new social and economic paradigm restructuring the traditional dimensions of time and space within which we live, work, and interact" (p. 3). That time and space may be the construct of the new community which may encompass countries, geographical regions such as Eurasia, continents, and planets. The new horizons of our knowledge access and dissemination is daunting but also an exciting opening to new communities.

New Horizons of Community

Just as the Internet has expanded our access to information, it has expanded our access to other people almost anywhere. However, this focus on communication and community must be given careful consideration. Barab, Kling, and Gray (2004) emphasize that "someone external cannot simply impose a pre-designed community onto a group, but rather community is something that must evolve from within a group around their particular needs and for purposes that they value as meaningful" (p. 5). Kling and Courtright (2004) consider that "the casual use of the term community to characterize groups that are engaged in learning, or groups that participate in e-forums, is seriously misguided. As we shall see, developing a group into a community is a major accomplishment that requires special processes and practices, and the experience is often both frustrating and satisfying for many of the participants" (p. 91).

Anderson and Wolff (2010) note that "the great virtue of today's Web is that so much of it is non-commercial. The wide-open Web of peer production, the so-called generative Web where everyone is free to create what they want, continues to thrive, driven by the nonmonetary incentives of expression, attention, reputation, and the like" (p. 164). Kelly (2010) provides an example in the statistic that "right now ordinary citizens compose 1.5 million blog posts per day" (p. 123). This new communication mode brings people together over a common interest or goal and can be an engaging experience for learning and developing sustainable growth.

Learner engagement might initially be considered a lofty goal and might be compared to Maslow's "self-actualization" at the very peak of his hierarchical triangle. The engaged learner asks insightful questions, searches for additional information, attends extra activities, and participates fully in discussions and building a sense of community within the classroom (Parker, 2012). Conrad's (2004) notes that "engaged learning stimulates learners to actively participate in the learning situation, and thus gain the most knowledge from being a member of an online community" (p. 7).

Engagement can be purely intellectual or it can be transformational at many levels. Mezirow (2009) explains that "Transformative learning is a rational, metacognitive process of reassessing reasons that support problematic meaning perspectives or frames of reference, including those representing such contextual cultural factors as ideology, religion, politics, class, race, gender and others. It is the process by which adults learn how to think critically for themselves rather than take assumptions supporting a point of view for granted" (p. 103). At its best, engaged learning would be transformational to both the learner and the organization that would benefit from this process.

This engagement can happen either because the topic is engaging or the methodology is engaging. Technology infused learning can enhance the engagement in almost any traditional methodology. Silberman (2006) lists active learning methods such as demonstration, case study, guided teaching, group inquiry, information search, study group, jigsaw learning, tournament learning, role playing, simulations, observation, mental imagery. Piskurich (2006) suggests that there are "only a half dozen or so general training delivery methods to choose from" (p. 93). Of these he focuses on instructor-led classrooms, on-the-job-training, self-instruction and technology-based training. He notes that "many of the most successful training processes combine delivery systems" (p. 97), a concept often termed blended learning. Nilson (2003) offers lecture, discussion, case method and experiential learning while Brookfield (2006) focuses on lectures and discussions. Brookfield (2006) warns that "one of the traps that advocates of discussion method often fall into is that of setting up a false dichotomy between lecturing and discussion" (p. 98). This warning should be expanded to include building false silos around any one method.

In an adult learning venue, an important role of the teacher is to create the environment for learning and sense of community. Illeris (2009) emphasizes the complexity of the classroom climate by noting that "all three learning dimensions must be taken into account, that the question of relevant learning types must be included, that possible defense or resistance must be considered and that internal as well as external learning conditions must also be dealt with" (p. 18). He focuses on the importance of both internal and external learning conditions. Intelligence, including Gardner's idea of multiple intelligences, and learning styles are examples of internal conditions. External conditions include the "features of the immediate learning situation and learning space and more general cultural and societal conditions" (p. 17). These are essential considerations for any initiative such as the Kazakhstan 2030 mentioned earlier.

Cranton (2006) emphasizes the importance of empowering the student by interactions in the learning environment and being aware of power relationships. "The creation of a learning community supports and encourages knowledge acquisition. It creates a sense of excitement about learning together and renews the passion involved with exploring new realms in education" (Palloff & Pratt, 1999, p. 163).

This interaction is best achieved when technology is infused in the development of the curriculum or program. Utilization of learning management systems such as Blackboard, ecollege, Moodle or university developed LMS facilitate the presentation of material, whole class or small group document sharing and text chatting. Farmer (2010) adds that "with today's changing technology, communication methods are now available for sophisticated interactive learning: among students, educators, and resources. Web 2.0, egaming, videoconferencing, and course management systems exemplify these delivery systems that incorporate learning activities" (p. 186).

Shea-Schultz and Fogarty (2002) put the topic in perspective. "The e in e-learning wasn't short for electronic or electric. It was for entropy, which is defined as (1) the capacity of a system to undergo spontaneous change and (2) a measure of the randomness, disorder, or chaos in a system" (p. 1). Accepting the reality of this statement will allow us the freedom to critically reflect on our options and enjoy the opportunity for spontaneity and creativity. Hakken (1999) suggests that the @ symbol used to indicate an electronic domain in an email address, is also an indication of the social space to which one is connected. Loader (1998) reminds us that numerous social scientists share the notion that "society is being transformed by a revolution in information technology which is creating an entirely new social structure" (p. 4).

On a more philosophical note, Maxine Greene (1995) comments that "We are in search of what John Dewey called 'the Great Community" but at the same time, we are challenged as never before to confront plurality and multiplicity" (p. 155). "To open up our experience to existential possibilities of multiple kinds is to extend and deepen what each of us thinks of when he or she speaks of a community" (p. 161). Kazakhstan can be an example of how to bring these ideas into the regional community of Eurasia in order to face its challenges and take advantage of the opportunities that require new skills and insights which could only be gained through adult learning.

The Community of Eurasia

The space that is the geography of our planet has been altered throughout history by political regimes and national borders. These make the space more supportive or repressive to transformative learning. Within the past century, Kazakhstan has seen the suppression of its long history of nomadic clans by the Russians, then emerged as an independent nation. After the collapse of the U.S.S.R., geographical regions became autonomous nations once again. One such example is the country of Kazakhstan.

Tazhina (2010) explains that Kazakhstan's independence in 1991 and resulting globalization created a conflict between the infiltrating western thought and traditional mentalities resulting in discomfort on both the personal and the familial level. She notes market competition, the collapse of Soviet values, individualization, uncertainty of the future, and aggravated social stress as areas of conflict. The previous Russian models of learning were no longer mandatory and a plethora of learning options became available. Within these over two decades of independence, this nation of rich and complex histories was developing models within its universities to educate leaders for all areas of government and industry in a world of rapid change and technology integration. Kazakhstan, like other countries around the world, has translated and adapted the traditionally Western models for human resource development and leadership. These models and the research instruments associated with them are used to educate emerging leaders.

Hofstede (2001) warns against the consequences of teaching foreign theories abroad. "What in fact happens when foreign theories are taught abroad – and this I have personally witnessed – is that the theories are preached but not practiced. Wise local managers silently adapt the foreign ideas to fit the values of their subordinates" (p. 389). This suggests the importance for a national culture to develop its own research instruments and analyze its own data. .

Historically Kazakhstan has experienced a series of crises. Within the past century, Kazakhstan has seen the suppression of its long history of nomadic clans by the Russians. Then it emerged as an independent nation after the fall of the U.S.S.R. When this collapse of the U.S.S.R. occurred, geographical regions became autonomous nations once again.

Tazhina (2010) explains that Kazakhstan's independence in 1991 and resulting globalization created a conflict between the infiltrating western thought and traditional mentalities resulting in discomfort on both personal and the familial level. She notes that market competition, the collapse of Soviet values, individualization, uncertainty of the future, and aggravated social stress as areas of conflict. In response to these needs, The Psychological Association for the Republic of Kazakhstan was founded in 1999 and in 2007 an organization of trainers for Kazakh business psychologists was opened in Almaty, Kazakhstan. The previous Russian models of learning were no longer mandatory and a plethora of learning options became available

During this past twenty years of independence, this nation of rich and complex histories was developing models within its universities to educate leaders for all areas of government and industry in a world of rapid change and technology integration. Kazakhstan, like other countries in Eurasia and around the world, has met this challenge by initially translating and adapting the traditionally Western models for human resource development and leadership. These models and the research instruments associated with them are used to gain insights into and educate emerging leaders.

This complex integration of national and organizational cultures and the increasing influence of Western models for leadership on Eurasian countries continues to be explored. Dorfman and House (2004) report that at the first GLOBE research conference in 1994, there was a consensus of the 54 researchers from 38 countries (of which Kazakhstan was one) that organizational leadership is defined as "the ability of an individual to influence, motivate, and enable others to contribute toward the effectiveness and success of the organizations of which they are members" (p. 56).

Latova and Latov (2007) report the findings of their study comparing Russia, Kazakhstan, Kyrgyzstan, and Turkey. They note that there are no Hofstede ratings for Kazakhstan but that most assume that Kazakh national mentalities are more oriental than Russian. However they found that students in Kazakhstan, as well as the other countries are more "westernized" than the population as a whole. They noted that particularly on Hofstede's power distance index, students in Central Asia republics such as Kazakhstan appear to be closer to the "European norm" than students of Russia. This confirmed their hypothesis that higher education in Oriental nations is a "translator" of western mental values.

Facing their challenges and taking advantage of the opportunities require new skills and insights which could only be gained through adult learning. One example in the region is the Kazakhstan project "Information Society 2030". This initiative highlights four main aspects of modern education:

The process of education - the interaction of society and the individual with the goal of improving the level of organization of the individual. Without the potential of the individual as an active creative subject of management, knowledge, skills can not be applied at a high, professional and ethical level.

The education system is not only educational institutions, but also all media, consulting, religious, non-governmental and even informal organizations such as the street and the family, if they provide the conditions for increasing the level of the personal potential of the society;

The result of education is an information personality capable of processing avalanche-like streams of information through scientific means of thinking and an objective system of values.

The value of education is the reproduction and development of the information society.

This project details the fact that because of the natural climate, geographic and demographic situation, Kazakhstan has very specific reasons to consider education to be the only competitive in the world market, a strategically important branch of the economy in terms of the country's economic development. Citizens of Kazakhstan should become global cultural leaders of the information age. It projects Kazakhstan in 40 years as a cultural leader of the global information society, the so-called "intellectual" society with an innovative "knowledge economy", which is at the head of world scientific and technological progress. This goal is supported by the fact that intellectual property is highly valued and tightly guarded in this intellectual society. This fact encourages a scientific environment where the scientific process of discovering new knowledge at the fundamental and applied levels is nurtured and the investment climate, where the innovative process of introducing scientific discoveries into business practice is carried out.

With this positive cultural foundation, Kazakhstan aimed at improving educational and business systems within the country by establishing more rigid requirements for professional certification in many areas. Geographical considerations for the population distribution and the location of institutions of higher learning pointed to the use of digital technologies and practices to achieve their goal.

FUTURE DIRECTIONS

In his publication "The Knowledge Web", Moe (2000) recounts that historically, "nations have developed based on their access to physical resources or their ability to surmount physical barriers" (p. 33). He then compares this to today's knowledge based economy in which the use of the Internet and electronic delivery of information relies on the "resources of brainpower and the ability to acquire, deliver and process information effectively" (p. 33). He suggests that the "Internet is to the Knowledge Revolution what the railroad was to the Industrial Revolution" (p.14). He notes widespread optimism surrounding the twenty-first century with "futurists predicting a period of rapid growth at the magnitude of the industrial revolution, if not greater, with the advent of the knowledge-based economy" (p. 33). Alheit (2009) suggests the "communication and interaction networks of the IT age" will "create the "future form of knowledge" which is "*doing knowledge*, a kind of lifestyle that determines the structures of society far beyond the purely occupational domain" (p. 119).

Further future predictions follow two themes. The first cautions that emerging new technologies will not replace the old. Valmont (2003) reminds us that "oral storytelling did not die when Gutenberg created the printing press" and "novels did not go away when films became popular. Literacies simply evolve" (p. 298).

Hubble's work with the Mount Wilson 100 inch telescope in the 1920's confirmed that most galaxies are rapidly receding from the Milky Way implying that the universe is expanding and later discoveries indicated that this expansion was actually accelerating. The discovery by the New Horizons spacecraft in 2019 of a new object beyond the current thinking of the edge of our solar system opened our thinking of a boundary to our solar system. Future research directions can be considered in light of Hubble's model of the expanding universe and the New Horizon's discovery. Hubble's model suggests four possibilities: the expansion can accelerate, the expansion can be constant, the present situation will remain, or the motion will reverse itself and result in the big crunch. Each of these possibilities will be examined for the expanding universe of technology infused adult learning.

If that expanding universe accelerates, it might seem almost out of control and almost uncomfortable. Yet it offers exciting possibilities. Hakken (1999) suggested that "we must come to terms…with an accelerated decoupling of space from place (p. 215). Maxine Greene (2001) challenges us to see the future as an opportunity for "thinking of things as if they could be otherwise" (p. 127). For specific examples of what is appearing on the horizon, Farmer (2010) provides the following list. Using "cloud computing", learners will be able to access learning objects anytime, anywhere, any way and store their own work on multi-purpose servers. She notes that the "Semantic Web" is becoming more accurate and multi-lingual and should "advance global learning dramatically" (p. 102). Talking computers would reduce the need for written literacy and require a focus on oral communication. She also predicts that learning will become more customized with "push" technologies delivering information to the user.

If the expansion is constant, it might appear more controlled and predictable yet still offering exciting possibilities. This would seem to put the internet into a long list of other technologies. Yermish reminds us that "ever since the advent of television, educators have wrestled with the viability of using this technology to reach wider audiences. Educational television facilitated the distribution of high-quality program content in a one-directional fashion" (p. 208). He defines a "passing of remoteness" as a "phenomenon of the rise of the Internet and other distance-shrinking technologies" (p. 208). Valmont (2003) reminds us that "oral storytelling did not die when Gutenberg created the printing press" and "novels did not go away when films became popular….Literacies simply evolve"(p. 298). So even an expanding universe would maintain the best of successful traditions. Barab, Kling, and Gray (2004) suggest that "we are currently in an exciting time in which pedagogical theory and technological advances have created an opportunity to design innovative and powerful environments to support learning" (p. 13). However they caution that it is important to remain "optimistic and visionary while at the same time avoiding hyperbole and unsubstantiated assumptions" (p. 13).

It is almost impossible to imagine a stationary universe. Standing still in the universe of technology really means going backwards. One would need to be content to live in the past. Anderson and Wolff (2010) offer a sobering thought. "The Web is now 18 years old. It has reached adulthood. An entire generation has grown up in front of a browser. The exploration of a new world has turned into business as usual. We get the Web. It's part of our life. And we just want to use the services that make our life better. Our appetite for discovery slows as our familiarity with the status quo grows" (p. 127). In a rapidly changing and fast paced world, it is difficult to imagine that the appetite for discovery will slow. But it is imperative that the momentum behind applying technology to learning in new and different ways does not slow.

If the expansion stops and the motion reverses, the result would inevitably be a Big Crunch. The luddites would have won and succeeded in putting the technology genie back in bottle.

The New Horizons discovery of breaking through boundaries and opening doors to new possibilities at further distances supports the investigation of the four possibilities of Hubble's universe.

While it might be interesting to suggest research on any one of these possibilities, clearly the most exciting would be that of a universe whose expansion is accelerating. Knowles (2005) sees technology as being in the "andragogoical tradition" (p. 237). Schein (2010) suggests the type of skills that the future will require. "As the world becomes more complex and interdependent, the ability to think systemically, to analyze fields of forces and understand their joint causal effects on each other, and to abandon simple linear causal logic in favor of complex mental models will become more critical to learning" (p. 371). Kelly (2010) notes that "book reading strengthened our analytical skills, encouraging us to pursue an observation all the way down to the footnote. Screen reading encourages rapid pattern making, associating this idea with another, equipping us to deal with the thousands of new thoughts expressed every day. The screen rewards and nurtures thinking in real time. In books we find a revealed truth; on the screen we assemble our truth from pieces" (p. 125). Further investigation of the connections between these two lists would be useful in planning future learning.

Jarvis (1985) echoes the sentiment that as society moves toward this new information technology society, it is essential that the designs of "learning be such that they encourage critical awareness about all forms of information they receive, whether their teacher is in the classroom, the purveyor of information through the media, or the billions of pages of circulars, or even the programmer of a computer learning package" (p. 14). At the end of the day, after all the analysis, how this is put into practice is the most important. Brookfield (2006) advises what "skillful teaching boils down to whatever helps students learn, that the best teachers adapt a critically reflective stance towards their practice, and that the most important knowledge we need to do good work is an awareness of how students are experiencing their learning and our teaching" (p. xvii).

Blumenfeld notes that "there is both an art and a science in examining what lies ahead. Such an exploration of future possibilities is integral to our modern consciousness. Any critical look at future projections, however, demands that one knows who is making predictions and what their motives are" (p. 11). He also notes that the visionary director of the Media Lab at Massachusetts Institute of Technology "stresses that the world of tomorrow means connectivity, or immediate access in communications. He is very much aware that futurologists can be led astray when they rely too heavily on technology and not enough on human values" (p. 21).

In considering the future, there are many areas with unanswered questions. The geographic distance encompassed by organizational learning communities will demand more use of technology as the major vehicle for training. Technology will increasingly enhance traditional face-to-face seminars and allow for the expansion of the course before and after the seminar. However, there is still a great deal to be learned in order to achieve optimal utility of technology-enhanced and technology delivered learning. Professional educators and society's change agents are poised at the doorstep of an exciting new horizon for sustainable growth.

While this chapter connects decades-old learning theories to today's technology rich classrooms, the concept of learning community in the world of adult learning is only a few decades old. Yet technology in the form of Web 2.0 is providing exciting options for enhancing and expanding learning communities across space and time for exploring new horizons beyond the known universe or even our own Solar System.

The author's predictions might be a future with even more connections, more blurring of boundaries; a future that values personal philosophies but shared experiences and goals. Maxine Greene (2001) challenges us to see the future as an opportunity for "thinking of things as if they could be otherwise" (Greene, 2001, p. 127).

CONCLUSION, RECOMMENDATIONS AND A LOOK FORWARD

As more decentralization occurs within organizations, it will likely mean more opportunities for emerging leaders in emerging economies in countries such as Kazakhstan and regions such as Eurasia. It will also provide more opportunities for theory development and more venue in which Transformational Learning can occur. Lojeski & Reilly (2008) suggest one such opportunity. They note that the collocation of workers and leaders is a characteristic of the workforce before the Digital Age. If the new Digital Age will disperse leaders throughout the geography of the organization, new leadership opportunities will become available across the globe in countries where new models of leadership are evolving. They note that transactional, charismatic, and transformational views of leadership were developed before the Digital Age, when organizations and teams were likely to be collocated and more culturally homogeneous. They suggest that today's organizations need the ambassadorial leader. "The ambassadorial leader is a boundary spanner. Like an ambassador, the leader must span geographic, cultural, and organizational boundaries and foster trusting relationships among disparate groups of people" (p. 130).

However, Hofstede (2001) warns against the consequences of teaching foreign theories abroad. "What in fact happens when foreign theories are taught abroad – and this I have personally witnessed – is that the theories are preached but not practiced. Wise local managers silently adapt the foreign ideas to fit the values of their subordinates" (p. 389). This suggests the importance for a national culture to develop its own research instruments and analyze its own data. The first step in this process is the work done with the research in Kazakhstan.

Tazhina (2010) provides specific recommendations for the future within the area of applied psychology and leadership. She notes that "While Kazakhstan has the necessary resources, it needs fundamental development in psychological research. Her recommendations follow:

- Psychological practices (ie: medical insurance coverage of psychological support and lower prices for counseling) from developed countries should be applied while taking into account the cultural peculiarities of Kazakhstan.
- An Employee Assistance Program, which has helped western countries in handling psychological problems of employees and their families, would be beneficial to Kazakhs as psychological support in the workplace increases productivity and lowers conflicts within companies.
- Applied psychology needs to become part of the president's anti-crisis strategy. Psychological knowledge will increase the efficacy of professional training and retraining.
- Development of competent psychological services within schools in order to ensure the psychological development of new generations" (p. 3).

These recommendations would likely be applicable to other countries in this Eurasia region.

Static situations can be comfortable. But static doesn't move any field forward whether it be astronomy or education. In the two decades at the beginning of the 1900's, people saw their world expand to include other galaxies, discovered that those galaxies were receding from our own galaxy, and that expansion was accelerating. This same sense of discomfort is present in the at many levels of every organizational structure. The rate at which communication and access to information is accelerating can be unsettling. The thought of 24/7 access to information and individuals can seem uncomfortable. This requires a new model for technology infused adult learning to guide the sustainable growth in today's world.

Mazarr (1999) suggests that "knowledge-era learning" must become more "holistic" and "high-tech"; must "emphasize creativity and participation" and be "characterized by more choice and competition" (p. 285). But it is good to remember the words of Shea-Schultz and Fogarty (2002) who suggest that "e-learning is an art, not a science (p. 168). Applying technology infused learning in curriculum and program development and delivery requires both art and science.

This chapter has connected decades old learning theories to today's technology rich environment. While the concept of the learning community in the world of adult education is only a few decades old, technology in the form of Web 2.0 is providing exciting options for enhancing and expanding learning communities across space and time to facilitate sustainable growth especially in regions such as Eurasia.

REFERENCES

Alheit, P. (2009). Biographical learning – within the new lifelong learning. In K. Illeris (Ed.), *Contemporary theories of learning: Learning theorists...in their own words* (pp. 116–128). New York: Routledge.

Anderson, C., & Wolff, M. (2010). The Web is dead. Long live the internet. *Wired, 18*(9), 118-127, 164, 166.

Barab, S., Kling, R., & Gray, J. (2004). *Designing for virtual communities in the service of learning*. Cambridge, UK: Cambridge University Press. doi:10.1017/CBO9780511805080

Bennett, E.E., & Bell, A. A. (2010). Paradox and promise in the knowledge society.

Blumenfeld, Y. (1999). *Scanning the future*. New York, NY: Thames & Hudson.

Brookfield, S. (1986). *Understanding and facilitating adult learning*. San Francisco, CA: Jossey-Bass.

Brookfield, S. (1987). *Developing critical thinkers*. San Francisco, CA: Jossey-Bass.

Brookfield, S. (2005). *The power of critical theory: liberating adult learning and teaching*. San Francisco, CA: Jossey-Bass.

Brookfield, S. (2006). *The skillful teacher*. San Francisco, CA: Jossey-Bass.

Cerf, V. (2010). Google's view. *Smithsonian, 41*(4), 120.

Comins, N., & Kaufmann, W. (2012). *Discovering the universe*. New York, NY: W. H. Freeman.

Cranton, P. (2006). *Understanding and promoting transformative learning*. San Francisco, CA: John Wiley & Sons.

Dorfman, P., & House, R. (2004). Cultural influences on organizational leadership: literature review, theoretical rationale, and GLOBE project goals. In R. House, P. Hanges, M. Javidan, P. Dorfman, & V. Gupta (Eds.), *Culture, leadership, and organizations: The GLOBE study of 62 societies* (pp. 51–73). Thousand Oaks, CA: Sage Publications.

Farmer, L. (2010). Innovative instructional strategies with the use of technology for adult learners. In V. Wang (Ed.), *Integrating adult learning and technologies for effective education* (pp. 170–188). Hershey, PA: IGI Global. doi:10.4018/978-1-61520-694-0.ch010

Greene, M. (1995). *Releasing the imagination.* San Francisco, CA: Jossey-Bass.

Hakken, D. (1999). *Cyborgs@cyberspace.* New York, NY: Routledge.

Hawking, S. W. (1988). *A brief history of time.* New York, NY: Bantam Books. doi:10.1063/1.2811637

Heaney, T. W. (2000). Adult education and society. In A. L. Wilson & A. R. Hayes, A. R. (Eds.), Handbook of adult and continuing education (pp. 559-572). San Francisco, CA: Jossey-Bass.

Hewitt, H. (2005). *Blog: Understanding the information reformation that's changing your world.* Nashville, TN: Thomas Nelson.

Hofstede, G. (2001). *Culture's consequences: comparing values, behaviors, institutions, and organizationa across nations.* Thousand Oaks, CA: Sage.

Illeris, K. (2004). A comprehensive understanding of human learning. In K. Illeris (Ed.), *Contemporary theories of learning: learning theorists...in their own words* (pp. 7–20). New York, NY: Routledge.

Jarvis, P. (1985). Thinking critically in an information society: A sociological Analysis. *Lifelong Learning,* 11-14.

Jarvis, P. (2009). Learning to be a person in society: Learning to be me. In K. Illeris (Ed.), *Contemporary theories of learning: learning theorists...in their own words* (pp. 21–34). New York, NY: Routledge.

Kasworm, C., & Londoner, C. A. (2000). Adult learning and technology. In A. L. Wilson & E. Hayes (Eds.), *Handbook of adult and continuing education* (pp. 224–242). San Francisco, CA: John Wiley & Sons.

Kasworm, C., Rose, A. D., & Ross-Gordon, J. M. (2010). Adult and continuing education as an intellectual commons. In C. E. Kasworm, A. D. Rose, & J. M. Ross-Gordon (Eds.), *Handbook of adult and continuing education* (pp. 1–12). Thousand Oaks, CA: Sage.

Kasworm, C. E., Rose, A. D., & Ross-Gordon, J. M. (2010). *Handbook of adult and continuing education.* Thousand Oaks, CA: Sage Publications.

Kelly, K. (2010). From print to pixel. *Smithsonian, 41*(4), 122–128.

Kling, R., & Courtright, C. (2004). Group behavior and learning in electronic forums. In S. Barab, R. Kling, & J. Gray (Eds.), *Designing for virtual communities in the service of learning* (pp. 91–119). Cambridge, UK: Cambridge University Press. doi:10.1017/CBO9780511805080.008

Knowles, M. (1989). *The making of an adult educator.* San Francisco, CA: Jossey-Bass.

Knowles, M., Holton, E., & Swanson, R. (2005). *The adult learner.* Burlington, MA: Elsevier. doi:10.4324/9780080481913

Latova, N.V. & Latov, Y.V. (2007). Peculiarities of "Westernization" of the Students' mentality in modernizing nations. *Sociological researches,* (11), 90-98.

Lesgold, A. (2000). What are the tools for? Revolutionary change does not follow the usual norms. In S. Lajoie (Ed.), *Computers as cognitive tools* (pp. 399–408). Manwah, NH: Lawrence Erlbaum Associates.

Loader, B. (1998). Cyberspace divide. In B. Loader (Ed.), *Cyberspace divide*. New York, NY: Routledge. doi:10.4324/9780203169537_chapter_1

Lojeski, K., & Reilly, R. (2008). *Transforming Leadership and Innovation in the Globally Integrated Enterprise*. Hoboken, NJ: John Wiley & Sons.

Mazarr, M. (1999). *Global trends 2005: An owner's manual for the next decade*. New York, NY: St. Martin's Press.

Merriam, S., Caffarella, R., & Baumgartner, L. (2006). *Learning in adulthood: a comprehensive guide*. San Francisco, CA: John Wiley & sons.

Merriam, S. B. (2008). *Adult learning theory for the twenty-first century in New Directions for adult and continuing education* (pp. 93–98). San Francisco, CA: Jossey-Bass.

Mezirow, J., & ... (2000). *Learning as transformation*. San Francisco, CA: Jossey-Bass.

Moe, M. (2000). *The knowledge web*. Beverly Hills, CA: Knowledge Enterprises Group.

Nilson, L. B. (2003). *Teaching at its best*. San Francisco, CA: Anker Publishing.

Pais, A. (1982). *Subtle is the Lord: The science and the life of Albert Einstein*. New York, NY: Oxford University Press.

Palloff, R., & Pratt, K. (1999). *Building learning communities in cyberspace*. San Francisco, CA: Jossey-Bass.

Parker, J. (2009). Adult learning and CTE: A shared history influenced by technology. In V. Wang (Ed.), *Definitive readings in the history, philosophy, practice and theories of career and technical education*. Hershey, PA: IGI Global.

Parker, J. (2012). *Engaging traditional learning and adult learning via information technologies. Pedagogical and andragogical teaching and learning with information communication technologies*. Hershey, PA: IGI Global.

Piskurich, G. (2006). *Rapid instructional design*. San Francisco, CA: John Wiley & Sons.

Rhoades, E., Friedel, C., & Morgan, A. (2009). Can Web 2.0 improve our collaboration? *Techniques*, *83*(9), 24–27.

Schein, E. (2010). *Organizational culture and leadership* (4th ed.). San Francisco, CA: Jossey-Bass.

Shea-Schultz, H., & Fogarty, J. (2002). *Online learning today: Strategies that work*. San Francisco, CA: Berrett-Koehler Publishers.

Silberman, M. (2006). *Active training*. San Francisco, CA: John Wiley & Sons.

Tazhina, G. (2010). Applied psychology in Kazakhstan. *Paper presented at the Kazakhstan in Globe: Socio-Economic and Cultural Aspects, Scientific congress*. Academic Press.

Tyson, N., Liu, C., & Irion, R. (2000). *The universe: at home in the cosmos*. Washington, D.C.: Joseph Henry Press.

Valmont, W. (2003). *Technology for literacy teaching and learning*. New York, NY: Houghton Mifflin.

Wheatley, M. (1999). *Leadership and the new science: Discovering order in a chaotic world*. San Francisco, CA: Berrett-Koehler Publishers.

White, B. A., & Bridwell, C. (2004). Distance learning techniques. In M. Galbraith (Ed.), *Adult learning methods: A guide for effective instruction* (pp. 273–288). Malabar, FL: Krieger.

Yermish, I. (2000). A case for case studies via video-conferencing. In L. Lau (Ed.), *Distance learning technologies: issues, trends and opportunities*. Hershey, PA: IGI Global. doi:10.4018/978-1-878289-80-3.ch015

Chapter 8
Educational Approaches and Strategies in the Knowledge Society:
University 4.0 and Academic Communication Models in Kazakhstan

Laura Turarbekova
https://orcid.org/0000-0003-3416-0160
Al-Farabi Kazakh National University, Kazakhstan

ABSTRACT

According to the theory of the link between democracy and society's need for educated citizens, the process of transmission of experiences is a basic activity for a society. The conditions of this transmission are the academic, institutional, and political freedom of that society's universities. This transmission takes the form of the communication model: a top-to-bottom form or a horizontal form. The form of transmission is a specific form of rationality expressed in a communicative action. To understand this rationality, it is necessary to analyze existing forms of communication in the context of the history of rationality itself. Today, the digitization of the higher education system has become a global trend, bringing with it new forms of communication. In the Republic of Kazakhstan, the "Industry 4.0" state program affirms that digital communication skills need to be implemented at all levels of social life. The chapter is devoted to the problem of which form of academic communication will be chosen and the consequences of this choice for the Kazakhstan in the future.

DOI: 10.4018/978-1-7998-2551-7.ch008

INTRODUCTION

Enlightenment, Enlightenment!

The study of the history of educational systems and its basic foundations cannot happen without making some comparisons between these systems and others. From a certain point of view, as soon as one looks at the history of education up close, unexpected parallels arise that can help in understanding the processes that occur in current educational policy. The history of education in Kazakhstan represents, from this point of view, a rich field in which to explore such parallels.

It is above all with questions about the Enlightenment and modernity, and the possibility of the application of these questions to the educational philosophy of Kazakhstan, that we must start our discourse about contemporary Kazakhstan. This line of questioning requires that the problem of the Enlightenment—and the possibility of applying the concept of "modernity" in the history of an atypical culture in relation to the history of the West—must be raised. The background of this questioning is philosophical and, at the same time, historical as well as political. Let us proceed to a consideration of these three components. They comprise the organizational background of this chapter.

It is philosophical in terms of its universality. Indeed, is the Enlightenment project universal? In terms of style, this line of questioning is very close and, at the same time, different from questioning initiated by French Theory (Foucault, 1984; Derrida, 1963), on the one hand, and different from questioning initiated by Critical philosophy (Habermas, 1987), on the other. Philosophers from these two theories, querying in the same direction, wondered whether modernity is a completed or an uncompleted project; and wondered whether we are living in modern or post-modern times. But the problem of completing or not completing modernity as a process does not exhaust the problem of the modern. The question should be asked about the universality of terms of modernity and the Enlightenment ideals.

This takes us back to the historical aspect of research. The question about the universality of the Enlightenment ideals would require not only knowledge of more or less accepted periodization in Western history and in the history of philosophy, but also knowledge of the historical and philosophical periodization that deserves the name "imitation of periodization." This is the period of the Kazakh Enlightenment. In Kazakh philosophy and history, it is widely recognized that the Kazakh Enlightenment has been in place since the first half of the 19th century. But why talk about the imitation of periodization?

For historical reasons—and before independence was gained in the 1990's—Kazakhstan followed the development paths of historical, political, economic, and social thought of Russia. From the 1840s to the 1850s, the intellectual discussion in Russia revolved around the question of the influence of the European Enlightenment on Russian society and on national identity. The two main intellectual fields—slavophilia and *zapadnichestvo* (westernism)—used an identical historical pattern to explain the difference between Russian culture and European culture. The Slavophiles supported the idea of the existence of an original and properly Russian historical developmental path. *Zapadnik*'s supported the idea of Russia's European ("western") way of historical development. Despite the opposing positions on how to interpret Russia's history and its relations with Europe, the European Enlightenment has instead been recognized as a gradual and desirable step of historical development (Pain & Volkogonova, 2008, p. 238). In this regard, let us note that this theory of the development of Russian culture's being in a state of constant catch-up with the European ("western") world was continued in the work of Eurasianist's thinker Nikolai Trubetzkoy. There, the application of the historical (and cultural) grid of the western world in relation to the historical and geographical reality of the Eurasian space carries in itself a negative and harmful connotation for an understanding of what the Russian Empire is (Trubetskoy, 1920; Trubetskoy, 1925; Trubetskoy, 1926, rep. 2000).

Oddly enough, [despite the fact that] now … the Russian government is making every effort to instill in Russia a worldview created by typical representatives of the European spirit, and to restructure [itself] according to the theories created by European publicists, it is now, despite this, that the spontaneous national identity and the non-European, semi-Asian face of Russia-Eurasia [comes out more than ever]. (…) Various Turan peoples [speak] their now[-]recognized official languages: Tatars, Kyrgyz, Bashkirs, Chuvash, Yakouts, Buryats, Mongols – [they have begun] to participate on a par with the Russians in the [project of] national construction; and [with regard to] Russian physiognomy, which used to seem purely Slavic, now you [also] notice something [of / akin to (?)] Turanian; […] most [notably (?), the] Russian language [now contains] some new sound combinations, [plus words that are otherwise foreign—i.e.] "barbaric," [and] also Turan [words as well. [It is as] if all over Russia again, as [had happened] seven hundred years ago, [wafts the smell] of burnt dog, [then the horse], [then] camel hair – [followed by the] Turan nomad [himself]. And the shadow of the great Genghis Khan, the unifier of Eurasia, rises over Russia [once more]. (Trubetskoy, 2015, p. 118)

Despite the strong imperial character of Trubetzkoy's work, his idea was almost the first effort to try to avoid the European historical penchant for marking periods in the history of the Eurasian space as such. Trubetzkoy was, from this point of view, a dark precursor to the visions that conquered Western thought following changes brought about by the Second World War. It is this idea of catching up to another culture which was expressed in 1963 by Derrida:

Perhaps this endless misfortune of the disciple is due to the fact that he does not yet know, or still hides from himself that, like in the real life, the master may still be absent. It is therefore necessary to break the ice[—]or rather[,] the mirror, the reflection, the infinite speculation of the disciple on the master[—and] start talking. (Derrida, 1963, p. 460)

But despite the existence of these "dark precursors" which proposed to consider the history of the Eurasian space as being separate from the widely accepted European-type periodization, the countries of Central Asia (including Kazakhstan) were widely considered as being those that follow after and repeat—with a delay of more than a century—the general stages of westernized history. Thus, the model of the Enlightenment of Europe (the West) is repeated in an almost oxymoronic term: the Kazakh Enlightenment. This oxymoron character of what is called "Kazakh Enlightenment" is the point that defines the whole nature of our research on communication in a digital university. The Enlightenment—this "sacred cow" in the history of Western thought—takes its own idea of the liberation of humanity by reason and creates a caricaturized form of that idea: the concept of "national" enlightenments (and thereby "national" reason?). This conceptual message would be much more readable in a place where its full background would be a long way distant from the circumstances from which the Enlightenment itself arose. The two arise from totally different circumstances, and that those who are aware of history know this distinction and realize that the term is anachronistic when compared to the present circumstance. In the absence of a revised lexicography in which the period from the late 17th and the 18th centuries would be termed "the pre-Kazakh Enlightenment, Kazakh philosophers, as well as all researchers in the humanities and social sciences, should make an effort to reconsider calling the role of this (very first) modernization of Kazakh society by the term "Kazakh Enlightenment."

The research reveals challenges facing the system of national education in the Republic of Kazakhstan in the field of digitization of academic communication as seen through the light of the objectives of the state program termed "Digital Kazakhstan" (2017) and its own hidden curriculum. This hidden meaning has analogous parallels with the hidden curriculum concept (*cf.*, for example, Kegan, 1994)—*i.e.* the concept that presupposes the transmission of norms and values in education with the help of non-explicit, but implicit, hidden forms—transmission by behaviors, cultural expectations, and cultural perspectives more than by official statements. The problem of the dependence of the university model/structure on its communicative practices is enshrined in a wider circle of questions regarding the Kazakh socio-political model and its current mutations—and the history of transformations of Kazakh society and its intellectual destiny.

These are the main concepts that follow the organizational background of the research. These are theories of Western intellectual history (especially the Enlightenment) and its influence all over the world. But the research is also about the possibility of applying these theories of the Enlightenment to atypical societies—doing so from historical, political, and social points of view. The case of Kazakhstan is ideal for analyzing changes in concepts such as modernity and modernization. This may be a task for the humanities and social sciences in Kazakhstan for years to come.

LEGAL REASON VS. ANTHROPOLOGICAL REASON: ON THE VALUE OF INTELLECTUAL LIFE IN SOCIETY

[We] believe that the assimilation of the European, universal education and the vigorous struggle against the obstacles to this goal should be the ultimate goal for any people capable of development and culture. ... To make the Kyrgyz capable of perceiving European transformative ideas, it is necessary to develop his skull and nervous system by education. (Walikhanov, 1985, p. 80)

The Kazakh Enlightenment is a time in the history of Kazakh thought that corresponds to roughly the first half of the late 19th century. The names of Shoqan Walikhanov, Ibyray Altynsarin, Abai are linked to the idea that, in order to bring the Kyrgyz (Kazakhs) out of the "wild" state, they should be educated and taught "culture." Except for the temporal distance that separates the European Enlightenment from the Kazakh Enlightenment, it is the source of the reception of education and culture that mainly distinguishes these two movements in the intellectual life of such different peoples. In the case of the first Kazakh educators, *kulturtrager* (transmitter of cultural ideal) refers to the Russian people; the Russian culture; the Russian language (Segizbayev, 1996). The character of the Kazakh Enlightenment is highly ethnic—or, at least, anthropological. It is not based on the idea of "reason" (*ratio*), but rather on the idea of "culture," which greatly changes the historical circumstances for all future modernizations.

This situation compounds the quirkiness associated with application of the term "Enlightenment" to the culture bordering the Russian Empire. Indeed, not only is the Enlightenment project termed as being "universal" in Walikhanov's interpretation (possible translations oscillate between the expression "universal European education" and "Universal European Enlightenment"; Walikhanov uses the second term, but with a semantic shadow of the first), but it is also Russian culture that acquires universal and "European" traits.

The very universality of the Enlightenment remains an unresolved question today. From its rejection by the philosophers of French theory (post-modern philosophers; the particle "post" claims a replacement of a certain outdated modernity) to the proclamation of the Enlightenment as an unfinished project by Habermas, we monitor the vivacity of the idea of the Enlightenment as the beginning of European civil societies today. The two poles of the debate over the question posed by Kant—"*Was ist Aufklärung*?" (*What is Enlightenment?*)—confirm this.

The first is the position of Michel Foucault who characterizes the Enlightenment thought as being primarily new ("modern") with regard to "the modification of the pre-existing relationship between will, authority, and the use of reason" as compared to the paradigm of previous eras. This modernity; this contemporaneity; is contained in Kant's "*Sapere aude!*" and is envisioned by Foucault as being a motto that proclaims the man as being himself responsible for his own exit from the minority state—by virtue of reason (Foucault, 1984). At the same time, a link that Foucault makes between the despotisms which had been a final result of revolutions of the twentieth century on the one hand, and the analytical reason of the Enlightenment on the other, is clear. In explaining why the Enlightenment theme reappears in European thought in the second half of the 20th century, Foucault notes:

Several processes, marking the second half of the twentieth century, have led to the heart of contemporary preoccupations concerning the question of the Enlightenment. The first is the importance acquired by scientific and technical rationality in the development of the productive forces and the play of political decisions. The second is the very history of a "revolution" whose hope, since the close of the eighteenth century, had been borne by a rationalism to which we are entitled to ask[] what part it could have in the effects of a despotism where that hope was lost. The third and last is the movement by which, at the end of the colonial era, people began to ask the West what rights its culture, its science, its social organization[,] and finally[,] its rationality itself could have to laying claim to a universal validity: is it not a mirage tied to an economic domination and a political hegemony? Two centuries later[,] the Enlightenment returns: but not at all as a way for the West to become conscious of its actual possibilities and freedoms to which it can have access, but as a way to question the limits and powers it has abused. Reason [—] the despotic enlightenment. (Foucault, 1991, p. 12)

By contrast, Habermas—a stalwart defender of modernity—characterizes the theories of the counter-Enlightenment as included in the dialectic of Enlightenment, so that these theories in question continue the ideas of the Enlightenment:

More and more elements of the critique of progress have been assimilated by the theory of progress: all in order to formulate an idea of progress that is subtle and resilient enough not to [(to not)] let itself be blinded by the mere illusion of emancipation. (Habermas, 1979, p. 182)

The Enlightenment, according to Habermas, is an unfinished project that dialectically absorbs anti-Enlightenment theories. It is a concept of specific rationality as a specific human capacity that appears spontaneously in a communicative action (and not a subject-centered rationality of the 18th century's Enlightenment, which is just a case of communicative action) (Habermas, 1987).

In any case, it is always a conception of rationality that is in question when it comes to the Enlightenment. But when we talk about the Kazakh Enlightenment, is there a question of any rationality or only the question of "skull change" (Walikhanov, 1985)? We will see below how national education has settled and developed in Kazakhstan from the arrival of Soviet power to the present day. Our theory is that the development of national education reflected the state of the public sphere. In any case, at the time when Walikhanov proposed to 'change the skulls' of the Central Asian nomads, the public sphere in the Habermasian sense did not exist in Kazakhstan.

The lack of knowledge of how to deal with the "public use of reason" or rationality (in Kantian and Habermasian terms) causes the situation in which, nowadays, bureaucratic power goes against digitalized power. The type of power that is exercised over the intellectual depends on this status of reason and on the value of intellectual life in society. If reason is seen as being a proper biological ability—a psycho-physiological ability (Walikhanov's "skull")—the power exerted over it is a repressive power ("*to develop his skull and nervous system by education*"), and the type of communicative action used to exert that power is a repressive communicative action. If reason is seen as being a socialization capacity (the "public use of reason," per Kant and Habermas) the repressive power has no domain, and there is no possibility of repression over reason. This idea may sound utopian, but the consequences are obvious: Kazakh society is not often ready to use reason publicly, in a transparent way. This unwillingness to engage in rational public discourse is the antithesis of the very meaning of a digital society.

If it is in communication that our rationality is expressed, we will have to analyze the types of communicative action in society. Such communication could be considered from the perspective of an "architectonic" model, *i.e.* the model of communication between its parts; of management principles; of organization. This conformity of models provides a continuity of "experience" in order to maintain the existence of the group throughout history/time. According to Dewey, the despotically organized government uses in its type of communication a "simply capacity for fear" (Dewey, 1916). There is no place for individuals to share conjoined communicative experience; to exchange information; and to engage in mutual and meaningful interaction. Then, in such a kind of society, subjected under a despotically organized government, communication takes a pyramidal and vertical (top-to-bottom) form of exchange of information.

In contrast, the democratically organized society needs, more than other types of government do, to have a deliberate and systematic form of education, because of its form of social life in which the interests of its members are mutually interpenetrating. This model has a "rhizomatic" form of transmission of experience—an *ipso facto* horizontal public sphere model. For instance, Deleuze and Guattari give us a philosophical description of the principles of rhizomatic models of communication/space distribution which serves as an example of the theory of the rhizomatic model of learning. According to Richard Rorty (Rorty, 1982), Deleuzian thought logically continues Dewey's pragmatism. The rhizomatic model corresponds to a few general principles that distinguish it from the so-called "*arborescent*" (vertical or top-to-bottom) model (Deleuze & Guattari, 1987). In the rhizomatic model of communication, horizontal links play the main role; and bureaucratic power, which is (by definition) vertical in nature, is reduced to its minimum extent, or may even be absent from this type of communication. The rhizomatic model has no center or periphery, but has several situational centers—and all the links in this communication model are situational.

This rhizomatic model is indeed a method and a model. If the virtual public sphere (especially the media, but also the Internet) is being criticized by Habermas when it comes to its democratic potential, we sustain the hopes of this horizontal model, which is a space for an ideal situation of exchange of arguments where the spontaneous rationality of communicative action has more channels to occur. To come to the end of our chapter topic, let us therefore summarize: The global development of the public space—specifically, the virtual and digital public sphere—leads to the creation of the horizontal public sphere that allows for the rapid and direct exchange of information, opinions, and arguments to occur. With the installation of communication instruments yet to be invented—technologies that will stimulate the processes in this sphere (seen as being an open, horizontal space of exchange)—a spontaneous, communicative rationality appears. Thus, by developing digital tools under the "Industry 4.0" program, Kazakhstan must—above all—put in place models of communication that allow the country's public space to be considered as being a rational public sphere, rather than being perceived merely as a simple space for a kind of communication perceived as being a unidirectional form of information transmission.

THE EMERGENCE OF UNIVERSITIES IN KAZAKHSTAN; KAZAHSTAN'S AFFINITY WITH GLOBAL TRENDS

The knowledge society presupposes that it is knowledge, as such, that becomes the key to success in all areas of human activity. In the knowledge society, it is continuous education, as well as the sharing of knowledge, that must meet the growing demand for innovation. When we are in the logic of innovation, it is the opposite of the idea of progress. Innovation is not subject to the teleological idea of good for all humankind—quite the contrary. In the logic of innovation, we are oriented towards "the here and now." Innovation is "creative destruction" in favor of another innovation that replaces the previous one (Schumpeter, 1942; Drucker, 1969).

In this logic of innovation, education acquires certain traits that did not exist before or that had not been so expressly obvious. The demand for professional knowledge in the knowledge society is constantly changing, and universities must be able to meet that demand. In addition, it is a link between innovations and education that the university in the knowledge society must provide. Universities (and educational organizations) are beginning to play an overarching role—responding to the demand of this capitalist society's logic of innovation.

To understand a country's chances of developing a competitive higher education system, one must first know the history of the universities of that country. As university culture and university history each differ from country to country, and as countries in a global world approach becoming mere regional variations of an almost identical educational system, the success of this undertaking depends on the capacity of the education system to adapt to the demands of the knowledge society. In the case of Central Asian countries—and, more concretely, in the case of Kazakhstan—we need to see the history of the university as an institution in order to lay the groundwork for future research.

The establishment and development of an educational system in Kazakhstan, and the formation of the Kazakh intelligentsia, were influenced by a number of factors.

Kazakh society is such that, even in the 19th century, it maintained a strong patriarchal tradition as a pledge of the stability of the nomadic economy.

After the end of the annexation of the territory of the former Kazakhstan to the Russian Empire, it is the interests of the metropole that the secular educative reform of education pursued in the 1860s. The reform had been marked by the creation of regional (*auyl*) schools for Kazakh and Russian children.

The integration of Kazakh culture into Russian culture was influenced by Tatar intelligentsia, who made up a kind of intellectual core. The Tatar intelligentsia actively spread the pan-Turkism ideological system advocating the unification of the Turks.

The Russian intelligentsia of Omsk and Orenburg played an important role in the development of education in the Steppe region. In this region, Kazakh newspapers and magazines such as *Dala Ualayatyn Gazeti* (the *Kirgiz Steppe Newspaper*), *Kazakh*, *Aikap*, and others are currently being published.

From this moment, the organizational and preparatory activity of creating a European-enlightened Kazakh intelligentsia began. Education reform primarily affected the northwestern regions of the region, bordering the regions of the metropolis. Initially, the reform covered only a small segment of the population.

Many of the Kazakh intelligentsia was imprisoned and shot during the first decades of the Soviet establishment of power. For example, consider the so-called "Alash case"—a mass repression, since 1928, against members of the Alash party. In April 1930, about 40 people were sentenced to various terms of imprisonment, and to execution (replaced by imprisonment for 10 years). They were charged with having participated in an armed struggle against the Soviet regime in order to overthrow it; having issued nationalist propaganda, and having links with foreign states fighting against the Soviet Union. Among them numbered Akhmet Baytursynov, Myrzhakip Dulatov, Myrzagali Espolov, Khalel Gabbasov, Gazambek Birimzhanov, and others (Aitmukhambetov, 2000).

The famine in Kazakhstan in the 1930s has also influenced the history of the establishment of higher education in Kazakhstan. This famine was caused by the common policy of the abolition of the *kou-laks*—farmers who owned the land privately—during the massive "collectivization" led by the Soviet power. *Golodomor* (the famine) was one of the crimes inflicted by the Soviet state in the 1930s against many ethnicities. This period in Kazakhstani history is relatively little studied in concrete detail. Thus, sometimes it is referred to as a "forgotten genocide." During the events related to the collectivization of 1925–1927, the nomadic pastoralists lost almost all their cattle, even though it was their main source of food and survival in nomadic conditions. As a result, the Kazakh nomadic peoples have lost up to 40% of their population. This tragic page in Kazakh history contributed to the creation of Soviet Kazakhstan—a stable territory with clearly defined boundaries and a sedentary population. Hunger dramatically changed the existing elements of Kazakh identity, such as kinship ties, loyalty to the hereditary elite, and the nomadic way of life itself, imposing the category of "Kazakh" nationality over these concepts (Cameron, 2016). Undoubtedly, massive settling of the population made sedentary-related objectives including industrialization, urbanization, and the development of higher education easier to implement. However, from the point of view of the loss of ethnic identity and autonomy, this put the development of Kazakh higher education and Kazakh scientific research definitively behind the imperial interests of Soviet Russia. As a long-term result, the situation of the Kazakh Academy and Kazakh science corresponded to the situation of the country itself— both were viewed as being a reservoir of natural resources to be exploited by the Empire that owned them (Medeuova, 2019).

The extermination of the thin layer of the Kazakh intelligentsia during the first decades of the Soviet establishment of power had led, among other things, to the problem of there being a lack of teaching staff with pedagogical training. The first universities centered on pedagogical training, therefore: the very first institution of higher education was the Kazakh Pedagogical Institute (now the Abaï Kazakh National Pedagogical University) which opened its doors in 1928. Then, in the 1930s, a few other institutions followed. For example, these included the Ural and Kyzyl-Orda Pedagogical Institutes (1931–1932), the Veterinary Institute (1929), the Agricultural Institute (1930), and the Medical Institute (1931). One of the most important universities, the Al-Farabi Kazakh National University, was opened in 1934. Thus, by the 1940s, on the eve of the Second World War, more than twenty higher educational institutions were operating in Soviet Kazakhstan.

During the post-Independence period, the establishment of the national education system went through a few stages. From 1991 to 1994—that is, in the first period after independence—the most urgent issue at hand was the formation of a legislative framework corresponding to the changed conditions. The main legislation regulating educational activities was the law entitled "On [the] Education of Kazakhstan," issued in 1992. On this period of transition from a command-and-control Soviet system to a market regulatory system, the situation of the national education of Kazakhstan was complicated by the lack of financial capacity of the national and local budget.

This period has had lasting impacts to this day. For instance, the system of pre-school and secondary vocational education adopted during the Soviet period has actually been destroyed. In addition, the quality of education has declined due to the outflow of teachers to other areas of activity.

However, since the second period (which lasted from 1995 to 1999), Kazakhstan's education system has seen positive developments due to the development of democratization and economic transformation.

One of the main tasks assigned to the education system by the Law of Education of June 7th, 1999 was the requirement of providing personnel to all sectors of the country's economy. A new model of the formative learning of students was developed at the government level. It was designed to select—by order of the state—the most gifted youth among those entering state universities.

The third period (which lasted from 1999 to 2010), was a period of a decentralization of management; a funding of education, and an expansion of the academic freedoms of educational organizations. It was an important stage in the reform of the education system. The State Education Development Program in the Republic of Kazakhstan was developed for 2005–2010. In this document, the priorities of educational policy were aimed at finding the best ways of adapting the higher educational system to the conditions of the market economy.

In 2010, a two-stage State program for the development of education was adopted in Kazakhstan for 2011–2020. The first stage was designed for 2011–2015; the second, for 2016–2020. This program provides for the development and introduction of a new, differentiated pay system, taking into account the specifics of teaching activities. The program supposes to combine school and university education, as well as higher education, science, and production. In addition, the program introduces gradations (levels) of universities: national research universities, national universities, research universities, institutes, and academies. Under this program, out of 140 existing universities (under different forms of ownership), only 50 universities and 30 institutes were permitted to remain. The rest were required to be categorized as academies. The total number of organizations of higher education were prohibited from exceeding 100 units.

According to the Center for Bologna Process and Academic Mobility's ENIC-Kazakhstan website (n.d.), in the present-day Republic of Kazakhstan, there are 131 higher educational institutions. Among them are universities with the status of national, public, private, or academy status. This includes both civilian and governmental universities.

However, a number of problems in higher education remain unresolved despite the measures taken in Kazakhstan. This is mainly due to the problem of the "aging" of teachers. The main reason for this is there being insufficient wages as compared to other sectors of the economy. In addition, the gap between universities and the science sector is leading to a decline in the quality of education. The largest number of specialists is those who finish their education after the first stage of higher education. This significantly reduces the overall level of higher-educated graduates in the country. In order to raise the quality of higher education in Kazakhstan to a new international level, permanent and stable investments in education and science are needed in order to help maximize opportunities to prepare a competitive domestic workforce.

We can therefore speak of a tradition of higher education—and, with it, a tradition of academic communication—which is not very old in modern Kazakhstan, especially in relation to countries where university cultures (and academic traditions) were born. That said—and notwithstanding the fact of the university institution's having had a relatively short history of in that country—Kazakhstan has been engaged in the Bologna Process since 2010. That process has set several objectives for internationalization and, with this, of reconciliation of academic standards with older, and therefore recognized, well-developed higher educational systems (Fiche Curie Kazakhstan, 2015).

Research Question

The research question of our study is whether, with the social and political transformations the nation has undergone, the country (in our case, Kazakhstan) is experiencing the transformation of all institutions not only in terms of their content (i.e. the particular, concrete discourse), but also as to their structure and the model of communication accepted in it.

Focus

The study focuses on how changing the communication model involves changing the communication practices and *vice versa* within the Kazakh university system—with the advent of digital technologies, in the context of the "University 4.0" approach/practice philosophically challenging formal and non-formal communicative academic approaches and practices.

DIGITAL CHALLENGES TO THE UNIVERSITY 4.0 CONCEPT IN KAZAKHSTAN

Thanks to its spontaneous nature, education has often been a natural object of reflection of the humanities. Several definitions have been given to what education and its objectives is and should be, starting with pedantic theories (παιδεία), medieval perennialism, and enlightenment pedagogical ideas, arriving today at the theories of education in democratic societies, the politicized and ideologized nature of education and its sometimes oppressive function, and opportunities to achieve insight by understanding the nature of this oppression itself (Freire, 2007). In the case of pre-Soviet, Soviet, and post-Soviet Kazakhstan, the problem of defining and understanding the character of the Kazakh educational system and its goals is complicated by its political history, in which the question of public spaces and its relationship to the norms of Western democracy is a foreign question planted in a theoretical soil that is both archaic and constantly flogged by the ideas of modernization (either with the arrival of Soviet-style democracy or with the establishment of post-Soviet democratic institutes).

We therefore assume that the form or model of national education as a digitized public space—and its democratic traditions and communicative rationality in Kazakhstan—could be discovered in existing communication practices. These are, for national education, the forms of communication that exist in primary, secondary, and higher education institutions. In short, this can include teaching methodology—not only documents of all kinds (student works, dissertations, textbooks, and conference papers), but also the forms and methodology of teaching; the kinds of problems posed in front of students, administrative practices; and the entire model of the educational institution. The field is wide; and any list of what constitutes communication practices in universities will never be exhaustive. Through textual, written communication practices—and, more specifically, school exercises (and the forms they take)—we will contextualize such practices through models of learning and training. The analysis will take place in the context of the state's commitments under the "University 4.0" program. This analysis will try to predict the consequences that such a commitment could bring.

Extensive and Intensive Models of Formal Written Communication

The analysis of existing school practices accepted in Soviet and post-Soviet Kazakhstan traces the first line of thought of this study. This is the common practice taken for the methodology of writing school exercises in post-Soviet schools. This methodology is based on what is called *referere* (Latin *referere*) which could be translated as a "summary." *Referat* is done to communicate; to report on the content of one or a few sources—a kind of school compilation with the aim of better studying a particular subject. *Referat* was often a most frequently requested exercise for undergraduate students and students in schools and universities in the Soviet Union and, consequently, in Soviet (and post-Soviet) Kazakhstan.

This type of methodology should be called extensive (Latin *extendere*—extend). It is about the action of extending; of lengthening; but also of the action of pushing the limits of something; enlarging; increasing the scope of something; increasing importance; increasing in volume; in scope. This practice of school communication has its traditions and forms. As for its form, the text is divided into three parts:

- **Introduction** (where information about the origin of the sources, the name and the greats of the source author is communicated, the problem and its relevance) is described.
- **Main part** (where the content of the text studied is communicated briefly, and the existing points of view are described; this part may contain an undefined number of parts and chapters, a balancing of the structure of the text is not required).
- **Conclusion** (a general conclusion of the issue announced).

Other types of written theoretical works, such as master or doctoral dissertations, are structured in the same way. In addition, the requirements for such works tend to be far more complicated as one proceeds from the conclusion of a bachelor's degree on to master-level and doctoral-level programs. Acknowledging this increased level of complexity as a given, this work (which is theoretical in nature) focuses on one facet of extensive methodology—specifically, the task of increasing volume. Volume is essential to success. For instance, such works require a large number of pages and a large bibliography. Success is based on the authority of the sources, and above all on the authority of many of the sources used, the number of which is gradually expanding.

The development of the Internet has led to the fact that at universities in post-Soviet countries (and all over the world), the active distribution of *referats* already prepared in different areas of knowledge has begun. Some resources offer to download ready-made works for money or for free, despite proclamations of academic powers on the unacceptableness of these practices. There are at least some kinds of problems that the *referat* as a model of academic and academic exercise poses: first, the problem of plagiarism; and second, the problem of students' losing the capacity for analysis and critical thinking.

Some pedagogical models at Kazakh universities of recent times provide for a "critical thinking" discipline. This discipline—relatively new from the point of view of methodological practice—is based on the model corresponding to the "dissertation." One could call it a model of intensive communication (one that manifests itself at high voltage, with great force; which gives the greatest performance). There is a pre-established text structure and a requirement to balance the plan. The structure traditionally includes an introduction; three core parts structured according to the principle of "thesis—antithesis—synthesis"; and a conclusion. An analytical effort is explicitly required of students.

There are also other approaches to the methodology of a school and university exercise and/or to the methodology of research in general. For example, some university programs are based on the practices advertised in university guides at universities in the Anglo-Saxon world (Harvard; Oxford; etc.). However, of these, we distinguish only two:

- **Extensive practice**, based on the potentially unlimited widening of sources, and with minimal analysis required; and
- **Intensive practice**, based on an intensive, analytical, and in-depth exploration of a minimum number of sources; putting forth an explicitly requested analytical (and speculative) effort.

These two primary practices, and uses of both, are done in parallel with the universities of Kazakhstan, and reflect the state of affairs of the smallest and most exemplary form of academic communication: formal communication in school. At the same time, the problematization of these pedagogical practices brings us back to a more global problem: namely, the problem of the democratization of university life in times of political transition in a post-Soviet country in development. The case of Kazakhstan is not only a special case of a country. It is also exemplary in terms of the processes of change in the post-Soviet space.

Academic Communication in University 4.0

According to the objectives of the "Digital Kazakhstan" program of December 12, 2017, "Industry 4.0" is one of the drivers of the digital transformation industry. In this concept of production, added value is ensured by the integration of physical objects, processes, and digital technologies. In it, physical processes are monitored in real time. Decentralized solutions are adopted. Also, the interaction between machines and human beings is emphasized. The program affirms:

Emphasis will be placed on the development of creative and critical thinking, as well as the use of modern educational technologies in the learning process. (Digital Kazakhstan, 2017)

It is clear that national education is one of those areas where digital communication skills need to be implemented at all levels, while providing youth education tasks, as well as adequate communication with the academia in the process of internationalizing higher education and research. The relationship between a model of academic communication and a university model gives us an image of society. In addition, this communication model shows us the future of the group and its ability to develop over historical time.

One of the fathers of the philosophy of education, John Dewey, envisions two main types of government: one despotic, and the other—as he calls it—"the democratic ideal." It would be a mistake, he notes, to assume that there is no common interest in a despotically governed society. The despotically governed state assumes, for its members, the common interest (as in all societies). But the main function of the type of communication accepted in a despotic state is a simple call to fear. It is not about 'the can' that makes us take care to prepare for the future. This fear is an isolated fear—fear as such (Dewey, 1916, p. 100). It is this isolated fear that affects all forms of communication, including those that serve the transfer of knowledge, information, and experience—that is, education.

In such a situation where fear becomes an individual's first motivation, the meaning of his activities is completely absorbed by his emotion. There is no need for the exchange of communicative experience between individuals. Communication assumes a pyramidal and vertical (top to bottom) form of information exchange (Figure 1).

In a democratically organized society, this is another type of communication that works, because of its being situated in such a form of social life in which the interests of its members are mutually shared.

Figure 1. Top-to-bottom form of communication"

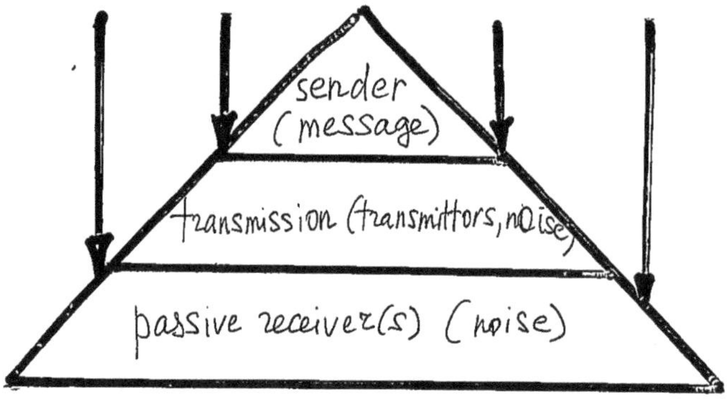

In the "ideal" democratic society, therefore, there is no room for barriers to free trade and the communication of experience. The digital communication model is one of the most progressive forms of communication. It corresponds to the ideal of a modern and mobile democratic society without artificial barriers. This model has a "rhizomatic" form of information transmission (Figure 2).

The digitization of the higher education system has become a trend. The use of digital technologies expands the possibilities for communication. The 21st century has given birth to a new generation whose childhood and youth have passed into the digital space. The American researcher Marc Prensky calls this generation born in 2000 *digital natives* (unlike today's teachers who remain, according to Prensky, *digital immigrants*) (Prensky, 2001). Between these two groups (digital natives and digital immigrants),

Figure 2. Rhizomatic communication model

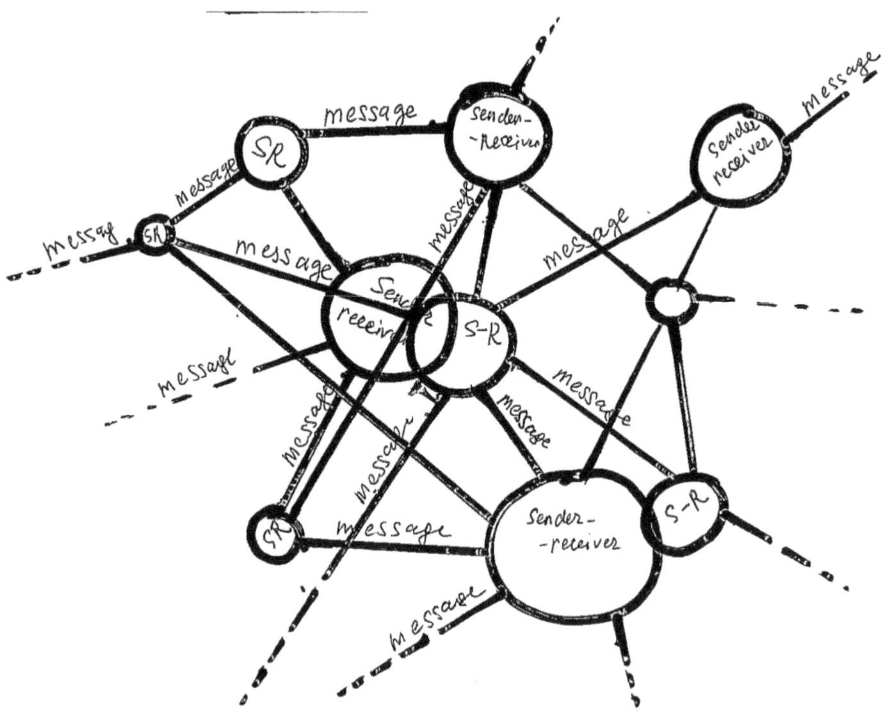

there is no common language of communication. Education in the new digital format is such that students often teach teachers how to obtain and process new information and how to critically select from information-gathering channels.

One of the main trends in modern higher education in the Republic of Kazakhstan is consistent with the objectives of the "University 4.0" concept. Responding to the challenges of the fourth industrial revolution, University 4.0 must integrate the digital ecosystem and a cyberphysical complex into a single world—a combination that simultaneously includes real academic work and research and their virtual counterparts. This model is being implemented in Kazakhstan, for example, by the Al Farabi Kazakh National University. The concept of "University 4.0" involves the use of cloud technologies; automation of the university's various activities; the introduction of intelligent technologies in campus infrastructure management; and the use of technologies Big Data to create an analytical base (Elizarov, 2000).

The main consequence of the introduction of digital communications into university life would be a change in the model of academic communication at all stages. There are two main types of academic communication: formal and non-formal communication. (This includes formal verbal and written; secondary primary and formal; direct non-formal; and non-direct communication). These two main types of communication (between at least two people) may involve vertical relationships (from a higher-level person to a subordinate). Or, it may involve horizontal relationships (at the "researcher to researcher," "teacher to student," or "department to department" level; etc.). This corresponds to the two aforementioned (pyramidal / rhizomatic) models of communication (Elizarov, 2000; Medvedeva, 2014).

The desired digital communication model that meets the requirements of the "University 4.0" concept can only reflect social and political trends. In this sense, "University 4.0" is both a consequence and a cause of certain socio-political attitudes, with its "hidden curriculum" of democratic education. Dewey affirms:

Society exists through a process of transmission quite as much as biological life [does]. This transmission occurs by means of communication of habits of doing, thinking, and feeling from the older to the younger. Without this communication of ideals, hopes, expectations, standards, [and] opinions, from those members of society who are passing out of the group life to those who are coming into it, social life could not survive.(…) Society not only continues to exist by transmission, by communication, but it may fairly be said to exist in transmission, in communication. (…) Not only is social life identical with communication, but all communication (and hence all genuine social life) is educative. (Dewey 1916, p. 4)

The powerful seek to form communication, but communicative action itself forms its own rationality. From this point of view, we can assume that changes in the public space (in the case of academic communication, in our study) are changing the social and political model of a country. This course of historical events gives hope that autocratic regimes, having become obsolete, are becoming a pure historical curiosity—and nothing more.

CONCLUSION, SOLUTIONS, AND RECOMMENDATIONS

The case of Kazakhstan could serve as a sample of historical processes in some countries in the post-Soviet space, particularly in Central Asia. An important aspect of modern socio-cultural development in this country is the transformation of the communication space. Widespread digitization has resulted in a number of changes in all areas of cultural and social life. The essence of modern academic communication is the ability to exchange information without restriction. "University 4.0" is a democratic model of the University, in which less space will remain for the negative costs associated with the education system (plagiarism; corruption; nepotism; etc.). "University 4.0" would serve as a means of building a modernized and democratic society, capable of being adequately represented on the world stage by the current and future specialists that the national education system is producing at this time. The major challenge of the years to come will be to produce tools designed to increase time for research and improve the conditions of producing collaborative knowledge. From a political, and even philosophical, point of view, the digital transition will be accomplished when digital science will produce more freedom in everything relating to knowledge.

Kazakhstan, which claims to have a kind of primacy among the countries of the Central Asian region, has acknowledged the field of education to be a significant national and international priority, being a one-party and unique-party national signatory to the Bologna Process. The *Astana Declaration of the Second Meeting of Ministers for Education of the Member States of the European Union and of the Central Asian Countries* (Astana, 2017) proclaims:

The participating Ministers and delegates reaffirmed their commitment to establish a strong, durable and stable relationship aiming at fostering a prosperous, sustainable and stable, socio-economic development of the Central Asia region in line with the global commitment to Sustainable Development Goals, in particular to "ensure inclusive and quality education for all and promote lifelong learning." (Astana, 2017, p. 1)

Along with taking leading roles in international cooperation in the fields of education and science with EU countries in the region, Kazakhstan is taking the most active part in international efforts to support Afghanistan. In particular, as part of the civil education program, Kazakhstan universities have enrolled about 1,000 Afghan students in the 2018–2019 academic school year (Shaukenova, 2018). Thus, it is necessary to state the important role that Kazakhstan plays in the Central Asian region in the development of international cooperation in order to preserve stability and ensure peace.

Strategic decisions on EU-Central Asia cooperation are focused on cooperation priorities such as security, the rule of law, good governance, human rights, youth and education, and the environment and energy. At the same time, the role of education in creating an open, knowledge-based society with a high level of employment is emphasized in all strategic documents of cooperation. The existing Central Asian Education Platform (CAPO)—a project funded by the European Commission—is a key element of the European Education Initiative for Central Asia. Thus, the main characteristics of the knowledge society are presented in the Central Asian region, which cannot avoid the process of adapting the education systems of Central Asian States to the needs of the globalized world.

As a region located with a specific geopolitical situation in the depths of the mainland, not only Kazakhstan, but the whole of Central Asia needs the development of communication technologies. An important aspect of modern socio-cultural development in this country is the transformation of the communication space. Widespread digitization has led to a number of changes in all areas of cultural and social life. Of course, the potential of this new digital space and its limits are not yet defined. For modern Kazakhstan, and for its national model of education, the correct approach to the complexity of digital communication and the place of the person in it is important.

We must not lose sight of the risks associated with the development of the digital communication environment. These risks are common to all areas of social life—including education and the scientific and academic environments. Such risks are highlighted by public space theorists. Warnings about concerns over the illusory involvement of others in the democratic and social life of an individual with unlimited access to information and concerns over his ability to lead a supposedly active social life by posting comments to potentially anonymous sources are all warnings which ought not to be overlooked.

The most important thing would be to make a constant effort of a theoretical reflection on the essence of the process, its consequences, and its possible risks. The essence of modern communication processes in general and academic communication, in particular, is the ability to exchange information without restriction. "University 4.0" is, from this point of view, a democratic model of the university. It is seen as being one in which less space will remain for the negative costs associated with the education system (plagiarism; corruption; nepotism; etc.) in Kazakhstan. "University 4.0" would serve as a means of building a modernized and democratic society—one capable of being adequately represented on the world stage by the present and future specialists that the national education system is currently producing.

In order to respond adequately to the ongoing processes in the field of education and science in Central Asian countries, it will be necessary not only to use sources of a geopolitical and purely technical and statistic character, but also to evaluate those geopolitical, technical, and statistic sources from an historically grounded and philosophically reflective perspective.

The research question of our study was whether, with the social and political transformations the nation has undergone, the country is experiencing the transformation of all institutions—not only in terms of their content (i.e. the particular, concrete discourse), but also as to their structure, and the model of communication accepted in it. In other words, we asked whether communication design is involved in the process of the practical implementation of the government programs of modern Kazakhstan's digitalization. The given answer is "yes"—communication design is possible, and it can and should be involved in facilitating the actual processes of academic communication, with the aim of forming a new digital university. And, even more, we would say that without changing the communicative model, there will be no 4.0 University in Kazakhstan, ever! But, observing this, it must be said that these communication practices are rooted in the past of the people—and it is by making a profound analysis of this historical past that the society could manage its present. Otherwise, in the face of modern technologies (with their capabilities of total control), we may become a society marked by even more repressive systems of control. It is not technology that makes society. It is human beings—with their history—who shape communicative practices.

Understanding communicative rationality involves changing one's perspective in understanding historical processes. The case of the Kazakh Enlightenment in the context of the call for increased modernization of contemporary Kazakhstan is one of the avenues to be explored in this case. The human sciences and the social sciences must work together to create not an ideological basis for fashionable slogans, but rather a consistent theory of communication based on a real and honest historical and philosophical theory.

REFERENCES

Aitmukhambetov, A. A. (2000). Public education and the formation of the Kazakh intelligentsia of North-West Kazakhstan in the second half of the 19th–early 20th centuries. Unpublished doctoral dissertation, Baitursynov Kostanay State University, Kostanay, Kazakhstan.

Astana. (2017, June 23). *Astana Declaration of the second meeting of ministers for education of the member states of the European Union and of the central Asian countries*. Retrieved from https://eeas.europa.eu/sites/eeas/files/01_astana_declaration_170623_final_en.pdf

Cameron, S. (2016). The Kazakh Famine of 1930–33: Current research and new directions. *East/West: Journal of Ukrainian Studies, 3*(2), 117–132. doi:10.21226/T2T59X

Deleuze, G., & Guattari, F. (1987). Rhizome (Introduction). In *A Thousand Plateaus* (pp. 7–13). Minneapolis, MN: University of Minnesota Press.

Derrida, J. (1963). Cogito et histoire de la folie. *Revue de Metaphysique et de Morale*, *4*, 460–494.

Dewey, J. (1916). *Democracy and education: An introduction to the philosophy of education*. New York: The Macmillan Company.

Digital Kazakhstan. (2017, December 12). Government of the Republic of Kazakhstan State Program. Retrieved from https://digitalkz.kz/en/human-level-development/

Drucker, P. F. (1969). *The age of discontinuity*. New York: Harper and Row.

Elizarov, V. (2000). The republic of scientists: The social space of an invisible community. In L. Kachanov (Ed.), *Space and time in modern sociological theory* (pp. 103–127). Moscow: IS RAS.

ENIC-Kazakhstan. (n.d.). Center for Bologna process and academic mobility. Retrieved from https://enic-kazakhstan.kz/ru/reference_information/universities

Fiche Curie Kazakhstan. (n.d.). French diplomacy. Retrieved from https://www.diplomatie.gouv.fr/IMG/pdf/KAZKHSTAN_Fihce_Curie_MARS_2015__cle06b53d.pdf

Foucault, M. (1984). Qu'est-ce que les lumières? In *Dits et Ecrits* (Vol. 4, pp. 562–578). Paris: Gallimard.

Foucault, M. (1991). Introduction (by Michel Foucault). In *G. Canguilhem (1991). The Normal and the Pathological* (pp. 7–25). New York: Zone Books.

Freire, P. (2007). *Pedagogy of the oppressed*. New York: Continuum.

Habermas, J. (1979, Spring). Consciousness – Raising or redemptive criticism – The contemporaneity of Walter Benjamin. *New German Critique, NGC, 17*, 56.

Habermas, J. (1981). *The theory of communicative action* (Vol. 1–2). New York: Beacon Press.

Habermas, J. (1987). *The philosophical discourse of modernity: Twelve lectures*. Cambridge, MA: MIT Press.

Kegan, R. (1994). *In over our heads: The mental demands of modern life*. Cambridge, MA: Harvard University Press.

Medeuova, K. (2019). Epistemological breaking and random anthropology. In L. Turarbekova et al. (Eds.), Materials of the second cycle of international scientific events—"The economic role of international educational projects in the global world"—within the framework of the project [regarding the] "Multidimensional study of the history, problems and prospects of the introduction of international educational projects in the Republic of Kazakhstan." Almaty: Ulagat.

Medvedeva, S. M. (2014). From scientific creativity to popularization: A theoretical model of scientific communication. *Bulletin of MGIMO-University*, *4*(37), 278–284.

Pain, E. A., & Volkogonova, O. D. (Eds.). (2008). Russian modernization: Reflecting on identity. Inst. Kennana. Moscow: Three Squares.

Prensky, M. (2001). Digital natives, digital immigrants. *On the Horizon*, *9*(5), 1–6. doi:10.1108/10748120110424816

Rorty, R. (1982). *Consequences of pragmatism: Essays, 1972–1980*. Minneapolis, MN: University of Minnesota Press.

Schumpeter, J. (1942). *Capitalism, socialism and democracy*. New York: Harper & Brothers.

Segizbayev, O. A. (1996). *Kazakh philosophy of the 15th–early 20th century*. Almaty: Gylym.

Shaukenova, Z. K. (2018). "Kazakhstan and Central Asian countries: Tomorrow will be lain today." Kazakhstan Institute for Strategic Studies, under the President of the Republic of Kazakhstan. Retrieved from http://www.kisi.kz/index.php/ru/publikatsii/25-shaukenova-zarema-kaukenovna/35-kazakhstan-i-strany-tsentralnoj-azii-zavtra-zakladyvaetsya-segodnya

Trubetskoy, N. S. (1920). *Europe and humanity*. Sofia: Russian-Bulgarian Book Publishing.

Trubetskoy, N. S. (1925). About the Turanian element in Russian culture. In P. N. Savitsky, P. P. Suvchinsky, & N. S. Trubetskoy (Eds.), *Eurasian Temporary* (pp. 351–377). Berlin.

Trubetskoy, N. S. (2000). *The legacy of Genghis Khan*. Moscow: Agraf. (Original work published 1926)

Trubetskoy, N. S. (2015). *A look at Russian history not from the West, but from the East*. Moscow: Direct Media.

Walikhanov, S. (1985). Judicial reform note. In S. Walikhanov (1985), Collected works in five volumes—Volume 4—Alma-Ata: The main edition of the Kazakh Soviet Encyclopedia (pp. 77–104). Academic PRess.

Walikhanov, S. (1835–1865). Collected writings.

Wikipedia. (2019). Rhizome. Retrieved from https://en.wikipedia.org/wiki/Rhizome

Wikipedia. (2019). The Soviet famine of 1932–33. Retrieved from https://en.wikipedia.org/wiki/Soviet_famine_of_1932%E2%80%9333

KEY TERMS AND DEFINITIONS

Auyl: A traditional village, a traditional encampment, a nomadic settlement in the past, and (now) the sedentary peoples of Central Asia (Kazakhs; Turkmens; etc.).

Alash: The name "*Alash*" was given to the movement within the Constitutional Democratic Party in Russia, in the early 20th century (until 1917); the *Alash* party (1917–1920) in Kazakhstan; and the Alash Autonomy (1917–1920) (a White-Army-controlled state located in the territory of present-day Kazakhstan).

Communicative Action: Habermas (*The Theory of Communicative Action*, 1981) defines communicative action as being an interaction between at least two individuals that is ordered according to those norms which are accepted as being mandatory norms. Habermas' communicative action is opposed to instrumental action. The area of instrumental action is one's sphere of work. Instrumental action has success as its primary goal. In turn, communicative action is aimed at achieving mutual understanding by coordinating the efforts of the participants by communication.

Communicative Rationality: In keeping with Habermas' difference between communicative and instrumental action, he distinguishes communicative rationality from instrumental rationality. The notion of instrumental rationality is borrowed, by Habermas, from Max Weber—who distinguished instrumental rationality from value rationality. Instrumental rationality is characterized by an emphasis on tools (instruments) to achieve set goals, but not on the rationality of the goals themselves. Unlike instrumental rationality, the consensus of actors is important for communicative rationality. Communication here is not a one-way presentation of information, but rather a way of interacting with people.

Golodomor (Holodomor): The Soviet famine of 1932–33 was a major famine that killed millions of people in the major grain-producing areas of the Soviet Union, including Ukraine, Northern Caucasus, Volga Region and Kazakhstan, the South Urals, and West Siberia. The Holodomor in Ukraine and Kazakh famine of 1932–33 have been seen as genocide committed by Joseph Stalin's government. It has been estimated that between 2, 3.3, and 3.9 million Kazakh people (40% of all Kazakhs) died in Kazakhstan. (Wikipedia, 2019).

Intelligentsia and Kazakh Intelligentsia: (Latin *intelligentia, intellegentia*—understanding, cognitive power, knowledge; from *intelligens, intellegens*—intelligent, knowledgeable, thinking, understanding). The word appeared in Russian language in the 1860s and was synonymous with the expressions "thinking man" and "thinking people." It refers to a social group which includes people who are professionally engaged in mental work and have the necessary special education for such work (engineers, technicians, doctors, teachers, lawyers, scientists, and the arts). The history of the Kazakh intelligentsia is tragic. Administrative reform carried out by the government of Tsarist Russia in Kazakhstan since the middle of the 19th century was accompanied by educational reform. This was due to the government's need for autochthons (people who could read and write in the Russian language and who could serve a kind of link between the local, mostly uneducated, population and the administrative leadership). This gradually formed, thin social layer of highly educated steppe intelligentsia was almost destroyed during repressions in the first decades of Soviet power in Kazakhstan. Further formation of the Kazakh intelligentsia is connected with the history of the formation of the Kazakh university.

Kazakh Enlightenment: Influenced by democratic Russian thought in the 19th century, the worldviews of prominent Kazakh educators such as Shoqan Walikhanov (1835–1865), Ybyrai (Ibrahim) Altynsarin (1841–1889), and Abai Kunanbayev (1845–1904) was formed. The Kazakh Enlightenment is inextricably linked to the history of Russian democratic thought.

Koulaks: Farmers who owned the land privately, during the policy of massive "collectivization" led by the Soviet power. The famine in Kazakhstan in the 1930s is part of a historical tragedy of several peoples together. The famine was caused by the common policy of the abolition of the *koulaks* and collectivization of lands and private proprieties.

Rhizome: In botany and dendrology, a rhizome (from Ancient Greek *rhízōma*—"mass of roots," from *rhizóō*—"cause to strike root") is a modified subterranean plant stem that sends out roots and shoots from its nodes (Wikipedia 2019). Deleuze and Guattari used this term to create the concept of rhizome as an architonic model that could describe specific states and/or the specific understanding of the different areas where this concept is applied (society; culture; thought; literature; politics; etc.). Deleuze and Guattari (1987), in *A Thousand Plateaus*, assert the difference between the rhizome and its opposite, the arborescent, which forms a model of domination and subordination like a tree with its root-pivot and its trunk.

Subject-Centered Rationality: Subject-centered rationality is a type of rationality related to subject-centered philosophy. From the Cartesian perspective, the subject is presented as a source of rationality, a 'philosopher sovereign' of his reason. It is a transcendent, autonomous and impersonal subject in search of absolute truth (the principle *a priori*). The philosophy of the twentieth century—especially postmodernist philosophy—criticizes this notion of the uncommitted and unstructured subject's not being involved in socio-historical processes. At the same time, it is the whole kind of rationality generated by the philosophy of the transcendent subject that is criticized.

Industry 4.0 and University 4.0: According to the objectives of the "Digital Kazakhstan" state program approved by the Government of the Republic of Kazakhstan No. 827 (December 12, 2017): Industry 4.0 is one of the drivers of digital transformation industry, is the concept of production, where additional value is provided by the integration of physical objects, processes and digital technologies, in which physical processes are monitored in real time, decentralized solutions are adopted, as well as the interaction of machines between themselves and people. (Digital Kazakhstan 2017)

Human-level development: The fourth most important dimension of Kazakhstan's digitization program, "Human-level development," proclaims: Evolution of the new competence and digital literacy of the population will become possible due to the innovations in education. (…) To create a digital society, it will be need to update the education system in accordance with the best world practices. Emphasis will be placed on the development of creative and critical thinking, as well as the use of modern educational technologies in the learning process. (ibid.)

Chapter 9
Regional University Partnership for Sustainable Development in the Age of Digital Technologies

Gainiya Tazhina
https://orcid.org/0000-0001-7500-5648
University of International Business, Kazakhstan

ABSTRACT

In the modern world, the sustainable development of higher education institutions is determined by their ability to integrate into the global digital knowledge. The study aimed to find out the needs of faculty in digital technologies for teaching and research. The study also aimed to find out the faculty's opinion about the building of Regional Universities' Partnership for Technical and Vocational Education and Training (TVET) in Information and Communication Technologies (ICT). The practical implementation of the study could be launching a regional universities' partnership and the development of a regional resource center, which will serve for internationalization, intercultural and interpersonal exchange, and provide long-term benefits to partner universities to improve their educational potential. Due to the uneven development of digital technologies in higher education, these conclusions apply to universities not only in Central Asia but throughout the Eurasian region.

INTRODUCTION

Modern education and higher education systems, both at the regional and international levels are developed in the context of integration into the global digital knowledge. Digital information technologies contribute to the efficiency and sustainability of all learning forms, enrich the educational process itself, and are an effective tool for moderation and coordination of the joint work of interested participants aimed at staffing and scientific support of education (Soghomonov, 2016; Sharonin, 2019; Desha & Hargroves, 2013; Jean-Francois, 2015; Springett, 2015; Schultz & Viczko, 2016).

Ongoing international cooperation in higher education is putting forward newest forms of the educational organization, such as network universities. The importance and best practices of this form of

DOI: 10.4018/978-1-7998-2551-7.ch009

higher education organization have already been studied and highlighted by several authors as a modern trend (Hagen, 2016; Belenov & Kirchanov, 2016). The authors point out that network universities provide more opportunities for high-grade education (Makoveeva, 2012; Selyanskaya, 2014), become effective in dealing with crisis trends (Endovitsky, 2015; Krasnova & Belous, 2016) faced by modern institutions of higher education.

Created and successfully operating network universities (or university networks) are not actually a traditional higher educational institution, but rather a form of educational programs, which provides special ways and strategies for its development and promotion. The central point in the definition of a network university is the multiplicity and heterogeneity of its participants, represented by individual classical universities or other specialized higher educational institutions.

University networks, as a rule, are several large and well-known universities, united by high standards of academic reputation and achievements in the field of various applied or fundamental research. University networks coordinate exchanges between students, but most of their efforts are focused on the development of basic research. Successful practices of university networks are UNIMED, the Mediterranean Universities Union that counts 124 Universities coming from 23 countries of both shores of Mediterranean (www.uni-med.net); The WUN, Worldwide Universities Network (WUN, 2019), that is a leading global higher education and research network made up of 23 universities, spanning 13 countries on six continents; Universitas 21, U21, a leading global network of research-intensive universities "that empowers its members to share excellence, collaborate across borders and nurture global knowledge exchange", focused on fostering global citizenship and encouraging institutional innovation (Teaching Practices Survey 2016: Compiled U21 Results, 2019).

At present two such large projects of network universities are being implemented in the Eurasian space - the University of Shanghai Cooperation Organization, SCO University, and Network University of the Commonwealth of Independent States (CIS). These universities primarily provide network educational services. University of Shanghai Cooperation Organization, SCO University operates as a network of existing universities in the member states of the SCO: Kazakhstan, China, Kyrgyzstan, Russia, Tajikistan, Uzbekistan (http://uni-sco.com). The Network University of the Commonwealth of Independent States (CIS) includes the universities of Russia, Belarus, Kazakhstan, Kyrgyzstan, Moldova, Tajikistan and Ukraine (http://ysu.am/international/en/1373369370).

The features of the SCO University project are bilingual education and teaching opportunities in the languages of the participating countries (http://uni-sco.com). The CIS Network University was created in 2010 and is an attempt to transfer the European experience of the Erasmus Mundus program to the development of higher education in the post-Soviet space. The goals of the CIS Network University were "to improve the quality and attractiveness of higher education, strengthen cooperation and inter-university relations in the CIS member states, organize and implement high-quality joint master's programs, strengthen international cooperation in training highly qualified specialists, facilitate exchange graduate students, and conduct joint research to prepare a dissertation" (http://ysu.am/international/en/1373369370).

The BRICS (Brazil, Russia, India, China, South Africa) Network University, BRICS NU, founded in the context of similar projects in 2016. This is the new network of the BRICS member countries' higher education institutions engaged in cooperation and joining the BRICS NU (https://we.hse.ru/en/brics). BRICS NU is an educational project aimed at developing, preferentially, bilateral/multilateral short-term joint training, master's and PhD programs along with joint research projects in various knowledge fields according to common standards and quality criteria, given the recognition of the learning outcomes by

BRICS NU participants as per national criteria. The group consists of two universities from Brazil, three from Russia, two from India, three from China and two from South Africa.

The newly created and already successfully operating network universities are one of the organizational forms in higher education, focusing on the provision of educational programs for different levels and knowledge areas. However, in the work of network universities, little attention is paid, or no attention is paid at all to the problems of network partnership for various fields' faculty vocational training/ retraining in the use of digital technologies in teaching. The issue of the short-term faculty training/ retraining programs' necessity is under-researched area and crucial for launching such projects. Faculty vocational training/retraining programs are a cornerstone of the universities' network implementation and partnership established between the universities.

The study aimed to find out the needs of faculty in digital technologies for teaching and research. Recent issues of the Networked Readiness Index (http://reports.weforum.org) have shown that countries in the Eurasian region, and Central Asian states (Kazakhstan, Kyrgyzstan, Uzbekistan, Tajikistan, Turkmenistan) are developing unevenly in digital universities' knowledge and technology. This research also aimed to study the prospects for developing partnerships between universities in the Central Asian space in the training /retraining of various specialties' faculty for the use of information technologies in their teaching. Thus, this study differed from the analogues already being implemented by its focus on the target audience of higher education teachers from different countries, represented by faculty with diverse experience in various disciplines who are interested in applying and expanding the application of digital technologies in their teaching and research, and correspondingly interested in evolving their ICT skills at partner universities.

LITERATURE REVIEW

In the modern world, the sustainable development of higher education institutions is determined by their ability to integrate into the global digital knowledge. In the light of the rapid transformation of digital technology in the 21st century, the need to develop the digital skills of the faculty is also sharply increasing. Recent issues of the Global Competitiveness Index and the Networked Readiness Index (http:// reports.weforum.org/) have shown that the Central Asian countries (https://express-k.kz) are developing unevenly in digital university knowledge and technology.

These Central Asian countries have a wide palette of cultural roots (https://caa-network.org/archives/9492; https://express-k.kz). Social, economic, political and other features of these countries have more a unifying rather than a disconnecting principle. The presence of a common regional identity, in fact, expresses the similarity of their national being and national spirit, the complementarity of cultures. This fact reflects cooperation in the field of science and education. The latest data and research in the field of international cultural relations and cultural diplomacy (British Council-Education Intelligence, 2013) showed the importance of cultural ties and forces that form the cultural relations of nations, their ability to achieve international goals through attraction and cooperation. The field report showed that there are a number of forces that shape a nation's cultural relations. Scholars depicted activity of four drivers from The Report such as the desire to create a good impression, cultural assets, language, and history (British Council -Education Intelligence, 2013).

Educational initiatives/exchanges are generally accepted to be one of the most powerful and long lasting influences on attitudes towards national culture. Therefore, investment in academic, research and teaching exchange is seen as a very important. Faculty choice of one training/retraining destination over another is greatly influenced by a nation's culture and the potential to experience other educational environments (Choudaha & Van Rest, 2018).

A study of the potential of Central Asian higher education institutions disclosed that the universities are developing unevenly in various aspects of educational activity, and in digital university knowledge and technology, in particular (https://caren.geant.org). The CAREN Central Asian Research and Education Network project, established in 2009, funded by the European Union (EU), considered the issue for building a network of high-performance Internet resources for research and educational communities in Central Asia (Tazhina, 2012). Several regional and cross-regional initiatives were launched, mainly with the involvement of Kazakhstan, Kyrgyzstan and Tajikistan. In July 2010, CAREN became operational, interlinking Kyrgyzstan, Tajikistan and Turkmenistan through their national research and education networks (NRENs). Kazakhstan joined in 2012, but Uzbekistan kept postponing the date. These projects included improving skills for sustainable development, promoting work-based learning and converting local Vocational education and training (VET) institutions into centers for lifelong learning. Although, from the outset, the Platform has been a means to facilitate interstate cooperation in an environment where not all actors are interested in regional formats. However, after evaluating the overall impact and progress of the Education Initiative, its actual added value remains questionable (Axyonova, 2013; Report: Overview of the Higher Education System Kazakhstan, 2017).

The 3rd project phase CAREN-3 was launched in June 2016, initially connecting Kyrgyzstan and Tajikistan where the governments have signed bilateral financing agreements with the European Commission (EC). The Kyrgyz and Tajik research and education communities have been connected to their peers in Europe and the rest of the world via links from Bishkek (Kyrgyzstan) and Dushanbe (Tajikistan) to the CAREN network hub in Frankfurt by high-speed Internet highway GÉANT (www.geant.org). Kazakhstan, Turkmenistan and Uzbekistan are also eligible to join the project subject to EC approval and similar government financing agreement. The success of this new phase mainly depends on the Uzbek government's willingness to cooperate and the ability of all participants to use the network in a meaningful way for innovative joint initiatives and (inter-) regional cooperation projects (https://caren.geant.org).

As emerging economies develop, greater emphasis is placed upon education, essentially higher education, as central to aiding progress and empowering further economic stability. The British Council describes great forces in societal development that will affect all areas of general human growth and progress in the years to come (British Council-Education Intelligence, 2013). These long-term driving forces, or Megatrends, have great importance now and certainly they will have great importance in the future. These conceptual strategies for the direction and growth of international higher education in the future apply to digital technology and the way it is expected to revolutionize teaching and learning.

University of Oxford Report (2018) has shown International Trends in Higher Education Technology is becoming central to the process of learning and teaching in higher education. As societies rapidly develop into knowledge-based information economies, information technology becomes a key driver of both economic competitiveness and social development. Fluency in information technology has thus become a central pillar of higher education, particularly for faculty in their teaching. Alongside classes taught wholly online, technology is also influencing traditional campus-based teaching and learning. Virtual learning environments, flipped classrooms and blended learning have all become an accepted part of the classroom lexicon over the past few years. All three offer new approaches to traditional campus-based teaching, with virtual learning environments such as Blackboard and Moodle primarily used for course administration, storage of course content and additional resources, while flipped classrooms have influenced pedagogical methodology by offering a way to blend online and class learning (http://global.oup.com/uk/orc/learnvle/; Horizon Report: Higher Education Edition, 2014).

The research (British Council-Education Intelligence, 2013) has shown that whilst digital technology and the opportunity for progress and access it is not doubted the experiential values of international education remain at the heart of individuals' aspirations to learn and grow. Technology is a tool as important as people/professionals/academicians/faculty make it.

What does the university faculty think about the application of information technologies to their teaching? What are the faculty needs for training or retraining in ICT? Because today's digital technologies affect the quality of higher education and play a predominant role in improving learning outcomes.

Assessment of the training needs for university teaching staff from public and private sectors revealed that university teachers need the training, including areas of professional competencies and trends, global innovations in teaching strategies, learning theories and supervision (Khan & Sarwar, 2011). Hamadneh (2015) found that faculty members' the most prominent training need of technological skills is the "Use virtual labs", while the "Analyze quantitative and qualitative data using statistical programs" was the most prominent training need of research skills. Abouelenein and Mohamed (2016) discovered the need for university faculty to be trained in surveying the Internet, designing educational websites, concurrent communication search engines, producing interactive multimedia, Photoshop, mastery learning, distance learning, communication technology, hypertext, virtual classes. A wide variety of lecturers, academic staff at Sofia University was surveyed in order to identify their skills, competencies, and needs in the field of e-learning (http://e-center.uni-sofia.bg). It showed that the technologies used at a very superficial level; e-learning exists only within the traditional teaching and learning process and is regarded as supplementary with a relatively small role. The use of the full potential of the digital technologies to change the learning and teaching is far from the desired level. Scholars concluded that this makes it imperative to design courses for training the academic staff in the field of using ICT in education context.

Several studies (Robert, 2014; Watty, McKay & Ngo, 2016; Vezirov, 2017) determine that one of the important tasks of the professionalism of the faculty is informational competence, as a component of their professional competence. For instance, Schlitz et al. (2009) illustrated the need for development of web-based assessment skills for faculty members through the process of adopting new technology. The implementation of a web-based rubric software in a faculty learning community enhanced student performance, augmented instructor evaluation of student performance, and facilitated outcomes.

The proficient level in the use of ICT helps the faculty in solving educational tasks, in vocational retraining and advanced training of personnel, and allows continuous self-improvement, technology's rapid acquisition, information processing, and its practical application (Tonkonog, 2017). At the same time, in the digital age, the requirements for the ICT competencies of faculty are constantly increasing (Salim, Mahmood & Ahmad, 2018; Sergeieva, 2018). The popular Internet-based technologies are social networking sites (SNS), attracted a great deal of scholarly attention and used as an educational tool for fast and effective communication in recent years (Akçayır, 2017). Competencies such as e-learning, the widespread use of massive open online courses, and virtual learning environments act as the needs of modern university faculty. That is why, one of the directions in the development of higher education in the field of information technology is founding of regional centers for vocational training and advanced retraining centers for faculty (Borshcheva, 2015) in different teaching fields and areas of knowledge.

It is suggested that ongoing professional development must be provided for faculty to model the new pedagogies and tools for learning with the aim of enhancing the teaching-learning process. However, it is important for teaching staff trainers and policy makers to understand the factors affecting the effectiveness of different approaches to ICT used in vocational retraining so education strategies can be appropriately explored to make such changes viable to all. ICT is seen as an important instrument to support new ways of teaching and learning. It should be used to develop student's skills for cooperation, communication, problem solving and lifelong learning (Agbo, 2015).

Glotova et al. (2015) suggested that personalization of training is needed for continuing education and training of a specialist. These researchers have developed components of a network information system to build and implement individual learning paths. The basics for these are the approaches to synchronizing the life cycles of a professional, educational programs and digital technology resources.

ICT resources, or technocratic, or expert-oriented indicators, belong to the group of criteria for a sustainable university. With all the multitude and variety of sustainability indicators of higher education institutions, operational and educational activities are recognized as vital important prerequisite to achieve sustainable competitive advantage in higher education (Fischer et al., 2015; Al Shobaki & Naser, 2017). As Springett (2015) emphasizes, the paradigm of higher education for sustainable development is transforming into the new paradigm of sustainable higher education, which is accompanied by the participation of universities in world university networks. Openness to the international and participation in the global education, orientation to global markets promise universities promising benefits. On the other hand, the universities themselves, which have chosen a sustainable development strategy in their activities, are more likely to face the local problems and interests (Soghomonov, 2016). Educational resources created in the regional network of universities' interactions allow the faculty to learn new qualifications in lifelong learning that meet the requirements of modern, sustainable higher education (Borshcheva, 2015), while the benefits of rich multimedia ICTs include the provision of opportunities for learners in social, economic, and environmental dimensions of sustainable development. (Caird & Roy, 2019)

New trends require partnership and concerted action at the national, regional and international levels to ensure the quality and sustainability of higher education systems. Assumed the need to increase funding for information technologies, research and higher education development in many countries, including the Central Asian states, universities should seek new ways to expand innovative information technologies through multilateral university partnerships.

SIGNIFICANCE OF THE STUDY

The study broadens the existing knowledge about regional universities' partnership in organization of ICT training courses for the educators in order to sustainably develop higher education institutions. Firstly, regional partnership amongst Central Asian universities is formed to integrate their digital resources. Although there are studies about the activities of the several universities' networks (Jean-Francois, 2015; BRICS Network University, 2019; Selyanskaya, 2014; Krasnova & Belous, 2016; Makoveeva, 2012), as well as the analyses of the criteria for sustainable development of universities (Teaching Practices Survey 2016: Compiled U21 Results, 2019; Fischer, Jenssen, & Tappeser, 2015; Caird & Roy, 2019), the previous researches (Hagen, 2016; Belenov & Kirchanov, 2016; Shanghai Cooperation Organization (SCO) University, 2019; Network University of the CIS, 2019) have provided little evidence on inclusion of Central Asian universities into the regional networks, analysis of their sustainable development and their participation in partnerships on upskilling higher education faculty. The uniqueness of the need for a regional partnership of universities is crystallized by the fact that in the social, economic, political and other features of these countries there is a unifying, common regional identity (https://caa-network.org/

archives/9492; https://express-k.kz). This fact is important in educational initiatives. The latter is widely recognized as the most powerful in influencing the attitudes (British Council-Education Intelligence, 2013). Project CAREN3 could have covered this problem to a certain extent, however, Uzbekistan, Turkmenistan and Kazakhstan have not been added to the network yet.

Secondly, in order to organize trainings and re-qualification courses in ICT for the university faculty in the Central Asia it is required to collect preliminary factual data on the needs of educators themselves. This initial stage of the study on the needs of training programs is based on researches of Borshcheva (2015), Vezirov (2017), Robert (2014), Khan and Sarwar (2011), Abouelenein & Mohamed (2016). This research deepens the existing knowledge about needs of university faculty in Central Asia in forming new skills for utilization of rich resources that digital technologies offer to the higher education sector and processes (https://caa-network.org/archives/9492; https://express-k.kz; https://caren.geant.org). In the current digital age professional duties of university faculty should include continuous upskilling in the application of information technologies to their respective fields of education and research. This, in turn, implies the development of their digital literacy and competency. Thus, the process of digitization of higher education depends considerably on each teacher's level of ICT competency, as true digitization will be possible only when each discipline and scientific findings are performed by a fully trained specialist in the application of information technologies in their field (Schlitz, 2009; John, 2015). Consequently, the actuality of training and requalification of educators from various backgrounds in usages of ICT in their professional activities is evident (Report: Overview of the Higher Education System of Kazakhstan, 2017). Literature review has shown that development stages of the given issue in different countries are unequal and uneven (http://reports.weforum.org). The knowledge of needs in ICT training programs is fragmented and has varied levels of intelligence on the path to sustainable development of higher education institutions. Therefore, by studying various perspectives of the faculty on needed types of ICT, this empirical research broadens current understanding of the needs of educators in Central Asia in ICT training programs and qualification courses.

In this study we assume that this type of universities' partnership provides more perspectives of the academic community and allows to develop a new way to urge higher education institutions to form network partnerships by utilizing information technology resources in order to upskill and raise competencies of their educators. Such approach is justified by the fact that currently higher level of digital literacy/competency is required for university faculty, who work with large amounts of data. Additional training and requalification of teaching staff in mastery of innovative information technologies in higher education will provide more benefits, when regional university partnerships bring teachers of the same discipline together for sharing and exchanging knowledge.

This research represents a step forward in studying and identifying the considerable factors of regional universities' partnership in organization of ICT training/retraining courses for the faculty in order to sustainably develop higher education institutions. The approach taken in this study is not blocked and not in any way a lineal one. The researchers from other universities in Central Asia or Eurasian region, who work on similar problems, can also use instruments of this study.

THEORETICAL BACKGROUND

In modern times of digital technologies and knowledge societies, continuous learning throughout one's life is becoming more significant (Merriam, Caffarella, & Baumgartner, 2006; Jarvis, 2007; Illeris,

2015; Baporikar, 2016; Gouthro, 2017; Chen & Liu, 2019). People must study throughout their whole lives in order to adapt to the changing nature of digital age (Fischer, 2000; Aspin & Chapman, 2001). In this context the competency levels of today's professional have become a widely discussed issue. There are numerous documents that have been published by world organizations (Latchem, 2017; University of Oxford. International Trends in Higher Education, 2018; Report: Overview of the Higher Education System Kazakhstan, 2017). These list key competencies of the 21st century, which must be developed through learning and technical and vocational education and training (Blaschke & Hase, 2015; Juvova, 2015; Volles, 2014; Parker & Tazhina, 2012).

Although, Connectivism Learning Theory has been proposed as basis for learning in digital age, it is not fully understood to what extent these are based on the learning theory and whether it truly reinforces learning (Steffens, 2015; Goldie, 2016). Hence, for our research model a classical theory of lifelong learning (LLL) and TVET (Merriam, Caffarella, & Baumgartner, 2006; Jarvis, 2007; Illeris, 2015) were chosen, as these can describe and explain learning better. These occurrences will be presented and discussed from the perspective of their actuality in lifelong learning as essential part of the professionalism of higher education faculty.

Sustainable development of higher education for everyone cannot be achieved without rapid expansion of high quality technical and vocational education and training (TVET). Today this issue is causing a big resonance. The TVET UNESCO strategy recommends an inclusive and holistic approach to management and delivery of TVET (Latchem, 2017). They carry the idea of not limiting TVET systems to simply teaching the skills required for an individual's job but allowing them to renew and adapt their skillset in rapidly changing work environment. In other words, professional training should cover the idea of sustainability. The notion of sustainability in this paper is used to describe TVET, which in turn, is renewable and adaptive to changing work requirements, and contributes to sustainable economic development of the society. While concepts of sustainable development and inclusive professional training are becoming more widely recognised in world-wide TVET community, the solutions for its realisation must be determined (Latchem, 2017). In case where TVET learners are university teachers these objectives gain a particular actuality and importance.

According to Schaffer and Richardson (2004), when information technologies are introduced to programs of faculty's requalification, an emphasis is often made on teaching the technology instead of teaching with through technology. The educators should have the opportunity to practise the application of technology during their training and requalification courses. This way they will be able to recognise how technologies can be used to boost their teaching activities/courses. They will have positive attitude towards ICT and will see it as useful instrument, that can integrate itself with their ongoing activities, is easy to use and can demonstrate noticeable results (Baylor & Ritchie, 2002). In addition, faculty will be more inclined to utilise ICT in their courses, when during professional training and requalification they given an opportunity to practice the new technology and to learn in collaborative environment with colleagues from other universities/countries (Schaffer & Richardson, 2004).

ICT allows for new innovative possibilities to be employed in professional education and learning (TVET). Digital technologies have revolutionised numerous organisations, created new jobs while replacing others. For employees this implies the need for reskilling in order to prosper in high tech work environment. For educators this entails integration of ICT not only with course materials and skills development, but with course delivery as well. Technologies allow to easily deliver TVET to wider audiences (Hyland, 2007; Jarvis, 2007; Baporikar, 2016; Chen & Liu, 2019; Blaschke & Hase, 2015; Volles, 2014; Latchem, 2017).

Therefore, having the power to alter the curriculum and to control learning and education processes, it is in the interest of faculty to be competent in application of ICT in their teaching and research activities, in order to train and prepare young professionals for the knowledge society and to be competent professional members of knowledge society themselves (Agbo, 2015).

Rapid development of information technologies challenges higher education providers to broaden their practices of continuous changes and anticipative lifelong learning and education, to utilise new technological advances, improvement of teaching methodologies. All these develop and complement continuous learning theory and TVET. Worldwide experience in organisation of learning and science at university level has also shown that sudden increase in applications of innovative technological potential of universities in both industries and regions is possible through formation of universities networks. In modern conditions in regional university partnerships a need arose for new models of educator's professionalism to be created, studied and realised. Such models of training and certification of educators is of similar nature to those of students. Introduction of ICT applications to higher education institutions of regional network TVET for higher education faculty is not only one of the means of universities sustainable development in the modern digital age, but also a contribution to continuous learning theory and TVET.

THE AIM AND METHODOLOGY OF THE STUDY

This study is aimed to determine the needs and priorities of university faculty in application of information technologies in education and science. Additionally, the research is purposed to discover through views of educators themselves about Regional Universities' Partnership formation for upskilling university faculty in applications of ICT.

The context of this research is represented by the fact countries of Central Asia: Kazakhstan, Kyrgyzstan, Uzbekistan, Tajikistan and Turkmenistan can be characterised by common regional self-identity, similarities in national day-to-day life and spirit, and complementary cultures (https://caa-network.org/archives/9492; https://express-k.kz). This fact is reinforced by cooperation in the areas of science and education. Studying the potentials of higher education institutions of Central Asian regions has demonstrated that universities in these countries are developing unevenly in various aspects of educational activities, particularly, in terms of digital technologies and knowledge (https://caren.geant.org). The purpose of Central Asian Research and Education Network (CAREN), which was founded in 2009 and financed by EU, was to form the networks of high-performance internet resources for the research and education communities across Central Asia (Tazhina, 2012). Several regional and cross-regional initiatives were launched, mainly with the involvement of Kazakhstan, Kyrgyzstan and Tajikistan. However, after evaluating the overall impact and progress of the Education Initiative, its actual added value remains questionable (Axyonova, 2013; Report: Overview of the Higher Education System Kazakhstan, 2017). The 3rd project phase CAREN-3 was launched in June 2016, initially connecting Kyrgyzstan and Tajikistan where the governments have signed bilateral financing agreements with the EC. Kazakhstan, Turkmenistan and Uzbekistan are also eligible to join the project subject to EC approval and similar government financing agreement. The success of this new phase mainly depends on the ability of all participants to use the network in a meaningful way for innovative joint initiatives and (inter-) regional cooperation projects (https://caren.geant.org). Holistically these reasons serve as a basis for the selection of universities in Central Asia in this study.

As the instrument for this study a questionnaire was created to measure four main research constructs: universities' faculty training needs in improving their ICT skills for teaching and research; universities' faculty interest in building the Regional Universities' Partnership of TVET in ICT; whether Regional Universities' Partnership is the criteria of universities' sustainable development; views of the educators on disseminating TVET in ICT at partner universities of Central Asia. The elements of the toolkit were based on respective confirmed measures from previous research (Borshcheva, 2015; Khan & Sarwar, 2011; Abouelenein & Mohamed, 2016; John, 2015; Hamadneh, 2015; Krasnova & Belous, 2016; Makoveeva, 2012; Teaching Practices Survey 2016: Compiled U21 Results, 2019; Hagen, 2016; Fischer, Jenssen, & Tappeser, 2015; Caird & Roy, 2019, Belenov & Kirchanov, 2016; Agbo, 2015; Blaschke & Hase, 2015; Hyland, 2007; Latchem, 2017).

The questionnaire consisted of 14 points. Six aspects were concerned with universities' faculty training needs in improving their ICT skills for teaching and research (Borshcheva, 2015; Vezirov, 2017; Khan & Sarwar, 2011; Abouelenein & Mohamed, 2016; John, 2015; Hamadneh, 2015). Next three measured universities' faculty interest in building the Regional Universities' Partnership of TVET in ICT (Krasnova & Belous, 2016; Makoveeva, 2012; Teaching Practices Survey 2016: Compiled U21 Results, 2019; Hagen, 2016). Other two elements evaluated whether Regional Universities' Partnership of TVET in ICT can be considered as the criteria for universities' sustainable development (Fischer, Jenssen, & Tappeser, 2015; Caird & Roy, 2019; Hagen, 2016; Belenov & Kirchanov, 2016). And final three assessed views of the educators on disseminating TVET in ICT at partner universities of Central Asia (Agbo, 2015; Blaschke & Hase, 2015; Hyland, 2007; Latchem, 2017).

All variables in this study based on Likert's 5-point scale with 1 being "fully agree" and 5 being "fully disagree". The first section of the questionnaire was comprised of four research variables mentioned above. The second section included demographic data of the respondents.

Quantitative approach was used as the control mechanism of the research aim. Data collection procedure based upon the quasi-experimental design was used to investigate the problem of the study, since the logic of the experimental approach in the natural group was preserved. In this study, the reverse translation method was used to adapt the elements of the scale for respondents, universities' faculty from Central Asia. An English linguistics expert has translated the English versions of the scale's elements to Russian, which is the language of international communication in this region. Next, a different expert has translated the questionnaire's Russian version to English. Two English versions were then compared, and adequate respective questions' translations were found. Before commencing a field research, a trial pilot study of 14 points was undertaken. The results have proven that all parts of the questionnaire were clear and well understood

A letter/email requesting participation in the research was sent out to social and professional contacts in Central Asia universities. This study has employed a purposeful methodology of data sample selection from the pool of responses of educators of all specialties from both state and private universities.

Overall, 326 university educators from Kazakhstan, Kyrgyzstan and Tajikistan took part in the survey. Unfortunately, faculty members of the universities in Uzbekistan and Turkmenistan did not participate. 290 valid responses were processed in this study, this comprises 89% of all responses.

LIMITATIONS OF THE STUDY

1. The study was limited to a sample of faculty members from Kazakhstan, Kirgiz Republic and Tajikistan universities, during the second semester of the academic year 2018-2019.
2. Citing and referencing prior research studies showed that despite the existence of the analysis of network universities' activities, the previous research has provided limited knowledge of the inclusion of universities in Central Asia in regional networks, the analysis of their sustainable development and their partnerships in upskilling the higher education faculty members.
3. The number of questions covered in the questionnaire is also a limiting factor. It was surmised that more questions could bring out a negative attitude from educators, whose spring semester schedule was tightly packed with their teaching load.

RESULTS AND ANALYSES

Table 1 comprises the demographic information of respondents. In the studied selection 32 respondents (11%) were university faculty aged below 29 years. The age of 78 participants (27%) varied between 30 and 39 years; age of 58 respondents (20%) was between 40 and 49 years; 87 educators (30%) in the selection belonged to 50-59 years age group; and final 35 (12%) were aged above 60 years.

116 (40%) of respondents out of 290 were males and 174 (60%) – females. In terms of higher education degrees, 12 participants (4%) had a bachelor's degree, 75 (26%) had a master's degree, 148 (51%)

Table 1. Demographic information of respondents.

Variable	Number of the respondents	Frequency	Variable	Number of the respondents	Frequency
Age			Gender		
£ 29	32	11	Male	116	40
30-39	78	27	Female	174	60
40-49	58	20	Total	290	100
50-59	87	30			
³ 60	35	12	Country		
Total	290	100	Kazakhstan	137	47
			Kyrgyziya	84	29
			Tajikistan	69	24
Educational level			Total	290	100
Bachelor	12	4			
Master	75	26	Type of university		
PhD/ Candidate/ Doctor of Science	148	51	State/National	183	65
Higher Education Diploma holder	55	19	Private	107	35
Total	290	100	Total	290	100

were PhD or Candidate/Doctor of Science, and 55 (19%) had the specialist's qualification with a higher education diploma.

A greater ratio of the respondents, namely 183 (65%), were State/National universities faculty members, while 107 of them (35%) were from private universities. About half of the participants, 137 (47%) were from Kazakhstani universities, 84 (29%) – Kyrgyzstan universities, and 69 (24%) – universities in Tajikistan.

Preliminary results analysis was carried out to verify the validity and credibility of the research procedure. A descriptive statistics and matrix of correlation of variables were calculated.

Cronbach's alpha was used to verify the consistency of questionnaire's elements. Table 2 demonstrates the results of the average, standard deviations and alpha coefficient, while table 3 lists the correlations. The alpha-value for all factors was higher than commonly used level of 0.70. These results signify the credibility of the research scales.

The correlation results in table 3 have a positive correlation on a significant level (0.01 and 0.05) for the majority of scales.

A factorial analysis was carried out. It did not suggest a prior separation of variables into dependent and independent, as all issues covered by this study were considered by us as equal. In this study the factorial analysis is exploited for the analysis of the measured variable in order to structure them.

As a result of using the Kaiser-Meyer-Olkin Measure of Sampling Adequacy criterion (Table 4), an acceptable adequacy of the applicability of factor analysis to the values of this sample was established (criterion value = 0.724).

Through utilization of Bartlett's Test of Sphericity (table 4) it was established that the dataset was acceptable for carrying out the factorial analysis with them (p £ 0,001).

Through Kaiser's criteria, it is established that values of the first four factors (table 5) were above one (1 - 3,626; 2 - 1,570; 3 - 1,315; 4 - 1,211). This signifies that emphasising these four factors is optimal.

Based on R. Kettler's screening criteria, the scree plot (figure 1) illustrates that inflection point occurs on the value of four, i.e. the slope of the curve is clearly leveling off on the value of four. This confirms the earlier conclusion of emphasizing four factors in the structure.

The correlation matrix of 14 variables was analyzed by the Principal Component Analysis method. Four factors with values above one were extracted. These factors were then evaluated using Varimax rotation (table 6).

Table 2. Descriptive statistics

Question	Mean	Std. Deviation	N	Question	Mean	Std. Deviation	N	Case processing summary		
Q1	2,06	,882	290	Q8	2,14	,970	290	Cases	N	%
Q2	2,21	1,067	290	Q9	2,63	1,140	290	Valid	288	99,3
Q3	2,06	1,044	290	Q10	1,57	,879	290	Excluded[a]	2	,7
Q4	2,03	1,039	288	Q11	2,57	,917	290	Total	290	100,0
Q5	1,93	,931	290	Q12	2,88	,983	290			
Q6	1,73	,809	290	Q13	2,26	,925	290	Reliability Statistics		
Q7	2,22	,930	290	Q14	3,52	1,104	290	Cronbach's Alpha		,714

a. Listwise deletion based on all variables in the procedure

Table 3. Correlations (N=290)

		Q1	Q2	Q3	Q4	Q5	Q6	Q7	Q8	Q9	Q10	Q11	Q12	Q13	Q14
Q1	Pearson Correlation	1													
Q2	Pearson Correlation	,207**	1												
Q3	Pearson Correlation	,297**	,375**	1											
Q4	Pearson Correlation	,339**	,201**	,441**	1										
Q5	Pearson Correlation	,342**	,099	,274**	,354**	1									
Q6	Pearson Correlation	,285**	,067	,304**	,260**	,324**	1								
Q7	Pearson Correlation	,135*	,169**	,230**	,201**	,233**	,374**	1							
Q8	Pearson Correlation	,264**	-,017	,081	,195**	,241**	,385**	,325**	1						
Q9	Pearson Correlation	,078	,088	,372**	,200**	,145*	,176**	,261**	,330**	1					
Q10	Pearson Correlation	,142*	,048	,381**	,451**	,420**	,439**	,296**	,301**	,370**	1				
Q11	Pearson Correlation	,324**	,131*	,184**	,111	,224**	,159**	,032	,219**	,056	,126*	1			
Q12	Pearson Correlation	,160**	,012	-,074	-,030	,096	,080	,128*	,142*	,131*	-,015	,139*	1		
Q13	Pearson Correlation	,014	,120*	,086	,187**	,173**	,157**	,272**	,244**	,156**	,052	,050	,324**	1	
Q14	Pearson Correlation	-,026	-,054	-,211**	-,137*	-,126*	-,338**	-,073	-,071	,029	-,214**	-,061	,111	,099	1

**. Correlation is significant at the 0.01 level (2-tailed).
*. Correlation is significant at the 0.05 level (2-tailed).

The first factor can be interpreted as "faculty training needs in improving their ICT skills for teaching and research", as the variables concerned with this aspect had the highest load levels (Q10=, 735; Q6=, 727; Q8=, 615; Q7=, 544; Q5=, 466; Q9=, 458).

The second one can be construed as "faculty interest in building the Regional Universities' Partnership on TVET in ICT", as its variables had the following high load levels: Q3=, 758; Q2=, 743; Q4=, 550.

The third can conditionally be interpreted as "Regional Universities' Partnership on TVET in ICT as the criteria of universities' sustainable development", as variables that revolved around this property had the highest load levels of Q11=, 742; Q1=, 731.

Table 4. KMO and Bartlett's test

Kaiser-Meyer-Olkin Measure of Sampling Adequacy		,724
Bartlett's Test of Sphericity	Approx. Chi-Square	860,421
	df	91
	Sig.	,000

Table 5. Total variance explained

Component	Initial Eigenvalues			Extraction Sums of Squared Loadings			Rotation Sums of Squared Loadings		
	Total	% of Variance	Cumulative %	Total	% of Variance	Cumulative %	Total	% of Variance	Cumulative %
1	3,626	25,898	25,898	3,626	25,898	25,898	2,701	19,295	19,295
2	1,570	11,215	37,113	1,570	11,215	37,113	1,816	12,974	32,269
3	1,315	9,396	46,509	1,315	9,396	46,509	1,606	11,468	43,737
4	1,211	8,649	55,159	1,211	8,649	55,159	1,599	11,421	55,159
5	,994	7,099	62,258						
6	,891	6,362	68,620						
7	,778	5,558	74,178						
8	,704	5,029	79,207						
9	,667	4,764	83,971						
10	,557	3,980	87,950						
11	,524	3,746	91,696						
12	,499	3,563	95,260						
13	,339	2,423	97,683						
14	,324	2,317	100,000						

Extraction Method: Principal Component Analysis

The fourth factor "dissemination of TVET in ICT at Central Asia partner universities" as the variables concerned with this reason had the highest load levels (Q13=, 702; Q12=,667; Q14=, 529).

The factors, which were determined as the result of Varimax rotation, can explain 55.2% of general dispersion (table 6). This includes "faculty training needs in improving their ICT skills for teaching and research" factor, which explains 25.9% of general dispersion; "faculty interest in building the Regional

Figure 1. The scree plot.

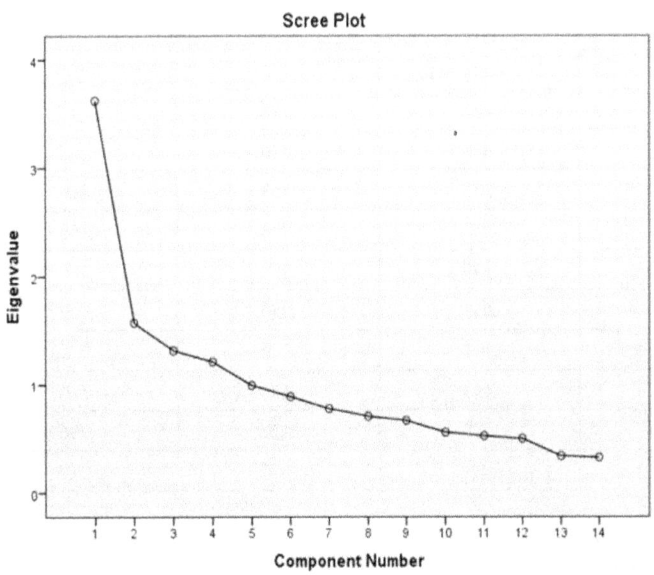

Universities' Partnership of TVET in ICT" factor explaining 11.2% of general dispersion; "Regional Universities' Partnership on TVET in ICT as the criteria of universities' sustainable development" factor that explains 9.4% of general dispersion; and "dissemination of TVET in ICT at Central Asia partner universities" factor explaining 8.6% of general dispersion.

This empirical study promotes further work on literature resources on sustainable development of higher education institutions through development and testing of the hypothesis on forming network universities partnerships in Central Asia in order to raise ICT competency levels among the faculty members. This research is the initial attempt to apply factorial analysis to views and perspectives of educators from various universities and countries with a common cultural background.

DISCUSSION AND CONCLUSION

The purpose of this research was to resolve the following issues: to determine universities' faculty training needs in improving their ICT skills for teaching and research; to define universities' faculty interest in building the Regional Universities' Partnership of TVET in ICT; whether the Regional Universities' Partnership of TVET in ICT can be considered as criteria for universities' sustainable development; whether the educators are open to and support the process of disseminating TVET in ICT at partner universities of Central Asia.

Via means of factorial analysis, it was possible to reduce and classify the variables, i.e. define the structures of interaction between the variables in the context of forming network universities' partner-

Table 6. Rotated component matrix[a]

Question	Component			
	1	2	3	4
Q10	,735	,259	,012	-,109
Q6	,727	,016	,255	-,053
Q8	,615	-,148	,238	,320
Q7	,544	,195	-,079	,350
Q5	,466	,198	,418	,038
Q9	,458	,330	-,221	,337
Q3	,320	,758	,109	-,101
Q2	-,157	,743	,163	,105
Q4	,399	,550	,180	-,030
Q11	,057	,050	,742	,043
Q1	,141	,270	,731	,057
Q13	,193	,108	-,007	,702
Q12	,027	-,156	,296	,667
Q14	-,427	,005	-,103	,529

Extraction Method: Principal Component Analysis.
Rotation Method: Varimax with Kaiser Normalization[a].
a. Rotation converged in 8 iterations.

ship in Central Asia. The collected data provides a deeper understanding about educators' perspectives on universities partnerships and professional trainings in ICT. The results of this research indicate that university faculty in Central Asia are interested in raising their ICT competences and building universities' partnership in Central Asia, view network partnerships as one of the criteria for higher education's sustainable development; and are assured in the need for dissemination of TVET in ICT throughout all partner universities in Central Asia. This is in agreement with the deductions of Borshcheva (2015), Abouelenein & Mohamed (2016) и Hamadneh (2015) about universities' faculty training needs in improving their ICT skills for teaching and research. It is worth noting that the supposed universities' faculty interest in building the Regional Universities' Partnership of TVET in ICT is confirmed in the works of Krasnova & Belous (2016), Hagen (2016) and the results of The Teaching Practices Survey 2016: Compiled U21 Results (2019). The results of this empirical study demonstrate that higher education teachers in Central Asia believe in considering the universities partnerships in expanding ICT as criteria for their sustainable development, what in turn, is also supported in data samples derived by Fischer, Jenssen,& Tappeser (2015) Caird & Roy (2019), Hagen (2016), and Belenov & Kirchanov (2016). These authors have also discovered that another criteria for universities' sustainable development is expanded and developed the application of ICT advances in the respective fields of higher education. According to Agbo (2015), Blaschke & Hase (2015) and Latchem (2017), using ICTs and Blended Learning in Transforming TVET is a success factor in the dissemination of ICT competencies among university faculty members; this affirms an important component on disseminating TVET in ICT at partner universities of Central Asia uncovered as part of this research.

The identified factors can serve as the argument in support of regional universities' partnership in Central Asia as means of their sustainable development in the modern age of digital technologies. First of all, universities in Central Asia should integrate their digital resources. This study takes into consideration the existing analysis of the activities of various network universities (Jean-Francois, 2015; BRICS Network University, 2019; Selyanskaya, 2014; Makoveeva, 2012), and the analysis of criteria of universities' sustainable development (Teaching Practices Survey 2016: Compiled U21 Results, 2019; Fischer, Jenssen, & Tappeser, 2015; Caird & Roy, 2019). The results of this paper complement prior research on inclusion of Central Asia universities into regional networks, the analysis of their sustainable development and their participation in partnerships on upskilling the higher education faculty (https://caren.geant.org; Hagen, 2016; Belenov & Kirchanov, 2016; SCO University, 2019; Network University of the CIS, 2019). The uniqueness of the need for a regional partnership of universities is crystallized by the fact that in the social, economic, political and other features of these countries there is a unifying, common regional identity (https://caa-network.org/archives/9492; https://express-k.kz). This is an important factor in education initiatives (British Council -Education Intelligence, 2013).

The results of this research deepen our knowledge about faculty needs in Central Asia in raising their competences in exploiting the vast capabilities that information technologies offer in the respective teaching and research fields (https://caa-network.org/archives/9492; https://express-k.kz; https://caren.geant.org). True digitization is performed by a specialist trained in ICT in respective subject area (Schlitz, 2009; John, 2015). According to Report: Overview of the Higher Education System Kazakhstan (2017), this is problem's actuality and its unequal and uneven development in different countries are evident (http://reports.weforum.org).

In this study it is assumed that a given type of universities partnership broadens the perspectives of academic community and allows to develop a new solution to encourage higher education institutions to integrate the ICT resources through forming regional network partnerships for upskilling and expanding competencies of the educators. Additional training and requalification of teaching staff in mastery of innovative educational digital technologies in their respective fields and research disciplines will be more beneficial only when regional university partnerships bring faculty of the same specialty together for learning and knowledge exchange.

This research represents a step forward in studying and identifying the considerable factors of regional universities' partnership in organization of ICT training courses for educators in order to sustainably develop higher education institutions. The approach taken in this study is not blocked and not in any way a lineal one. The researchers from other universities in Central Asia or Eurasian region, who work on similar problems, can also use instruments of this study.

IMPLICATIONS

The author's conclusions about regional universities' partnerships in Central Asia and their role in universities' sustainable development in the modern age of digital technologies are supported by concepts of continuous learning and TVET. In current times of digital technologies and knowledge societies lifelong learning matches the nature of the digital age (Fischer, 2000; Illeris, 2015; Gouthro, 2017; Chen and Liu, 2019; Report: Overview of the Higher Education System Kazakhstan, 2017; Latchem, 2017; University of Oxford. International Trends in Higher Education, 2018). Sustainable development of higher education for everyone cannot be achieved without a rapid expansion of high quality technical and vocational education and training (TVET). Today this issue is causing a big resonance.

The TVET UNESCO strategy recommends an inclusive and holistic approach to management and delivery of TVET (Latchem, 2017). In case where TVET students are university teachers these objectives gain an actuality and importance.

The results of this empirical study carry a practical importance for strategies in higher education and administrative staff members of universities in Central Asia with the authority to make relevant decisions. Views and beliefs of the academic community, faculty members of universities in Central Asia should be the basis for further strategies on universities' sustainable development in the region. The academic communities may organize events and meetings in order to evaluate the contribution of their professionals and to understand achievements and share ideas and concerns around organization of such activities. This improves the overall quality and stability of higher education institutions. Based on the data in table 5, managers and leaders of higher education institutes may involve ICT resources and specialists of their universities in such initiatives and meetings. Doing so allows them to discuss and evaluate the possibilities of real contributions from community members to the sustainable development model in both face-to-face and online modes. All members of the regional universities' partnerships will have the opportunity to benefit from significant advantages of the partnership.

REFERENCES

Abouelenein, Y., & Mohamed, A. (2016). Training needs for faculty members: Towards achieving quality of university education in the light of technological innovations. *Educational Research Review, 11*(13), 1180–1193. doi:10.5897/ERR2015.2377

Agbo, I. (2015). Factors influencing the use of information and communication technology (ICT) in teaching and learning computer studies in Ohaukwu local government area of Ebonyi state-Nigeria. *Journal of Education and Practice*, *6*(7), 71–86. Retrieved from https://files.eric.ed.gov/fulltext/EJ1083136.pdf

Akçayır, G. (2017). Why do faculty members use or not use social networking sites for education? *Computers in Human Behavior*, *71*, 378–385. doi:10.1016/j.chb.2017.02.028

Al Shobaki, M. J., & Naser, S. S. A. (2017) The role of the practice of excellence strategies in education to achieve sustainable competitive advantage to institutions of higher education-faculty of engineering and information technology at Al-Azhar university in Gaza a model. *International journal of digital publication technology*, *1*(2), 135-157. Retrieved from https://philarchive.org/archive/ALSTRO-9

Aspin, D., & Chapman, J. (2001, July). Lifelong learning: concepts, theories and values. *Paper presented at the SCUTREA 31st annual conference*. Academic Press.

Axyonova, V. (2013, February). The EU education initiative for Central Asia five years on: Lessons learnt? *EUCAM Policy Brief, 30*. Retrieved from http://eeas.europa.eu/central_asia/docs/2010_strategy_eu_centralasia_en.pdf

Baidarov, Y. (2017, June 21). Cultural and civilizational grounds for regional integration in Central Asia. *Central Asian analytical network CAAN*. Retrieved from https://caa-network.org/archives/9492

Baporikar, N. (2016). Lifelong learning in knowledge society. In P. O. Pablos & R. D. Tennyson (Eds.), *Impact of economic crisis on education and the next-generation workforce* (pp. 263–284). Hershey, PA: IGI Global. doi:10.4018/978-1-4666-9455-2.ch012

Baylor, A. L., & Ritchie, D. (2002). What factors facilitate teacher skill, teacher morale, and perceived student learning in technology using classrooms? *Computers & Education*, *39*(4), 395–414. doi:10.1016/S0360-1315(02)00075-1

Belenov, O. & Kirchanov, M. (2016). Network of universities as a form of development of higher education: forms, organization features and prospects. *Bulletin of Voronezh State Un. Ser.: The problems of Higher Education*, *1*, 114-118.

Blaschke, L. M., & Hase, S. (2015). Heutagogy, technology, and lifelong learning for professional and part-time learners. In *Transformative perspectives and processes in higher education* (pp. 75-94). Academic Press. Retrieved from https://www.academia.edu/23356035/Heutagogy_technology_and_lifelong_learning_Curriculum_geared_for_professional_and_part-time_learners

Borshcheva, E. A. (2015). Further professional education as a factor in the development of professional competence of a specialist. *Bulletin of the Orenburg State University*, *2*(177), 4–9. Retrieved from https://cyberleninka.ru/article/n/dopolnitelnoe-professionalnoe-obrazovanie-kak-faktor-razvitiya-professionalnoy-kompetentnosti-spetsialista

BRICS Network University. (2019, August). Retrieved from https://we.hse.ru/en/brics/

British Council -Education Intelligence. (2013, November). *MEGATRENDS - The future of international education.* Retrieved from https://www.britishcouncil.org/sites/default/files/megatrends_v1_1.pdf

Caird, S., & Roy, R. (2019). Blended learning and sustainable development. In W. Leal Filho (Ed.), *Encyclopedia of Sustainability in Higher Education*. Cham: Springer. doi:10.1007/978-3-319-63951-2_197-1

CAREN Project. (2019, August). Retrieved from https://caren.geant.org/Pages/Home.aspx

Chen, Z., & Liu, Y. (2019). The different style of lifelong learning in China and the USA based on influencing motivations and factors. *International Journal of Educational Research*, *95*, 13–25. doi:10.1016/j.ijer.2019.03.005

Choudaha, R., & Van Rest, E. (2018). Envisioning pathways to 2030: Megatrends shaping the future of global higher education and international student mobility. Retrieved from https://www.studyportals.com/report-envisioning-pathways-to-2030-studyportals-2018/

Desha, Ch., & Hargroves, K. (2013). *Higher education and sustainable development: A model for curriculum renewal*. London, New York: Routledge. doi:10.4324/9781315883953

Endovitsky, D. A. (2015). Resist the crisis tendencies, stick to the path of development. *Proceedings of Voronezh State University. Series: Problems of higher education, 2*, 5–8. Retrieved from http://www.vestnik.vsu.ru/content/educ/2015/02/toc_en.asp

Fischer, D., Jenssen, S., & Tappeser, V. (2015). Getting an empirical hold of the sustainable university: A comparative analysis of evaluation frameworks across 12 contemporary sustainability assessment tools. *Assessment & Evaluation in Higher Education*, *40*(6), 785–800. doi:10.1080/02602938.2015.1043234

Fischer, G. (2000). Lifelong Learning - more than training. *Journal of interactive learning research*, 11(3), 265-294. Retrieved from https://www.learntechlib.org/primary/p/8380/

GÉANT network. (2019, August). Retrieved from https://www.geant.org/News_and_Events/CONNECT/Pages/CAREN_project.aspx

Glotova, T., Deev, M., Krevskiy, I., Matukin, S., Mkrttchian, V., & Sheremeteva, E. (2015). Individualized learning trajectories using distance education technologies. In A. Kravets, M. Shcherbakov, M. Kultsova & O. Shabalina (Eds.), Creativity in intelligent technologies and data science (pp. 778-792). Springer. doi:10.1007/978-3-319-23766-4_62

Goldie, J. G. S. (2016). Connectivism: A knowledge learning theory for the digital age? *Medical Teacher*, *38*(10), 1064–1069. doi:10.3109/0142159X.2016.1173661 PMID:27128290

Gouthro, P. A. (2017). The promise of lifelong learning. *International Journal of Lifelong Education*, *36*(1-2), 45–59. doi:10.1080/02601370.2017.1270067

Hagen, S. (2016). *Study of the achievements of tempus iv projects on the internationalization of higher education in Central Asia*. UK: Semantica Ltd. doi:10.2797/88130

Hamadneh, I. M. (2015). Training needs for faculty members at Al-Albayt university from their perspectives in the light of some variables. *European Scientific Journal, 11*(25), 177–195. Retrieved from https://eujournal.org/index.php/esj/article/view/6212

Hyland, T. (2007). Lifelong learning and vocational education and training: values, social capital and caring in work-based learning provision. doi:10.1007/978-1-4020-6193-6_3

Illeris, K. (2015). The development of a comprehensive and coherent theory of learning. *European Journal of Education, 50*(1), 29–40. doi:10.1111/ejed.12103

Jarvis, P. (2007). *Globalization, lifelong learning and the learning society: Sociological perspectives*. London: Routledge. doi:10.4324/9780203964408

Jean-Francois, E. (2015). *Building global education with a local perspective. An introduction to glocal higher education*. New York: Palgrave-Macmillan.

John, S. P. (2015). The integration of information technology in higher education: A study of faculty's attitude towards IT adoption in the teaching process. *Contaduría y Administración, 60*, 230–252. doi:10.1016/j.cya.2015.08.004

Juvova, A., Chudy, S., Neumeister, P., Plischke, J., & Kvintovaet, J. (2015). Reflection of constructivist theories in current educational practice. *Universal Journal of Educational Research, 3*(5), 345–349. doi:10.13189/ujer.2015.030506

Khan, M., & Sarwar, M. (2011). Needs assessment of university teachers for professional enhancement. *International Journal of Business and Management, 6*(2), 208–212. doi:10.5539/ijbm.v6n2p208

Kirby, J. R., Knapper, C., Lamon, P., & Egnatoff, W. J. (2010). Development of a scale to measure lifelong learning. *International Journal of Lifelong Education, 29*(3), 291–302. doi:10.1080/02601371003700584

Krasnova, G. A., & Belous, V. V. (2016). Network universities: international experience and trends. *Bulletin of Russian Peoples' Friendship University (RUDN), 4*, 22-30. Retrieved from https://cyberleninka.ru/article/n/setevye-universitety-zarubezhnyy-opyt-i-mezhdunarodnye-tendentsii

Latchem, C. (2017). Using ICTs and blended learning in transforming TVET. UNESCO and Commonwealth of learning. Retrieved from https://unesdoc.unesco.org/ark:/48223/pf0000247495

Makoveeva, V. V. (2012). Network interaction: The key factor of education, science and business integration. *Bulletin of Tomsk State University, 354*(1), 163–166.

Mediterranean Universities Union. (2019, August). Retrieved from http://www.uni-med.net

Merriam, S. B., Caffarella, R. S., & Baumgartner, L. M. (2006). *Learning in adulthood: A comprehensive guide* (3rd ed.). San Francisco: Jossey-Bass.

Network University of the CIS. (2019, July). Retrieved from http://www.ido.rudn.ru/su_sng/

Parker, J., & Tazhina, G. (2012). Improving the Workforce in Kazakhstan through Distance Learning Technologies. In Handbook of Research on Technologies for Improving the 21st Century Workforce: Tools for Lifelong Learning. Academic Press. doi:10.4018/978-1-4666-2181-7.ch023

Preparing TVET for the digital age: Explainer. (2019, August). *Development Asia*. Retrieved from https://development.asia/explainer/preparing-tvet-digital-age

Rasul, A. (2019, June 5). Central Asia: problems and solutions. *Express K. Part ten*. Retrieved from https://expressk.kz/news/politekonomiya/tsentralnaya_aziya_problemy_i_resheniya_chast_desyataya-142135

Report, H. (2014). *Higher education edition:* New media consortium. Retrieved from http://global.oup.com/uk/orc/learnvle/

Report: *Overview of the Higher Education System Kazakhstan*. (2017, February). Education, Audiovisual and Culture Executive Agency (EACEA). doi:10.2797/985596

Robert, I.V. (2014). *Theory and methodology of education informatization (psycho-pedagogical and technological aspects)*. Moscow: BINOM - Laboratoriya znaniy.

Salim, S. F. M. Y. S., Mahmood, M. F., & Ahmad, A. B. (2018). The importance of information literacy to support lifelong learning in convergence era. *Development*, *7*(3), 353–362. Retrieved from http://hrmars.com/hrmars_papers/The_Importance_of_Information_Literacy_to_Support_Lifelong_Learning_in_Convergence_Era.pdf

Schaffer, S. P., & Richardson, J. C. (2004). Supporting technology integration within a teacher education system. *Educational computing research*, *3*(4), 423-435. Retrieved from https://eric.ed.gov/?id=EJ683701

Schlitz, S. A. (2009). Developing a culture of assessment through a faculty learning community: a case study. *International journal of teaching and learning in higher education, 21*(1), 133-147. Retrieved from http://www.isetl.org/ijtlhe/

Schultz, L., & Viczko, M. (2016). Assembling and governing the higher education institution. democracy, social justice and leadership in global higher education. London: Palgrave-Macmillan.

Selyanskaya, G. N. (2014). Distributed university: from the university branch network to the electronic network universities. *Modern problems of science and education*, *5*, 1-14. doi:10.17513pno.119-14862

Sergeieva, L. (2018). Modern professional education and educational services market. *Fundamental and applied researches in practice of leading scientific schools*, *28*(4), 122-126. Retrieved from https://www.farplss.org/index.php/journal/article/download/518/481

Shanghai Cooperation Organisation (SCO) University. (2019, June). Retrieved from http://uni-sco.com/?lang=EN

Sharonin, Yu. V. (2019, January 29). Digital technologies in higher and professional education: from personally oriented smart didactics to blockchain in purpose training of specialists. *Modern problems of science and education*, *1*. Retrieved from http://science-education.ru/ru/article/view?id=28507

Siemens, G. (2008). About: Description of connectivism. *Connectivism: A learning theory for today's learner, website*. Retrieved from http://www.connectivism.ca/about.html

Soghomonov, A.Y. (2016). Sustainable university (mission, meanings, programs, cases). *Journal of applied ethics*, *49*, 151-170.

Springett, D. (2015). Education for sustainable development. Challenges of a critical pedagogy. In M. Redclift & D. Springett (Eds.), *Routledge international handbook of sustainable development*. London, New York: Routledge.

Steffens, K. (2015). Competences, learning theories and MOOCs: Recent developments in lifelong learning. *European Journal of Education*, *50*(1), 41–59. doi:10.1111/ejed.12102

Tazhina, G. (2012). Kazakhstani e-learning experience in higher education. *International journal of multidisciplinary thought*, *2*(2), 435-441.

Teaching practices survey 2016: Compiled U21 results. (2019). Universitas 21. Retrieved from https://universitas21.com/sites/default/files/2019-2/TPS%20compiled%20results%20logo.pdf

Tonkonog, V. (2017). Topical issues of application of distance learning technologies in the system of development of the Russian Federation. *Editura Universităţii Naţionale de Apărare*, *1*(1), 544-549. doi:10.12753/2066-026X-17-080

Training needs analysis of Sofia University staff. (2014, November). Retrieved from http://e-center.uni-sofia.bg/TNA_vocational_trainers_en.pdf

University of Oxford. *International trends in higher education: Report 2016-17*. (2018, June). Retrieved from http://www.ox.ac.uk/sites/files/oxford/trends%20in%20globalisation_WEB.pdf

Vezirov, G. (2017). Pedagogical conditions of informational competence development of pedagogical workers in the advanced training system. *Scientific support of the system of advanced training of personnel*, *2*(31), 44-50.

Volles, N. (2014, July 18). Lifelong learning in the EU: Changing conceptualisations, actors, and policies. *Studies in Higher Education*, 1–21. doi:10.1080/03075079.2014.927852

Watty, K., McKay, J., & Ngo, L. (2016). Innovators or inhibitors? Accounting faculty resistance to new educational technologies in higher education. *Journal of Accounting Education*, *36*(C), 1–15. doi:10.1016/j.jaccedu.2016.03.003

World Economic Forum report: Shaping the future of education, gender and work. (2019, June). Retrieved from http://reports.weforum.org

WUN. (2019, June). Worldwide Universities Network Annual Report. Retrieved from https://wun.ac.uk/files/annual_reports/wun_report-final_(medium-res).pdf

Yurdakul, C. (2017, January 1). An investigation of the relationship between autonomous learning and lifelong learning. *International journal of educational research review*, *2*(1), 15-20. Retrieved from https://dergipark.org.tr/download/article-file/298782

KEY TERMS AND DEFINITIONS

Information and Communication Technology (ICT): A broad term including communication devices, various services, video conferencing, online learning, etc. to enable users to access, store, transmit, and manipulate information.

Life Long Learning (LLL): Self-initiated learning that is centered on personal development outside of a formal educational institution.

Regional Resource Center: The organization that responds to the needs of its regional partners in developing and disseminating a scope of training materials and curricula to various social and professional groups in these areas.

Technical and Vocational Education and Training (TVET): Education and training for employment knowledge and skills with the purpose of social equity, inclusion, and sustainable development.

Universities' Partnership: Partnerships between universities worldwide to fostering relationships on research and teaching.

Chapter 10
The Impact of the Flipped Classroom on Students' Academic Achievements in Secondary Schools

Meruyert Koshegulova
https://orcid.org/0000-0001-8505-7142
Dongguk University, South Korea

Yerkhan Mindetbay
University of Southampton, UK

ABSTRACT

The purpose of this study is to analyze the effects of flipped learning on students' academic achievements in the subject of science at Bilim Innovation Lyceums (BIL) in Kazakhstan. For this purpose, pre and post surveys were conducted on 168 students who were divided into two groups; the experimental group consisting of 84 students who took part in flipped learning classes for seven weeks and the control group consisting of 84 students who experienced the traditional method of classroom instruction at the same period. To achieve the objectives of the study, a final placement test score was used before and after the introduction of the flipped classroom model. The results of the study are summarized as follows. There were a significant difference between the two groups in terms of academic achievement when it measured by test scores before and after the concerned semester. On the basis of these findings, several suggestions were made for the schools to utilize innovative instructional methods including flipped learning for sustainable education in the future.

DOI: 10.4018/978-1-7998-2551-7.ch010

INTRODUCTION

Since 2000, various efforts have been undertaken to provide quality education to children, youth and adults around the world (UNESCO, 2008). UNESCO announced the 'Incheon Declaration' at the 2015 World Education Forum, proclaiming 'Equal, and inclusive quality education for all, and improving lifelong learning opportunities' by 2030 (UNESCO, 2015). Education Goal in Sustainable Development Goals (SDGs) is aimed at working towards quality. At this point, education institutions play an important role in society supporting sustainable development, and economic growth and education could be a strategic sector for development cooperation between countries in the Eurasian region. In the context of globalization, international cooperation partnerships between education institutions in the Eurasian region are becoming increasingly important for better responsiveness of the education to the changing needs of the labor market in this region (Asia Education, 2019).

Recent decades have witnessed huge technological progress in the education system, whereby technology has become one of the powerful tools due to its ability to increase efficiency and improve the quality of overall outcomes (Alamri, 2019). And the role of technology in reaching sustainable goals can play an important role. Huawei (2019) analyzed the correlation between SDGs and ICT and, SDG4 got 72%, which was the highest correlation with ICT (See Figure 1). The high correlation between SDG4 and ICT skills shows that a country's overall education level is closely related to its ICT education and training level (Huawei, 2019).

There are several cases where access to quality education was made through implementing ICT in lots of developing countries. For example, the African countries are implementing various forms of education programs and initiatives using ICTs to improve access to educational resources through open educational resources (OERs) (Islam & Knezevic, 2019). Using ICT by implementing eLearning through OERs and online courses can be an alternative way of making education accessible and for providing scale for skill-based training at a minimum cost.

The Eurasian region is making efforts to digitalize the education system and pays lots of attention to implement ICTs in education (Avetisyan et al., 2015). The educational use of ICT is a theme that the international community is paying attention to as a key mechanism for expanding educational opportunities, providing quality education, and promoting lifelong learning societies (UNESCO, 2015). But UNESCO IITE (2012) pointed out that despite significant progress in recent years regarding the gaps in ICT development among Eurasian countries, ICT access and use by their populations is relatively low.

Analyzing the successful cases of ICT implementation into K-12, FC could be an efficient way to accelerate sustainability in education in the Eurasian regions. The use of FC as an alternative to the traditional classroom has been attracting the attention of educators. The latest advancements in technological tools such as interactive videos, video conference systems make a way to spread the use of FC (Cabi, 2018). Recent researches stated that FC is the best model for using technology in education (Hamdan et al., 2013). Also, Fabrega et al. (2019) suggested FC as an active learning methodology in sustainable development curricula.

Figure 1. SDGs and ICT correlation
Source: Huawei, 2019

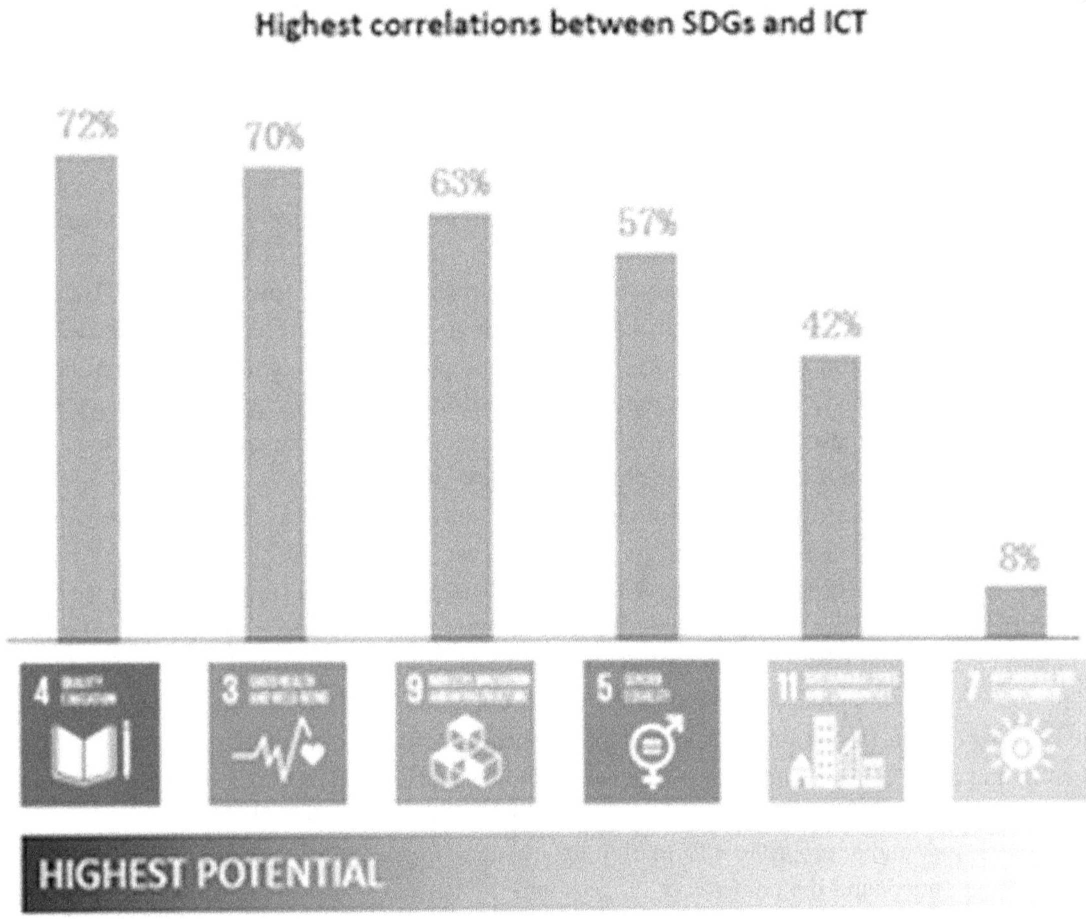

BACKGROUND

Flipped Classroom

Many countries in the world attempted to make structural changes in teaching methods to be prepared for the acceleration from the tremendous changes in knowledge and informational fields (Elian & Hamaidi, 2018). These kinds of challenges demand to do a in-depth review of the educational system in most countries in the world. This makes to find new approaches to develop and update the teaching and learning process. And these approaches focus on the role of learner where s/he is the center of the learning process (Elian & Hamaidi, 2018).

Making a student the center of the learning process makes him/her reach the proficiency level in case if teaching and learning environments and teaching methods are suitable to the student's abilities and needs. One of such methods is the Flipped Classroom (FC) model. The FC model is a new pedagogical model where the teacher shares prepared in advance digital resources with students through a platform outside the classroom, and related content is also taught through this outside platform asynchronously (Cabi, 2018). Flipped learning is done by learners individually in advance through videos and text, and in the class, it is conducted as a learner-oriented participatory type, such as discussion and questioning. These methods are reported to have positive effects, such as strengthening learners' learning motivation and collaboration skills (Park, 2014). According to the Flipped Learning Network Committee, flipped learning allows a variety of learning methods and it has characteristics such as flexible environment which means creating a flexible learning space, learner-centered learning culture, intentional contents that have intention by learner-led learning culture or instructor's sophisticated instructional design, a professional educator who means that the instructor should have professional knowledge of technology as well as pedagogical knowledge (FLN, 2014).

Flipped learning and traditional classes show various differences in terms of teaching-learning activities and class structure. The traditional class consists mainly of instructor-led lecture sessions in the classroom, and activities such as learner-oriented tasks and problem solving are performed outside the classroom. On the contrary, flipped learning takes place first through various materials such as video and text prepared by the teacher outside the classroom, followed by learning activities such as student-centered discussion and questioning in the classroom (Park, 2014).

The differences between flipped learning and traditional classes are as follows in terms of class structure. The structure of the class consists of four stages: 'before class', 'introduction of class', 'in class' and 'after class' (Korea U Learning Association, 2014). Traditional lessons and flipped learning make a difference in all four of these stages. First of all, traditional classes are prepared by teachers at the 'before class' stage. By contrast, in flipped learning, the learner is to study ahead of the class by himself according to the procedure provided by the teacher, and keep a record of the questions related to the learning content. In the 'introduction of class' phase, traditional classes offer limited information, with teachers giving one-way, instructor-led classes. However, flipped learning teaching methods allow learners to interact with teachers in class to ask learning-related questions, allowing them to anticipate the most necessary and appropriate information for learners. In a traditional class, 'in class' is a step in which learners understand the contents of a class, and the teacher tries to help the learner understand through additional learning materials. On the other hand, in classes using flipped learning methods, the teacher presents tasks and applies what the learner has learned through discussion or project learning. Finally, in the 'after class' phase, the teacher evaluates the past assignments in traditional classes and the learners perform the tasks. On the contrary, in the flipped learning class, the teacher organizes the information related to the contents of the lecture with the learner and carries out the activity of providing feedback individually to the necessary learner. As a result, the traditional teaching method is a way of conveying the knowledge necessary for learners, while flipped learning is possible for further learning.

Impacts of the FC on Student Learning

The prior studies on flipped learning can be largely divided into theoretical and empirical studies. There are theoretical studies that suggest the applicability of flipped learning classes and the model of classes that can be introduced in various subjects (Lee, 2013; Kim, 2018). Empirical studies have demonstrated the effectiveness of flipped learning in school sites, mainly from a variety of perspectives: students' academic performance, interest, and motivation in flipped learning, flipped learning classes' impact on the classroom environment and atmosphere in the classroom, improvement of relationships between students, and relationships between teachers and students (Lee, 2014; Velegol & Zappe, 2016; Strayer, 2007). In most studies, students' attitudes, motivations, and participation in classes are selected as independent variables and the effect of these variables on their academic performance and academic performance are analyzed (Lee & Kim, 2015; Jung, Bae, & So, 2015; Choi, 2015). The related prior studies are mainly those that analyzed students' perception of the classroom environment in which flipped learning was introduced in the class (Velegol & Zappe, 2016; Strayer, 2007).

FC is reported to have a positive effect on the classroom environment when introduced into the classroom in the following respects. First, FC increases students' motivation for learning. The study, which analyzed the impact of FC on learning motivations, found that positive results were seen in areas such as attention, relevance, confidence, and satisfaction and that students were not only given a right to speak, but also various student-oriented activities were carried out (Jung, Bae, & So, 2015; Lee, 2014). Second, the students' attitude toward the subjects they taught with FC turned out to be positive. For example, in a study that analyzed the scientific attitudes of elementary school students, flipped learning has positive effects on factors such as curiosity, co-operation, spontaneity, and persistence (Lee, 2015). Third, FC improves the classroom atmosphere. In a study of humanities middle school students, it was reported that the atmosphere in the classroom has changed into a real learning space with a living atmosphere as a result of introducing flipped learning for one semester in the Korean language subject (Lee, 2014). Fourth, FC has been able to increase students' interest because it requires active participation from students. Through this, the students responded positively that it was easier to remember the contents of the flipped learning class than the ones in the traditional classroom, and that they wanted to participate more actively in the FC in the future. A study of high school students found that students actively participated in flipped learning classes and that the atmosphere in the classroom was upbeat (Ryu, 2015). FC has changed the learning atmosphere so that learners can self-directed learning (Oderesa, 2015; KBS, 2014). Finally, flipped learning has the effect of improving the interaction between teachers and students, students and students (Lee, 2014). The students responded that the classroom environment improved positively through various learning activities with the help of the teacher in flipped learning classes compared to traditional classes (Velegol & Zappe, 2016; Strayer, 2007). Also, the increased interaction between teachers and students in flipped learning classes has increased the effectiveness of teachers and the opportunity to reflect on classes on their own (Jin, 2016).

Flipped Classroom and Students' Academic Achievement

The study on the effectiveness of FC is largely divided into studies related to academic achievement and motivation. However, studies of learning motivations showed mostly positive results, but studies of academic performance did not show consistent results. In the case of a positive effect, as a result of the introduction of FC to elementary school social studies classes, the academic performance of students in the low level has increased (Lee & Kim, 2015). Also, as a result of applying FC in chemistry classes, the academic performance of elementary school students has increased compared to that of traditional students. And there were significant differences between experimental and control groups in students' scientific attitudes, exploration skills, and class satisfaction as well as academic achievement. It was analyzed that FC, as well as academic achievement, affects the formation of self-directed learning habits of elementary school students (Song, 2016).

On the other hand, studies are showing that FC has a minor or no significant effect on academic performance (Choi, 2015; Lee et al., 2015; Jung, Bae, & So, 2015). For example, as a result of introducing FC to social classes of elementary school students, there were positive results in learning motivation, but there was no difference in academic performance (Lee et al., 2015). Also, as a result of applying FC to middle school students, participation in the class was high, but the student's academic performance was not effective (Choi, 2015). In the middle school student's math class, there were significant differences in mathematical attitudes between experimental and control groups, but no significant differences in academic performance (Hwang, 2017; Scott, 2011).

Researchers believe that there are three main reasons for the conflicting results in terms of academic performance (Jung, Bae, & So, 2015; Jung, 2014; Choi, 2015). First, the study period is set too short for students to get used to the new teaching-learning method. For students who have been familiar with traditional classes for many years, FC seems to be fresh, requiring time before they get used to it and having an immediate effect after adjusting. Second, it may be because of differences in the learning environment or the various characteristics of students (Jung, 2014). In FC, student-oriented classes take place, so they are no longer in the teacher-centered classroom structure of the past. In some cases, it is not a row of desks, but rather a space for group activities to create a separate space for studying individually.

In FC the learning environment is changed so that students can learn at their own pace at any time. Therefore, it is necessary to carefully design classes before flipped learning in consideration of various variables such as situations, classroom environment, teachers, and educational content to improve students' academic performance (Jung, Bae, & So, 2015). Finally, there may also be a limit to how to measure academic performance in FC (Lee et al., 2014). When FC is introduced, test scores are sometimes used for academic achievement before and after FC because of the concern that there will be a score gap between the experimental and control group students (Lee, 2014; Ruddick, 2012). Because of the limitations of these paper-based exams, the effects of flipped learning may not be properly assessed (Lee et al., 2014).

Flipped learning has been a huge sensation and major impact on the way of teaching, and it started in the U.S. and spread all over the world. Flipped learning has become an important way for learners, who have been passively sidelined from the one-sided lecture-oriented classes, to become the center of classroom activity again and build learner-oriented classroom culture. With the introduction of flipped learning, the academic performance of top-ranked learners rose, and those who were passive in classes became actively involved. There was a change in the interaction between learners and learners, between teachers and learners (KBS, 2014).

As flipped learning has become a worldwide teaching-learning trend, Kazakhstan, the hub of the Eurasian Region, has also introduced flipped learning on a trial basis to the Bilim Innovation Lyceum (BIL). In 2003, the Kazakh government began to create policies focused on the digitalization of all sectors, including the education system (UNESCO IITE, 2012). In 2007, Kazakhstan's Law on Education pointed out an important mechanism for the realization of national education policies, and eLearning and distance learning are defined as new innovative learning technologies (Kazakhstan Act on Education, 2007). The Kazakhstan-2011-2020 Development Strategic Plan, approved in 2010, focuses on the large-scale adoption of digitalization and eLearning of the entire education system (UNESCO IITE, 2012). To achieve the introduction of the eLearning education system mentioned in the Kazakhstan-2011-2020 Development Strategic Plan, regulations were developed for the development and activation of open education materials (OER). Flipped Classrooms can be an effective way to introduce this eLearning education system.

In the flipped classroom, learner-centered education can be achieved by increasing the efficiency of providing learning materials by suing eLearning class materials as pre-learning. The problem is that in the context of Kazakhstan K-12, there is a lack of relevant research and practice and there is a lack of resources for reference.

Therefore, to identify the effects of FC Model on students' academic achievement, this study aims to answer the following research question:

- To what extent does the Flipped Classroom Model affect students' academic achievement?

General Educational Institutions in Kazakhstan and the BIL

The main educational policy tasks of the government of Kazakhstan are 'flexibility', 'diversity' and 'choice'. Independent from the collapse of the Soviet Union, Kazakhstan created new policies for the establishment of a national system and established the Act on Education to lay the foundation for national education. Kazakhstan's education policy has repeatedly changed in consideration of changes in its political, economic and social environment, a transition to democracy, transition to a market competition system and inclusion into the world order. The '2010-2020 Kazakhstan Development Strategy' was presented as a policy to fulfill the challenges required by changes in the times while maintaining the unique experience and advantages accumulated in Kazakhstan's historical development process, and aims to foster experts suitable for the free economic market through diverse and flexible education courses. The main objectives of Kazakhstan's education system include the formation of learners' general knowledge of academic and cultural studies, social adaptation of primary and secondary school learners, education of civil spirit and love of the country, and the re-education and improvement of qualifications, such as meeting the social needs of qualified workers and professionals (Government of Kazakhstan, 2019). To achieve these educational goals, Chapter 2 section 30 of the Kazakhstan Constitution states several basic principles related to education.

First, secondary education is compulsory education, guaranteeing free secondary education through national educational institutions. Second, citizens have the right to receive free higher education based on competitive principles in national higher education institutions. Third, the paid education at the private school institution proceeds according to the principles and procedures set by the law. Fourth, the state should establish general education standards and all educational institutions should operate by these standards. Under these educational goals and basic principles, the education structure according to age in Kazakhstan's education system is as follows.

The educational system shown in Table 1 was established under the Education Act 1997 as a basic framework. Children in Kazakhstan attend kindergarten, which is equivalent to pre-school education, from the age of 3 to 6, and enter elementary school at the age of 7 and receive elementary education from the first to the fourth grade until the age of 10. Students from 11 to 15 years of age will be admitted to junior high school and receive basic secondary education from grade 5 to grade 9. Students will take the entrance exam after the basic curriculum has been completed, after which the students will have two options for future careers. The first is to enter general high school and receive general secondary education from 16 to 18 years of age, the second to enter vocational-technical school without going to high school and receive secondary or elementary vocational education for 4 to 5 years. The compulsory education period in Kazakhstan is 11 years, and students who have completed compulsory education take the Unified National Test (UNT), which is a high school graduation examination and entrance examination for higher education institutions. Higher education has four years of college; two years of master's and three years of doctorate, and different periods are applied like the course.

Table 1. Kazakhstan education system

<table>
<tr><th>Age</th><th>3~6 years</th><th>7~10 years</th><th>11~15 years</th><th>16~18 years</th><th>19~21 years</th><th>22 years~</th></tr>
<tr><td rowspan="2">level</td><td rowspan="2">preschool education/ kindergarten</td><td rowspan="2">elementary education (1~4 grade)</td><td rowspan="2">basic secondary education (5~9 grade)</td><td>General Secondary Education (10~11 grade) (3 years)</td><td rowspan="2">Higher Education (Bachelor, Master's, PhD)</td><td rowspan="2">post-graduate</td></tr>
<tr><td>Secondary primary vocational education (2 years)</td></tr>
</table>

Source: (Kazakhstan Education Act, 2007)

Kazakhstan has selected development in the education sector as a major task for national development since independence, increased the budget size in the education sector every year, and in 2015, 3.5 percent of GDP was invested in education. The Kazakh government's interest in education can be seen in the following development of education. In 1999, Kazakhstan became the first Central Asian country to include preschool education as a one-year course in compulsory education. Since 2000, the government has focused on ICT-enabled education and eLearning to ensure that at least one computer room has been installed in all schools nationwide (Korean Embassy, 2017.11.18.) In 2003, Kazakhstan's Education Ministry established a phased strategy to switch from the existing 11-year school curriculum to the 12-year school curriculum operated worldwide and is currently running on a trial basis. As part of the pilot project, the Kazakhstan school year transition process has been applied to 54 selected schools in major parts of the country, increasing the number of participating schools each year. Under the Kazakhstan Education Ministry's plan, the 12th-grade transition process for school education will be completed by 2020. The new curriculum will apply to the existing '11th-grade school curriculum' plus the pre-school preparation stage of '0th-grade'. Mandatory '0th-grade' education for 5-year-olds began in September 2017. In '0th-grade'classes are conducted by taking 3-4 subjects a day with 35 minutes.

In Kazakhstan, education takes place in general educational institutions and special purpose educational institutions. General education institutions refer to national and public schools and provide primary, basic and general secondary education based on national education courses. Special purpose education institutions can learn fields such as science, culture, art, sports, and military from the ground up to the advanced stage, and operate education courses to foster experts in specific fields. Under the Kazakhstan Education Act (2007), special purpose education institutions are classified as Gymnasium, Lyceum, Small School, Profile School, and International School, and the characteristics of each school are shown in Table 2. In addition to the national education curriculum in all special purpose schools except for international schools, international education courses are integrated according to the purpose of school operation. In Gymnasium, Small School and International School, education will continue from elementary school to high school, and in Lyceum and schools by field, students can enter the school through exams from middle school.

In Kazakhstan, general national and public schools are set up in each region (there are 14 main regions), but in the case of schools that fall into special-purpose education institutions, students are free to move to schools in their preferred areas and can transfer as many as possible. In this study Bilim Innovation Lyceum, a special purpose school was selected. The reason why BIL was chosen is that the school was

Table 2. Types of special purpose institutions in Kazakhstan

	Characteristics	School Year
Gymnasium	It is an educational institution that provides deep education expanded in the fields of education such as social and humanitarian according to learners' trends and abilities based on national education courses, elementary and secondary schools, and general secondary education and additional education programs.	From 0th grade or 1st grade to 11th or 12th grade of high school
Lyceum	It is an educational institution that provides basic secondary, general, and additional education programs to provide scientific and mathematical expansion and deepening education programs according to learners' orientation and ability.	From 5th grade of middle school to 11th or 12th grade of high school
Small School	It is a general elementary and secondary school that provides a particular type of class by combining a set of classes for a small number of learners	From 0th grade or 1st grade to 11th or 12th grade of high school
Profile School	It is an educational institution that provides intensive education on special areas such as music, sports, and science based on national education courses.	From 5th grade of middle school to 11th or 12th grade of high school
International School	An educational institution that provides specially designed integrated programs certified by the International Baccalaureate Organization or international organizations.	From 0th grade or 1st grade to 11th or 12th grade of high school

Source: (Kazakhstan Education Act, 2007)

interested in digitalization secondary education at that time, such as trying to introduce Massive Open Online Courses (MOOCs).

BIL is a network of public middle and high schools led by Kazakhstan's KATEV International Public Foundation, formerly called Kazakh-Turkish Lyceum (KTL). The KATEV Foundation was established in 1992 by Kazakhstan President Nazarbayev and Turkish President Ozal in 1997 through a cooperative effort to coordinate Ozal's efforts to link educational institutions between countries. The KATEV Foundation operates Turkish schools in 170 countries around the world. In 2016, the 'KATEV' foundation was separated into two foundations and renamed as 'Bilim-Innovation' and 'Bilim-Orda'. The Bilim-Innovation Foundation currently operates 27 BIL middle and high school networks in Kazakhstan and is supported by state and local budgets.

BIL's distinguishing characteristics compared to general national and public schools are as follows. First, BIL operates an integrated curriculum. BIL's curriculum has a form of integrating national and international education courses. The use of extended program material due to curriculum and interdisciplinary integration in science and math subjects, as well as the elements of lyceum and innovative technology. Second, BIL's classes run in multiple languages. In the BIL, education is conducted in multilingual languages, such as in Kazakh, Russian, English, and Turkish. Third, BIL is also distinguished from ordinary schools in terms of the operation schedule and structure of the semester. In general schools, education is made up of six days a week, and classes are five days a week at BIL, and students are required to stay in dormitories for the semester. And while Kazakhstan's general schools are all coeducational, BIL is divided into male and female schools and integrated schools. Fourth, the BIL enters through tests and has a pre-season training course. (BIL, 2019).

RESEARCH METHOD

Participants of the Study

This study was conducted on 168 students attending eighth, ninth and tenth grades at Bilim Innovation Lyceums (BILs) located in 4 out of 14 regions of Kazakhstan. For empirical research, three grades consisting of two classes were divided into experimental groups (the flipped classroom (FC) group) and comparative groups (the traditional class (TC) group). A total of 168 students participated in the study, with 84 students in the flipped learning class and 84 in the traditional class group, all participants are males since schools that participated in the research are Boys Schools. Information about the students who participated in the study is given in Table 3.

Among those surveyed, the region accounted for 53 percent of the total from Almaty. The majority was 64.9 percent for eighth-graders and Biology accounted for a majority of 64.9 percent of the subjects.

Content and Procedure

The academic performance of FC and TC groups was measured by the students' final exam results. Before the introduction of FC, the results of eighth-grade biology, ninth grade computer science, and tenth-grade algebra were used for each final exam subject in the first semester of 2016-2017 academic years. Tests after the introduction of FC used final exam scores for the second semester of 2016-2017 academic years. Students' grades were used after they were officially allowed to use their grades for research by sending a letter to Darkhan Ote, the head of the BIL Network, to use them for research purposes.

This study introduced FC in BIL for seven weeks from November 16 to December 30, 2016, in three subjects: biology, computer science, and algebra, to analyze how flipped learning can affect students' academic performance. To introduce FC to the BIL, the meeting was held through a video conference in August 2016 by recruiting teachers from BIL across the country who wanted to try flipped learning. The video conference was held through Skype and was selected by Yerkhan Mindetbay, a computer sci-

Table 3. The Information about the Participants of the study

		FC (%)	TC (%)	Total (%)
Region	Aktobe	9 (5.4)	11 (6.5)	20 (11.9)
	Almaty	46 (27.4)	43 (25.6)	89 (53.0)
	Pavlodar	19 (11.3)	16 (9.5)	35 (20.8)
	Shymkent	10 (6.0)	14 (8.3)	24 (14.3)
Grade	8th grade	56 (33.3)	53 (31.5)	109 (64.9)
	9th grade	14 (8.3)	17 (10.1)	31 (18.5)
	10th grade	14 (8.3)	14 (8.3)	28 (16.7)
Subject	Computer Science	14 (8.3)	17 (10.1)	31 (18.5)
	Biology	56 (33.3)	53 (31.5)	109 (64.9)
	Algebra	14 (8.3)	14 (8.3)	28 (16.7)
Total (%)		84 (50)	84 (50)	168 (100)

ence teacher at Pavlodar BIL. Yerkhan Mindetbay was the initiator of digitalization of middle and high school education and introduced the Massive Open Online Courses to BILs, which began to emerge at that time, and flipped learning was implemented as the first step in its attempt.

In Kazakhstan, flipped learning was a new concept of the teaching-learning method. Studies conducted on the FC Model (Chen et al, 2017; Song & Kapur, 2017; Bergman & Sams, 2012; Khan, 2016; KBS, 2014) have led to the development of an appropriate form for BIL flipped learning environment. This form includes out-of-class activities and in-class activities which focus on understanding, remembering and applying, also analyzing, evaluating and creating (Anderson, 2005). The teachers participating in the experiment designed a model suitable for BIL's classes, looking at Khan Academy (2016) and Bergman & Sams's (2012) use of FC through constant video meetings. The classes of experimental and control groups were set up with the same teacher teaching. Because the variable "teacher" can affect the effectiveness of flipped learning, flipped learning classes and traditional classes are taught by the same teacher and the teacher created the required activity area for the in-class. Videos of out-of-class activity were made in a 10- to 15-minute length, and teachers participating in the operation of flipped learning classes used the video as class material in all 4 BILs. The videos were posted on a YouTube channel called LEARNERS. Students watched the lecture video on YouTube before the class, and then took part in the class. BIL teachers shared roles through video meetings, designed material preparation, and classes, and applied flipped learning classes in the second semester of fall (November-December).

At the pre-class stage, the teacher uploaded a pre-teaching lecture for flipped learning to YouTube and delivered the link to the class leader in each grade. On the eve of the flipped learning class, the class leader prepared a pre-teaching lecture for flipped learning for easy access from the computer room. Since BIL is a dormitory school and due to school internal regulations, students in flipped learning classes were prevented from using smart devices inside the school, so students studied video clips of pre-teaching classes on the day before class at the computer room. The YouTube channel interface produced for this study is shown in Figure 2.

During the class, the teacher asked the students questions related to the pre-teaching videos to find out how much the students understood the new topic on their own, and then gave supplementary explanations if any misinterpreted the contents of the out-of-class video and distributed prepared in-class activities by individuals or groups. The teacher was mainly a helper when the students asked for help. In the post-class phase, the teacher asked the students additional questions about the topic they had learned that day, gave them supplemental explanations related to the subject mainly to the students in need, and presented them with the task of making questions by watching the next pre-teaching session.

For traditional classes that took part in the comparative group, the same learning content as the flipped learning experimental group was conducted with a teacher-centered teaching method. And a group-specific project task used during flipped learning in-class activity was presented as a homework assignment due to lack of class time so that it could be solved outside the classroom.

Data Collection Tool

As a data collection tool after the introduction of the FC Model was used a final placement test score results from the prior 1st semester and after 2nd semesters of 2016-2017 academic years to answer the research question.

Figure 2. Screenshot of a video view from LEARNERS YouTube channel for FC at BIL.

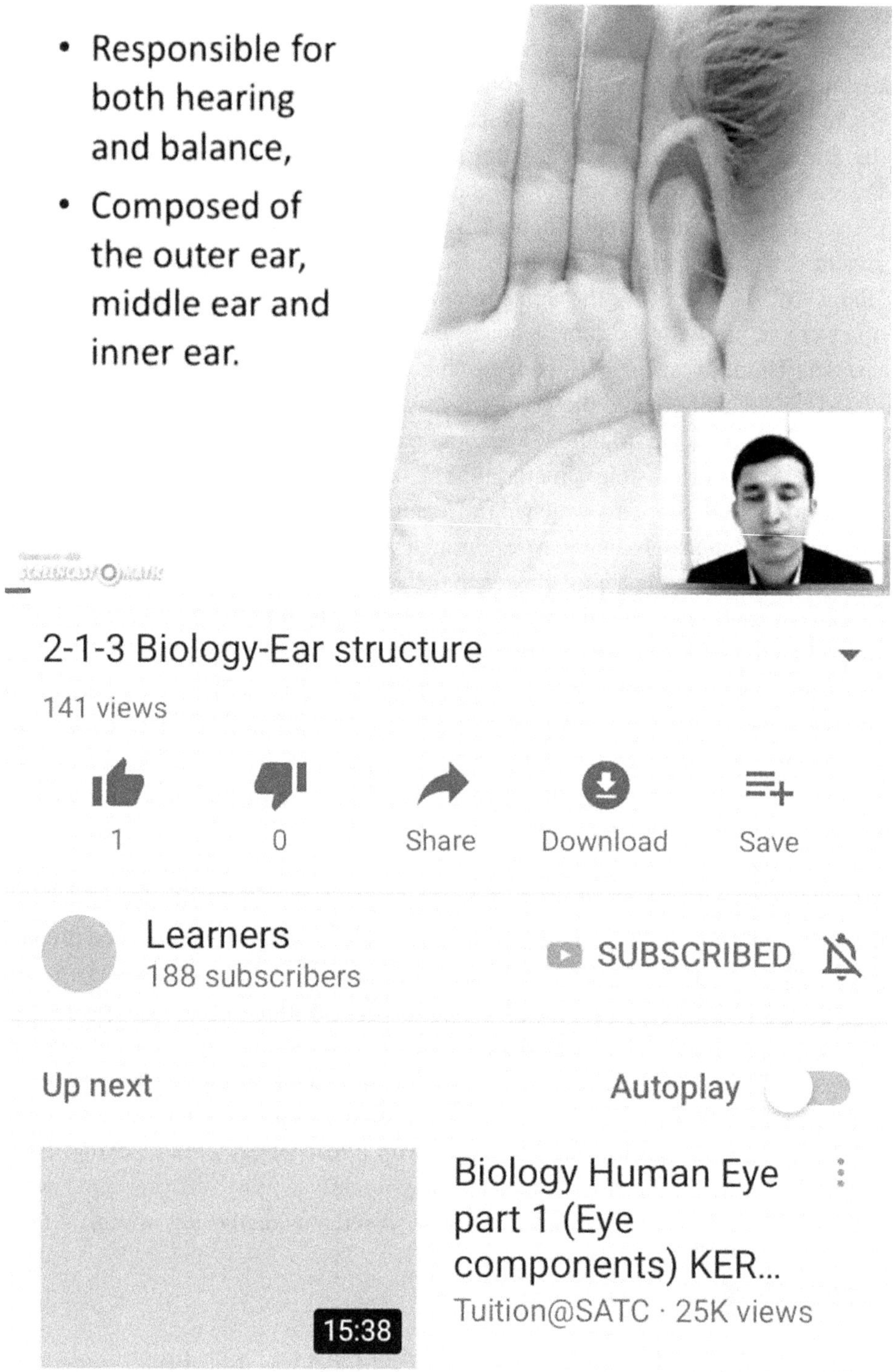

Analysis

The collected data were analyzed as follows. The statistical processing of the collected data was performed by utilizing the SPSS 21.0 statistical package program through the data coding and data cleaning process. First, frequency analysis was conducted to find out about the general characteristics of the participants. Second, to verify equalization of the study groups (control, experimental), a t-test was applied to students' scores in the two groups in the achievement pretest and to see if there any change between the two groups in the post-test, also t-test was applied. Finally, the response sample t-test was conducted for pre- and post-verification of the academic performance by the group.

RESULTS

A t-test was performed to identify whether there was any statistically significant difference between the pre-test scores of the two groups. Table 4 displays the results t-test to check the equalization of the study groups.

Table 4 indicates that there were no statistically significant differences between the mean scores of the students (t=.553, p>0.05). Based on this finding, it can be stated that both groups can participate in the experimental process. Table 5 shows the means and standard deviation values, t-values of the pre- and post-test academic scores that were calculated according to the groups (flipped classroom, traditional classroom).

Table 5 demonstrates that the mean of a pre-test for the Traditional Classroom is (8.27) and the standard deviation is (2.485), and the mean of post-test is (8.55) and the standard deviation is (2.310). The analysis results showed an increase in the average of 0.28, but no statistically significant difference was found (p>0.05). Also, the mean of the pre-test for the Flipped Classroom group students is (8.54) and the standard deviation is (3.562), the means of the post-test is (9.89) and the standard deviation is (3.159). For Flipped Classroom 1.35 was increased on average, and there is also a statistically significant

Table 4. Results of t-test on scores of achievement pre-test of FC and TC groups

Group	N	M	SD	*t*	*p*
Flipped Classroom	84	8.54	3.562	.553	.581
Traditional Classroom	84	8.27	2.485		

Table 5. Pre-test and Post-test achievement scores within the groups

Group	Pre-test		Post-test		t	*p*
	M	SD	M	SD		
FC	8.54	3.562	9.89	3.159	-8.416*	.000
TC	8.27	2.485	8.55	2.310	-1.365	.176

* Statistically significant at the level of significance (* p < 0.05)

difference (t=-8.416*, p<0.05). In other words, the Flipped Classroom, as a whole, did significantly affect the change in academic performance.

To check the differences between the two groups in the post-test scores t-test was applied and the results are shown in Table 6.

As observed in Table 6, there is significant difference was found in the means of post-test scores of the two groups (t=3.151*, p<.005).

CONCLUSION

In this study, it was analyzed eighth, ninth and tenth graders attending Bilim Innovative Schools in Kazakhstan through seven weeks of Flipped Classroom in biology, computer science, and algebra to the influence of academic performance. In this study, the results of final placement test scores for the semester before and after the introduction of flipped learning were analyzed with data. Consequently, the results of comparing the pre-test and post-test scores after the introduction of the Flipped Classroom showed statistically significant differences in the experimental group (t=-8.416*, p<0.05). Also, there was a statistically significant difference in post-test scores between experimental and control groups (t=3.151*, p<.005). The findings suggest that learning in a Flipped Classroom increases students' academic performance, compared with the Traditional Classroom environment.

Despite the limitations regarding the small sample size of Secondary Male School students, the findings of this study are consistent with those of other studies that have been investigated the efficacy of the flipped classroom approach for enhancing student engagement and increasing of key concepts (Bergman & Sams, 2012; Khan, 2016; Davies et al., 2013; Al-Zahrani, 2015; Alamri, 2019). The researchers consider that the findings of this study will encourage teachers of science subjects to teach students by using modern teaching strategies, in particularly the Flipped Classroom Model as it helped to improve the academic achievement of students at BILs.

LIMITATIONS AND FUTURE RESEARCH DIRECTIONS

In addition to these findings, the following points should be considered when introducing new teaching-learning methods into K-12 education in Kazakhstan. First, a new teaching method needs to be fully orientated with the teacher. During this study, it was found that there was a great difference in the level of understanding of the flipped classroom of participating teachers. For example, questions have arisen about what teachers need to do when students have not seen the pre-video before class and when they have not completed the group activities.

Table 6. Post-test achievement scores between two groups

Group	N	M	SD	*t*	*p*
Flipped Classroom	84	9.89	3.159	3.151*	.002
Traditional Classroom	84	8.55	2.310		

* Statistically significant at the level of significance (*p < 0.05)

Second, since students rarely experience self-directed learning before class, they need to be explained and taught new teaching-learning methods. Third, an understanding of the information technology environment available to students is essential. In the case of the Bilim Innovation Lyceum, the school regulations prohibit the use of smartphones in the school, so the pre-class videos were viewed in the computer lab. However, there were other classes or projects in the computer lab, which caused students to enter the class without watching the video. Fourth, the government's support for the school's ICT technology needs to be strengthened. In some cases, there were no technical tools needed to create video classes, no internet connection at school, or no free use of computers or smart devices.

The limitations of this study and suggestions for future research are as follows. First, the fact that this study was conducted for a relatively short period of seven weeks is a big limitation. If FC classes are conducted for a long time, the perception of the teaching-learning environment and the effects on the students' academic achievement could be different. Second, it is necessary to analyze the differences among groups by conducting studies with more student sample cases. Statistical analysis may have different effects depending on the number of cases. Third, it was a pity that the students who participated in the study were all boys, and the researchers could not see the results of the girls. Further research is needed to explore the effects of FC in not only the Bilim Innovation Lyceum, but also the general public school, and the boys as well as girls. Accumulating these studies will help to find ways in which FC classes can be applied more effectively to Kazakhstan's school culture and educational reality.

Further, the findings recommended providing schools with technology tools, modern laboratory devices, and high-speed internet to help teachers to prepare the needed materials according to the Flipped Classroom Model. Furthermore, the study suggests conducting future research to investigate the effect of new teaching-learning methods, including flipped learning, which could be applicable in Sustainable Development Curricula and help in cooperation between countries in Eurasian region through more systematic and rigorous research designs on other variables such as other content subjects, region, mixed-gender schools and other grades from different academic stages.

REFERENCES

Al-Zahrani, A. M. (2015). 'From passive to active: The impact of the flipped classroom through social learning platforms on higher education students' creative thinking'. *British Journal of Educational Technology*, *46*(6), 1134–1150. doi:10.1111/bjet.12353

Alamri, M. M. (2019). Students' academic achievement performance and satisfaction in a flipped classroom in Saudi Arabia. *International Journal of Technology Enhanced Learning*, *11*(1), 103–119. doi:10.1504/IJTEL.2019.096786

Anderson, L. W. (2005). Objectives, evaluation, and the improvement of education. *Studies in Educational Evaluation*, *31*(2), 102–113. doi:10.1016/j.stueduc.2005.05.004

Asia Education. (2019). Retrieved from https://ec.europa.eu/europeaid/regions/asia/eu-support-education-and-science-collaboration-asia_en

Avetisyan, P. S., Zaslavskaya, M. I., Galikyan, G. E., Gevorkyan, N. M., Arutyunyan, M. L., Movsisyan, M. S., . . . Matevosyan, B. G. (2015). Modernization of Higher Education in the context of integration processes. Publishing center RAU.

Bergmann, J., & Sams, A. (2012). *Flip your classroom: Reach every student in every class every day.* Washington, DC: Internal Society for Technology in Education.

BIL. (2019). International Educational Fund 'Bilim Innovation'. Retrieved from www.bil.edu.kz

Buli-Fabrega, M., & Casanovas, M. M. (2019). Flipped Classroom as an Active Learning Methodology in Sustainable Development Curricula. *Sustainability, 11*(17), 4577. doi:10.3390u11174577

Cabi, E. (2018). The Impact of the Flipped Classroom Model on Students' Academic Achievement. *International Review of Research in Open and Distance Learning, 19*(3), 202–221. doi:10.19173/irrodl.v19i3.3482

Chen Hsieh, J. S., Wu, W. C. V., & Marek, M. W. (2017). Using the flipped classroom to enhance EFL learning. *Computer Assisted Language Learning, 30*(1-2), 1–21. doi:10.1080/09588221.2015.1111910

Choi, J. E. (2015). *The effect of the Flipped learning in the science class on the science achievement and class participation of middle school students* [Master's thesis]. Seoul, Soongsil University.

Davies, R. S., Dean, D. L., & Ball, N. (2013). Flipping the classroom and instructional technology integration in a college-level information systems spreadsheet course. *Educational Technology Research and Development, 61*(4), 563–580. doi:10.100711423-013-9305-6

Elian, S. A., & Hamaidi, D.A. (2018). The Effect of Using Flipped Classroom Strategy on the Academic Achievement of Fourth Grade Students in Jordan, *iJET, 13*(2), 110-125.

FLN. (2014). Flipped Learning Network. Retrieved from http://flippedlearning.org/definition-of-flipped-learning/

Government of Kazakhstan. (2019). State Programme for education development of Kazakhstan. Retrieved from www.open.egov.kz

Hamdan, N., McKnight, P., McKnight, K., & Arfstrom, K. M. (2013). *The flipped learning model: A white paper based on the literature review titled "A review of flipped learning."* Arlington, VA: Flipped Learning Network.

Huawei. (2019). 2019 Huawei ICT Sustainable Development Goals Benchmark. Retrieved from https://www.huawei.com/en/about-huawei/sustainability/sdg

Hwang, J. W. (2017). *The effects of mathematics learning using flipped classroom on underachieved students' mathematics learning attitude and academic achievement - Focusing on Operations on Real Numbers, Third Grade, Middle School* [Master's thesis]. Seoul, Korea University.

Islam, M. F., & Knezevic, R. (2019). The role of MOOCs in achieving the Sustainable Development Goal Four. In *Proceedings of the Western Balkan Information and Media Literacy Conference* (pp. 53-66). Academic Press.

Jin, H. K. (2016). *Application Method of Flipped Learning in Korean Language Instruction* [Master's thesis]. Seoul, Dongguk University.

Jung, J. A., Bae, J. H., & So, K. H. (2015). Biology Education: The Effect of Flipped Learning of Elementary Science Class on Learning Motivation and Academic Achievement of Elementary Students. *Biology Education, 43*(4), 333–343. doi:10.15717/bioedu.2015.43.4.333

Jung, M. (2014). *The Effects of Flipped Classroom on Elementary Learner's Mathematics Academic Achievement and Attitude* [Master's thesis]. Korea National University of Education, Seoul.

Kazakhstan Education Act. (2007). Law of the Republic of Kazakhstan about education. Retrieved from https://cis-legislation.com/document.fwx?rgn=18150

KBS. (2014). KBS Panorama. Retrieved from www.kbs.co.kr

Khan Academy. (2016). Retrieved from https://www.khanacademy.org/

Kim, J. S. (2018). *A Study of instructional procedures and material development for flipped classroom according to science instructional models* [Master's thesis]. Korea National University of Education.

Korea U learning Association. (2014). *Flipped Learning.* Seoul: Contents Media, 201p.

Lee, B. H., & Lee, H. C. (2016). The Effects of Science Lesson with the Application of Flipped Learning on Science Academic Achievement and Scientific Attitude. *KESES, 35*(1), 78–88.

Lee, D. Y. (2013). Research on Developing Instructional Design Models for Flipped Learning. *The Journal of Digital Policy & Management, 11*(12), 83–92.

Lee, H. S., & Kim, C. S. (2015). A study on the Effect of Flipped Learning on Learning Motivation and Academic Achievement. *Korean Computer Education, 19*(1), 143–147.

Lee, J. Y., Kim, Y. H., & Kim, Y. B. (2014). A Study on Application of Learner-Centered Flipped Learning Model. *Educational Technology, 30*(2), 163–191. doi:10.17232/KSET.30.2.163

Lee, M. K. (2014). Case Study on Effects and Signification of Flipped Classroom. *Korean Educational Development Institute, 41*(1), 87–116.

Oderesa, (2015). *Math Class Method of Students Participation through Flipped Classroom Practice* [Master's Thesis]. Busan University.

Park, K. B. (2014). Exploration of the possibility of Flipped Learning in social studies. *Social Studies Education, 53*(3), 107–120.

Ruddick, K. W. (2012). *Improving chemical education from high school to college using a more hands on approach.* Unpublished doctoral dissertation, University of Memphis.

Scott, A.J. (2011). In-class versus online video lectures: similar learning outcomes, but a preference for in-class. *Society for the teaching of psychology, 38*(4), 298-302.

Song, E. J., Lee, C.H. (2016). Effect of flipped learning STEAM applied to science and sound chapter on academic achievement and motivation of elementary school student. *The Korean Association of Practical Arts education, 2*, 297-301.

Song, Y., & Kapur, M. (2017). How to flip the classroom- "Productive failure or traditional flipped classroom" pedagogical design? *Journal of Educational Technology & Society, 20*(1), 292.

Strayer, J. F. (2007). *The effect of the classroom flip on the learning environment: A comparison of learning activity in a traditional classroom and a flip classroom that uses an intelligent tutoring system* [Doctoral thesis]. The Ohio State University.

UNESCO. (2008). *2008-Education for All by 2015 –Will we make it?* Background papers for the Education for All global monitoring report.

UNESCO. (2015). [*Incheon Declaration and Framework for Action.* Retrieved from http://unesdoc.unesco.org/images/0024/002456/245656e.pdf

UNESCO IITE. (2012). *Promotion of the Use of ICTs in TVET in CIS Countries.* Special Report on the Activities Implemented within the joint IFESCCO/UNESCO IITE project. Retrieved from https://iite.unesco.org/publications/3214702/

Velegol, S. B., & Zappe, S. E. (2016). How does a flipped classroom impact classroom climate? In *Proceedings of the ASEE 123rd Annual Conference & exposition.* Academic Press. 10.18260/p.25479

KEY TERMS AND DEFINITIONS

eLearning: A learning system which is obtained through the internet using an electronic device.

Eurasian Region: The alignment of the former USSR countries underpinned by historical, geographical, economic and geopolitical factors.

Flipped Classroom: One of the latest eLearning model that sets out to reverse the role of teaching with homework, whereby learners would typically digest new educational content outside their classroom. Teachers would then use their classroom sessions to allow learners to apply the information learned through a series of practical assignments.

Flipped Learning: An Interactive learning where teacher is a facilitator who gives directions to students apply concepts and engage creativity in the subject matter.

Massive Open Online Courses (MOOCs): A learning model for delivering learning content online to anyone who wants to take a course with no limit on attendance.

Open Educational Resources (OERs): A teaching and learning resources in any way that can be found in the public domain or introduced with an open license to freely copy, use, adapt and re-share them.

Sustainable Development Goals (SDGs): A blueprint that address the global challenges related to poverty, inequality, climate change, environmental degradation, peach and justice to achieve a better and more sustainable future for all.

Chapter 11
How Social Media Usage Influences Student Learning Outcomes

Uldana Baizyldayeva
KIMEP University, Kazakhstan

ABSTRACT

The development of new information and communication technologies and their utilization in everyday lives and especially the involvement of new generation in the usage of these technologies for communication, for entertainment, for education, and other activities has raised a real problem of distracting of young generation from necessary information for professional and intellectual development. In this chapter, the influence of social networks on higher institution students' academic performance is considered. There is a trial to build analytical models and estimate the degree of social networks impact on student academic performance by using GPA grades. The problem of involvedness of young people in social networks and its impact on the study process and academic performance brought concern towards the quality of professional development in the Central Asian region. As it is a sustainable development provided by the country's economy, the educational system directly depends on younger generation's interest in study and wellbeing.

INTRODUCTION

There is a problem about the future of youth and their development, active usage of Social media leads the indefiniteness of expectations in lives, but it is known that good knowledge is the best valuable contribution for everybody. Good GPA level is one of the main indicators of university's quality and reputation. This research should be directed to define the social media usage impact's degree (positive or negative) on students' study outcomes.

The relevance of this topic today is quite broad, day by day there is so much information in the world. The task is to help students to filter only the necessary information, make it accessible and understandable for its further conversion to knowledge.

DOI: 10.4018/978-1-7998-2551-7.ch011

Social networks penetrate into the peoples' daily life very deeply. The social media users of Central Asian countries compose 21% of the total population (Prins, 2019). The telecom companies of the Central Asian countries represent the social media penetration separately in December 2018. There are almost 1,263 thousand internet users in the republic of Turkmenistan, 21.2% of penetration rate (per internet users), 20 thousand Facebook subscribers (0.3% penetration); more than 17,161 thousand internet users in the republic of Uzbekistan, 52.3% of penetration rate (per internet users), 800 thousand Facebook subscribers (2.4% penetration); a few more than 3,013 thousand internet users in the republic of Tajikistan, 32.4% of penetration rate (per Internet World Stats), some more than 2,493 thousand internet users in Kyrgyzstan republic, 170 thousand subscribers (1.8% penetration); 40.1% penetration (per Internet World Stats), almost 14,470 thousand internet users, 650 thousand Facebook subscribers (10.5% penetration); 78.9 penetration rate(per Internet World Stats) in the republic of Kazakhstan, 2.500 Facebook subscribers (13.4% penetration).

The source of Statcounter.com shows the most popular Social Media sites in Kazakhstan. Since 2009 Facebook, VKontakte, YouTube occupy the first places and Instagram is on one of the last places in the list (Figure1).

As it is seen in the histogram the leader of sites in the period of 2009-2019 is Facebook -36,42%, then Vkontakte -26,2% and YouTube -15,43%. For the last year within 2018-2019 there is some change in results. The leader of Social Media sites in Kazakhstan is YouTube and Twitter is one of the last in the list. (Baizyldayeva, Nurmagambetova, 2019)

The most of all people use the site of Pinterest 23,32%, different from the previous chart, Pinterest has occupied the 5th place, then Vkontakte has stayed on the second place 22,15%, Facebook has become on the 3rd place 14,78%, YouTube and Instagram are on the 4th and 5th places 14.54% and 14.55% accordingly. Twitter is not so popular 8,1% in the country. (Figure2).

Social network sites join people. Their own opinion can be shared not only with friends, but with the whole world. Using social media tools, it can be organized a video call, meeting, event, protest, conference or donation program. Most social networking sites are free for users. Youth can work for the good of society, using social media tools to participate in volunteer initiatives. Social networking sites are used for communication, but unfortunately not for it, for spam too, cybercrime and fraud. There are

Figure 1. Social media usage in Kazakhstan," Market Share Perc. (2009 - 2019)"
Note: the histogram chart was created by author based on the data from Statcounter.com

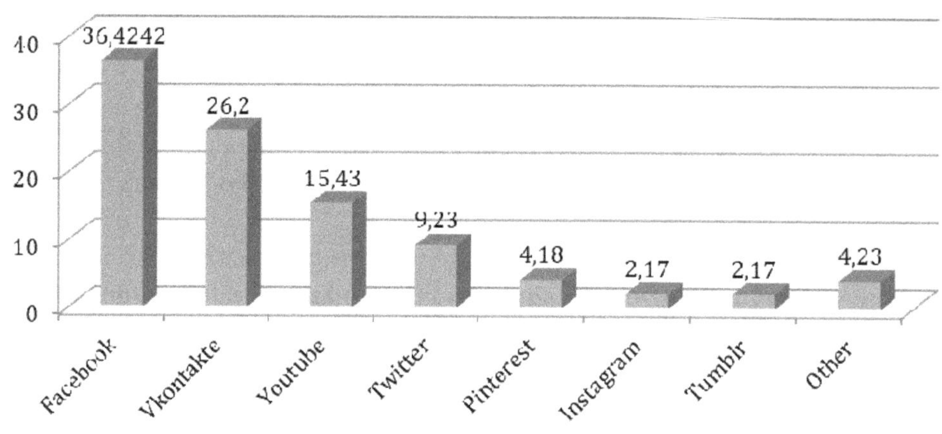

Figure 2. Social media usage in Kazakhstan in the period from October 2018- to October 2019
Note: the bar chart was created by author based on data from Statcounter.com

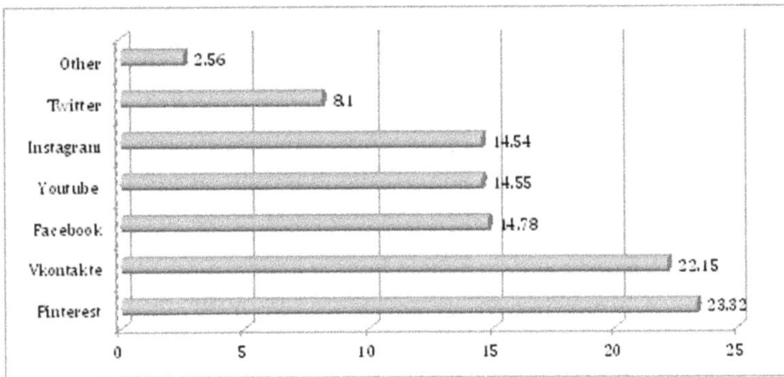

not all people have enough knowledge and skills needed to use computer technology and tools. Young people can use the social networking sites not only for leisure activities, but also to unite young people for initiatives to improve society.

Social media play a crucial role in improving governance and reducing corruption, increasing economic efficiency and stability, and creating positive social and environmental changes. The only way to make the country's development sustainable is to increase the participation of youth and the media in society. The main task of society is the formation of a person with a systemic worldview, an active civic position and critical, socially and environmentally oriented thinking. We can talk about the existence of a stable relationship between the orientation and content of social changes on the one hand and changes in the system of value orientations of youth on the other. Successful state reform is possible only with the active participation of young people, which requires new approaches to the development and implementation of youth policy. Conditions should be created for the acquisition of new knowledge and skills conducive to the sustainable development of society.

This topic is researched in other countries, but for Kazakhstan it is new. It is learnt thoroughly other countries' experience and apply positive and useful things to Kazakhstani education. Most of studies show the negative influence of social media usage to the students' academic performance and they suggest different ways for avoiding or reducing such negativity in their countries. Ketari and Khanum (2013) defined the relationship between the use of Facebook and the students' assessments in Saudi Arabia. Camilia et al. (2013) in his work provided the similar study, where conducted with Nigerian students and reported the absence of social networks usage frequency's influence on students' outcomes.

The authors of Junco et al., 2011, Tariq et al., 2012, Sampson et al., 2004, García-Peñalvo et al., 2012, Camilia et al., 2013, found the negativity in impact of social media usage on academic outcomes. They also signified the possibility of its influence on their lives in the countries of the United States, Nigeria and Pakistan.

There is no secret that the social media often violate generally accepted moral standards, use various manipulative technologies to influence the consciousness of the viewer, reader. If the young generation is a passive consumer of any kind of media information, that is, the information transmitted through the channels of the media does not expose it to independent, critical reflection, gradually, in the process of close communication with the media, its values and attitudes change.

For example, on average over a year, young viewers see about 20 thousand advertisements, convincing them to make the right choice in purchasing various goods. The passive consumption of such media information contributes to the emergence of stereotyped judgments, according to which, only by purchasing advertised goods, you can become like an ideal person who succeeds in life. But at the same time, according to numerous modern studies, the younger generation has a decrease in volitional abilities, unwillingness to achieve their goal with honest work. On the contrary, passivity and infantilism are characteristic of many young people. The reason for this passivity is seen, among social, pedagogical and other reasons, in the accessibility of satisfying desires due to the abundance of internet programs, computer games, advertising, etc.

The purpose of the study is to identify the influence of social media usage on students' academic performance (GPA) in institutions of higher education.

For identifying this phenomenon, the survey was conducted among students from various institutions of higher education in Kazakhstan.

Research Questions

- Does the usage of social networks influence to the Kazakhstani students' GPAs.
- Do the factors relate to each other? Is the relationship positive or negative?
- Do the students' grades increase or decrease while the usage time of social networks increase? (Baizyldayeva & Nurmagambetova, 2019)

LITERATURE REVIEW

The study is about how social media influence to the young people, what are the main points of this impact and what kind of young people and how they react to the influence. These are the affordable questions that have been answered in studies where they say that social media gives young people the new educational opportunities to explore new trends, develop writing and communication skills, cultural advancement, religious and political information, collect and send links, change the life style, growth and development of society (Merriam Encyclopedia, 2001). Ghulam Shabir's either mentioned the negative impact of the social media usage on young people, and in particular, on the results of students' education, on the active lifestyle of students (reduction of sports). He paid attention at socially - unethical norms of communication on the Internet, switching the use of SMM into a hobby for wasting time, ambiguity and confusion of youth thinking, promotion of unethical pictures, videos, clips, etc. - all of them are the downside of the benefits of social media, which is recommended for young people to avoid themselves and block access to educational institutions, or limit the use of the Internet as a whole (Ghulam Shabir, 2014).

Media culture assimilates the norms and values of a particular social group, develops attitudes and considers media information through the prism of these values and orientations. In this regard, the understanding of the problems of media violence in the works of modern media culture is extremely relevant.

The reality is that everybody faces violence in many everyday situations, regularly become spectators and users of screen violence, which are abundant in mass media: television, the press, the Internet, cinema, etc. The basic theories of "media effects" as follows describe the mechanisms of influence of audiovisual works containing scenes of violence: manipulating a sense of fear (for example, stimulating a sense of fear of aggression and violence); teaching the audience violent / aggressive actions with their subsequent commission in real life (violence as an acceptable way to solve any problems); stimulation, arousal of aggressive, imitative instincts of the audience, its appetite in relation to scenes of violence (especially in relation to an audience with a disturbed psyche); "Vaccinating" the audience with a sense of indifference, indifference to the victims of violence, lowering the threshold of sensitivity in relation to the manifestation of violence in real life; virtual and safe for others, the release of aggressive emotions that do not lead to negative consequences in real life.

Currently, in the world practice of media education, numerous media education programs have been developed that contribute to the development of independent, critical thinking, creativity, communication skills, aesthetic tastes, and value orientations of a young audience. Through media education, the younger generation learns to work with information, to understand how, through media information, an impact on the consciousness of the audience is carried out, what manipulative and technological methods are used.

Thinking about reality and the picture of the world being created has always been a part of socio-historical development and an important component of philosophical knowledge. Accordingly, at each historical stage, their ideas about the social and moral social ideal developed. The intensive development of new information technologies and the widespread distribution of media products creates new problems related to understanding the media reality, how people interact with the world of the media, how social, moral, moral choices are made in a world where the media are perceived as an integral part of life. This made possible the emergence and development of a society of mass consumption, mass values, mass holidays, mass emotions of a society of the twentieth century, the habitat of which is media reality.

In the reality created by cinema and television, a new world of visual images was constructed, where fantasy exists along with the proposed depicted objects. In a post-industrial society, a person got the opportunity to independently model completely new constructs of media reality, in which everyone has the right to see and design their own media reality.

That is why the works of media culture are becoming in modern conditions a sociocultural environment, the living space of a person. "Continuously expanding media have become a real habitat - a space as real and, apparently, open as the globe was five hundred years ago". The world of media is increasingly associated with consumption, including social, cultural, spiritual consumption: in the words of Guy Debord, "a real consumer becomes a consumer of illusions". In a world of illusions and media manipulations, it is difficult for a person saturated with ready-made mosaic images of the media world to understand: "How can you resist the consumption of information that daily tempts with an increase in the degree of sensation, speed of presentation of an event, catastrophes and horrors? This degree rises to a boiling point, that is, the point of non-perception and we become indifferent to everything surrounding us directly, but dependent on what happens far, beyond the bounds of visibility, feelings, experiences."

M. McLuhan, considering the means of communication as a kind of continuation of the senses and expanding the capabilities of the nervous system, was one of the first to consider the processes of mass communication in the world of culture. Jean Baudrillard, developing the idea of M. McLuhan about the expansion of a person in space with the help of technological "prostheses", wrote: "everything that exists in a human being — its biological, muscular, brain substance — hangs around him in the form of mechanical or informational prostheses." Thus, a person of the media age of the post-industrial world, who had previously used a prosthesis for "expansion", himself becomes a prosthesis - a prosthesis of the body and a prosthesis of consciousness.

In turn, the media field creates a special world around modern man, the basis of which is publicity. According to M. Heidegger's definition, publicity in a special way "rules the whole interpretation of the world and presence and turns out to be right in everything. And this is not on the basis of some kind of exclusive and primary existential attitude towards "things", not because she has at her disposal a clearly adequate transparency of presence, but on the basis of non-entry "into the essence of the matter", because she is insensitive to all level differences and authenticity. Publicity obscures everything and gives the hidden as known and accessible to everyone." At the same time, "groundless explanations do not block their access to publicity, but favor it. The interpretations that anyone can pick up, not only eliminate the task of real understanding, but also form an indifferent intelligibility, from which nothing is already closed".

Along with the accumulation of experience in communicating with media reality, the media consumer is growing self-confidence in the sophistication and completeness of understanding of the information media field, which, according to M. Heidegger, allows spreading "growing unnecessarily in one's own understanding. The imagination of people that they support and lead a complete and genuine "life" brings calm to the presence, for which everything is "in the best order" and with which all doors are open. " Indeed, why bother trying to understand something when all events are very clearly shown, already understood for you, commented and analyzed? And if something was not shown there, then TV, maybe this was not there at all? The illusory reality created by the media allows the modern media consumer to "dream and know that you are dreaming" (F. Nietzsche), but do nothing to wake up (or not know what to do if you wake up?).

All aspects of the existence of media subjects are reflected in media reality, and human interaction with the media world determines consciousness, feelings, life strategies and value orientations of society as a whole. In a tense struggle, there is a clash of alternative video projects depicting the past, present and future, the authors of which are trying to convince the audience that what is shown on the screen is fully consistent with objective truth.

The transformational processes of attitude towards media reality in a post-industrial society lead to the understanding that the goal of the creators of media works is no longer to depict directly observable reality with a claim to objectivity. An increasingly significant role in television projects, cinematic art is given to the personality of the author, interpreter, interpreter, building a picture of video reality. In other words, not only and not so much what is shown comes to the fore, but who comments on the video. One of the central points of understanding the structure of media reality and comprehending the processes that occur with a person "freed from the fetters of reality" (P. Sloterdijk), living in the era of media technology, is the analysis of media culture works - a method of studying the media text by studying its individual sides, its constituent parts, artistic identity, sociocultural context, etc.

Media text, which is a complex sign complex, carries not only the information load, but also is the result of communication and creative understanding of its essence by the subjects involved in the process of creating and perceiving media information. In this regard, a creative understanding of media reality is inconceivable without a critical assessment of the works of media culture, identifying their properties and characteristics, components and elements in the context of a personal, sociocultural and author's position, which involves the ability to group facts, properties and phenomena, classify them, and reveal the essential aspects of the studied media products, its internal structure. Only on the basis of the system-forming characteristics of the media text can the recipient make independent and informed conclusions, which are the basis for the interpretation and reflection of media information.

The world has become different, people live in conditions of a tremendous congestion in the information space, not without reason modern society is increasingly called "super-informed." And an inherent characteristic of this world is uncertainty. The idea that uncertainty plays an important motivational role in human behavior is not new. Uncertainty is multifaceted: it can be weak or strong, temporary or stable, important or trivial. People can feel uncertainty in general or in specific things, for example, in their beliefs, views, values, relationships with other people, in their future and their place in the world, and more fundamentally - in themselves, in their identity. And today, radicalization is a dangerous consequence of uncertainty; the history of the twentieth century provides a significant number of examples of the growth of extremism as a reaction to this phenomenon. Modern life is hard to imagine without social media. This phenomenon has tightly entered our life, first of all, the life of modern youth, and entailed the transformation of the communication process. To indicate changes in the communicative process that is unfolding in social networks, one can appeal to the idea of F. Bushini. He suggests using the concept of effusion, which indicates the specifics of communication through new media, because the participants are in symmetrical relationships; by default, all participants in this process have equal access to knowledge, to information. The situation of interaction requires not only to have an opinion, but also to express it, act, giving advice to each other and making assessments, making judgments, in a word, to actively participate in this communicative process. Moreover, the reactions of the participants should be instantaneous. A number of studies have pointed out the relegation to the background of traditional leisure activities by new, mediated Internet technologies. D. Boyd draws attention to the fact that it was always typical for adolescents to be in the so-called networked social environments. Previously, such an environment included parks and courtyards, but for modern youth, the Internet has become such an environment, namely, social media. So, D. Korolyeva in a study of the everyday life of modern adolescents notes that checking personal messages on social networks, updating a news feed is an integral part of everyday life of adolescents. P. Arsand noted that the events taking place in the life of modern youth "online" are of equal importance with the events that take place "offline". In this way, adolescents satisfy the need for "constant events," that is, the need for new impressions. Thus, according to D.O. Korolyeva, checking news and messages on social networks today can be regarded as a new ritual characteristic of adolescent everyday life, as an attempt to solve the time gap. According to T.D. Marcinkowska, "... the younger generation is developing in a fundamentally new social and information space in which the words" information culture "are not an abstract concept, but a living reality".

According to Ostapenko's work, the emptiness formed due to the lack of events is filled either with boredom or with vanity. The incompleteness of time, the absence of eventuality can become causes of boredom as a special mental state of a person developing in connection with a deficit of external and internal activity. According to the research results of Posokhova and Rohina, adolescents experience boredom as a result of a lack of new experiences, a desire to experience positive emotions, and also because of dissatisfaction with the current state of affairs (social environment, monotony of life, its monotony). Teenagers experience a state of boredom because they don't know how to solve the problem of lack of time, while at present, adolescents most often use social media to overcome boredom. Thus, the experience of boredom provokes a search for new sensations, new information, for which modern young people go to social media. It should be noted that under the influence of social media, young people can form a picture of the world that does not always adequately reflect reality. As a result, the impossibility of embodying certain ideas can lead to a violation of expectations (in relation to one's own culture), loss of a sense of self-identification and, as a result, the appearance of uncertainty, which is beneficial for those involved in involving young people in illegal activities. Thus, social media is turning into an effective tool for radicalization, which has recently been puzzled in European countries, in particular in France. Today, the Internet allows people to create not only professional media sites that are edited by specialist journalists, but also unprofessional independent Internet resources, the contents of which are regulated by ordinary users. It should be noted that such popular social media as Facebook, Twitter, LiveJournal, Wikipedia, YouTube, etc. due to the special capabilities of the interface are a unique means of communication. The peculiarity of such social media, their uniqueness lies in the fact that, in combination with the development of mobile technologies, today we can find out about the resonant event much earlier than it will be announced in the official media.

Kates' results of his study demonstrate that the use of mobile smartphones has a small negative impact on students' grades. The author was not satisfied with the results and recommended in subsequent works to pay attention to the moderators of the goals of using smartphones: in pursuit of fashion and prestige, or for training. (Kates A.W., Wu H. & Coryn C.L.S., 2018).

There is so much social media diversity today that students spend time to simultaneously communicate in several of it. On the one hand, it is said that this is good, they develop skills of fast typing, quick response when switching, be aware of all current events, but is it so simple, because the main task of students is learning, and often using of social media becomes a priority for most students. Considering the preferences of multitasking and self-regulation, the results of hierarchical regression analysis showed that neither the multitasking preferences nor the control of self-regulation contribute to the determination of student academic performance after controlling such well-known variables as age, gender and year of study. Despite multi-tasking with different media and technologies and individual control of self-regulation, the use of media has increased, leading to a decrease in academic performance (Uzun & Kilis, 2019).

Galla and Duckworth provide the experiments from different literature about the understanding of students' behavior during study, particularly self - control. It is the wrong approach to count the time student spent for doing his homework, it depends on many factors and it doesn't give the objective result of self-control (Galla & Duckworth, 2015). Then the study describes the experiment with small children ("the preschool delay-of-gratification paradigm") which is called "marshmallow test". The children were presented different sweets: marshmallow, biscuits, candies and other things (Mischel, 2014). The child was asked to prefer what would he or she has the small set of sweets right away or to wait for the big set of sweets "after the experimenter comes back from doing something unrelated in the hallway". Nearly all children chose the bigger set, "delayed treat (National Institute of Child Health and Human Development, 1999)". Most children preferred bigger set, that shows the children's opportunity of self-control behavior. "Wait time in this standardized situation correlates positively with self-control ratings by parents…and predicts higher report card grades and standardized test scores, lower self-reported reckless behavior". (Mischel, 2014; Tsukayama et al., 2013).

Students who understand the negative impact of media multitasking on academic performance will potentially contribute to self-awareness and, possibly, self-regulation of multitasking habits. So the self-regulation of multitasking habits and the necessary range of skills become the attractive qualities of the modern student, graduate and modern professional. Developing the self-regulation skills and positive technology habits throughout school to balance the modern workplace. (Kaitlyn E. May and Anastasia D. Elder, 2018).

In the study of Ewa Szumowska we could acquaint with the experiment where the authors gave the possibility for the participants to use 6 different social media resources simultaneously to understand the degree of media multitasking influence on students' academic outcomes. For one part of participants they did not signify any limits but to the another part they limited time of using social media. Ewa Szumowska has defined that the frequency of social media multitasking is related to many switches in different media tasks for the participants who are poorer in self-regulation and the frequency of social media multitasking is related to strong multitasking usage but only when students have been allowed freely switch between tasks. While participants have worked sequentially, their frequency of media multitasking is not related negatively to the multitasking outcomes (Szumowska, Popławska-Boruc, Kus, Osowiecka, & Kramarczyk, 2018).

In the study of Wu it became clear that the time pressure is the most significant predictor of students' academic outcomes. Also, he used the method of writing notes. Some students did not use any notes, others used unstructured and matrix-structured notes. Using matrix-structured notes helped students to absorb maximum value of information during the lesson, so their outcomes showed better results than others and the worst results were at students who did not use any notes at all. High time pressure requirement reduced the irrelevant browsing rates and increased the results of outcomes (Wu & Xie, 2018). In the study authors supposed that performance motivated students had the positive affect on the academic outcomes of students, but not for long term, because it is difficult to attract students' attention without any interest (Harackiewicz, Barron, Tauer, Carter, & Elliot, 2000). In another study authors applied the cases from the life and encouraged the students for solving problems following the examples from their lives. These class activities increased students' interests to study and affect positively to academic performance (Chris S. Hulleman, Judith M. Harackiewicz). Thus, today teachers should change methodic and look for new approaches to decrease the students' distraction from the study to decline the negative affect to the academic performance. *Hypothesis in the model 1* (Figure3,4): Null hypothesis supposes the absence of relationship between Social media usage and academic performance (GPA) through the students' interest to study.

Alternative hypothesis supposes the presence of relationship between Social media usage and academic performance (GPA) through the students' interest to study.

Implementation

To conclude all of the knowledge on the topic the scheme of the model is constructed where the main independent factor is the social media usage and additional (moderators) are the indicators of self-regulation, social media multitasking, impulsivity/non-impulsivity. Theoretically proposed hypothesis provides for the determination of the existence of a relationship between the frequency of users of social networks and their academic performance (GPA). So, the null hypothesis H_0, will deny the existence of a relationship between these factors, and the alternative hypothesis H_1 will recognize its existence. So, the constructed model 2 is in (Figure 3).

Figure 3. Model 2
Note: the figure was created by author

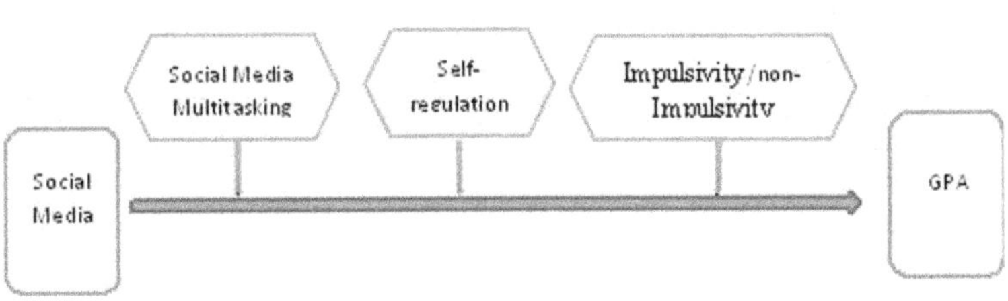

Figure 4. Model1
Note: the figure was created by author

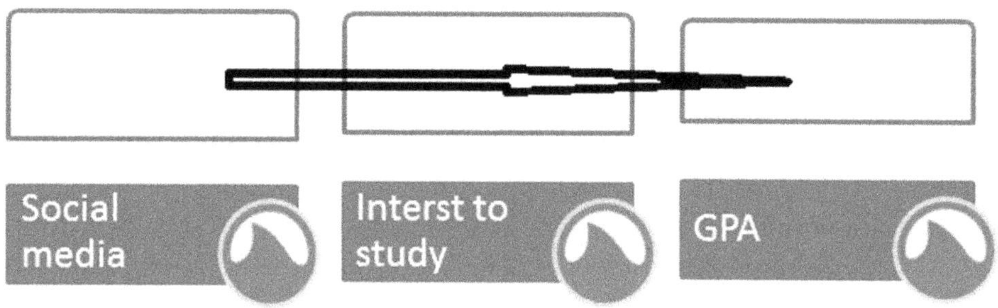

METHODOLOGY

The main problem of students' distraction during the study is the absence of their interests in studying subject or topic.

The online Google form survey was conducted among 104 undergraduate students from Narxoz university, 70 females, 34 males. Then checked data and extracted 23 incorrect answers and worked with 81 answers. Below they are represented some models of research, analysis of which were done in Gretl. Also, for checking the reliability of data Cronbach alpha test was calculated, it equaled 0,98. The first model is aimed to define the relationship between students' interests in study and their academic performance.

Model1

H0: There is no relationship (R=0) between students' interest to study and average GPA, the parameters of model are statistically insignificant (b0=b1=0).

H1: There is positive relationship ($R^{1}0$) between students' interest to study and average GPA, the parameters of model are statistically significant ($b0^{1}b1^{1}0$). See Table 1.

Table 1. Model 1: OLS, using observations 1-81

	Coefficient	*Std. Error*	*t-ratio*	*p-value*	
Const	3.17832	0.0639613	49.69	<0.0001	***
Areyouinterestedinthestudyofyou	0.0890710	0.0370810	2.402	0.0187	**

Mean dependent var	3.313580	S.D. dependent var	0.281071
Sum squared resid	5.889882	S.E. of regression	0.273048
R-squared	0.068066	Adjusted R-squared	0.056269
F(1, 79)	5.769934	P-value(F)	0.018650
Log-likelihood	−8.774884	Akaike criterion	21.54977
Schwarz criterion	26.33867	Hannan-Quinn	23.47114

Dependent variable: WhatisyouraverageGPA.
Note: table was compiled by the author

Results

The results show the positive relationship between students' interest to study and average GPA, where R = 0,24 (R squared =0,06), b0 = 3,178, b1 = 0,089, also the Fisher criterion F(1,79) = 5, 77, which is greater than F table = 3, it tells us about statistical significance of the model. So we can reject the null hypothesis. In fact we confirm the positive influence of students' studying interest on GPA level.

ANALYSIS OF QUANTITATIVE DATA

Model2

ANOVA is the analysis of variance. This method is used to find the statistically significant difference between three variables: Social media multitasking (distraction), Students' impulsivity/non-impulsitivity in character and students' self-regulation skills, influencing their academic performance (GPA) (see Tables 2, 3, and 4). The means of variables will be denoted: self-regulation skills mean is μ 1, impulsitivity/ non-impulsitivity mean is μ2, Social media multitasking (distraction) mean is μ3.

H0: Absence of statistically significant difference between students' impulsitivity/ non-impulsitivity, social media multitasking (distraction) and self-regulation skills: μ1= μ2= μ3

H1: Presence of statistically significant difference between students' impulsitivity/ non-impulsitivity, social media multitasking (distraction) and self-regulation skills: $\mu 1^{1}$ $\mu 2^{1}$ μ3.

Table 2. Analysis of variance, response = WhatisyouraverageGPA, treatment = Doyouconsideryourselfasapersonw (self-regulation skills)

	Sum of squares	df	Mean square
Treatment	0.118206	2	0.059103 (mean 0,243)
Block	0.334062	2	0.167031
Residual	5.86779	76	0.0772078
Total	6.32006	80	0.0790008

Note: table was compiled by the author
F(2, 76) = 0.059103 / 0.0772078 = 0.765505 [p-value 0.4687]

Table 3. Analysis of variance, response = WhatisyouraverageGPA, treatment = Doyouconsideryouareimpulsiveorn (students' impulsitivity/ non-impulsitivity)

	Sum of squares	df	Mean square
Treatment	0.387869	2	0.193935 (mean 0,44)
Block	0.334062	2	0.167031
Residual	5.59813	76	0.0736596
Total	6.32006	80	0.0790008

Note: table was compiled by the author
F(2, 76) = 0.193935 / 0.0736596 = 2.63285 [p-value 0.0784]

Table 4. Analysis of Variance, response = WhatisyouraverageGPA, treatment = Can you sit in Social media play comp (social media multitasking (distraction))

	Sum of squares	df	Mean square
Treatment	0.25132	2	0.12566 (mean 0,354)
Block	0.334062	2	0.167031
Residual	5.73468	76	0.0754563
Total	6.32006	80	0.0790008

Note: table was compiled by the author
F(2, 76) = 0.12566 / 0.0754563 = 1.66533 [p-value 0.1960]

Comparing means of three variables we see that µ1= 0,243, µ2 = 0,44, µ3 = 0,354, they are all different, not equal µ1[1] µ 2[1] µ 3, so the absence of difference between three means (null hypothesis) can be rejected, but not all of means are statistically significant. The most statistically significant mean in probability of 90% (α = 0,1) is the impusitivity/non-impulsitivity mean p value 0,078, the others are statistically insignificant. Thus it can be concluded that the factor of impusitivity/non-impulsitivity impacts the academic performance more than other factors.

In addition to reported analysis the relationship between two of research variables – "Number_of_hours_a_day_you_use_social_media" and "GPA" with calculation of correlation coefficient in IBM SPSS system was investigated. It is obtained as result negative value of relationship, which equals -0.172. From such correlation coefficient between two mentioned variables it may be concluded, that the more hours student spend in social networks, the lower is the student's GPA score (see Table 5).

Table 5. Pearson correlation analysis

Correlations			
		Your_average_GPA	Number_of_hours_a_day_you_use_social_media
Your_average_GPA	Pearson Correlation	1	-.172
	Sig. (2-tailed)		.125
	Sum of Squares and Cross-products	6.320	-2.915
	Covariance	.079	-.036
	N	81	81
Number_of_hours_a_day_you_use_social_media	Pearson Correlation	-.172	1
	Sig. (2-tailed)	.125	
	Sum of Squares and Cross-products	-2.915	45.556
	Covariance	-.036	.569
	N	81	81

Note: Correlation analysis was done in IBM SPSS 20

CONCLUSION AND DISCUSSION

In this study they are represented two models, each of them had separate goals. In the first model there is shown the direct and positive connection of the study interest and GPA, but the initial point of this connection starts from the Social media usage. This problem was risen some years ago, when the people (students) were not so active in social media. But there is understood the necessity of returning to this item because it one of the most important things in defending students from huge attack of Social media distraction. The results confirm the positive affect of study interest on GPA.

Model two demonstrated the analysis of variance to determine the significant difference between moderated factors of impulsivity, self-regulation and Social media multitasking impacting simultaneously to students' GPA and it should be remembered the initiative point of the model is social media usage. Totally it can be seen that there was the difference between three factors' means however the most significant seemed the factor of impulsivity which influences more powerful on the academic performance than the other two.

Limitations. The main limitation of this research is the cross-sectional type of regression analysis. In the future work it is suggested to represent the time-series type. The GPA value was asked from the students themselves, not from official resources, so their representation could not be objective.

REFERENCES

Al-Khalifa, H. S., & Garcia, R. A. (2013). The state of social media in Saudi Arabia's higher education. *International Journal of Technology and Educational Marketing*, *3*(1), 65–76. doi:10.4018/ijtem.2013010105

Baizyldayeva, U., & Nurmagambetova, G. (2019). The Influences of the Social Media on the Students'. *Academic Outcomes*, *1*, 296–307.

Bajdarov, E. U. (2009). Informacionno-obrazovatelnye i vospitatelnye strategii v sovremennom obshestve: nacionalnyj i globalnyj kontekst. In Materialy mezhdunarodnoj nauchnoj konferencii. Minsk: Pravo i ekonomika.

Camilia, N., Ibrahim, S., & Dalhatu, B. (2013). The effect of social networking sites usage on the studies of Nigerian students. *International Journal of Engineering Science*, *2*, 39–46.

Galla, B. M., & Duckworth, A. L. (2015). More than resisting temptation: Beneficial habits mediate the relationship between self control and positive life outcomes. *Journal of Personality and Social Psychology*, *109*(3), 508–525; Advance online publication. doi:10.1037/pspp0000026 PMID:25643222

García-Peñalvo, F. J., Colomo-Palacios, R., & Lytras, M. D. (2012). Informal learning in work environments: Training with the soci.al web in the workplace. *Behaviour & Information Technology*, *31*(8), 753–755. doi:10.1080/0144929X.2012.661548

Harris, R. (2002). *Psihologiya massovyh kommunikacij*. Retrieved from https://uchebnikfree.com/svyazi-obschestvennostyu-upravlenie/sravnenie-razlichnyih-mass-media-mentalnyie-34500.html

Internet World Stats. (n.d.). Asia. Retrieved from https://www.internetworldstats.com/asia.htm

Junco, R. G., Heiberger, G., & Loken, E. (2011). The effect of Twitter on college student engagement and grades. *Journal of Computer Assisted Learning*, *27*(2), 119–132. doi:10.1111/j.1365-2729.2010.00387.x

Kaitlyn, E. M., & Anastasia, D. E. (2018). *Efficient, helpful, or distracting? A literature review of media multitasking in relation to academic performance*. International Journal of Educational Technology in Higher Education. doi:10.118641239-018-0096-z

Kates, A. W., Wu, H., & Coryn, C. L. S. (2018). (2018). *The effects of mobile phone use on academic performance: A meta-analysis*. *Computers & Education*, *127*, 107–112. doi:10.1016/j.compedu.2018.08.012

Ketari, L. M., & Khanum, M. A. (2013). Impact of Facebook usage on the academic grades: A case study. *Journal of Computers*, *5*(1), 44–48.

Mischel, W. (2014). *The Marshmallow Test: Mastering self-control*. New York, NY: Little, Brown.

Prins, N. (n.d.). *An Analysis of the Russian Social Media Landscape in 2019*. Retrieved from https://www.linkfluence.com/blog/russian-social-media-landscape

Shabir, G., Hameed, Y. M. Y., Safdar, G., & Gilani, S. M. F. S. (2014). The impact of social media on youth: A case study of bahawalpur city. *Asian Journal of Social Sciences & Humanities*, *3*(4), 132–151.

Sheluho, M. V. (2012). Vliyanie socialnyh media na sferu obrazovaniya. In *Pedagogicheskoe masterstvo: materialy II Mezhdunar. nauch. konf.* (pp. 26-32). Moscow: Buki-Vedi. Retrieved from https://moluch.ru/conf/ped/archive/65/3189/

Szumowska, E., Popławska-Boruc, A., Kuś, J., Osowiecka, M., & Kramarczyk, J. (2018). When frequent media multitaskers perform worse and when they do not: The role of self-regulation ability and strategy manipulation. *Computers in Human Behavior*, *83*, 184–193.

Tariq, W., Mehboob, M., Khan, M. A., & Ullah, F. (2012). The impact of social media and social networks on education and students of Pakistan. *International Journal of Computer Science Issues*, *9*, 407–411.

Teryakova, A. S., & Bobrova, I. I. (2014) *Vliyanie socialnyh setej na molodyozh* // Portal nauchno-prakticheskih publikacij. Retrieved from http://portalnp.ru/2014/12/2243

Tikhonova, A. D. (2018). *Social media and youth: the risk of radicalization. Psychology and law*, *8*(4), 55-64.

Tsukayama, E., Duckworth, A. L., & Kim, B. E. (2013). Domain specific impulsivity in school-age children. *Developmental Science*, *16*(6), 879–893. PMID:24118714

Wu, J. Y., & Xie, C. (2018). Using Time Pressure and Note-Taking to Prevent Digital Distraction Behavior and Enhance Online Search Performance: Perspectives from the Load Theory of Attention and Cognitive Control. *Computers in Human Behavior, 88, 244-254.* doi:10.1016/j.chb.2018.07.008

Uzun, A. M., & Kilis, S. (2019). Does persistent involvement in media and technology lead to lower academic performance? Evaluating media and technology use in relation to multitasking, self-regulation and academic performance. *Computers in Human Behavior*, *90*, 196–203. doi:10.1016/j.chb.2018.08.045

Vladimirova, T. N., & Zhilavskaya, I. V. (2011). *Molodezh i media. Celi i cennosti. In materialov I Vserossijskoj nauchno-prakticheskoj konferencii*. Moscow: RIC.

Yandex. (n.d.). Retrieved from https://zen.yandex.ru/media/id/5abb502655876be3093d2ea4/-sovremennye-media-i-rol-molodeji-v-jizni-obscestva-5abd2c05d7bf214e3a1ff6bd

Zhilavskaya I. V., Avgustevich S. I. (2012). M. Ekologiya mediaprostranstva. In *materialov II Mezhdunarodnoj nauchno-prakticheskoj konferencii*. Academic Press.

Chapter 12
Mobile Devices in Education

Anastassiya Khalikova
https://orcid.org/0000-0002-5086-7396
University of International Business, Kazakhstan

Svetlana Silkina
University of International Business, Kazakhstan

ABSTRACT

This chapter reviewed the importance of using ICT in the educational process with the example of mobile devices. Mobile devices as teaching tools are becoming a more and more common part of the educational process in classrooms. Every day the share of mobile Internet and mobile device users are increasing. The level of introduction of mobile devices into the educational environment at the leading universities worldwide is quite high. In Kazakhstan, this system is spread slightly. However, the University of International Business implemented the application for learning the English language which is called "The UIB English." It is obvious that the use of mobile learning in the educational process requires organizational, research and methodological work. Universities should create and implement projects to operate the mobile version of the portal; identify and develop the most popular mobile services integrated with the information system of the university; develop and implement a mobile security policy; and create its own applications.

INTRODUCTION

The importance of using ICT in the educational process is reviewed on the example of mobile devices.

Later, people will not need to travel to other cities or countries to get an education. With the development of technology, you can learn anywhere, having a phone in your pocket and a good LTE signal.

Mobile learning is a relatively new way of learning, in which people get knowledge through gadgets: smartphone, tablet or laptop. A few years ago, special devices were introduced and developed for this purpose: something like e-books containing training programs. With the development of the Internet and phones, the latter took on the role of "teacher." And the curriculum consists of applications that the user downloads.

DOI: 10.4018/978-1-7998-2551-7.ch012

Another aspect of mobile learning is organizational. Gradually, the study or transfer of some information "remotely" are introduced in schools and Universities. Electronic diaries, groups in social networks, documents with open access-all this allows gadgets to help with the studies.

Mobile devices as teaching tools are becoming a more and more common part of the education process in classrooms. Every day the share of mobile Internet and the number of users of mobile devices are increasing. Such changes are quite conditioned – now everyone is striving for convenience and mobility in all spheres of life. With the advent of communicators and tablets, there is no need to take "bulky" laptops and other devices on the road, on business trips, at meetings, and for other purposes. However, mobile devices would not bring so much benefit without special add-ons – mobile applications. The importance of mobile applications in education is growing, and the main reason for this is the opportunities they provide:

- Collaboration of students on tasks during the lesson and in extracurricular activities.
- File exchange.
- Organization of distance learning.
- Interaction with students all the time.

BACKGROUND

Let's take a closer look at the concept of "mobile learning." Mobile learning (M-Learning) - the ability to learn regardless of place and time, through a number of mobile devices.

Mobile learning – e-learning through mobile devices, not limited to the location or change of location of the student.

Thus, mobile learning involves the use of mobile technology both individually and in conjunction with other information and communication technologies (ICT), for the organization of the educational process, regardless of place and time.

With the transition to the mobile sphere, education adapts to the conditions of this environment, becoming more compact, narrowly focused and interactive. On the mobile web, it is important that the information can be assimilated in small pieces, as clearly as possible correspond to the situation and, at the same time, that the process of interaction with the product is fun. Accordingly, user habits are changing, students increasingly want education to be simple, effective and fun. It becomes possible to study where you are at any time. Therefore, learning has become much easier, and the opportunity to do it little by little, but often that in the learning process is very important. The growth of mobile technologies is making constant changes in education. Education is no longer limited to space or tools such as desks, computers or expensive textbooks. Instead, all the power of learning-focused at everyone's fingertips with instant access and unlimited possibilities. In Strategy "Kazakhstan 2050" is written about the modernization of methods of teaching. It is necessary to modernize teaching methods and actively develop online education systems, creating regional school centers, intensively introduce innovative methods, solutions, and tools into the domestic education system, including distance learning and online learning, available to everyone. It is necessary to get rid of outdated or unclaimed scientific and educational disciplines while strengthening the popular and promising areas. It is better to change the focus and emphasis of secondary and higher education curricula to include practical skills and practical qualification programs, to create entrepreneurship-oriented curricula, educational courses, and institutes.

Laliberte (2010) defines the term as: "Educational technology is a tool that increases performance levels while allowing the use of innovative approaches with regard to teaching and learning" (p. 53). Yet due to the broadness of the field, one can find different and sometimes contradictory definitions for it (Schneider, 2013).

John Traxler (2009) argues that mobile learning completely changes the learning process, as mobile devices modify not only the forms of presentation and access to it but also contribute to the new forms of knowledge and mentality creation. Training becomes timely, sufficient and personalized.

There are different ways to use mobile technology in the classroom. What can be done and what cannot be done is limited mainly by the creative approach of the teacher. Thus, the more creative and innovative people become, the more results they will get when using technology in the classroom. Here are a few examples to help you understand what effective use would look like.

1. Live polls, when you get an instant result, can be used both after the introduction of a new topic and as a final control of the knowledge and skills of students. Teachers can use these tools (many of which are free) to determine what students already know and what to focus on. It can also provide insight into each student's strengths and weaknesses and, if necessary, help with individual learning.
2. The creation of the video. Instead of students writing an essay or article on a topic where some simply copy and paste paragraphs without necessarily understanding the content, the teacher may ask students to create a video recording of what they have researched.
3. The use of QR codes. Quick response codes (QR) are another great way to use mobile technology in the classroom. By generating QR codes, you can provide information, tasks, links to additional resources, images, solutions to tasks that can be read by students ' smartphones.
4. Use the audio recording function. Students often need personal and quality feedback about the work they are doing. Teachers can use the audio recording feature built into most smartphones to provide this connection for all students.

The mobile learning organization as a new technology in the following categories of mobile education are distinguished:

- **Technology:** Driven mobile learning-Some specific technological innovations are located in the academic environment to demonstrate the technical feasibility and pedagogical opportunities.
- **Miniature but Portable E-Learning:** Mobile, wireless and portable technologies used to replicate approaches and solutions that are already in use in conventional e-learning tools. For example, transferring some e-learning technologies, such as a virtual learning environment, these technologies or, for example, flexible replacement of static desktop technologies mobile technology.
- **Connected Classroom Learning:** The same technologies are used in the classroom to support collaborative learning, possibly, in connection with other technologies in the classroom, such as interactive whiteboards.
- **Informal, Personalized, Situated Mobile Learning:** The same technologies are enhanced additional functionality, such as local awareness or video transmission, and aimed at educational activities, which in otherwise it will be difficult or impossible.

- **Mobile Training/Performance Support:** Technologies are used to improve performance and mobile workforce efficiencies by providing information and support, right on time and in the context of their immediate priorities.
- **Remote/Rural/Development Mobile Learning:** Technologies are used to solve environmental and infrastructure issues, provide education and support it where conventional e-learning technologies might not work that often accepted in developing or evolutionary paradigms.

So, what are the benefits of learning through mobile devices?

1. Digital thinking. The current staff consists of a large number of millennials. These are employees who have grown up on technology and are used to using them in everyday life. They are comfortable working with digital devices. Why shouldn't it start at school? This makes learning more accessible to them and prepares them to become ready for the real world. Mobile learning is at the heart of a visionary digital approach to life. This ensures that students will be ready for the real world and will be able to deal with it better than those who are afraid of technology.
2. Flexibility for students. Mobile learning gives students tremendous flexibility in choosing the device they want to learn from when they want to study, and, most importantly, at a pace that is comfortable for them. Students are not limited to a classroom or a set timetable to be able to study. Mobile learning means that students can, at their discretion, log into applications to view course materials, complete assignments, or take the test.
3. Convenience to the teacher. The easiest way for mobile learning is to share learning material with students. You can offer texts, video or audio. And this can be done at any time. Students can prepare their homework by watching a video that a teacher shares with them. Interaction during the lessons is another plus for the teacher. An example of this might be questioned during a lesson. Teachers ask questions, and students answer them on their mobile devices. Teachers can get immediate feedback, which is especially useful when teaching large groups.
4. Interesting formats for learning. Mobile learning includes formats that students enjoy and provide a better perception and memorization of learning material. These include the formats that are often used on our smartphones (videos, interactive videos, games, etc.).
5. Micro-learning. This type of training content is designed to be accessed and explored in the short series. People often use their mobile phones when they have a few free minutes. Micro-learning allows them to immerse themselves in learning material without worrying about time-consuming.

However, there are drawbacks to mobile learning.

1. Distraction. Mobile devices can be a great temptation to switch in the lesson to something more interesting. Children love to learn on tablets and phones, but playing on these devices seems even more fun! As a teacher, you cannot always control what your students are doing on their gadgets.
2. Lack of standardization. Device compatibility issues may arise due to the lack of standardization in smartphones. Students may have mobile devices with different operating systems, different versions of this operating system, battery life, and so on. As a result, some students may not be able to work with educational content.

This system helps students to carry out educational activities without the participation of another person. In a mobile learning environment, students use an app to guide the user through a sequence of activities that helps them complete learning tasks. Examples include intelligent databases used to solve problems with typical learning tasks and research progress maps to guide day-to-day activities. The system provides support for the execution of the request and identifies the steps required to perform the learning task.

Implementing any innovation you need to be prepared for the negative side, so it was considered both the undoubted advantages and negative aspects of mobile learning. Thus, the undoubted advantages of using mobile devices and technologies in the educational process of the school are: Quick access to authentic educational and reference resources and programs at any time and in any place; constant feedback from the teacher and the educational community; taking into account the individual characteristics of the student - diagnosis of problems, individual learning pace; increasing motivation of students through the use of familiar technical means and virtual environment; organization of autonomous learning; creating a personalized professionally-oriented learning space of the student; development of skills and abilities for continuous learning during life.

The negative aspects of mobile learning in the first place should include difficulties not so much technical and financial as administrative, organizational and methodological. First, it is difficult to convince both teachers and the administration of educational institutions that this form of training contributes to the optimization of the educational process, because the execution of tasks takes place on devices (phones), which are usually prohibited at schools and universities for using in the classroom, because all mobile devices act as an electronic cheat sheet. Secondly, teachers do not possess (unlike students) the appropriate level of ICT competence that would allow them to implement in the traditional form of tasks based on mobile technologies, to use existing educational applications for mobile devices, to provide interactive support for the educational process, to develop ICT competence of students in this field. Third, there are not enough ready-made mobile learning resources and programs for students and schoolchildren of different levels and specialties, but at the same time English teachers are in a better position: there is a wide variety of different applications and games in English, on the basis of which you can create grammar tests, search and game tasks. Technical and financial problems are reduced to the high cost of some mobile devices (there are already cheap alternatives to iPhone), small screen and small font, which is used again not on all mobile devices. Today, a modern teacher is able to turn mobile devices and technologies from a threat to learning in to help and support.

An example of a successful application of this method of training is a number of educational programs at universities in Japan and China. Considering mobile technology, the teachers of these universities consider them very promising in terms of informatization of modern society. National Cyber Institute in Japan, specializing in remote training through the Internet, in 2008 offered an innovative training system- with a mobile phone that allows you to study any discipline as at home, as in a cafe or in the subway. If your computer is in the middle of the screen during a lesson the text of the lecture and all the necessary drawings are shown, and in the corner there are a broadcast video recordings of the lecture itself, that version for mobile phone is based on video streaming technologies, and all texts and drawings are downloaded additionally. Students were invited to study about 100 different subjects, including ancient Chinese culture, journalism, and English literature.

Nowadays many universities in Russian Federation have a special mobile app for their students or even for enrollees. They give opportunity to watch timetable, information about events, staff, and faculties. The app for enrollees of St. Petersburg national research university of information technology, mechanics and optics provides such features as always be aware of the events of the admission campaign and quickly understand the procedure for admission, get acquainted with training programs, noting favorites, study the steps of admission, calculate exam's all possible options, learn the answers to frequently asked questions, be aware of news and ratings, get quick access to important contacts.

Today there are several popular mobile applications, containing information about universities. It can be said that each of them does not have any clear classification. Each of them is unique with original design and content.

The ex-president of Kazakhstan was also for the usage of mobile devices during the education process. Nazarbayev(2012) emphasizes the modernization of teaching methods and the development of an online educational system. The use of mobile technologies and training applications allows us to further improve the pedagogical process. Many scientists and educators are confident that the future of training with ICT support is connected and depends on the spread of mobile communications, the popularity of smartphones and gadgets, the emergence of a large number of educational applications and programs, as well as new technologies that expand the possibilities and quality of education. Unfortunately, not all Kazakh universities have their own apps for learning.

A mobile application is a program installed on a particular platform that has certain functionality that allows you to perform various actions.

The importance of mobile applications for education is growing not only because of their accessibility and attractiveness in terms of new technologies, but also because of the opportunities they provide: students working together on tasks, taking learning outside the school, everyone have the opportunity to speak out, to participate (as opposed to the system with a show of hands). The use of mobile applications for educational institutions allows:

- Implement unified control over the level of knowledge of students.
- To simplify carrying out offsets and control works.
- Speed up the exchange of information between all participants of the educational process, simplify the process of interaction between teachers and students.
- To intensify and modernize the educational process.
- Organize a distributed educational resource.
- Provide joint activities of students without reference to the location of participants in the educational process.
- Use your mobile device as a personal library of educational, methodical and reference materials.
- Connect the mobile device to the devices and devices in the network of the educational institution for educational and research purposes.
- With the help of mobile applications and embedded sensors to gather information about the environment in educational and research purposes.

Speaking about mobile applications for education, it is worth noting their ability to access cloud services, which are used as a single information field to store information about students and teachers, indicators of educational activity.

It is an indisputable fact that the smartphone is part of the image of a modern schoolboy or student. Smartphones, tablets and other digital devices, of course, will not replace the classical teaching of academic disciplines. But the full integration of digital learning can be done as a didactic addition to the classroom learning scenario and beyond. Due to copyright data protection, the use of smartphones in European schools often difficult, this is debated by many German scientists.

Mobile learning can be seen as an integral part of the future e-learning process with the growing technological competencies of the infrastructure, the positive attitude that is formed in people, and many other features. This process of change presents many new problem situations that need to be addressed. Therefore, the importance of scientific research in this area is great. It is worth noting that in the design of mobile learning technologies and learning environments can be chosen according to students' individual ways of perception. Active learning and socio-constructivist learning were preferred as mobile technologies adapted to their competencies and were able to use features specific to mobile technologies. In addition, in the process of evaluating the elements that need to be taken into account in the development of these environments, research is also conducted based on the fundamental principles of the theory of multimedia learning and the theory of media wealth. While these projects were completed, a study that looked at cognitive load theory, which argued that staying within certain limits is important for students to make the most of their cognitive abilities, was considered important in terms of developing the design process. As a result, there are many variables to consider when developing mobile learning environments as well as other learning environments. They include student profile, attitude to mobile technologies, subject compliance, existing technical infrastructure. decompression is what you want. So, instead of sticking to a single theory or learning model, using learning theory or models that can meet the needs of existing conditions, working through different stages of the design and learning process, would be the right approach.

Thus, the use of ICT allows conducting classes at a high scientific, educational, aesthetic and emotional level (photography, animation, music); provides visibility; allows the use of a large amount of didactic material, in general, improves the quality of education in accordance with the requirements of Ministry of Education.

Advantages of using information technologies in comparison with the traditional methods are used in combination with audio and video clarity, the possibility of using interactive whiteboard, ensuring the effectiveness of perception and memorization of educational material, and also it saves study time. The strength of mobile learning is its ability to shape thoughts immediately. You can get ideas from other people and share them with the world in seconds; get feedback, clarifications, materials, and so on. Also, connections and cross-links are easily established between mobile students, forming learning communities. Enthusiasm increases when students manage the information materials they write, edit, review and publish. In the future, training can be carried out through the formation of personal digital sets of projects.

Mobile learning is seen as more measurable, as it provides the necessary training to the people who need it in the shortest possible time, and measures the results in order to make sure that the goals are achieved. However, it would be shortsighted to believe that mobile learning will replace traditional classroom learning. In a traditional classroom, people have the opportunity to get to know each other and develop relationships. Due to the fact that more time is spent on independent processing of information, rather than on interaction in a dialogue, such a tool is naturally suitable for more introverted people.

The use of innovative forms of learning in contrast to traditional methods assigns the student a major role on the way to the assimilation of knowledge, in which the teacher assistants, organizes, directs and stimulates learning activities.

The use of mobile technologies as a support of the educational process can improve the quality of education and the attractiveness of the provided educational services for University students. Training becomes timely, sufficient and personalized. In connection with the above, it can be concluded that at the moment the research related to the methods and techniques of using mobile technologies are timely, promising and relevant.

But not all agree with all advantages of mobile device in education. French education Minister Jean-Michel Blanquer (2017) announced a total ban on mobile phones in primary and secondary classes. In a statement, the official sounds concerned that because of the gadgets, the attention of students is scattered, and they lose the thread of the lesson. All modern gadgets have their pros and cons-it all depends on how they are used. Smartphones help to stay connected, find the necessary information and organize social events, but at the same time can negatively affect concentration, communication skills, contribute to the development of lost profits syndrome, procrastination and stress.

Most of today's students are technically and psychologically ready to use mobile technologies in education, and new opportunities need to be considered to make better use of the potential of mobile learning. The solution of this problem requires organizational efforts on the part of education managers, research and methodological work of scientists and teachers to implement strategies, forms and methods of mobile learning in the educational process of higher education institutions.

There are some negative effects from mobile devices in the article "Do smartphones interfere with learning" (2017):

1. **The Deterioration of Concentration:** It takes 25 minutes to concentrate on the original task if you are distracted by a text message or e-mail, according to the latest research on the phenomenon of distracted attention. That's why doing homework with a phone lying nearby causes so many problems. A person's ability to multitask is a myth. In fact, it takes a lot of time, effort and concentration to perform two tasks at the same time.
2. **Lack of Personal Communication:** Using a mobile phone can affect the quality of communication in real life, even if you don't realize it. There were many different studies on this topic. For the studies, the researchers decided to conduct an experiment: they divided the participants into two groups and asked them to talk to strangers for 10 minutes. Participants of the first group were allowed to carry smartphones; the second group had notebooks instead of phones. What did the results of the experiments show? Participants from the first group were less sympathetic to their interlocutors, felt less desire to make friends with them than participants from the second group.
3. **The Development of the Syndrome of Loss of Profits:** The hallmark of lost profits syndrome (Fomo) is the need to be aware of what other people are doing now and the worry that they are spending time much more fun and interesting. Gadgets can contribute to the development of lost profits syndrome in someone who has a predisposition to it – such people are more likely to experience mood decline, increased anxiety and several times more likely to check social networks during classes.
4. **Sleep Disturbance:** Using the phone in the evening is bad for the amount and quality of sleep. Why is this happening? The sleep hormone, melatonin, begins to be produced by the body about 9 o'clock in the evening. However, the light coming from the screen of a mobile phone can "trick" the body and send a signal to the brain that it is day, suppressing the production of melatonin. Thus, the use of the phone in the evening does not allow the body to relax and tune in to rest. Scientists advise not to use gadgets an hour before bedtime or put them into night mode.
5. **Procrastination:** The tendency to postpone difficult or important things is common among modern students-according to statistics, about 75% of American students suffer from it. The answer to the

question, what do you do when you procrastinate, is most often associated with the use of a mobile phone: correspondence, checking social networks, games and shopping. Of course, mobile phones will not turn you into a procrastinator, but they can greatly affect the development of the tendency to postpone things "for later".

6. **Stress:** Dependence on a mobile phone can have a negative impact on a person's psychological health. Too frequent use of a smartphone is often associated with anxiety, irritability, frustration and impatience. According to the latest research, 60% of teenagers experience a strong excitement when they cannot use their gadgets. By the way, that is why the ban on gadgets during lessons can have a negative impact on students. Researchers from Singapore found that students who had their devices removed during the test had 17% worse use of their working memory and had a harder time switching from one task to another than those students whose gadgets were just lying around. The researchers suggested that the problem was anxiety due to the lack of a smartphone.

There are considered a number of negative factors that gadgets can have on human perception, but is it really so negative devices affect cognitive abilities? Researchers of the Higher school of Economics Polivanova and Koroleva (2017) in a survey of adolescents 16-18 years found that the estimates do not depend on the frequency of smartphone use in the classroom. Everything from honors to students, and they begin to glance at the screen of the smartphone when they get bored. The only exception is the participants of the Olympics, whose focus on ultra-high results does not allow to be distracted for a minute. The researchers also found that teenagers forget about smartphones when the lesson is really interesting or difficult: after all, before the advent of gadgets, students also found ways to distract from the tedious lessons. The most effective way to pull a student away from flipping through profiles in social networks is to arouse curiosity and actively engage in the lesson. Only a strong and caring teacher can defeat the useless use of gadgets during training.

METHODS

The level of introduction of mobile devices into the educational environment of the world's leading universities is quite high. In Kazakhstan, this system is spread slightly, however, the University of International Business implemented the application for learning the English language which is called "UIB English".

There are only two universities in Almaty which use mobile devices in the education process: Kazakh National University named after Al Farabi (KazNU) and The University of International Business(UIB). KazNU's mobile application is called UNIVER. The UNIVER mobile application is the official mobile client of the UNIVER system. The application provides the student with the most necessary data related to his/her studies. It is specially adapted for use on mobile devices and has several advantages and new features compared to the web version on the device. These include:

1. Display of news data, schedules, current certification, magazine, teaching materials, student profiles.
2. Offline work.
3. Receiving notifications of changes in user data.
4. Data synchronization on different devices.
5. Saving web traffic.

According to students' feedbacks from App Store and Google Play, they are satisfied with the quality of the app and they see the benefits from the usage of it. They say that this app helps to economize time because they can use it at any time and place. By the way, they do not need an Internet connection to look through some lectures or presentations. UNIVER helps to make education in this university more up-to-date.

The University of International Business is the first university in Kazakhstan which has created its own application for studying English "Uib English". This app allows to increase vocabulary, develop reading and listening skills and to check grammar accuracy. Anastassiya A. Khalikova (2019) studied the advantages of using this app for the presentation of new words in her thesis work. This study was held at the University of International Business (UIB). In this study, fifty-three the first, the second and third-year students of University of International Business with Elementary level of the English language took part. The average age is 18. All of them were from Kazakhstan. Their majors were various: HoReCa (hotel, restaurant, and café), Tourism, Logistics, Assessment, Finance, Accounting and Audit, Journalism and Entrepreneurship and Innovation. This information is very important because the person-oriented approach was widely used in the research in order to achieve success, to interest and to motivate our students to learn a foreign language hardly.

During the research, the experimental research design was used. At the beginning of the research, students were given some kind of questionnaire which had the following questions:

1. How do you memorize new words? What helps you in doing this?
2. How were the words introduced to you when you were at school?
3. How would you like to learn English words?

This questionnaire helped to understand the past experience of students in learning words and to see their opinion, preferences, and view about learning.

Different methods and techniques were used during the research for improving and developing the ability to use vocabulary. Of course, technical progress cannot be ignored that is why CALL and ICT also played an important and integral part of the research.

FINDINGS AND DISCUSSION

The examination was done for three months. Many ethical issues were considered while conducting research to protect the participants. Students were informed that they are going to become a part of an experiment which helps them to learn the English language more effectively. Different methods and techniques were tried for acquiring vocabulary. Special attention was paid to the "UIB English" app. For the students of University of International Business, "UIB English app", games, and PowerPoint presentation proved itself to be the most effective. Thanks to the app, students could memorize the graphical and phonological forms of the words. They could write words. Their speaking abilities also increased with the help of all methods and techniques which were tried during the research. So, it can be concluded that learning through mobile devices makes the process more interesting and productive.

One of the features of this app is that it is available not only for students of the university but also to school children. UIB also widely uses it in different competitions among people who would like to study at the university in the future and to get a scholarship.

From the Khalikova's survey (2019), it can be noticed that this app help to improve students' vocabulary skills. The comparison results of students' grades are shown in the tables 1,2, and 3 below.

It is obvious that the use of mobile learning in the educational process requires organizational, research and methodological work. The Universities should create and implement projects to operate the mobile version of the portal; identify and develop the most popular mobile services integrated with the information systems of the University; develop and implement a mobile security policy; create its own applications, etc. All of these points are very important.

Every year, modern society develops and progresses in almost all sectors of our life. Thus, there is a huge amount of information that cannot be stored only in one's head or written down on paper. Information is a kind of baggage of knowledge that people pass from generation to generation, update, process, and supplement. It is impossible to imagine a modern person who would not seek to replenish his knowledge and improve existing ones. Now there are many sources for obtaining information, and, first of all, the main source, as well as affordable and, perhaps, indispensable, is the Internet. The World Wide Web covers global space, and computer technology, which has the strongest influence in our time, allows us to provide informational support to absolutely everyone

Table 1. Comparison table of the first year students' grades

Midterm 1	Midterm 2
70	75
51	35
52	57
5	0
62	53
79	76
71	65
81	71
53	48
65	55
5	0
54	49
14	44
76	78
74	66
69	70
50	50
0	5
70	64

Table 2. Comparison table of the second year students' grades

Midterm 1	Midterm 2
50	52
0	0
44	58
50	50
63	72
52	50
10	0
39	46
51	62
37	63
9	0
79	85
50	54
74	75
68	70
65	77
64	83
60	79
37	64
63	54

Table 3. Comparison table of the third year students' grades

Midterm 1	Midterm 2
67	76
66	69
50	32
64	77
52	53
86	93
51	56
30	73
51	49
50	55
59	79
36	35
51	33
60	67
50	41
73	69
51	51

While talking about knowledge, the word education always comes to mind. As the proverb says: "Learning is an eye of the mind". To be educated is to live a full life, to be a self-confident person, versatile, and also to be useful to society. Thanks to the development of computerization, the advent of new technology, information and knowledge have become available to everyone. Accessibility is the main indicator by which we simply must be educated, replenish our "baggage" of knowledge and keep pace with the times.

Modern educational institutions need to become places where people not only study but at the same time see the advanced technologies. Without the usage of information and communication technology (ICT), society cannot raise the up to date generation of the 21st century. Currently, much attention is paid to innovative educational technologies. Innovation is a new idea or method, or the use of new ideas and methods (Cambridge Dictionary, n.d.). It turns out that innovations are ideas, processes and means, and the results taken in the unity of qualitative improvement of the pedagogical system.

Dictionary of methodological terms gives the following definition of ICT: "information technology is a system of methods and methods of collection, accumulation, storage, search, transmission, processing and delivery of information using computers and computer communication lines" (Azimov & Shchukin, 1999, p. 90).

According to the classification of Voitko (2005), there are the five main areas of ICT use in the classroom:

1. Usage of ready-made multimedia products and computer training systems;
2. Creating your own multimedia and training programs;

3. Creating your own multimedia presentations;
4. Usage of ICT in extracurricular activities;
5. Usage of Internet resources.

ICT can be a way for presenting something or way of controlling. It provides a high quality of presentation and usage of various communication channels (text, sound, graphic, touch, etc.). New technologies allow making the learning process individual according to the pace and depth of the course. This differentiated approach gives a great positive result, because it creates conditions for the success of each student, causing students positive emotions, and thus affects their learning motivation.

The following digital educational resources are used on English lessons: presentations in Power Point (PP), text editors, spreadsheets, tests, training programs on CD-ROM, electronic textbooks, educational Internet resources (Mukovnikova, 2008). But now there are also add mobile devices to this list.

The modern lesson is impossible without the use of information and communication technologies. Every day the Internet community has new educational resources, new software tools which come to education institution. The teacher cannot stay away from these processes. The introduction of information technology is on the way to increase the methodological material of each teacher in the framework of its subject.

Nowadays, the issues of efficiency of use information and communication technologies (ICT) in education increasingly, scientists from different countries are trying to determine under what conditions the use of ICT will be more effective in the training of graduates. ICT can be a way of presenting something or a way of controlling. It provides a high quality of presentation and usage of various communication channels (text, sound, graphic, touch, etc.). New technologies allow making the learning process individual according to the pace and depth of the course. This differentiated approach gives a great positive result, because it creates conditions for the success of each student, causing students positive emotions, and thus affects their learning motivation.

Unlike traditional methods, when using interactive forms of learning, the student himself becomes the main acting figure and opens the way to the assimilation of knowledge. The teacher acts in this situation as an active assistant, and his main function is the organization and stimulation of the educational process.

In the work programs of various disciplines, hours are necessarily allocated not only for classroom, but also for independent work, which

It plays a decisive role in the development of the material, especially in the situation of the first-year students in higher education, different levels of knowledge of the material by students and the lack of classroom hours. The role of mobile phones as learning devices is increasing, contributing to the spread of mobile learning is ubiquitous. In addition, the emergence of the Internet made distance learning available for education in all parts of the light. In a short period of time the appeal of distance learning has led to the realization that a variety of mobile devices are an effective means for obtaining and assimilation of information. Thus, many the researchers proposed mobile devices for teaching and learning (Kukulska-Hulme& Shield,2008).

The introduction of the latest technologies, informatization, and computerization at the moment are an integral part of education and the educational process as a whole. Thus, “education” and “information and communication technologies” become one step in the acquisition of knowledge.

SOLUTIONS AND RECOMMENDATIONS

There are both positive and negative sides of using mobile device in education. Some countries (i.e. France) ban usage of mobile phones in the classroom because of their negative effects. But still there are some positive feedbacks. It can be recommended to universities, especially universities in Kazakhstan and Central Asia, to create certain educational applications for all of the courses according to the requests of the department's instructors which are suitable and meaningful for the instructors and students' specializations. But educational applications absence is not the main problem. Some Kazakh universities still do not have a good internet connection, so this problem needs to be solved first. The internet should be available in any place at the universities to make for student a comfortable environment to study.

Although it should be considered the quality and spontaneity of the given material. It must be taken the fact of back and forth between teachers of subjects and programmers. Accessibility and control of performance of the work in these apps are also played significant role for qualitative transition from traditional education to digital form of it. It is necessary to understand the fact of transition cannot be done instantaneous. It requires time, financial resources and educators and educational organizations' willingness.

FUTURE RESEARCH DIRECTIONS

The development of applications for mobile devices in higher education has become a common thing. For many people, who work in the education field, mobile technology has recently become one of the most important areas of research. Also the increasing availability of open educational resources for mobile technology is making access to learning more affordable for anyone who wants to learn. Today, mobile learning is a very important topic for many educational institutions. Mobile learning can be disruptive to education or add another layer to the learning and teaching processes. In the future, more research should be conducted in order to prevent some negative effects. A thorough analysis, from a pedagogical and technological perspective, is the main thing to do to ensuring proper usage and implementation of mobile learning. Digitalization is something that cannot be ignored in the 21st century. That is why it is very important to study and be prepared to possible difficulties that can appear in the future.

CONCLUSION

The relevance and practical significance of this article are due to the process of modernization of Kazakhstan's education related to the introduction to information opportunities, as well as the introduction of a wide practice of teaching fundamentally a new media. Digital education, actively implemented over the past decade, has the following settings: the development of information and communication competence, self-organization in the educational process, independent critical thinking, and, accordingly, the development of students such knowledge, skills and abilities that will allow them to successfully carry out professional activities and to be competitive in a multicultural world society. As a result, it is necessary to understand the methodology and didactic organization of digital learning to use mobile effectively apps and tablets in the educational process.

According to rough estimates, the total number of mobile phone users in the world is several times more than the number of Internet users. One recent and significant change in the learning environment has been the need for mobility. Smartphones are becoming cheaper and more popular in society. In addition to this, the exponential growth of wireless and mobile networks leads to significant changes in mobile devices, protocol development, standardization and network implementation, user acceptance. Mobile learning is carried out mainly through a wireless network. It can be quickly adapted to meet changing learning needs. Students have the opportunity to find and learn what they need, at the pace and in the place that suits them. Mobile learners can work together with teachers and other learners to learn better. With mobile learning, learning materials can be delivered in a quick and cost-effective way in a multimedia format.

This year, the number of connected mobile devices, most of which are mobile phones, will surpass the number of inhabitants of the planet for the first time in history. Despite such widespread and unique learning opportunities, these technologies are often banned or ignored by official education systems. This potential cannot be used. The possibilities of mobile technologies in the field of education are impressive and in many cases well-founded. While not a panacea, mobile technology will help to address some of the pressing problems of education through a new and effective approach. In a world that is increasingly dependent on communications and access to information, mobile devices will not be a transient phenomenon. As the power and capabilities of mobile devices are constantly growing, they can be used more widely as educational tools and take center stage in both formal and non-formal education.

REFERENCES

Azimov, E. G., & Shchukin, A. N. (1999). *Dictionary of methodological terms (theory and practice of language teaching)*. Moscow: IKAR Press.

Blanquer, J. M. (2017). Ban students from using mobile phones in the country's primary, junior and middle schools. The Guardian. Retrieved from https://www.theguardian.com/world/2017/dec/11/france-to-ban-mobile-phones-in-schools-from-september

Cambridge dictionary (n.d.). Retrieved from https://dictionary.cambridge.org/

Do smartphones interfere with learning (2017). Teach Me Please. Retrieved from https://blog.teachme-please.ru/posts/meshajut-li-smatphony-uchjobe

Education in Japan. (2011). Orientalica. Retrieved from http://www.orientalica.com/lofiversion/index.php?t203.html

Khalikova, A.A. (2019). Methods of boosting vocabulary skills of elementary level students in the process of foreign language education.

Koroleva, K., & Polivanova, D. (2017). How smartphones help study. Retrieved from https://iq.hse.ru/en/news/201806836.html

Kukulska-Hulme, A., & Shield, L. (2008). An overview of mobile assisted language learning: From content delivery to supported collaboration and interaction. Retrieved from https://goo.gl/kgcsrC

Laliberte, T. R. (2010). *Mixed method study: Exploring the use of educational technology tools in K-12 classrooms* [Doctoral Dissertation]. University of Phoenix.

Mukovnikova, E. V. (2008). Effective use of digital educational resources in English lessons.

Nazarbayev, N. A. (2012) *Kazakhstan 2050*. Retrieved from http://adilet.zan.kz/rus/docs/K1200002050

Pfeil, A. (2015). Digitale und analoge Lernwelten im Deutsch als Fremdsprache-Unterricht Informelles Lernen. *Fremdsprache Deutsch, 53*.

Schneider, D. K. (n.d.). *Educational technology*. EduTech Wiki. Retrieved from http://edutechwiki.unige.ch/en/Educational_technology

Traxler, J. (2009). *Mobile Learning: Transforming the Delivery of Education and Training*. Retrieved from http://www.aupress.ca/index.php/books/120155

Voitko, S. A. (2005). On the use of information and communication technologies in English lessons. *Festival of pedagogical ideas*. Retrieved from http://scientificjournal.ru/a/114-fil/1036-the-use-and.html

KEY TERMS AND DEFINITIONS

App: An application downloaded by a user to a mobile device.

CALL: Study with the help of computers.

Experimental Research Design: Study that includes a hypothesis, a variable that can be manipulated by the researcher, and variables that can be measured, calculated and compared.

ICT: Activities or studies involving computers and other electronic technology.

Interactive Form: A form of study when students completely involved into learning process.

Midterm: An exam at the middle of study (In Kazakhstan it is usually after 7th and 15th weeks).

Mobile Learning: Education conducted by means of smartphones or tablet computers.

Chapter 13
Implementation of Multilingual Education for Sustainable Development in the Netherlands and Kazakhstan

Fatima Duisebayeva
Kazakh National Agrarian University, Kazakhstan

Assel Imasheva
S.Seifullin Kazakh Agritechnical University, Kazakhstan

ABSTRACT

The chapter presents a comparative analysis of the implementation of multilingual/bilingual education in Kazakhstan and the Netherlands. The study explores the origin and role of multilingualism, for socio-economic development, relevant regional and international practices in multilingual education, the growth of trilingual instruction, English language training and the use of digital technologies (distant, e-learning programs) in the Eurasian region, Major common features and differences of implementing multilingual/bilingual teaching between the two case studies and the main findings from research trips are identified. A theoretical analysis of scholarly approaches, as well as practical and methodological implications, are made on the example of implementing multilingual instruction at the Kazakhstani agricultural higher educational institutions, particularly Kazakh National Agrarian University and Kazakh S. Seifullin Agritechnical University and Dutch counterparts - Wageningen University, and the Hague University of Applied Sciences.

INTRODUCTION

The situation when an individual or a group of people use more than one language while interacting with other people is widely called as polylingualism, multilingualism and/or plurilingualism. The terms "multicultural" and "polycultural" education are used interchangeably as they differ primarily by lin-

DOI: 10.4018/978-1-7998-2551-7.ch013

guistic origins (Latin "multum" and Greek "poly" both meaning "many"). These terms are derived from French "multilinguisme" and "plurilinguisme", which were widely used in research since the 1950s (Cohen, 1956).

Multilingual education means using of at least three languages as tool of instruction in education: first, the mother tongue, second, a regional or national language and, the third, an international language (UNESCO, 2003).

English language is often being used as a medium for international communication, the leading language of business, science and socio-economic development. (Samuelson and Freedman, 2010).

English has been the official language of the European Central Bank since 1998, with press conferences held in English, despite the fact that the United Kingdom has a special opt-out from the EU treaties and the Economic and Monetary Union (Dor, 2004).

In the USA multicultural and multilingual education was developed intensively in response to demands to end racial discrimination, inequality and segregation in the 1960s-1970, during the so-called "Black Revolution", accompanied by the civil rights movement and supported by the state laws to merge public schools for white and black students (e.g. the lawsuit "Brown vs. Board of Education of Topeka"). In the 1980 - 2000s American scholars supported multicultural and multilingual education as one of the fundamental principles of democratic society (Nieto, 2008, Banks, 2008; Campbell, 2010; Glazer, 1998)

On the other hand, in some countries like Australia the concept of multilingualism is slowly losing its ground, although in the 1990s, it was on top of governmental agenda. (Heugh, 2014).

Politically multilingualism promotes increasing of linguistic capital and establishing interethnic dialogue between nationalities, particularly in Kazakhstan. The strategic policy goal of multilingual education (MLE) is achieving social justice, equity and human rights (Duisebayeva, 2018).

MLE unites different disciplines that come together through language and education, such as sociology, pedagogy, psychology, linguistics, methodology, etc. Multilingual pedagogy builds bridges between cultures, schools and countries and is relevant to primary and secondary school pupils and teachers, university students and professors; it promotes overcoming barriers of monolingualism and transforming without privileging a language. Its major principles are Mother Tongue Instruction (MTI), support and/or revival of other languages and language transfer (Harrison, 2013).

MLE could also be combined with Foreign Language and Intercultural Communication Learning for the dominant language and monolingual speakers, allowing all students to learn in more than one language.

THEORETICAL BACKGROUNDS OF MULTILINGUALISM AND MLE

Multilingualism Policy as Social and Economic Indicator of Sustainable Development

Multilingualism plays an essential role in socio-economic development of a number of countries. Duchene and Heller (2012) believe that multilingualism not only facilitates economic growth but also is a product of "new" economy, which is based on competitive production in a global system and economic organization on a global scale. Transformation of economic systems from extracting raw materials to information and services is essential for many countries, especially Kazakhstan. Recent policies on higher education system in Kazakhstan (such as 2010 State Program for Education Development for

2011 – 2020) aim to contribute to economic innovations, raise quality of education and improve staff training (Lukashova et al., 2015).

Speaking two, three or four languages is common for many Europeans. (Baker, 2011) Speaking several languages not only increases opportunities for work and education within European Union, but also improves trade within Europe, and between Europe and the rest of the world (Tinsley, 2011).

A recent survey across small and medium enterprises (SMEs) in European countries illustrated that many business opportunities were lost due to shortage of language skills, for example, 11% of respondents lost a contract due to a shortage of language competence, with an average business loss of €325,000 per enterprise over a three years period (Hagen et al., 2006).

English language was extensively used in SMEs, however, demand for other languages, such as Spanish, was also necessary alongside with English language skills. In addition, companies employing several languages, improved their export sales by 45% (Tinsley, 2011).

A number of policies supporting multilingual education for economic development were established in Europe in the last decade. For example, the Lisbon Agenda (Lisbon Strategy) was launched in 2000 with an aim to make the EU "the most competitive and dynamic knowledge-based economy by embedding foreign language into general education system (Smokotin, 2010) This objective was further supported by European Council meeting in Barcelona in 2002, which aimed to make European training and education systems a "world quality reference". (European Commission, 2005).

International Practices of Multilingual Education

Currently, multilingualism is gaining support at all levels in ethnically heterogeneous countries of Europe (e.g. Belgium and Switzerland), Asia (e.g. Singapore and Malaysia), Africa and the Commonwealth of Independent States (CIS). For example, multilingual education in the mother tongue (Russian) and foreign languages has been historically developed in many regions of Russia, such as Crimea and Republic of Sakha (Yakutia). Multilingualism issues were widely explored by a number of Russian and Kazakhstani scholars, who acknowledged the importance of cultural and linguistic diversity in a multicultural environment (Galskova, Baryshnikov, Evdokimova, Zhetpisbayeva, Mazhitaeva, Smagulova, Tuleuova, Duisebayeva, Imasheva).

The main goal of multilingual education (MLE) is pursuit of social justice and equity. MLE unites different disciplines that come together through language and education, such as linguistics, psychology and education. MLE builds bridges between schools, cultures and countries without favouring one language over another, which helps to overcome monolingualism barriers. Three major principles of MLE are mother tongue instructions (MTI), support and/or revival of other languages and language transfer (Harrison, 2013).

Multilingualism as the act of using multiple languages, either by an individual speaker or by a community of speakers, is becoming a social phenomenon governed by the needs of globalization, cultural diversity and openness._Multilingual speakers outnumber monolingual speakers in the world's population (Tucker, 1999).

Europe is at the forefront of the development of policies that promote multilingualism in its member states, both on the social and the institutional level, as well as plurilingualism on the individual level. Europe faces the challenge of multilingual education and diversity on various and exceedingly heterogeneous levels. Recent research demonstrates that multilingualism is one of significant functional realities in today's European societies. These realities challenge traditional visions of language education, where each language is taught one after another as first and successive foreign languages. Owing to the ease of access to information facilitated by the Internet, individuals' exposure to multiple languages is becoming increasingly frequent thereby promoting a need to acquire additional languages. Multilingual education typically refers to "first-language-first" education, that is, schooling which begins in the mother tongue and transitions to additional languages (Ziegler, 2013).

Typically, MLE programs are situated in developing countries where speakers of minority languages tend to be disadvantaged in the mainstream education system as in the case with Eurasian countries and Kazakhstan. Though there are cases related to the Netherlands, Spain and some other developed European and Asian countries.

However, not all speakers need to be multilingual in multilingual societies. Some states can have multilingual policies and recognise several official languages, such as Canada (English and French). In some states, particular languages may be associated with particular regions in the state (e.g., Canada) or with particular ethnicities (Malaysia/Singapore). When all speakers are multilingual, linguists classify the community according to the functional distribution of the involved languages.

Recent research reveals that multilingualism was more common in the past than is usually supposed: in early times, when most people were members of small language communities, it was necessary to know two or more languages for trade or any other dealings outside one's own town or village, and this holds good today in places of high linguistic diversity such as Sub-Saharan Africa and India. Ekkehard Wolff estimates that 50% of the population of Africa is multilingual (Wolff, 2000).

Some multilingualism experts use the term code-switching, that describes the process of 'swapping' between languages. In many cases, code-switching is motivated by the wish to express loyalty to some cultural group in immigrant communities of the New World or may also function as a strategy where proficiency is lacking. Such strategies are common if the vocabulary of one of the languages is not very elaborated for certain fields, or if the speakers have not developed proficiency in certain lexical domains, as in the case of immigrant languages.

Bilingualism is defines as an ability to use two languages. However, individuals with varying bilingual characteristics may be classified as bilingual. Bilingualism encompasses a range of proficiencies and contexts from a minimal proficiency in two languages, to an advanced level of proficiency which allows the speaker to function and appear as a native-like speaker of two languages. For some, it means an equal ability to communicate in two languages. For others, it simply means the ability to communicate in two languages, but with greater skills in one language. In fact, it is more common for bilingual people, even those who have been bilingual since birth, to be somewhat "dominant" in one language. Bilinguals who are highly proficient in two or more languages are reported to have enhanced executive function and are better at some aspects of language learning compared to monolinguals. In the bilingual model, the native language and the community language are simultaneously taught. However, teachers should be well-qualified in both languages, in techniques and methods for teaching a second language (Romaine, 1995)

Trilingual education is a growing phenomenon all over Europe and Asia. Many new trilingual initiatives at primary level relate to the trends of growing recognition of regional and minority languages and increasing internationalization. Trilingual schooling in bilingual areas offers a challenge to fulfil the widely held concept of 'unity in diversity.' This type of education often pays attention to (a) the region's own language, (b) the state language and (c) a foreign language.

Most member states of the European Union are multilingual, trilingual or bilingual. Trilingual education in Europe is practiced in Finland (Vaasa), Spain (Basque county, Catalonia, Valencia) the Netherlands (Friesland).

English is the second language for a large number of Europeans, but there are several regions in the European context where English is the third language. In regions where three languages are spoken in daily life, English is even the fourth language. The people in these regions already speak the national or majority language(s) and the regional or minority language/s (Beetsma, 2001).

In recent years, linguistic research has focused attention on the use of widely known world languages such as English as lingua franca, or the shared common language of professional and commercial communities. In lingua franca situations, most speakers of the common language are functionally multilingual. Now that English has become the most important language of global science and technology and is the number one international means of communication, it is expanding into many countries where it is not spoken traditionally. It can therefore be considered important to teach English at all education levels in the European member states (Komorowska, 2011).

In Kazakhstan the term "multilingual education" has been used since the 2000s. However nowadays the term "trilingual education' is more common due to identification of specific languages. Kazakhstani government emphasized the importance of learning three languages – Kazakh, Russian and English – for training multilingual specialists in the country (State of the Nation Address by the President of the Republic of Kazakhstan Nursultan Nazarbayev, January 10, 2018). multilingual instruction was supported within the "Trinity of languages" project and identified both theoretical framework and methodological principles for multilingual and vocational education in Kazakhstan (Zhetpisbayeva, 2009; Mazhitayeva et al., 2012).

According to the State Program on Education Development for 2011-2020 and Program "Trinity of Languages" (2007), by 2020 100% percent people in Kazakhstan shall speak Kazakh, 95% - shall speak Russian and 25% - shall speak English language (The State Program of Development and Functioning of Languages of Kazakhstan for 2011- 2020, 2010).

Kazakhstan is implementing multilingual education through integration to the world scientific and educational space. The importance of learning three specific languages is emphasized on the state level; the proportion of languages is regulated by state decrees.

MULTILINGUAL EDUCATION IN KAZAKHSTAN AND THE NETHERLANDS

Comparative analysis of MLE in Kazakhstan and the Netherlands

The theme of the present comparative research was chosen based on the fact that multilingual/ trilingual education or the use of three languages is peculiar to both countries- Kazakhstan and the Netherlands. Kazakhstan is just starting to develop the principles of MLE on the experimental level while the Netherlands has a long history of successful MLE implementation. Therefore, the authors of the chapter strongly believe that this comparative approach would be useful from both theoretical and practical points of view.

The analysis of the education system in Kazakhstan and the Netherlands revealed contextual similarities and differences between Dutch and Kazakhstani educational systems based on language policies, role of national languages and the increasing role of English, as well as specific implementation issues.

Similarities regard state regulation of language policies in both countries, growth of English language use alongside with existing priority of the national languages.

Nowadays multilingual education is one of the priority trends of educational system development in Kazakhstan, having been initiated and supported by the government and the Ministry of Education and Science of the RK during the last decade. Actually, the development of multilingual education in Kazakhstan is based on a number of the state decrees such as The development of MLE in Kazakhstan, the 1996 Language Policy Strategy, the 1997 Law on Languages, the 2001 State Program of Development and Functioning of Languages for 2011-2020 and the 2012 Strategy for Development of the Republic of Kazakhstan Until 2030.

These policies are aimed at the internationalization of Kazakhstani higher education system, its integration into world educational and scientific community, transfer of technologies to the country, expanding employment opportunities in the world labor market, competitiveness advantages, improvement of the faculty's and students' study, research and intercultural communication at an international scale.

MLE implementation measures in Kazakhstani agricultural universities comprise reforming state standards and curricula with the aim of introducing new interdisciplinary, gender-sensitive courses and electives, distant, e- learning programs, promoting professional development and international academic mobility programs, English language courses, which contribute to faculty's and students' succeeding in academic, scientific, and professional settings, internationalization of the higher education (Duisebayeva, 2018).

The analysis of multilingualism and bilingualism in the Netherlands demonstrates the presence of state policy in this field until the 1990s; however, since then the situation has been changing. The European Commission, European Parliament, European Platform and Government of the Netherlands issued various state acts and resolutions, regulating the use of languages, mostly Dutch and English languages, at different education levels.

The most significant and explicit was the 1992 Law on Higher Education declaring that "Classes should be taught and exams should be offered in Dutch", although there were two exceptions possible:

a. if teaching concerns the language in question,
b. if the specific nature, the structure or the quality of the teaching, or otherwise the origin of the participants required such, conforming a code of conduct which has been established by the authorities" The "specific nature" of the education requires using a different language (for example, when books are only in English, or when there is a foreigner in the audience) (Law on Higher Education, 1992).

The analysis of of MLE implementation Kazakhstan and the Netherlands revealed that there are contextual differences in Dutch and Kazakhstani educational systems. These differences are related to discrepancies of history, culture, economy, state education policies (especially between centralised and decentralised systems) as well as implementation practices and different roles and proportion of languages. Multilingual education is practiced in a different way because of the different socio-political context.

In Kazakhstan the state policy is trilingualism, i.e. learning and teaching in three languages (Kazakh, Russian and English) simultaneously and on equal basis in the whole sector of higher education. In the Netherlands it is mostly the policy of bilingualism (with the exception of Frisian language), which starts at primary and secondary education level, rather than at university level. Therefore, some educational issues like education management, development of curriculum, methodology and leaning styles at university and secondary school levels are solved in a different way.

Bilingual tuition is mainly conducted at graduate studies level, while there are special multilingual groups at the undergraduate level. It was found that the driving force of Dutch higher education was to attract foreign students and develop advanced technologies by means of English language. The proportion and percentage of courses taught in Dutch and English vary in different universities.

Bilingual/Trilingual Education in the Netherlands

Bilingual education in the Netherlands historically started with the Resolution of European Council "Plurilingual Educaton in Europe" (Strasburg, 1969). The European Platform, an autonomous Dutch organisation mandated by the government, oversees the quality of bilingual education in the country by setting standards for bilingual schools and teachers. Currently bilingual education is successfully implemented at all education levels from primary schools to universities in the Netherlands. In fact, bilingual teaching starts at primary and secondary levels, rather than at higher education level. There were around 100 bilingual schools in 2007, 133 in 2011, 250 schools in 2013 (out of a total 6,913). In these schools, the first language (L1) was Dutch, whereas the second language (L2) was usually English (Kuiken and Linden, 2013).

At present bilingual education is already very well established in the Netherlands, and many Dutch people speak English to a high standard and prefer to study in English. Most bilingual secondary schools are Bilingual Preparatory Scientific Education (TVWO) and Bilingual Higher General Secondary Education (THAVO). The following subjects are taught in English: Arts, Chemistry, Physics, Biology, Geography, Economics, Physical education, Drama, English, Mathematics, History, Music, Social sciences and Religious studies, but some variation may exist among schools (Oostendorp, 2012).

Dutch secondary schools practicing bilingual education offer part of their classes (e.g. Mathematics, Geography and Chemistry) in other languages. In 2011, this other language was English (in 132 schools) and German (in 1 school). Nowadays, a few dozen primary schools are also experimenting with teaching part of their classes in English. After six years of secondary schooling, Dutch students are supposed to be able to operate their language in question at level B1/B2 (according to the European reference scale), which means they should be able to use their language in question independently in everyday contexts and situations (Oostendorp, 2012).

In the province of Friesland, which has its own official language (West Frisian language), there are some trilingual primary schools, where children are taught in Dutch, Frisian and English. The 2013-2018 Administrative Agreement of Frisian Language and Culture contains a number of regulations aimed at stimulating the Frisian language and culture, specifically in the fields of education, media and culture (Nusche, 2014).

In Friesland the linguistic situation differs per school. Some are predominantly Dutch, others Frisian. In the seven experimental schools, both Frisian and Dutch are equally often used as medium of instruction, whereas English is used as the third language of instruction. Elementary schools in the province of Friesland (The Netherlands) have been confronted for over a decade with three compulsory school languages: Frisian (the regional language), Dutch (the national language) and English (the foreign language). Since 1980 Frisian has legally been an obligatory language for primary schooling in Friesland, and English became legally obligatory in primary education in the Netherlands in 1986. In the early nineties, national core-objectives were formulated for most school subjects at primary level. In line with this, core-objectives have been officially defined for the teaching of Dutch (national), English (national) and Frisian (regional).

Dutch is in principle the language that is legally prescribed as medium of instruction in primary education in The Netherlands. For the schools in Friesland province, Frisian is also legally allowed as medium of instruction (in addition to Dutch) since 1980. Strictly speaking, the use of English as medium of instruction is not legally permitted at primary level in Dutch primary schools. In practice, primary schools do use English as medium of instruction however, albeit exclusively for teaching English as school subject. Within the framework of the trilingual project, English will be used as medium of instruction for other school subjects as well at an experimental basis (Beetsma, 2001).

Use of English Language in the Netherlands and Kazakhstan

Higher education in the Netherlands and Kazakhstan is characterised by increasing significance and use of the English language. In the Netherlands instruction is partly conducted in English language. The use of English as a language of education is no longer restricted to higher education. Implementation of bilingual and multilingual education in the Netherlands is regulated to a certain degree by various acts and resolutions of the Dutch government and European Commission/ Europarliament. However, its major principles are defined by demands of business, technologies transfer and labor market (Extra and Yagmur, 2012).

As a result, nowadays about 80% of graduate level education in the Netherlands is conducted in English. Obviously, the Netherlands is a multilingual country as it hosts a number of minority languages, both local and those brought by immigration. On the other hand, the Netherlands is considered a bilingual rather than a multilingual country, where people use the native Dutch and the second English languages. There are several indications that the Dutch are moving from being a traditionally multilingual population, to being bilingual with their knowledge of English.

The rise of English as an international "lingua franca" (i.e. common language or dialect used systematically for communication) is especially noticeable in the last decades. The 2006 Special Eurobarometer report for the European Commission noted that 87% of Dutch citizens speak English as a second language, while the average in the European Union was 38%. The percentage of the second language speakers of English in the Netherlands is very high, compared only with the Scandinavian countries. The status of English as an international "lingua franca" has become undeniable and the widespread bilingualism of the Dutch population means that many people have access to international cultural resources in English language, without giving up their own cultural heritage in return (Oostendorp, 2012).

English is widely used for professional and career development both in the Netherlands and Kazakhstan. There are, however, certain common features, justified by globalisation, education internationalisation and labour market development. For example, learning English as the language of education, business and technologies, teaching and learning of English in secondary schools, capacity building facilities of language training at linguistic centres of Kazakhstani universities are similar to Leiden University's Talencentrum/Academic Language Centre and Linguistic Centre. There is also a common issue of professional and career development for multilingual teachers in both countries. Therefore, the professional development units like Graduate School of Learning (ICLON) have been organised at Kazakhstani universities and separately at the national level, e.g. Orleu – National Centre for Professional Development/ Almaty, Kazakhstan.

The use of Digital Technologies for Multilingual Instruction

Digital technologies are used for multilingual instruction of agricultural specialties in Kazakhstan. S. Seifullin Kazakh Agritechnical University has introduced e- learning (DLS) on the basis of the learning management system (LMS) Moodle (Modular Object-Oriented Dynamic Learning Environment) since November 2018. The system allows to provide course and lecture materials, tests, to examine knowledge and to control students' progress using different languages and correspondingly making this learning environment convenient for all users, both tutors and students. New courses/disciplines have been designed for undergraduate and postgraduate studies in the framework of this distant learning platform. LMS is characterized by a course content creation (SCORM or HTML), videoconferencing (BigBlueButton или Webex), analytics and graphic reporting, learning trajectory management, support of multilingual instruction and numerous trainees. The system operates in 154 languages including Kazakh, English, and Russian languages.

There are five main types of users (roles) in the system: administrators, course makers, teachers (tutors), students and guests. Moodle has a wide module (course elements) variety that can be used to develop courses of any type in three languages. Depending on the course content and the teaching concept, the course creator includes the most appropriate elements and resources provided by the Moodle system. One can separate the Moodle tools (modules) for presenting course materials into static (course resources) and interactive (course elements) modes. The system operates both in content and test mode and allows to minimize the hardware requirements for the student's workplace. It is enough to have a web browser for using Moodle and it makes this learning environment convenient for both students and tutors. This system also has quite a lot of technological advantages, which include such important characteristics for users as an intuitive, simple interface, broad communication capabilities (feedback organization). The Moodle interface is easy to use and to navigating on both desktop and mobile devices. The interactive elements of the course include: Questionnaire, Database; Wiki, External tool, Glossary, Task, Lecture, Feedback, Survey, Seminar, Test, Forum, Chat, etc. The general principles of Moodle system are demonstrated on the example of the courses "Professionally Oriented Foreign Language/ English, "Mathematical Modeling in Power Engineering" for the specialty "Agrarian Technologies" designed and conducted in English by the associate professor of Kazakh S.Seifullin Agritechnical University Assel Imasheva (Imasheva, 2019).

S.Seifullin Kazakh Agrotechnical University plans to further develop the system of multilingual instruction using the Moodle and other digital technologies in the linguistic, technological, qualitative, legal and organizational aspects. They are being adapted to the requirements of Kazakhstan's education market and have unlimited modification opportunities for all universities.

Moreover, other digital technical means are being used for facilitating the work between a student and a teacher. Mobile devices are getting practiced in the educational process: mobile learning or e-learning through mobile devices is applied regardless of location of both a student and a teacher. Various mobile applications, such as Edusoft, make possible to use practical materials outside the classroom via Internet or WiFi. Both universities – Kazakh National Agrarian University and Kazakh S. Seifullin Agrotechnical University – apply new programs "Unihub.kz" and "Antiplagiat.vuz with the aim of evaluating students' written works (essays, diploma papers, dissertations, etc.) for plagiarism, including those in English language. In the study of disciplines using the CLIL method, different modern auxiliary tools are applied, such as 3D visualization simulators and mobile applications.

The difficulty arising in the process of instruction is that the interface in these tools operates only in English or Kazakh/Russian languages. Therefore, currently KazATU researchers are developing the mobile application "Farmer" with the ability to switch the interface to English, Russian, Kazakh languages, render the corresponding language support and assure broad availability of multilingual applications based on the works of Microsoft engineers and inventors of MAT, Jan A. Nelson and Camerum Lerum (Nelson, 2015).

With emerging markets, expanding international cooperation and internationalization of education, computer technologies users expect to be able to use software and applications in their own language (Dedić and Stanier, 2016).

Actually, the issue of multilingualization of computer systems, its internationalization and localization is acquiring the growing significance alongside with the development of information technologies. Translating the user interface is usually part of the software localization process, which also includes adaptations such as units and date conversion. Many software applications are available in several languages, ranging from a few, the most spoken languages to dozens for the most popular applications (such as office suites, web browsers, etc.). Due to the status of English in computing, software development nearly always uses it though there are also Non-English-based programming languages. So almost all software is initially available in an English version, and multilingual versions, if any, may be produced as alternative options based on the English original (Multilingual Functionality, 2016).

Thus, new digital technologies are getting introduced and applied for the needs of multilingual instruction process in the Kazakhstani university system in general and at agricultural universities in particular with account of modern multilingual systems and applications. However, there is still a lack of digital technical means and the need to develop modern multilingualized applications.

FINDINGS OF THE EMPIRICAL RESEARCH AND TRIPS

The major findings of the research are based on qualitative and quantitative analysis, interviews with the major stakeholders - administrators, faculty and students of Kazakhstani (Kazakh National Agrarian University, Kazakh S.Seifullin Agritechnical University) and Dutch universities (Wageningen University, the Hague University of Applied Sciences and Dalton den Haag School) carried out during research trips to universities and colleges in the Netherlands.

In the process of research, interviews of students, faculty and stakeholders have been conducted as the part of the primary research tool. Interviews were conducted in a relaxed atmosphere according to a well-thought-out plan with the identification of questions prepared for each focus group. Planned respondents- students, faculty and stakeholders – revealed sufficient knowledge of the subject and great interest to the research. During the interview, questions were asked from easy to difficult questions; each interview lasted for 15-20 minutes and a voice recorder was used.

Research trips to universities and secondary schools in the Netherlands in 2014-2016 were funded by the Bolashak scholarship (Kazakhstan). Discussions with administration and faculty staff facilitated comprehension of the Dutch university system peculiarities in terms of trilingual and bilingual teaching and learning, including structure, management and languages taught.

Research interviews and analysis of the major stakeholders at Wageningen University revealed that bilingual tuition was mostly conducted at graduate studies level, combined with English language training at the Linguistic Centre. There were special multilingual groups at the undergraduate level (mostly for foreign students) and few undergraduate programs and courses in English, e.g. Tourism, Computer Science, etc.

Research trip to the Hague University of Applied Sciences illustrated that all undergraduate programs were conducted in English, which was justified by the goal to attract foreign students and acquire advanced technologies. Personal meetings and interviews with the university scholars and faculty including program manager Johan Krop and lecturer of English Tatyana Vladimirova, along with research of their curricula and syllabi confirmed the university's tendency to bilingual instruction.

Another research trip to Dalton den Haag School with its complete English language instruction demonstrated the tendency of Dutch secondary education to internationalisation and meeting labour market demands. There were also some courses in English at Leiden University Computer Science program. The proportion and percentage of courses taught in Dutch and English vary in different universities, based on students' language proficiency and career needs. Attendance of a symposium on Multilingualism in Hogeschool (Leiden) and its Information Market (November 2017) confirmed once again the tendency of the Dutch higher education to technologies transfer by means of English language tuition.

FUTURE RESEARCH DIRECTIONS

The research "Implementation of multilingual education for sustainable development in the Netherlands and Kazakhstan" was conducted in 2016-2019 by Kazakhstani scholars Fatima Duisebayeva and Assel Imasheva on the basis of the research trip to the Netherlands in the framework of Kazakhstani Presidential "Bolashak" program.

In future research will be proceeded at a larger scale including multilingual education implementation in other Eurasian countries such as Kyrgyzstan and Uzbekistan. Future research directions also comprise the study of the multilingual education issues in combination with national, identity and language policies and realities in Eurasian countries with account of migration. Interesting materials regarding MLE implementation in the USA are also being identified, maintained and introduced to scientific circulation and will be included in the future research activity.

CONCLUSION

Since the 1960s, multilingualism has played an important role in both socio-economic development and effective communication between persons, who otherwise do not share a native dialect or language. A number of relevant state and international treaties (such as Lisbon Strategy) were established in Europe, Asia and the USA, promoting bilingual/multilingual practices. Despite growth in English language use, demand for other languages was sometimes greater than demand for English language, especially for European SMEs to boost their exports and reduce business expenditures.

The main goal of multilingual education is pursuit of equity and social justice. In Kazakhstan, the significance of learning Kazakh, Russian and English was emphasized on the state level within the "Trinity of languages" program. In Kazakhstan, the state policy is to teach and learn three languages simultaneously and equally, while in the Netherlands, it is mostly bilingualism, which starts at primary and secondary education level, rather than at higher education level.

Research trips to the Netherlands in 2014-2016 illustrated that bilingual tuition was primarily run at graduate studies level, while there were special multilingual groups at the undergraduate level. The percentage and proportion of courses taught in English and Dutch vary in different universities. The driving force was to attract foreign students and develop advanced technologies transfer by means of English language.

The study is carried out during the authors' internship at ICLON (Graduate School of Learning, Leiden University, the Netherlands), research trips to Dutch universities, attendance of DRONGO Festival in Amstersdam, Diversity Symposium and international conferences at Leiden University.

The works of Dutch scholars M. van Oostendorp, G. Extra, K. Yagmur, S. Kroon, J. Bezemer, F. Kuiken, E., Linden were used as the main sources for the analysis of multilingual/bilingual education peculiarities in the Netherlands._

Having analysed multilingualism and MLE policies and practices in two case study countries, the following measures are recommended for successful implementation of MLE in Kazakhstan:

- Development of multilingualism at the primary and secondary school levels in order to prepare students for trilingual tuition at university level;
- Reforming curricula of higher educational institutions by Ministry of Education and Science, i.e. increasing academic hours for teaching English language and introducing special disciplines in English at undergraduate level, as well as transfer of postgraduate education to complete multilingual tuition;
- Promotion of faculty's and students' knowledge of English through facilitation of various extra-curricular activities at university language centers.
- Introducing innovative digital technologies and multilingual applications into the teaching process.

ACKNOWLEDGMENT

The research project was funded by the Kazakhstani Presidential Fellowship program "Bolashak" and supported by the Dutch counterparts – Dutch Academic Services (DAAS) and Leiden University Graduate School of Learning (ICLON).

REFERENCES

Banks, J. A. (2008). *An Introduction to Multicultural Education*. Boston, MA: Pearson/Allyn and Bacon.

Baryshnikov, N.V. (2004). Multilingvodidaktika. Inostrannyye yazyki v shkole. *Foreign languages in school*, *5*, 19-27. (in Russian)

Beetsma, D. (Ed.). (2001). *Trilingual Primary Education in Europe*. Mercator-Education.

Bezemer, J. (2003). *Dealing with multilingualism in education: a case study of a Dutch primary school classroom*. Amsterdam: Aksant Academic Publishers.

Campbell, D. (2010). *Choosing Democracy: A Practical Guide to Multicultural Education*. Sacramento.

Cohen, M. (1956). On the Sociology of Language. Pour une sociologie du langage. Academic Press.

Curtis, G. E. (1996). *Russia: A Country Study*. Washington: Library of Congress. Retrieved from http://countrystudies.us/russia/

Dedić, N., & Stanier, C. (2016). An Evaluation of the Challenges of Multilingualism in Data Warehouse Development. In *Proceedings of the 18th International Conference on Enterprise Information Systems ICEIS 2016* (pp. 190-196). Academic Press.

Dor, D. (2004). From Englishization to Imposed Multilingualism: Globalization, the Internet, and the Political Economy of the Linguistic Code. *Public Culture*, *16*(1), 97–118. doi:10.1215/08992363-16-1-97

Duchene, A., & Heller, M. (2012). Multilingualism and the new economy. In M. Martin-Jones, A. Blackledge, & A. Creese (Eds.), The Routledge Handbook of Multilingualism (pp. 369-383). Academic Press.

Duisebayeva, F. (2018). Workforce development in Kazakhstan: The Role of Multilingual Instruction. *Paper presented at CESS 2018 conference*. Academic Press. Retrieved from https://www.centraleurasia.org/conferences/annual/past/cess-2018-panels/#6932

European Commission. (2005). Realising the European Higher Education Area - Achieving the Goals. Conference of European Higher Education Ministers.

European Parliament. (2009). *EP Resolution on Multilingualism: An Asset for Europe and a Shared Commitment*. Brussels: European Parliament.

Evdokimova, N. V. (2008). Formirovaniye osnov mnogoyazychiya (in Russian). Formation of multilingualism principles. Rostov State Economic University.

Extra, G., & Yagmur, K. (2012). Language Rich Europe. Trends in Policies and Practices for Multilingualism in Europe.

Functionality, M. (2016). New in Wolfram Language 11. Retrieved from www.wolfram.com

Galskova, N.D. (2003). Obucheniye na bilingval'noy osnove. Inostrannyye yazyki v shkole. Education on bilingual basis. *Foreign languages in school*, *2*, 3. (in Russian)

Glazer, N. (1998). *We Are All Multiculturalists Now*. Cambridge, MA: Harvard University Press.

Hagen, S., Foreman-Peck, J., Davila-Philippon, S., Nordgren, B. (2006). ELAN: Effects on the European economy of shortages of foreign language skills in enterprise.

Harrison, K. (2013). Multilingual Education. In F. V. Tochon (Ed.), *Language Education Policy Studies*. Madison, WI: University of Wisconsin. Retrieved from http://www.languageeducationpolicy.org

Heugh, K. (2014). Turbulence and dilemma: Implications of diversity and multilingualism in Australian education. *International Journal of Multilingualism*, *11*(3), 347–363. doi:10.1080/14790718.2014.921180

Imasheva, A. (2019). *Professionally Oriented Foreign Language/English for the specialty "Agrarian Technologies". Kazakh S.* Astana: Seifullin Agritechnical University. Retrieved from http://agr.cskz.kz/

Komorowska, H. (2011). *Issues in Promoting Multilingualism. Teaching – Learning – Assessment*. Warsaw: Foundation for the Development of the Education System.

Kuiken, F., & Linden, E. (2013). *Language policy and language education in the Netherlands and Romania*. Amsterdam Center for Language and Communication. doi:10.1075/dujal.2.2.06kui

Lukashova, S., Omirzhanov, Y., & Chongarov, Y. (2015). Prospects and realia of establishing international universities in Kazakhstan. *Concorde*, *4*, 68–74.

Mazhitaeva, S., Smagulova, G., & Tuleuova, B. (2012). Multilingual Education as One of Priority Directions of Educational System Development in the Republic of Kazakhstan. *European Researcher*, *33*(11), 1.

Message to the People of Kazakhstan. (2012). Sotsial'no-ekonomicheskaya modernizatsiya – glavnyi vector razitiya Kazakhstana [Socioeconomic modernisation is a main direction of development of Kazakhstan]. (in Russian)

Nelson J. (2015). The Multilingual App Toolkit Version 3.0.

Nieto, S. (2008). *Affirming Diversity: The Sociopolitical Context of Multicultural Education*. Boston, MA: Pearson/Allyn and Bacon.

Nusche, D., Braun, H., Halasz, G., & Santiago, P. (2014). *OECD Reviews of Evaluation and Assessment in Education: Netherlands*. Retrieved from www.oecd.org/edu/school/OECD-Evaluation-Assessment-Review-Netherlands. pdf

Oostendorp, M. (2012). Bilingualism versus multilingualism in the Netherlands. *Language Problems and Language Planning*, *36*(3), 252–272. doi:10.1075/lplp.36.3.04van

Romaine, S. (1995). *Bilingualism*. Oxford: Blackwell.

Samuelson, B. L., & Freedman, S. W. (2010). Language policy, multilingual education, and power in Rwanda. *Language Policy*, *9*(3), 191–215. doi:10.100710993-010-9170-7

Schwinge, D. (2011). *Bilingual Learning*. Garden City, NY: Adelphi University.

Smokotin, V. M. (2010). Novyi etap v razvitiyi printsipa mnogoyazychiya v Evrope: Postroyeniye mnogoyazychnogo i politkul'turnogo obschestva. Vestnik Tomskogo gosudarstvennogo universiteta [New stage in development of multilingualism principles in Europe: establishment of multilingual, political and cultural society]. *Herald of Tomsk State University*, *333*, 61–66. (in Russian)

State of the Nation Address by the President of the Republic of Kazakhstan Nursultan Nazarbayev. (2018, January 10).

The Law on Higher Education. (1992, October 8). *Wet op Hoger Onderwijs en Wetenschappelijk Onderzoek*.

The State Program of Development and Functioning of Languages of Kazakhstan for 2011 - 2020. (2010). Government of Kazakhstan. Retrieved from http://www.primeminister.kz/page/article_item-86

The Strategy for Development of the Republic of Kazakhstan until 2030. (n.d.). Akorda. Retrieved from http://www.akorda.kz/ru/category/gos_programmi_razvitiya

Tinsley, T. (2011). The importance of languages for business. In Towards a language rich Europe. Multilingual essays on language policies and practices (pp. 58-61). Academic Press.

Tucker, G. R. (1999). *A Global Perspective on Bilingualism and Bilingual Education*. Carnegie Mellon University Press.

United Nations Educational, Scientific and Cultural Organisation [UNESCO]. (2003). Education in a Multilingual World.

Wolff, E. (2000). Language and Society. In B. Heine & D. Nurse (Eds.), *African Languages - An Introduction, 317*. Cambridge University Press.

Zhetpisbayeva, B. (2009). Teoretiko-metodologicheskiye osnovy poliyazychnogo obrazovaniya [Theoretical and methodological principles of multilingual education]. Academic Press. (in Russian)

Ziegler, G. (2013). Multilingualism and the language education landscape: Challenges for teacher training in Europe. *Multilingual Education*, *3*(1), 1. doi:10.1186/2191-5059-3-1

KEY TERMS AND DEFINITIONS

Multilingualism: Using of more than one language.

Bilingualism: Using two languages.

Trilingualism: Using three languages.

Bolashak Scholarship: International Scholarship was established on 1993 by the Decree of First President of the Republic of Kazakhstan N. A. Nazarbayev for training personnel and specialists for priority sectors of the Kazakhstani economy.

Chapter 14
English as a Medium of Instruction on the Way to Sustainability and Internationalization in Non-English-Speaking Countries

Aizhan Daukenova
University of International Business, Kazakhstan

Ainur Askhatova
University of International Business, Kazakhstan

Zhibek Kaisar
University of International Business, Kazakhstan

ABSTRACT

The present chapter describes the comparative analysis of the implementation of English as a medium of instruction in Kazakhstan and other non-English speaking countries by presenting a small-scale study of revealing the attitudes of graduate students and lecturers towards EMI in Kazakhstan. Compared to other countries, Kazakhstan has a number of similar issues in the implementation of English as a medium of instruction, which creates the possibility of performing a practice based on the experience of others. The research on English as a medium of instruction has revealed that EMI in Kazakhstan is in need of further guidance and investigation.

DOI: 10.4018/978-1-7998-2551-7.ch014

INTRODUCTION

English as a tool of teaching academic subjects in non-Anglophone countries is an international trend of the current century. Since English has become a language of technology, political and economic relationship, web communication, necessity of being part of global community has considerably increased. It resulted in conducting academic subjects in English, in countries where it is non-native language. It leads to the question of the presented research regarding how English as a medium of instruction is being implemented in Kazakhstan in comparison with other non-English speaking countries.

Educational programs in English as a medium of instruction are considered as one of the most expanded in the majority of countries of Europe, Asia-Pacific, Africa and Latin America (Dearden, 2014, p. 5). Kazakhstan also officially expands EMI within the policy of trilingual education – in Kazakh, Russian, and English. According to the policy, majority of subjects at schools and universities, as well as some bachelor and master's degree programs are conducted in English, guiding to the globalization of education and enhancement of international relations (Nazarbayev's Address to the Nation of Kazakhstan, 2017). As the President said, "Today I pose a challenge of carrying out the implementation of Kazakhstan's third modernization. It is necessary to create a new model of economic growth that will provide the country's global competitiveness" (Nazarbayev's Address to the Nation of Kazakhstan, 2017).

Qualitative usage of English as a medium of instruction is not investigated properly (Macaro, 2015, p. 4-7). EMI in the course of its development contradicts with the actual obstacles, such as incompliant conduction of the system; specifically, it is the lack of trained specialists, low mastery of English among teachers and students, deficient support of government, technology decay (Mousumi & Kusakabe, 2017, p. 2). English-medium schools (EMSs) in most of non-English speaking countries experience a remarkable inquiry among population, which entails fixing high tuition fee. It makes EMI accessible only to certain social classes (Murugesan, 2015, p. 10). Regarding all above stated, it could be concluded that the problem of English-medium education evolvement and proliferation represents significant importance.

In order to implement the analysis, various countries of Europe, Asia and Pacific were chosen, as Bangladesh, Japan, Turkey, Korea, Sri Lanka, Thailand, Brazil, Nepal, African and European countries. The history of the most of Asian-Pacific countries tightly correlates with the British rule expansion, which led to the massive popularization of EMSs (English-medium schools) and English language (Mousumi & Kusakabe, 2017, p. 3). There are peculiar backgrounds, advantages and downsides of EMI international system that can be compared and analyzed with the purpose of applying qualitative educational practices in Kazakhstan.

The present research states on the comparative analysis of implementation of English medium instruction in Kazakhstan and other non-English speaking countries by presenting a small-scale study of revealing the attitudes of graduate students and lecturers towards EMI in Kazakhstan.

BACKGROUND

On the way of globalization majority of countries, especially non-English speaking countries, attempt to be the part of developed countries' community (Galloway, Kriukow, & Numajiri, 2017, p. 9). In this regard, mastery of English provides the knowledge in order to achieve required international correlation. According to Galloway et al. (2017), the fair necessity of comprehension of English language is not sufficient. It leads to the correspondingly rising education through English (p. 9). Conversely, spheres of political and economic relationships, technology and worldwide network have contributed to globalization (Macaro, 2015, p. 6). Mastery of English language is the core in upgrading specialists in the mentioned spheres to enhance international relations and world economy. It resulted in the usage of medium language in communication (Mousumi & Kusakabe, 2017). The swift development of English in non-English speaking countries closely relates to the worldwide globalization and a significant increase of web-communication.

Higher education institutions (HEIs), based on certain reasons, are interested in attraction of international students. In order to optimize education among both international and home students they need to enhance skills of English language comprehension (Dearden, 2014). In addition, it is necessary for them to be able to provide education through English, due to the equality of knowledge acceptance by all students. In developing countries, the main reason for choosing English as a medium of instruction is the desire to advance the future career and purpose of moving abroad (Galloway et al., 2017, p. 10). Due to the fact, that parents strive to educate their children in English-medium schools from early age, English became demandable among students of secondary education (Mousumi & Kusakabe, 2017).

Current situation with non-availability of required academic information in home-languages in many developing countries is also considered as a reason of increasing English language skills. According to Dearden (2014), the obstacles, students face in the course of education mainly refer to the lack of academic subjects' knowledge in their home-languages (p. 7). Consequently, deficiency of knowledge leads to the regress of academic performance that would make great contribution to humanity. It is necessary for non-Anglophone countries to be able to conduct education through English to avoid this problem (Dearden, 2014).

As the result of all above mentioned, reasons influenced on rising English language necessity were the causes for development of English language as a medium of instruction (EMI). English as a medium of instruction is the phenomenon that is rapidly rising and taking huge part in the current educational system (Galloway et al., 2017, p. 9).

As Dearden mentioned (2014), "Definition of English as a medium of instruction was the use of English language to teach academic subjects in countries or jurisdictions where the first language (L1) of the majority of the population is not English" (p. 2). Considering the researches, the analysis demonstrated that even if EMI is spreading and proliferating as an indicator of higher quality of education, there are unreported objects of inappropriate improvement of EMI (Macaro, 2015, p. 5).

The purpose of one of several researches is to demonstrate significance of English as a medium of instruction at Japanese universities and the process of internationalizing higher education, scrutinize its effect for language teaching (Brown, 2015). According to Keio, despite the fact that EMI development commenced emerging and spreading in the late 1990s, full-degree English-taught programs (ETPs) in Japan remain considerably uncommon (p. 4). Altering the role of language teachers is one of essential implications of EMI, as the innovative approach is in demand of well-qualified specialists. According to the statistics of 2015, the amount of Japanese and international faculty members turned into approximately equal (Brown, 2015). The leading quantity of students in EMI undergraduate programs is in Humanities and Social sciences. Content-based instruction (CBI), content and language integrated learning (CLIL) are two programs of EMI expanding largely (Lee, 2014). According to Brown (2015), EMI is an outstanding tendency in current educational system of Japan. It does not only guide to a contemporary role of English in teaching, but also constructs positive cooperation and modification in mastering English as a foreign language (p. 419-423). The deficiency of education in Japan can be explained with several reasons (Keio Research Center for Foreign Language Education, n.d., p. 4). According to the author, firstly, it can be explained by the dissimilarities of English and Japanese languages, so that acquiring proficiency in English is more challenging for Japanese learners rather than for Indo-European family language speakers. Secondly, the reason lies in putting larger scope of emphasis on grammar skills in comparison with communicative skills (Keio Research Center for Foreign Language Education, n.d., p. 4).

Another research scrutinizes the objectives of English-medium schools' selection in Dhaka, Bangladesh by investigating the Clientele in teaching process of Bengali and English-medium schools (Mousumi & Kusakabe, 2017, p. 4). Unequal from other countries, typically only the representatives of higher social class have access to education in English-medium schools of Bangladesh. English-Medium Schools in Bangladesh have undergone a considerable proliferation in the last years. According to Rahman (2005), EMSs in Pakistan were called as "Passports to Privilege" (as cited in Mousumi & Kusakabe, 2017, p. 1). One of the study goals is to penetrate proliferation roots of such schools, despite the countless types of other schools and the struggles of Bangladeshi people for their native tongue Bengali with West Pakistan. Authors state that British dominion first initiated English-medium education in the Indian subcontinent. In a study, Rahman (2005) outlines that colonialism ensued on two kinds of school: chiefs' colleges for aristocracy, and English or European schools for professional classes, comprising English teaching schools and English as a medium of instruction school of armed forces (as cited in Mousumi & Kusakabe, 2017, p. 2). Prevailing trend of the elite to acquire English-medium education and the deficiency of schools were the roots for the rapid spread of EMSs. As authors claim, the peculiar attributes of EMSs such as quality and medium of instruction have contributed into the popularization of these schools in urban and semi-urban areas of Bangladesh. It is concluded in this research, that the English-medium schools extend vigorously in quantity, credibility and liability, and are in need of crucial research, rather than being in shade from people and government (Mousumi & Kusakabe, 2017, p. 12).

While researching about English as a medium of instruction in the higher education of Brazil, it is intended to present the contemporary challenges and opportunities. EMI system in the most of non-English speaking countries, as well as in Brazil, is a relatively new phenomenon (Martinez, 2016, p. 15). It is commonly regarded that in order to gain modern relevant experience, developing countries should trace the model of developed countries, specifically European. In contrast, Martinez (2016) states that Brazilian EMI system is distinctive in its own way and institutions are supposed to select the growth perspectives independently. Soren (2013) pays special attention to EMI professor's professional, personal and institutional identity, regarding this notion as a key figure in the learning process, possessing the demand for constant qualification and personal enhancement, EMI evaluation by the institution (as cited in Martinez, 2016, p. 20). Another remarkable point, according to the study statistics, is that the lower was the students' socio-economic status (SES) and English proficiency level, the more they preferred native language medium programs, mainly for the reason of getting higher academic results. Finally, it is deduced that Brazilian English-medium education system is still progressing, which allows it to learn from other countries' experience and actively participate in the further investigation (Martinez, 2016, p. 15).

The study in Turkey states that lecturers and students in HEIs support the idea of EMI implementation. Majority of universities in this country applied partial EMI programs, providing thirty per cent of their subjects through English language (Başıbek, Dolmacı, Cengiz, Bür, Dilek, & Kara, 2013, p. 1822). According to Başıbek et al., (2013), lecturer cling to the notion that there are much more materials and information in English rather than in Turkish language (p. 1824). As well as this research showed, that lecturers support teaching by method of EMI. Moreover, relying on the research, majority of lecturers think they are proficient enough for applying EMI in undergraduate education. They also support conduction of lectures in Turkish. They explained it as it is deeper and convenient for students to understand. In their point of view, EMI does not damage Turkish culture and mentality, and there are no conflicts between EMI and Turkish scientists regarding the latter's national interests (Başıbek et al., 2013, p. 1824). According to the study, in the field of perspectives of learners they hold an opinion that EMI would help to improve their English proficiency. As well as they can use their academic and social relations to obtain success in business after university. Otherwise, as it is shown in the research, due to the incompetent English level of students and teachers it is difficult for them to obtain academic knowledge of science through EMI (Başıbek et al., 2013, pp. 1819-1824).

The following research reports on the analysis of English-medium education effectiveness comparing the students' academic outcomes in India. The background of Indian English as a medium of instruction closely correlates with the British colonialism (Murugesan, 2015). According to Viswanathan (2014), British education policy's core purpose was to turn the middle class into a retainer of imperialist rule, launching social change (as cited in Murugesan, 2015, p. 10). The increasing request for English-medium schools is explained by the desire of individuals to improve earning perspectives and ability to involve in the worldwide economy. Nevertheless, the question of proliferating EMS is still arguable. After analyzing several studies, Murugesan (2015) comes to the opinion that "The results from the propensity score analysis suggest that there is no significant difference in the learning outcomes between the students who attend EMS and RMS [regional medium schools]" (p. 9). Thus, the medium of instruction is not an important factor in assessing learning results and more studies on English education in RMS need to be conducted (Murugesan, 2015, p. 11).

The research conducted among Southern Taiwan University of Science and Technology with participation of local and foreign students reported that local students prefer EMI to their native language (Huang, 2015, p. 72). As Huang (2015) stated, the questionnaire has been carried out to reveal availability of students to perceive English as a medium of instruction. Results of research said that students in this university support EMI courses and considered, as they are helpful for enhancing communication skills and professional knowledge (p. 76). As well as, it is also shown in the research that many students participate in the EMI courses on a voluntary basis to communicate with foreign students (Huang, 2015, p. 76). Whereas, students face with number of difficulties related to English and in their point of view low level of English comprehension is obstacle in the way of obtaining professional knowledge through EMI. However, majority of students can ask help from their classmates to overcome obstacles. Despite obstacles, almost all students hold that EMI courses helped them in forming good habits such as reading professional literature and learning materials in English. As well as the research applied Person correlation to find out correlation between different variables such constructs as Anxiety and Achievement (Huang, 2015, p. 78). It can be explained as this method showed that the lower participants think their English skills are, the less they can comprehend the course and the cause that they find EMI courses difficult. Overall, the author proposed in his research to establish courses that will help increase students' English skills and improve EMI in this university completely (Huang, 2015, p. 71-78).

In the research paper "Teaching in English on the rise in European Education" author Wachter (2015) states that considerable increase of international students took place worldwide in the last 5 decades (p. 3). As a result, English-medium education spread out across Europe, turning European countries into one of the prevailing destinations to study. Higher institutions of the Netherlands, Germany and the Nordic countries actively conduct English-medium programs, whilst in this case southern European countries lag behind. Teaching in English dominants in postgraduate studies, having the largest figures of students on Engineering and Technology faculties, and the least index in Social sciences. On average, Europeans and Asians comprise the substantial majority of students. Wachter (2015) claims that recently there had been a criticism of English-medium education, which was predicted to leading to unsatisfactory quality due to teachers' and students' insufficient level of English (p. 4). The evidence of 2002 experiment reveals that only a few percentage of students encounter the lack of foreign language command (Wachter, 2015, p. 4).

The investigation of EMI in African countries, displays that education policy of these countries extremely needs improvement regarding secondary education (Sibomana, 2015, p. 35). Commonly, African countries have three usable languages, first is their vernacular, generally used within tribes, second is Kiswahili, that is well-known for many people, the third is English. At the State level, there are two languages that are considered as officially: English and Kiswahili. In Kenya the issue, connected with language-in-education presents, due to the deficiency of knowledge in Kiswahili and English languages among majority of school children, especially rural habitants (Sibomana, 2015, p. 35). According to Sibomana (2015), the language-connected education policy of Kenya applies vernacular and Kiswahili from Grade 1 to 3, but from Grade 4 they additionally use English for teaching subjects (p. 36). Materials for Grades 1-3 are available only in 22 indigenous languages, while in general there are 40 indigenous languages (Sibomana, 2015, p. 37). It is stated, that "If it is a linguistic human right in education for one to be taught his/her mother tongue (Skutnabb-Kangas, 2000), then many children's rights are being violated in Kenya, because learners whose languages do not have literacy materials are not taught literacy in their mother tongue, or it is taught inappropriately" (Sibomana, 2015, p. 37). At schools, it is applied method to select for English language as a medium teaching from Grade 1, in the belief that it would help children to enhance English proficiency. Even in several schools of Kenya, it is prohibited for students to use their mother-tongue at schools, in order to spread usage of English language (Sibomana, 2015, p. 37). As Muthwii (2002) says, that as a result, children face two problems, non-comprehension of subject content, and disability to improve English communicative skills (as cited in Sibomana, 2015, p. 38). Besides that, Sibomana (2015) demonstrates the other problem in education with usage of this method presents as well: without studying their vernaculars and without contribution to them, there is a danger of their dwarfing (p. 38). Explaining that, the education in these countries is being performed concerning political interests of certain groups. In this regard, the evolvement of EMI in Kenya is conducting inappropriately, due to the reasons mentioned above.

According to Khati (2016), Nepal experienced discouraging of all languages except Nepali, during 1952-1990 years, when the slogan "one language, one costume, one religion, one nation" is widely spread at all territory of Nepal (p. 24). After gaining democracy, Nepal firstly started practicing EMI at private schools. Then state schools also began using EMI. According to the research, there are several reasons of applying English as a medium instruction in Nepal. First reason is connected with the fact that English is an international language that applied in technology and science. Consequently, knowledge and appropriate usage of English as a medium instruction can serve students to find new opportunities. Second reason is connected with political issues. While in Nepal there are many private schools that offer education in English, parents and students prefer them to state schools with education in Nepali language. As a result, teachers of public schools can lose their quotas from government. The implementation of EMI is performed in public schools. Thirdly, parents opt for English as a medium of teaching, because it may give better professional and academic knowledge for their children (Khati, 2016, p. 26).

The hasty growth of teaching academic subject through English language in courtiers, where population does not speak in English as well as it is spoken in native-countries is observed in our generation. Ernesto Macaro (2015), Professor in the Oxford University Department of Education, considers that "EMI is a growing global phenomenon taking place primarily in tertiary education" (p. 4). Macaro in his research (2015) notes several reasons of why EMI is not sufficient to enable students in learning academic subjects (p. 4). First reason is if students are taught in English, they should also discuss and even assessment system should be in English. Next reason is taken in medicine. There is no doubt that doctors have to read large scope of academic material published in English, but they also should be able to explain it to their patients. Another reason is shown within the class with three frequent consequences. First, if home students are large in number rather than L1 students, so there is a temptation for teacher to provide material and information in home-language for students in disregard for those who are few in number. Second consequence is if international students are in majority, teacher should have both experience, fluent English and pedagogically expert in own field. The third scenery looks like if internationalization is spread so much and English L1 students are present in EMI classes while there are home-language students, who cannot comprehend English are present as well. In the last case teacher faces the problem of who care about (Macaro, 2015, p. 4-7). Investigations show that the insufficient knowledge of English among students and teachers leads to non-qualitative conduction of lessons. Specifically, it reflects in shifting of medium language from English to native, as the result of which, the notion of EMI is distorted. If a teacher does not specialize only on EMI programs, there is a chance of disorder in transferring material for students. The reason for this is that the majority of current teachers who use EMI, were educated on their native language, and gained the qualification of EMI tutor within a short period.

Considering research papers, it is concluded that English is rapidly growing as a medium language in many developing countries. On the one hand, implementation of this phenomenon in non-Anglophone countries is the rational use due to such reasons as necessity of globalization, adoption of internationalization by HEIs, and exchange information and knowledge, available only in English language (Galloway et al., 2017, p. 9). The English language is becoming the language of the whole world, and most developing countries are endeavoring to be in progress with other developed countries. Spread of EMI all over the world is a result of the fact, that English language as a medium of instruction has been making great contribution for enhancement of international relationship between people of each country. On the other hand, some researchers hold the opinion that English as a medium of instruction has number of shortcomings, which will be followed by complications, if they are not eliminated on time. Teachers' insufficient knowledge of English language may cause to circumstances, that there would be temptation for them to conduct lesson on home-languages (Macaro, 2015, p. 5). Secondly, it is also connected with low level of English among students, so that they are not able to accept necessary information in the course of lessons. Besides, it should be considered as well, that teachers of academic subjects are not linguistic masters (Macaro, 2015, p. 5).

Governments of many Asian countries are implementing EMI to attract international students and also to perform proper environment for national students to avoid their mass immigration (Khati, 2016, p. 26). According to some researchers, as a result of all specified infirmities, EMI is not properly evolving. In many developing countries, there is a tendency that EMI is only adopted in private schools. It reflects negatively on EMI evolving in particular and in countries' evolving in whole. It can be explained with several realities. Firstly, although most parents wish their children to learn in English, not all of them have the possibility because the majority of them come from lower social classes (Mousumi & Kusakabe, 2017, p. 4). Secondly, the more students study in private schools, the fewer students leave in state schools, so that it badly reflects on state schools' teachers (Khati, 2016, p. 28). As studies showed, despite all shortcomings there are number of profits that EMI positively influenced. For example, in Taiwan, students choose EMI because it helps them for communication between foreign and home students

(Huang, 2015, p. 77). Lecturers of Turkey state universities also prefer EMI rather than home-language by virtue of availability of materials in English (Başıbek et al., 2013, p. 1822). The presented research figured out that the phenomenon of English as a medium of instruction is a necessary concept for future of the whole world on the way towards internationalization, globalization and relationships between all countries. The current aim for educational system is to find appropriate direction of EMI enhancement in developing countries, eliminating shortcomings that these countries face.

Overall, it can be claimed that the present research can assist in the implementation of the following study of English as a medium of instruction in the educational process of Kazakhstan.

METHODS

Instruments

The applied methodological approach is a quantitative analysis of study on students' and lecturers' viewpoints on learning and teaching process in English as a medium of instruction.

The study was presented in the form of questionnaire on the digital resource "Survey Monkey" and required participants to rate a given statement according to a specified Likert-type scale, applied in the research of Tung, Raymond, and Tsang (1997), and used in the study of Başıbek, et al. (2013) with some modifications (as cited in Başıbek et al., 2013). The questionnaire devised for the study was anonymous and consisted of 15 questions for university lecturers (Table 1) and 10 questions for graduate students (Table 2) with 5 options in each question. Participants were instructed to indicate the degree to which they agreed with each statement from 1 to 5 (1 – strongly agree, 2 – agree, 3 – neutral, 4 – disagree, 5 – strongly disagree).

The respondents were encouraged to answer the questions individually and demonstrate their unbiased and independent views on the use of English and native (Kazakh) or Russian as a medium of instruction at university. The students and lecturers were requested not to reveal their identity and personal information in the questionnaire. The responses were accumulated online via the digital resource "Survey Monkey" and statistically analyzed to enumerate the findings using Microsoft Excel.

Participants

Participants included 38 graduate students and 4 lecturers of the University of International Business in the Republic of Kazakhstan, who completed a digital questionnaire on attitude towards the English as a medium of instruction. Initially, it was planned to question 60 students and 5 lecturers, however some participants withdrew from the study due to private circumstances. Consent form was granted that lecturers and students could be approached and asked to take part in the study. There were 20% of responded students, who were in-serve teachers of subjects as physics, mathematics in native (Kazakh) or Russian languages at municipal schools. 80% of respondents among students were current teachers of English language at schools and language centers. The respondents were questioned in order to figure out their attitude towards perception of lectures in English language. Students' average age was 22-30 years old, the outcomes of older age students is also presented in the study. Lecturers, involved in the investigation, include 50% of social-humanitarian or pedagogical science teachers, such as history and philosophy of science, modern methodology of foreign language education, 50% are teachers of foreign languages,

Table 1. Lecturers' viewpoints on teaching and learning process in English as a medium of instruction (%)

Question	Strongly agree	Agree	Neutral	Disagree	Strongly disagree
1. Resources for teaching, e.g., textbooks and reference books, are in equal amount in English and in Russian/Kazakh.	0	50	0	50	0
2. Lecturing in Russian/Kazakh allows the lesson to progress faster than lecturing in English.	0	25	50	25	0
3. I support adopting English medium instruction at UIB.	0	50	25	25	0
4. It is difficult to express myself fully in lecturing in English.	0	25	50	0	25
5. Lecturing in Russian/Kazakh allows a teacher to go deeper into the content of the lesson than lecturing in English.	0	75	25	0	0
6. It is appropriate for instructors to teach the same lesson mixing English and Russian/Kazakh.	25	25	0	50	0
7. I think I am proficient enough to lecture in English.	50	25	25	0	0
8. Lecturing in Russian/Kazakh can promote students' interest in learning more than lecturing in English.	0	25	25	50	0
9. English medium instruction will not help students to obtain successful career after university.	0	25	0	50	25
10. Students give more importance to subjects taught in English.	0	25	75	0	0
11. Using English medium instruction will not contribute to English proficiency of the students.	0	0	25	25	50
12. Students' knowledge in their fields of study increases via English medium instruction.	0	50	25	25	0
13. Lecturing in Russian/Kazakh produces a better classroom atmosphere than lecturing in English.	0	25	25	50	0
14. Teaching a class in Russian/Kazakh encourages students to speak freely.	0	75	25	0	0
15. The English proficiency of the students I teach is adequate for them to study in English.	0	75	25	0	0

as academic English and French. 25% of respondents were current lecturers holding Master's degree at the time of study; 75% of respondents were in-service lecturers with the degree of PhD. Lecturers were implicated to the study in order to reveal their viewpoints on teaching academic disciplines in English language. The respondents were chosen as they deal with English as a medium of instruction and have required experience in education through English language. In the research, teachers and pupils of schools were excluded for the purpose of purity of investigation, since teaching and learning process in English as a medium of instruction at school needs special through investigation.

Procedure

At the initial stage, participants were divided into two main sections, lecturers and graduate students. Participants were asked to take part in the study by having conversation separately with each of them. At the beginning of the study, the pilot testing was experimented. In this experiment, the questionnaire was prepared for two sections, lecturers and graduate students. Questions were inconvenient to understand by participants and the study was conducted within 10 minutes. In order to perceive the neutrality

Table 2. Students' viewpoints on learning process in English as a medium of instruction (%)

Question	Strongly agree	Agree	Neutral	Disagree	Strongly disagree
1. Lectures in Russian/Kazakh can promote my interest in learning more than lectures in English.	10,53	28,95	34,21	13,16	13,16
2. English medium instruction will not help me to obtain successful career after university.	2,63	15,79	13,16	52,63	15,79
3. I give more importance to subjects taught in English.	21,05	60,53	10,53	7,89	0
4. Using English medium instruction will not contribute to my English proficiency.	2,63	21,05	23,68	39,47	13,16
5. I tend to give less importance to those subjects taught in Russian/ Kazakh.	2,63	34,21	34,21	21,05	7,89
6. Knowledge in my field of study does not increase via English medium instruction.	5,26	26,32	21,05	34,21	13,16
7. Lectures in Russian/Kazakh produce a better classroom atmosphere than lectures in English.	5,26	18,42	28,95	42,11	5,26
8. Learning in Russian/Kazakh encourages me to speak freely in the class.	7,89	42,11	26,32	18,42	5,26
9. My English proficiency is adequate to study in English.	10,53	65,79	10,53	7,89	5,26
10. The English proficiency of students in my group is not adequate to study in English.	0	31,58	28,95	36,84	2,63

and purity of investigation as well as to achieve the convenience in study conduction, it was decided to re-prepare the questionnaire.

Before starting the study, all participants were given an informed consent form for the purpose of their appropriate comprehension of the information about research and what data were required from them. The consent form was signed in 2 copies by participant, one copy was delivered to investigators and one copy was submitted to the participant.

Participants were asked to complete the questionnaire on the digital recourse "Survey Monkey". The link to the study was sent either by "WhatsApp" messenger or by e-mail to the participants' groups. There were two types of questionnaire prepared for participants: for lecturers and for graduate students. Average duration of the study conduction was 3 minutes by the students and 7 minutes by the lecturers. All participants could ask the researchers if they have problems with the digital resource or with comprehension of the questions. At the end of the study, the participants were given an oral debriefing, thanked for their participation, and were dismissed.

FINDINGS

The study focused on the viewpoints of students and lecturers regarding the learning and teaching process using English as a medium of instruction. As mentioned above, the participants were separated in two groups: university lecturers and graduate students.

Questionnaire among lecturers on their viewpoint towards learning process in English medium instruction included a number of points. The questionnaire of university lecturers' revealed the following results. In the first item, 50% of the lecturers stated that study material, such as textbooks and references are in equal amount in English and native medium instruction (Kazakh) or Russian, while the rest of university lecturers (50%) had the opposite opinion. The next question of the study aimed at if lecturing in Kazakh or Russian allows the lesson to progress faster than lecturing in English. Most of the university teachers (50%) were neutral towards this statement, whereas 25% agreed and the other 25% of the interviewees disagreed. Regarding the question of adopting English as a medium of instruction at the University of International Business (UIB), 50% of lecturers opted for adopting it, while the rest had neutral position (25%) or were against (25%) English as a medium of instruction at the University. In the next enquiry of the study, the half of the respondents (50%) could not give a definite answer whether it is difficult to express themselves fully while they lecture in English, 25% of the university teachers agreed and the other 25% strongly disagreed with the given statement. The upcoming question aimed at whether lecturing in native medium instruction allows going deeper into the content of the lesson than lecturing in English or not. Concerning this matter, 75% of the university lecturers agreed, while 25% of the teachers had neutral view towards this statement.

The following question of the study claimed that it is appropriate to teach the same lesson mixing English and Kazakh or Russian, 50% of lecturers disagreed with this, 25% of interviewees agreed and strongly agreed (25%). In the question about whether the lecturers are professionally proficient enough to lecture in English, there were the following responses: 50% of teachers strongly agreed that they are proficient, 25% agreed, 25% of the lecturers demonstrated neutral position towards this enquiry. Half of the interviewees (50%) did not hold the opinion that lecturing in native medium instruction could promote students' interest in learning more than in English, whereas the rest of the university lecturers agreed (25%) or were neutral (25%). In the upcoming statement that English medium instruction will not help students to obtain a successful career after graduating from university, 50% of the respondents disagreed, 25% strongly disagreed, the rest 25% of the university teachers agreed with this claim.

The upcoming item of the questionnaire figured out that the most of the lecturers (75%) held neutral position towards the statement that students give more importance to subjects taught in English, the rest 25% agreed with this. Further, 50% of the interviewees strongly disagreed with the claim that English as a medium instruction will not contribute to English proficiency of students, 25% disagreed and the rest 25% of the lecturers could give a definite answer to this question. In the next item, half of the responded university teachers (50%) held the opinion that students' knowledge in their fields of study increases via English as a medium of instruction, while the rest of the lecturers were neutral (25%) or disagreed (25%) with the given claim. The following question aimed at whether lecturing in Kazakh or Russian produces a better classroom atmosphere in comparison with lecturing in English as a medium of instruction. Regarding this matter, 50% of the lecturers disagreed, 25% agreed and the other 25% of the university teachers presented their neutral position. 75% of the questionnaire respondents agreed with the statement that teaching a class in native medium instruction (Kazakh) or Russian encourages students to speak freely than in English as a medium of instruction, while 25% of the lecturers had neutral opinion regarding this. The last question of the study questionnaire concerned the level of English proficiency of university students learning via EMI. On this matter, the majority of the university teachers (75%) claimed that the English proficiency level of students was adequate enough for them to study in English; the other 25% of the interviewees possessed neutral view towards this item.

The study among students on their viewpoint towards learning process in English medium instruction included a number of questions. Majority of students adhere to neutral viewpoint with respect to the first item of questionnaire (34%). Despite the fact that all students are able to sufficiently comprehend the information via English language, 28% of students agree, and 10% of students strongly agree that lectures in native (Kazakh) and Russian languages can promote their interest in learning more than lectures in English. There are 13% of students, who adhere to viewpoint that English language may facilitate their interests in learning process more than native languages. Similar indicator is shown by students, who strongly agree with the specified item (13%).

The next question was given to reveal the attitude of students on English as a medium of instruction assisting in obtainment of successful career after university. More than half part of students agrees with this statement (52%), while several students adhere to the opposite viewpoint (15%). The significant fact was revealed during the study, where the similar number of students replied that strongly agree with maintaining English for successful career (15%). The neutral view was upheld by 13% of students.

All the responses of lecturers and graduate students were thoroughly compared and analyzed. The overall findings regarding attitude of lecturers towards English as a medium of instruction can be defined as follows: 45% of lecturers support adopting EMI, 35% of university teachers have neutral position, 25% of lecturers are for the native medium instruction in Kazakh or Russian languages (Figure 1).

The result of the study, conducted among lecturers of the University of International Business was not exactly clear due to the fact that there were insufficient number of lecturers (4 persons), who completed the study. Before starting the present research, there was a prediction that the lecturers participated in this study have negative attitudes towards adopting EMI, due to the fact that lecturing in Kazakh or Russian provides deeper understanding and some students do not have proficiency in English. However, the study herein, shows that the majority of lecturers support adoption of English as a medium of instruction, although in most situations, they prefer adhering to neutral position. In general, the lecturers participated in this study have positive attitude towards adopting English as a medium of instruction in Kazakhstan. They hold an opinion that although learners are not appropriately proficient to learn subjects in English, implementation of this program may promote students for using English in their specific area in the future career. On the other hand, lecturers support the idea that lecturing in Kazakh or Russian provides deeper and clearer understanding in terms of the content of the lesson, due to the insufficient knowledge of English language by students. They also think that lecturing in mother tongue helps learners to acquire enough knowledge about the content of the lesson.

Figure 1. Overall attitude of lecturers towards EMI based on performed study

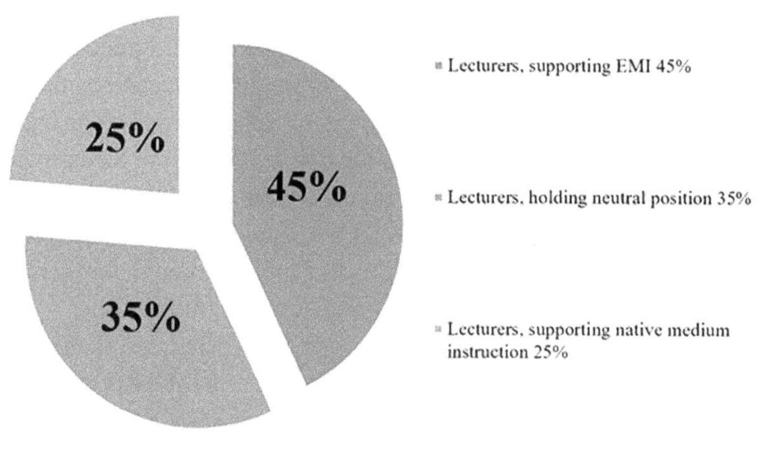

Figure 2. Overall attitude of students towards EMI based on performed study

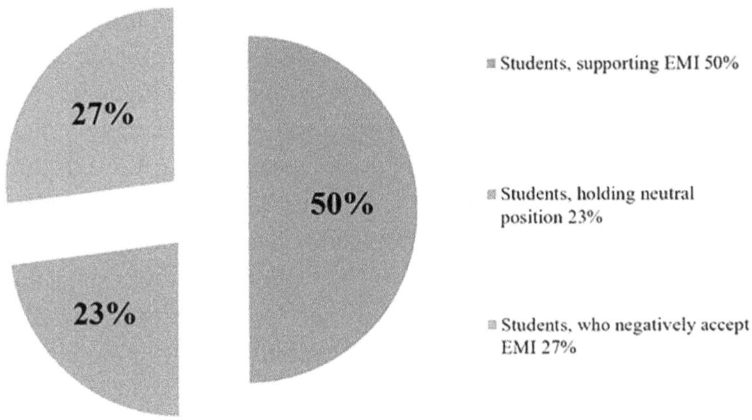

Regarding the responses of graduate students, the findings demonstrate that 50% of them adhere to studying in English as a medium of instruction, 23% hold neutral view, 27% of graduate students negatively accept learning process in English as a medium of instruction (Figure 2).

The study, conducted among students, showed significant results. Gaining results from the questionnaire among students was unhampered in comparison with study among lecturers, by virtue of the fact that the number of students, intended to participate was much more than number of lecturers (38 persons). Correlation of answers was also based on different situations, including self-assessment and assessment of other students of group on English proficiency. Students, who took part in the study, mostly have positive attitude towards English-medium instruction, although in some cases, they encourage Russian or Kazakh languages due to deeper comprehension of information during lectures. The fact that materials and information related to specific area of their profession are more available in English rather than in Russian or Kazakh languages makes students opt for English language. This case is similar to that, which is shown in the study among lecturers. Nevertheless, more than half the students consider that they are proficient enough in the English language to comprehend materials.

In general, the presented findings guided the implementation of the further part of research on comparison of learning process in English as a medium of instruction in Kazakhstan with other non-English speaking countries.

DISCUSSION

The purpose of the present research is to compare implementation of English medium instruction in Kazakhstan with other non-English speaking countries. Revealing attitude of graduate students and lecturers assisted to create a general model of how English as a medium of instruction is being implemented in Kazakhstan. In addition, the research is aimed at showing the key challenges that have been encountered in the course of its implementation.

As previously mentioned, the findings demonstrate that the majority of graduate students adhere to studying in English as a medium of instruction, almost a quarter of them hold neutral view and, approximately, the same number of graduate students negatively accept learning process in English as a medium of instruction. Similarly as shown in the research findings, more than half of total amount of lecturers participated in the study, support development of English as a medium of instruction in their university. In this regard, the answers of Kazakhstani lecturers were similar to answers of Turkish lecturers. However, the difference in attitude between these countries was in the fact that Turkish lecturers supporting English as a medium of instruction rely on English proficiency of students and feel more comfortable lecturing in English rather than in native language, since Kazakhstan lecturers consider otherwise. Students participated in this research have positive opinion toward English as a medium of instruction as well. The notable result has been revealed, when students questioned the English proficiency of lecturers, while in their opinion, their own English proficiency is sufficient.

Students of Taiwan University participated in study had similar answers as students of Kazakhstan. Students of both countries consider that English as a medium of instruction may help them in future career, as well as may assist them in obtaining new good habits, like reading professional literature in English. However, the research showed that students of Taiwan faced obstacles related to English proficiency. In this regard, it was advised to establish an English course that may help Taiwan students to be more proficient in comprehension of lectures in English. This practice is beneficial for Kazakhstan students, due to the fact that they also have several obstacles in comprehension of information via English. Although students consider that they are properly proficient in English the perception of information in native languages is more convenient for them. On the other hand, it can be connected with proficiency of lecturers. As students answered that some lecturers are not proficient in lecturing in English, the course for enhancing English proficiency should be available for lecturers as well.

Brown (2015) stated that English as a medium of instruction is becoming an outstanding tendency in the modern educational system of Japan (p. 419). Significance of English as a medium of instruction in Japan universities is connected with internationalizing higher education institutions, which resulted in spread of English as a medium of instruction among both, local and international students. The statistics carried out in Japan in 2015 showed that international faculty members became equal with members of national faculty members (Brown, 2015). The similar situation has place in the educational system of Kazakhstan. The essential role of adoption of English as a medium of instruction is internationalization of Kazakhstan education system, establishing competitive institutions for the nation (Dearden, 2014). At the current time, government attempts to enhance adoption of English as a medium of instruction in universities and schools of Kazakhstan. English as a medium of instruction has started taking place and playing significant role in higher education system of Kazakhstan several years ago, while schools started this program on an experimental basis in 2018 (Tenizbayeva, 2018). However, the current results of English as a medium of instruction demonstrated the rightness of Dearden (2014), who predicted that further development of English as a medium of instruction in Kazakhstan might assist in internationalization of the country (p. 15).

Compared to the spread of English as a medium of instruction in Bangladesh, Kazakhstan students at schools and universities have more opportunities to learn using English as a medium of instruction. However, using English for teaching students was firstly initiated by British dominion, Bangladesh has class separation in English as a medium of instruction and so only higher classes have possibility to learn English (Mousumi & Kusakabe, 2017). On the one hand, English as a medium of instruction may assist students and nation to obtain qualitative knowledge, on the other hand, class separation and privilege for higher classes in Bangladesh negatively influences on education system of Bangladesh in whole (Mousumi & Kusakabe, 2017). Although there are numbers of private schools and universities, where English as a medium of instruction is certainly strong developed, and English as a medium of instruction started being adopted in educational system a few years ago, the government of Kazakhstan gives more opportunities for talented students to learn using English as a medium of instruction in certain schools and universities. Therefore, class separation because of education possibilities in Kazakhstan is less developed than in Bangladesh.

Despite that, English medium adoption in Kazakhstan is at the initial stage of its development, government, on the way of implementation of the program, attempts to adopt English medium courses, considering less about English proficiency of participants of the program. It was proved by the present research, in which lecturers and students were questioned about the English proficiency of each other. As stated above, Korean government in the course of implementation of English medium instruction pays more attention on quantity of English medium courses in universities, while quality of these courses is a question of less priority. It is resulted by virtue of the fact that universities need reputation, and in their point of view, the more English medium courses are there, the higher reputation educational institutions present. As a result, this rush toward reputation destructs properly development of English as a medium of instruction (Lee, 2014, p. 110). This sample should be taken into consideration for country that recently started English medium instruction. Quality of courses plays significant role in future development of English as a medium of instruction in a way of internationalization.

According to Murugesan (2015), the significant difference is not placed between learning using EMS (English medium schools) or RMS (regional medium schools), so the medium instruction is not a basis for learning assessment. This statement is necessary in development of English as a medium of instruction in Kazakhstan. Believing that English may give more opportunities may harm learning native language. Thus, development of English as a medium of instruction should be conducted combining with native language and with ethnical norms of linguistics.

For reasons of economic policy, many European countries actively develop English as a medium of instruction in their educational system. As English turned to the preferable medium instruction not only within Europe, but also far from it, such countries as the Netherlands, Germany and Poland started proposing English medium programs for international students (Wachter, 2015). This is the sample of how English as a medium of instruction may influence on economic policy of the country. As stated above, Kazakhstan began implementation of English as a medium of instruction for the economic and political purposes as well (Dearden, 2014).

Besides that, European educational system also fears from insufficient English proficiency of students and lecturers. Nevertheless, research of Wachter (2015) showed only a few percent of learners with insufficient proficiency in English (p. 4). As shown in many researches, the key obstacle in proper development of English as a medium of instruction is insufficient proficiency in English language, and Kazakhstan, as it is indicated in the present research, is not exclusion. In comparison with European countries, Kazakhstan need decades of experience, and also support for development of English medium instruction, to achieve the same goals in internationalization and globalization.

As stated in the literature review, Nepal started its experience of English as a medium of instruction on a governmental basis after spread of program in private schools and its preference among people. Although this program, as in Kazakhstan, is supported by the government, it has number of discrepancies. English proficiency among teachers and students may harm learning process. Teachers of Nepal state that even if they have decades of experience in teaching their disciplines, it is hard for them to learn English to be able to teach disciplines in English. Moreover, students also do not have appropriate English proficiency. It is needed to learn English first, but it is not enough for them to be able to comprehend academic subjects in English (Khati, 2016, p. 27). Kazakhstan has similar situation in spread of

English as a medium of instruction in schools. Although the present research does not concern English as a medium of instruction implementation at schools, some researches demonstrated that insufficient mastering English language by teachers might harm learning process, because teachers should choose to deliver knowledge on discipline, or to choose to develop English comprehension (Dearden, 2014).

Despite the fact that Kazakhstan recently started implementation of English as a medium of instruction comparing with other countries, one of the main perspective aims of this program is achievement of increasing number of competitive universities of the world level with high qualitative knowledge. Increased competitiveness of higher education institutions assisted to achieve main aims of internationalization and globalization of the country. However, in the process of implementation of English as a medium of instruction the obstacles are faced. In general, these obstacles are related to English proficiency of students and lecturers. As Macaro stated (2015), English as a medium of instruction is the phenomenon that is not sufficiently investigated. He also stated that insufficient English proficiency might lead to non-qualitative learning process (p. 4).

Question of the present research was the process of how English as a medium of instruction is being implemented in comparison with other non-English speaking countries. Compared to other countries, Kazakhstan has a number of similar issues in the implementation of English medium instruction, which creates the possibility of conducting a practice based on the experience of others.

CONCLUSION

The present research paper intended to investigate how English as a medium of instruction is implemented in Kazakhstan in comparison with other non-English speaking countries. The study consisted of collection of research conducted in the following countries throughout the world: Japan, Bangladesh, Korea, Brazil, Turkey, India, Taiwan, Kenya, Nepal, European countries and Sri Lanka. It was followed by performing a small-scale research on the attitude of graduate students and lecturers towards English as a medium of instruction at the University of International Business in the Republic of Kazakhstan, discussion of the study findings, comparing them with the results of research in other non-English speaking countries and presenting suggested guidance.

The research paper represents a significant value. The impact of English in the most of international educational contexts means that there is a rapidly growing tendency for English to be adopted as a medium of instruction, though a majority of the population speaks a local language. In such situations, English has played a central role as an international language more than ever. Since the beginning of the XXI century there has been a sharp increase in the number of universities across the world that offer degree courses which are taught through the medium of English, although these universities are located in countries where English is not an official language. As stated before, educational programs taught in English as a medium of instruction are considered as one of the most expanded in the majority of countries of the European Union, Asia-Pacific region, Africa and Latin America. Kazakhstan also expands the usage of English as a medium of instruction, as today the majority of subjects at schools and universities, a number of bachelor's and master's degree programs are conducted in English. Still, the phenomenon of English as a medium of instruction is not investigated properly, as some non-English speaking countries tend to encounter a number of obstacles during implementation of EMI in the learning process.

The conduction of small-scale study highlighted the current state of teaching and learning process through English as a medium of instruction in Kazakhstan and allowed to compare it with other non-

English speaking countries. Overall, the attitude of lecturers and students towards English as a medium of instruction in Kazakhstan was positive, as they realize the considerable importance of English in today's globalized environment and labor market.

The research on English as a medium of instruction has revealed that EMI in Kazakhstan is in need of further guidance and investigation. The initial step is introducing courses of English proficiency among students and lecturers, which is a basis leading to effective usage of EMI. Further, the research paper has shown that in comparison with other countries, English as a medium of instruction in Kazakhstan does not harm the native language and culture. In general, the small-scale study demonstrated that issues that EMI in Kazakhstan faces are alike to the process of development of English as a medium of instruction in some other non-Anglophone countries. Hence, there is an opportunity in Kazakhstan to learn from the experiences of others in the world, who have already achieved success in the implementation of English as a medium of instruction in the educational process.

REFERENCES

Balakrishnar, J., & Thanaraj, T. (2011). Instruction in the English medium: A Sri Lankan case study. In *Proceedings of the Language and Social Cohesion in the Developing World conference* (pp. 166-177). Academic Press. Retrieved from http://www.langdevconferences.org/

Başıbek, N., Dolmacı, M., Cengiz, B., Bür, B., Dilek, Y., & Kara, B. (2013). Lecturers' Perceptions of English as a medium of instruction at Engineering Departments of Higher Education. *Procedia, 116*, 1819-1825. Retrieved from https://www.sciencedirect.com/

Brown, H. (2015). English as a medium of instruction in Japan: Discussing Implications for Language Teaching. *Focus on the learner,* (1), 419-423. Retrieved from https://jalt-publications.org/

Dearden, J. (2014). English as a medium of instruction – a global growing phenomenon. *British Council, 761*(3), 2-34. Retrieved from https://www.teachingenglish.org.uk/

Galloway, N., Kriukow, J., & Numajiri, T. (2017). Internationalization, higher education and the growing demand for English: an investigation into the English medium of instruction (EMI) movement in China and Japan. *Teaching English, 7*, 4-9. Retrieved from https://www.teachingenglish.org.uk/

Huang, D. (2015). Exploring and assessing effectiveness of English as a medium of instruction courses: The students' perspectives. *Procedia, 173*, 71–78. doi:10.1016/j.sbspro.2015.02.033

Keio Research Center for Foreign Language Education. (n.d.). *What is the Problem of English Education Japan?* Retrieved from http://www.flang.keio.ac.jp/en/support/event/contest2007.html

Khati, A. R. (2016). English as a medium of instruction: My Experience from a Nepali Hinterland. *Journal of NELTA, 21*(1-2), 23–29. doi:10.3126/nelta.v21i1-2.20198

Lee, J. (2014). Why Students Don't Participate in English as a medium of instruction Classes in a Korean University: A Case Study. *English Teaching, 69*(1), 91–117. doi:10.15858/engtea.69.1.201403.91

Macaro, E. (2015). English as a medium of instruction: Time to start asking some difficult questions. *Modern. English Teaching, 24*(2), 4–7. Retrieved from https://www.modernenglishteacher.com/

Martinez, R. (2016). English as Medium of Instruction (EMI) in Brazilian Higher Education: Challenges and Opportunities. *English in Brazil: Views Policies and Programs, 2*(81), 191-228. Retrieved from https://www.researchgate.net/

Mousumi, M., & Kusakabe, T. (2017). Proliferating English-Medium Schools in Bangladesh and Their Educational Significance among the "Clientele". *Journal of International Development and Cooperation, 23*(1), 1–13. Retrieved from https://ir.lib.hiroshimau.ac.jp/

Murugesan, S. (2015). Does Medium of Instruction matter? A propensity score analysis of the effect of English Medium Education on students learning outcomes in India. Retrieved from https://pdfs.semanticscholar.org/b874/647eb6bfb6073f90d86b8a1fae9a72cffc1f.pdf

Sibomana, E. (2015). Postcolonial language-in-education policies in Africa: The case of Kenya. *Rwandan Journal of Education, 3*, 37-47. Retrieved from https://www.ajol.info/

Tenizbayeva, M. (2018). 27 schools of Kazakhstan started to learn subjects in English in Almaty. Retrieved from https://www.inform.kz/ru/

The President of Kazakhstan Nursultan Nazarbayev's Address to the Nation of Kazakhstan. (2017). Retrieved from http://www.akorda.kz/en/

Wachter, B. (2015). Teaching in English on the Rise in European Higher Education. *International Higher Education,* (52), 3-4. Retrieved from https://ejournals.bc.edu/ojs/index.php/ihe/article/viewFile/8028/7179

KEY TERMS AND DEFINITIONS

Attitude: A tendency to respond positively or negatively towards a certain idea, object, person, or situation.

English as a Medium of Instruction (EMI): The use of English in the classroom by the teacher to teach.

Higher Educational Institutions (HEIs): Universities, colleges, and further education institutions offering and delivering higher education.

Lecturer: A teacher at a university or college.

Mother Tongue: A language learned from birth.

Non-English-Speaking Country: A country where English is not spoken as official or second language.

Viewpoints: The way people think about things in general, or the way they think about a particular thing.

Compilation of References

Abouelenein, Y., & Mohamed, A. (2016). Training needs for faculty members: Towards achieving quality of university education in the light of technological innovations. *Educational Research Review*, *11*(13), 1180–1193. doi:10.5897/ERR2015.2377

Afanasyeva O.V. (2010). Access to information: Russian and international legislation. Social sciences and modernity.

Afanasyeva O.V. (2012). Postmodernity as a crisis. Toward a new understanding of social openness. The policy.

Agbo, I. (2015). Factors influencing the use of information and communication technology (ICT) in teaching and learning computer studies in Ohaukwu local government area of Ebonyi state-Nigeria. *Journal of Education and Practice*, *6*(7), 71–86. Retrieved from https://files.eric.ed.gov/fulltext/EJ1083136.pdf

Agriculture in Central Asia Unlocking the Potential (Interview with Irna Hofman, Leiden University). (2018, October 11). *Voices on Central Asia.* Retrieved from https://voicesoncentralasia.org/agriculture-in-central-asia-unlocking-the-potential-interview-with-irna-hofman

Aitmukhambetov, A. A. (2000). Public education and the formation of the Kazakh intelligentsia of North-West Kazakhstan in the second half of the 19th–early 20th centuries. Unpublished doctoral dissertation, Baitursynov Kostanay State University, Kostanay, Kazakhstan.

Akçayır, G. (2017). Why do faculty members use or not use social networking sites for education? *Computers in Human Behavior*, *71*, 378–385. doi:10.1016/j.chb.2017.02.028

Akhmedov, M. Z. (2018). *Improvement of the mechanism for interaction of banking sector and the real sector in Tajikistan (the case of bank loans) (PhD dissertation).* Khujand State University named after Gaforov, Khujand, Tajikistan.

AkopovA.K. (2013). Модель глобального электронного правительства.

Al Shobaki, M. J., & Naser, S. S. A. (2017) The role of the practice of excellence strategies in education to achieve sustainable competitive advantage to institutions of higher education-faculty of engineering and information technology at Al-Azhar university in Gaza a model. *International journal of digital publication technology*, *1*(2), 135-157. Retrieved from https://philarchive.org/archive/ALSTRO-9

Alamri, M. M. (2019). Students' academic achievement performance and satisfaction in a flipped classroom in Saudi Arabia. *International Journal of Technology Enhanced Learning*, *11*(1), 103–119. doi:10.1504/IJTEL.2019.096786

Aldoshenko, E. V. (2014). Electronic government as a stage of formation of electronic democracy. Retrieved from www.cyberleninka.ru

Alexandros, A., & Paraskevi, D. (2019). Cases on corporate social responsibility and contemporary issues in organizations. Hershey, PA: IGI Global.

Alheit, P. (2009). Biographical learning – within the new lifelong learning. In K. Illeris (Ed.), *Contemporary theories of learning: Learning theorists...in their own words* (pp. 116–128). New York: Routledge.

Al-Khalifa, H. S., & Garcia, R. A. (2013). The state of social media in Saudi Arabia's higher education. *International Journal of Technology and Educational Marketing*, *3*(1), 65–76. doi:10.4018/ijtem.2013010105

Alpen-Adria-Universität Klagenfurt. (2017, November 15). Organic farming can make an important contribution to world nutrition, research shows. *ScienceDaily*. Retrieved from www.sciencedaily.com/releases/2017/11/171115092144.htm

Al-Zahrani, A. M. (2015). 'From passive to active: The impact of the flipped classroom through social learning platforms on higher education students' creative thinking'. *British Journal of Educational Technology*, *46*(6), 1134–1150. doi:10.1111/bjet.12353

Amba-Rao, S. (1993). Multinational corporate social responsibility, ethics, interaction and Third World governments. *Journal of Business Ethics*, *12*(7), 553–572. doi:10.1007/BF00872380

Aminov, Kh. I. (2010). *Modelling and information technology of the assessment of the credit risk of the commercial bank in the Republic of Tajikistan*. Dushanbe, Tajikistan: Monographiya.

Anderson, C., & Wolff, M. (2010). The Web is dead. Long live the internet. *Wired*, *18*(9), 118-127, 164, 166.

Anderson, L. W. (2005). Objectives, evaluation, and the improvement of education. *Studies in Educational Evaluation*, *31*(2), 102–113. doi:10.1016/j.stueduc.2005.05.004

Anderson, L., Earley, J., Feketekuty, G., & Williamson, I. (2004). *Legal analysis in commercial diplomacy analyzing applicable domestic laws and international agreements. ITCD*. San Diego Global University.

Antle, J. M., Jones, J. W., & Rosenzweig, C. E. (2017). Next generation agricultural system data, models and knowledge products: Introduction. *Agricultural Systems*, *155*, 186–190. doi:10.1016/j.agsy.2016.09.003 PMID:28701811

Arakeri, M., & Lakshmana. (2016). Computer Vision Based Fruit Grading System for Quality Evaluation of Tomato in Agriculture industry. *Procedia Computer Science*, *79*, 426–433. doi:10.1016/j.procs.2016.03.055

Arkhipova, Z. V. (2016). Transformation of E-Government into Digital Government. Retrieved from: https://cyberleninka.ru/

Asgher, U., Babar Rasheed, M., Al-Sumaiti, A. S., Ur-Rahman, A., Ali, I., Alzaidi, A., & Alamri, A. (2018). Smart Energy Optimization Using Heuristic Algorithm in Smart Grid with Integration of Solar Energy Sources. *Energies*, *11*(12), 3494. doi:10.3390/en11123494

Asia Education. (2019). Retrieved from https://ec.europa.eu/europeaid/regions/asia/eu-support-education-and-science-collaboration-asia_en

Asian Development Bank. (2016). *Tajikistan Promoting Export Diversification and Growth*. Philippines: Asian Development Bank.

Aspin, D., & Chapman, J. (2001, July). Lifelong learning: concepts, theories and values. *Paper presented at the SCUTREA 31st annual conference*. Academic Press.

Assylbekova, A. (2010). Investigation of landscapes of the northern slope of Alatau Mountains using satellite imagery. Almaty, Kazakhstan: Kazakh Universiteti.

Astana. (2017, June 23). *Astana Declaration of the second meeting of ministers for education of the member states of the European Union and of the central Asian countries*. Retrieved from https://eeas.europa.eu/sites/eeas/files/01_astana_declaration_170623_final_en.pdf

Avetisyan, P. S., Zaslavskaya, M. I., Galikyan, G. E., Gevorkyan, N. M., Arutyunyan, M. L., Movsisyan, M. S., . . . Matevosyan, B. G. (2015). Modernization of Higher Education in the context of integration processes. Publishing center RAU.

Axyonova, V. (2013, February). The EU education initiative for Central Asia five years on: Lessons learnt? *EUCAM Policy Brief, 30*. Retrieved from http://eeas.europa.eu/central_asia/docs/2010_strategy_eu_centralasia_en.pdf

Azimov, E. G., & Shchukin, A. N. (1999). *Dictionary of methodological terms (theory and practice of language teaching)*. Moscow: IKAR Press.

Baidarov, Y. (2017, June 21). Cultural and civilizational grounds for regional integration in Central Asia. *Central Asian analytical network CAAN*. Retrieved from https://caa-network.org/archives/9492

Baizyldayeva, U., & Nurmagambetova, G. (2019). The Influences of the Social Media on the Students'. *Academic Outcomes*, *1*, 296–307.

Bajdarov, E. U. (2009). Informacionno-obrazovatelnye i vospitatelnye strategii v sovremennom obshestve: nacionalnyj i globalnyj kontekst. In Materialy mezhdunarodnoj nauchnoj konferencii. Minsk: Pravo i ekonomika.

Balakrishnar, J., & Thanaraj, T. (2011). Instruction in the English medium: A Sri Lankan case study. In *Proceedings of the Language and Social Cohesion in the Developing World conference* (pp. 166-177). Academic Press. Retrieved from http://www.langdevconferences.org/

Banks, J. A. (2008). *An Introduction to Multicultural Education*. Boston, MA: Pearson/Allyn and Bacon.

Bannerman, L. (2009, August 7). Silvio Berlusconi Ridiculed Over Gas Pipe Diplomacy Claims. *The Times*.

Baporikar, N. (2016). Lifelong learning in knowledge society. In P. O. Pablos & R. D. Tennyson (Eds.), *Impact of economic crisis on education and the next-generation workforce* (pp. 263–284). Hershey, PA: IGI Global. doi:10.4018/978-1-4666-9455-2.ch012

Barab, S., Kling, R., & Gray, J. (2004). *Designing for virtual communities in the service of learning*. Cambridge, UK: Cambridge University Press. doi:10.1017/CBO9780511805080

Baranov, A. V. (2011). On the problems of formation of "Electronic state."

Bartalev, S., Yegorov, V., Jarko, V., Lupyan, E., & Plotnikov, S. (2016). *Satellite mapping of the vegetation cover of Russia*. Moscow, Russia: IKI RAN.

Baryshnikov, N.V. (2004). Multilingvodidaktika. Inostrannyye yazyki v shkole. *Foreign languages in school*, *5*, 19-27. (in Russian)

Başıbek, N., Dolmacı, M., Cengiz, B., Bür, B., Dilek, Y., & Kara, B. (2013). Lecturers' Perceptions of English as a medium of instruction at Engineering Departments of Higher Education. *Procedia, 116*, 1819-1825. Retrieved from https://www.sciencedirect.com/

Baylor, A. L., & Ritchie, D. (2002). What factors facilitate teacher skill, teacher morale, and perceived student learning in technology using classrooms? *Computers & Education*, *39*(4), 395–414. doi:10.1016/S0360-1315(02)00075-1

Bayne, N., & Woolcock, S. (2003). *The new economic diplomacy: Decision-making and negotiation in international economic relations.*

Beetsma, D. (Ed.). (2001). *Trilingual Primary Education in Europe*. Mercator-Education.

Belenov, O. & Kirchanov, M. (2016). Network of universities as a form of development of higher education: forms, organization features and prospects. *Bulletin of Voronezh State Un. Ser.: The problems of Higher Education*, *1*, 114-118.

Benedek, J., Sebestyén, T.-T., & Bartók, B. (2018). Evaluation of renewable energy sources in peripheral areas and renewable energy-based rural development. *Renewable & Sustainable Energy Reviews*, *90*, 516–535. doi:10.1016/j.rser.2018.03.020

Bennett, E.E., & Bell, A. A. (2010). Paradox and promise in the knowledge society.

Bergmann, J., & Sams, A. (2012). *Flip your classroom: Reach every student in every class every day*. Washington, DC: Internal Society for Technology in Education.

Bezemer, J. (2003). *Dealing with multilingualism in education: a case study of a Dutch primary school classroom*. Amsterdam: Aksant Academic Publishers.

Bhamra, A. (2018). *India Green Economy Barometer 2018*. Green Economy Coalition. Retrieved from https://www.greeneconomycoalition.org/assets/reports/Barometers-2018/India-Barometer-2018-Full-November-Draft.pdf

BIL. (2019). International Educational Fund 'Bilim Innovation'. Retrieved from www.bil.edu.kz

Blanquer, J. M. (2017). Ban students from using mobile phones in the country's primary, junior and middle schools. The Guardian. Retrieved from https://www.theguardian.com/world/2017/dec/11/france-to-ban-mobile-phones-in-schools-from-september

Blaschke, L. M., & Hase, S. (2015). Heutagogy, technology, and lifelong learning for professional and part-time learners. In *Transformative perspectives and processes in higher education* (pp. 75-94). Academic Press. Retrieved from https://www.academia.edu/23356035/Heutagogy_technology_and_lifelong_learning_Curriculum_geared_for_professional_and_part-time_learners

Bloom, P. (2017). *The Ethics of Neoliberalism: The Business of Making Capitalism Moral*. Routledge. doi:10.4324/9781315619019

Blumenfeld, Y. (1999). *Scanning the future*. New York, NY: Thames & Hudson.

Bolch, T. (2007). Climate change and glacier retreat in northern Tien Shan (Kazakhstan/Kyrgyzstan) using remote sensing data. *Global and Planetary Change*, *56*(1–2), 1–12. doi:10.1016/j.gloplacha.2006.07.009

Borshcheva, E. A. (2015). Further professional education as a factor in the development of professional competence of a specialist. *Bulletin of the Orenburg State University*, *2*(177), 4–9. Retrieved from https://cyberleninka.ru/article/n/dopolnitelnoe-professionalnoe-obrazovanie-kak-faktor-razvitiya-professionalnoy-kompetentnosti-spetsialista

Boyar, L., & Davis-Friday, P. (2019). Assessing a golden opportunity: CEO performance at McDonald's. *The CASE Journal, 15*(5), 397-415.

BRICS Network University. (2019, August). Retrieved from https://we.hse.ru/en/brics/

British Council -Education Intelligence. (2013, November). *MEGATRENDS - The future of international education*. Retrieved from https://www.britishcouncil.org/sites/default/files/megatrends_v1_1.pdf

Brookfield, S. (1986). *Understanding and facilitating adult learning*. San Francisco, CA: Jossey-Bass.

Brookfield, S. (1987). *Developing critical thinkers*. San Francisco, CA: Jossey-Bass.

Brookfield, S. (2005). *The power of critical theory: liberating adult learning and teaching*. San Francisco, CA: Jossey-Bass.

Brookfield, S. (2006). *The skillful teacher*. San Francisco, CA: Jossey-Bass.

Brown, H. (2015). English as a medium of instruction in Japan: Discussing Implications for Language Teaching. *Focus on the learner,* (1), 419-423. Retrieved from https://jalt-publications.org/

Bulgakova, A. (2019). *Food security and nationalism: Case of import substitution project in the Russian Federation.* Budapest: Central European University.

Buli-Fabrega, M., & Casanovas, M. M. (2019). Flipped Classroom as an Active Learning Methodology in Sustainable Development Curricula. *Sustainability, 11*(17), 4577. doi:10.3390u11174577

Cabi, E. (2018). The Impact of the Flipped Classroom Model on Students' Academic Achievement. *International Review of Research in Open and Distance Learning, 19*(3), 202–221. doi:10.19173/irrodl.v19i3.3482

Caird, S., & Roy, R. (2019). Blended learning and sustainable development. In W. Leal Filho (Ed.), *Encyclopedia of Sustainability in Higher Education.* Cham: Springer. doi:10.1007/978-3-319-63951-2_197-1

Camargo, L., & Stoeglehner, G. (2018). Spatiotemporal modelling for integrated spatial and energy planning. *Energy, Sustainability and Society, 8*(1), 32. doi:10.118613705-018-0174-z

Cambridge dictionary (n.d.). Retrieved from https://dictionary.cambridge.org/

Cameron, S. (2016). The Kazakh Famine of 1930–33: Current research and new directions. *East/West: Journal of Ukrainian Studies, 3*(2), 117–132. doi:10.21226/T2T59X

Camilia, N., Ibrahim, S., & Dalhatu, B. (2013). The effect of social networking sites usage on the studies of Nigerian students. *International Journal of Engineering Science, 2*, 39–46.

Campbell, D. (2010). *Choosing Democracy: A Practical Guide to Multicultural Education.* Sacramento.

Capelle-Blancard, G., & Petit, A. (2012). The Weighting of CSR dimensions: Does one size fit all? *SAGE Journals, 59*(6), 919-943.

Capelle-Blancard, G. (2016). The abrogation of the "Impôt sur les opérations de bourse" did not foster the French stock market. *Finance Research Letters, 17*(C), 257–266. doi:10.1016/j.frl.2016.03.024

CAREN Project. (2019, August). Retrieved from https://caren.geant.org/Pages/Home.aspx

Cassini, G. (2007). *Gli anni del declino. La politica estera del governo Berlusconi (2001-2006)* [*The Years of Decline: The Foreign Policy of Berlusconi's Government, 2001-2006*]. Milano: Bruno Mondadori.

Cerf, V. (2010). Google's view. *Smithsonian, 41*(4), 120.

Černič, L. (2018). *Corporate responsibility in the framework of socio-economic rights.* Routledge.

Cerny, P. (2010). *Rethinking World Politics: A Theory of Transnational Neopluralism.* New York: Oxford University Press. doi:10.1093/acprof:oso/9780199733699.001.0001

Chen Hsieh, J. S., Wu, W. C. V., & Marek, M. W. (2017). Using the flipped classroom to enhance EFL learning. *Computer Assisted Language Learning, 30*(1-2), 1–21. doi:10.1080/09588221.2015.1111910

Chen, Z., & Liu, Y. (2019). The different style of lifelong learning in China and the USA based on influencing motivations and factors. *International Journal of Educational Research, 95*, 13–25. doi:10.1016/j.ijer.2019.03.005

Chernysheva, T. K. (2018). Implementation of the E-Government concept in the context of the transition to a digital economy in the Russian Federation. Retrieved from: https://cyberleninka.ru/

Chetvernin, V. A. (2003). *Introduction to the course of the general theory of state and law.* Moscow: Institute of State and Law, Russian Academy of Sciences.

Chew, K. W., Chia, S. R., Yen, H.-W., Nomanbhay, S., Ho, Y.-C., & Show, P. L. (2019). Transformation of Biomass Waste into Sustainable Organic Fertilizers. *Sustainability*, *11*(8), 2266. doi:10.3390u11082266

Choi, J. E. (2015). *The effect of the Flipped learning in the science class on the science achievement and class participation of middle school students* [Master's thesis]. Seoul, Soongsil University.

Chorshanbiev, P. (2019, June 30). Predpriyatie v Tadzhikistane bol'she zakrivayut, chem otkrivayut (in Tajikistan, enterprises are more closed down than established). The Asia Plus.

Choudaha, R., & Van Rest, E. (2018). Envisioning pathways to 2030: Megatrends shaping the future of global higher education and international student mobility. Retrieved from https://www.studyportals.com/report-envisioning-pathways-to-2030-studyportals-2018/

Ciurzyńska, A., & Lenart, A. (2011). Freeze-Drying – Application in Food Processing and Biotechnology – A Review. *Polish Journal of Food and Nutrition Sciences*, *61*(3), 165–171. doi:10.2478/v10222-011-0017-5

Climate Handbook of Kazakhstan. (2004). *Long-term data*.

Cohen, M. (1956). On the Sociology of Language. Pour une sociologie du langage. Academic Press.

Comins, N., & Kaufmann, W. (2012). *Discovering the universe*. New York, NY: W. H. Freeman.

Cranton, P. (2006). *Understanding and promoting transformative learning*. San Francisco, CA: John Wiley & Sons.

Curtis, G. E. (1996). *Russia: A Country Study*. Washington: Library of Congress. Retrieved from http://countrystudies.us/russia/

Davies, R. S., Dean, D. L., & Ball, N. (2013). Flipping the classroom and instructional technology integration in a college-level information systems spreadsheet course. *Educational Technology Research and Development*, *61*(4), 563–580. doi:10.100711423-013-9305-6

Dearden, J. (2014). English as a medium of instruction – a global growing phenomenon. *British Council, 761*(3), 2-34. Retrieved from https://www.teachingenglish.org.uk/

Dedić, N., & Stanier, C. (2016). An Evaluation of the Challenges of Multilingualism in Data Warehouse Development. In *Proceedings of the 18th International Conference on Enterprise Information Systems ICEIS 2016* (pp. 190-196). Academic Press.

Deleuze, G., & Guattari, F. (1987). Rhizome (Introduction). In *A Thousand Plateaus* (pp. 7–13). Minneapolis, MN: University of Minnesota Press.

Derrida, J. (1963). Cogito et histoire de la folie. *Revue de Metaphysique et de Morale*, *4*, 460–494.

Desha, Ch., & Hargroves, K. (2013). *Higher education and sustainable development: A model for curriculum renewal*. London, New York: Routledge. doi:10.4324/9781315883953

Dewey, J. (1916). *Democracy and education: An introduction to the philosophy of education*. New York: The Macmillan Company.

Digital Kazakhstan. (2017, December 12). Government of the Republic of Kazakhstan State Program. Retrieved from https://digitalkz.kz/en/human-level-development/

Digital soil mapping: theoretical and experimental studies. (2011). Collection of articles. Russia, Moscow: Soil Institute.

Do smartphones interfere with learning (2017). Teach Me Please. Retrieved from https://blog.teachmeplease.ru/posts/meshajut-li-smatphony-uchjobe

Doing Business. (2014). Annual Report. Retrieved from https://www.doingbusiness.org/content/dam/doingBusiness/media/Annual-Reports/English/DB15-Full-Report.pdf

Dor, D. (2004). From Englishization to Imposed Multilingualism: Globalization, the Internet, and the Political Economy of the Linguistic Code. *Public Culture*, *16*(1), 97–118. doi:10.1215/08992363-16-1-97

Dorfman, P., & House, R. (2004). Cultural influences on organizational leadership: literature review, theoretical rationale, and GLOBE project goals. In R. House, P. Hanges, M. Javidan, P. Dorfman, & V. Gupta (Eds.), *Culture, leadership, and organizations: The GLOBE study of 62 societies* (pp. 51–73). Thousand Oaks, CA: Sage Publications.

Dorosh, S. (2016, December). Sanctions against Russia: was there any effect? *BBC News –Ukraine.* Retrieved from https://www.bbc.com/ukrainian/features-russian-38265024

Draft programme of industrial-innovative development of Kazakhstan for 2020-2025 presented in Nur-Sultan (2019). Atameken. Retrieved from https://atameken.kz/en/news/32482-proekt-gpiir-00-0-prezentovali-na-ploshadke-atamekena

Drucker, P. F. (1969). *The age of discontinuity.* New York: Harper and Row.

Duchene, A., & Heller, M. (2012). Multilingualism and the new economy. In M. Martin-Jones, A. Blackledge, & A. Creese (Eds.), The Routledge Handbook of Multilingualism (pp. 369-383). Academic Press.

Duisebayeva, F. (2018). Workforce development in Kazakhstan: The Role of Multilingual Instruction. *Paper presented at CESS 2018 conference.* Academic Press. Retrieved from https://www.centraleurasia.org/conferences/annual/past/cess-2018-panels/#6932

Du, S., & Luo, X. (2015). Exploring the relationship between corporate social responsibility and firm innovation. *Marketing Letters*, *26*(4), 703–714. doi:10.100711002-014-9302-5

Ease of Doing Business rankings. (2015). Doing Business. Retrieved from https://www.doingbusiness.org/en/rankings

Education in Japan. (2011). Orientalica. Retrieved from http://www.orientalica.com/lofiversion/index.php?t203.html

Elian, S. A., & Hamaidi, D.A. (2018). The Effect of Using Flipped Classroom Strategy on the Academic Achievement of Fourth Grade Students in Jordan, *iJET, 13*(2), 110-125.

Elizarov, V. (2000). The republic of scientists: The social space of an invisible community. In L. Kachanov (Ed.), *Space and time in modern sociological theory* (pp. 103–127). Moscow: IS RAS.

Endovitsky, D. A. (2015). Resist the crisis tendencies, stick to the path of development. *Proceedings of Voronezh State University. Series: Problems of higher education, 2*, 5–8. Retrieved from http://www.vestnik.vsu.ru/content/educ/2015/02/toc_en.asp

ENIC-Kazakhstan. (n.d.). Center for Bologna process and academic mobility. Retrieved from https://enic-kazakhstan.kz/ru/reference_information/universities

European Commission. (2005). Realising the European Higher Education Area - Achieving the Goals. Conference of European Higher Education Ministers.

European Parliament. (2009). *EP Resolution on Multilingualism: An Asset for Europe and a Shared Commitment.* Brussels: European Parliament.

Evdokimova, N. V. (2008). Formirovaniye osnov mnogoyazychiya (in Russian). Formation of multilingualism principles. Rostov State Economic University.

Extra, G., & Yagmur, K. (2012). Language Rich Europe. Trends in Policies and Practices for Multilingualism in Europe.

Farmer, L. (2010). Innovative instructional strategies with the use of technology for adult learners. In V. Wang (Ed.), *Integrating adult learning and technologies for effective education* (pp. 170–188). Hershey, PA: IGI Global. doi:10.4018/978-1-61520-694-0.ch010

Fiche Curie Kazakhstan. (n.d.). French diplomacy. Retrieved from https://www.diplomatie.gouv.fr/IMG/pdf/KAZKHSTAN_Fihce_Curie_MARS_2015__cle06b53d.pdf

Financial Times. (2015, January 29). McDonald's and its challenges worldwide: a market-by-market look. Retrieved from https://www.ft.com/content/f8ac22fc-a7c1-11e4-8e78-00144feab7de

Fischer, G. (2000). Lifelong Learning - more than training. *Journal of interactive learning research*, 11(3), 265-294. Retrieved from https://www.learntechlib.org/primary/p/8380/

Fischer, D., Jenssen, S., & Tappeser, V. (2015). Getting an empirical hold of the sustainable university: A comparative analysis of evaluation frameworks across 12 contemporary sustainability assessment tools. *Assessment & Evaluation in Higher Education*, *40*(6), 785–800. doi:10.1080/02602938.2015.1043234

Fisher, M. (2009). *Capitalist Realism. Is There No Alternative?* (p. 8). Oxford Books.

FLN. (2014). Flipped Learning Network. Retrieved from http://flippedlearning.org/definition-of-flipped-learning/

Forkuor, G., Hounkpatin, O. K. L., Welp, G., & Thiel, M. (2017). High Resolution Mapping of Soil Properties Using Remote Sensing Variables in South-Western Burkina Faso: A Comparison of Machine Learning and Multiple Linear Regression Models. *PLoS One*, *12*(1). doi:10.1371/journal.pone.0170478 PMID:28114334

Foucault, M. (1984). Qu'est-ce que les lumières? In *Dits et Ecrits* (Vol. 4, pp. 562–578). Paris: Gallimard.

Foucault, M. (1991). Introduction (by Michel Foucault). In *G. Canguilhem (1991). The Normal and the Pathological* (pp. 7–25). New York: Zone Books.

Francesco, S., Petrozzi, A., & Montesarchio, V. (2014). An Integrated System for the Energy Production and Accumulation from Renewable Sources: A Rural Tower Prototype. *Energy Procedia*, *59*, 205–212. doi:10.1016/j.egypro.2014.10.368

Francisca, F., Grigore, G., Stancu, A., & McQueen, D. (2019). *Responsible people: The role of the individual in CSR, entrepreneurship and management education*. Springer.

Freire, P. (2007). *Pedagogy of the oppressed*. New York: Continuum.

Friedman, T. (2000). *The lexus and the olive tree*. London: HarperCollins.

Functionality, M. (2016). New in Wolfram Language 11. Retrieved from www.wolfram.com

Galla, B. M., & Duckworth, A. L. (2015). More than resisting temptation: Beneficial habits mediate the relationship between self control and positive life outcomes. *Journal of Personality and Social Psychology*, *109*(3), 508–525; Advance online publication. doi:10.1037/pspp0000026 PMID:25643222

Galloway, N., Kriukow, J., & Numajiri, T. (2017). Internationalization, higher education and the growing demand for English: an investigation into the English medium of instruction (EMI) movement in China and Japan. *Teaching English, 7*, 4-9. Retrieved from https://www.teachingenglish.org.uk/

Galskova, N.D. (2003). Obucheniye na bilingval'noy osnove. Inostrannyye yazyki v shkole. Education on bilingual basis. *Foreign languages in school*, *2*, 3. (in Russian)

García-Peñalvo, F. J., Colomo-Palacios, R., & Lytras, M. D. (2012). Informal learning in work environments: Training with the soci.al web in the workplace. *Behaviour & Information Technology*, *31*(8), 753–755. doi:10.1080/0144929X.2012.661548

Gayurov, G. H. (2019). *Organizational and economic aspects of the use of banking potential in the Republic of Tajikistan] (PhD dissertation).* Tajik National University, Dushanbe, Tajikistan.

GÉANT network. (2019, August). Retrieved from https://www.geant.org/News_and_Events/CONNECT/Pages/CAREN_project.aspx

Geldyeva, G., & Veselova, L. (1992). *Landscapes of Kazakhstan. Kazakhstan, Alma-Ata*. Nauka.

Gladov, A. V., & … . (2008). Foreign experience in the implementation of public-private partnership: General characteristics and organizational and institutional framework. *Bulletin of SamSU*, *7*, 36–55.

Glazer, N. (1998). *We Are All Multiculturalists Now*. Cambridge, MA: Harvard University Press.

Glazyev, S.Y. (2012). Modern theory of long waves in economic development. *Economic science of modern Russia,* 2(57), 8-27.

Global Report on Food Crises 2019. (2019). FSIN Platform. Retrieved from http://www.fsinplatform.org/sites/default/files/resources/files/GRFC%202019_Full%20Report.pdf

Glotova, T., Deev, M., Krevskiy, I., Matukin, S., Mkrttchian, V., & Sheremeteva, E. (2015). Individualized learning trajectories using distance education technologies. In A. Kravets, M. Shcherbakov, M. Kultsova & O. Shabalina (Eds.), Creativity in intelligent technologies and data science (pp. 778-792). Springer. doi:10.1007/978-3-319-23766-4_62

Goldie, J. G. S. (2016). Connectivism: A knowledge learning theory for the digital age? *Medical Teacher*, *38*(10), 1064–1069. doi:10.3109/0142159X.2016.1173661 PMID:27128290

Gopp, N., Nechaeva, T., & Savenkov, O. (2017) Indicative capacity of NDVI in predictive mapping of the properties of plow horizons of soils on slopes in the south of Western Siberia. *Eurasian Soil*, *50*, 1332-1343. doi:10.1134/S1064229317110060

Gouthro, P. A. (2017). The promise of lifelong learning. *International Journal of Lifelong Education*, *36*(1-2), 45–59. doi:10.1080/02601370.2017.1270067

Government of Kazakhstan. (2019). State Programme for education development of Kazakhstan. Retrieved from www.open.egov.kz

Greene, M. (1995). *Releasing the imagination*. San Francisco, CA: Jossey-Bass.

Griffith, W. (2008). *McDonald's has a big appetite for China*. CNBC News.

Gvozdetsky, N. (1963). *On the altitudinal zonation as the basic laws of landscape differentiation of mountainous countries/Questions of the landscapes. Kazakhstan, Alma-Ata*. Nauka.

Habermas, J. (1979, Spring). Consciousness – Raising or redemptive criticism – The contemporaneity of Walter Benjamin. *New German Critique, NGC*, *17*, 56.

Habermas, J. (1981). *The theory of communicative action* (Vol. 1–2). New York: Beacon Press.

Habermas, J. (1987). *The philosophical discourse of modernity: Twelve lectures*. Cambridge, MA: MIT Press.

Hagen, S., Foreman-Peck, J., Davila-Philippon, S., Nordgren, B. (2006). ELAN: Effects on the European economy of shortages of foreign language skills in enterprise.

Hagen, S. (2016). *Study of the achievements of tempus iv projects on the internationalization of higher education in Central Asia*. UK: Semantica Ltd. doi:10.2797/88130

Hakken, D. (1999). *Cyborgs@cyberspace*. New York, NY: Routledge.

Hamadneh, I. M. (2015). Training needs for faculty members at Al-Albayt university from their perspectives in the light of some variables. *European Scientific Journal, 11*(25), 177–195. Retrieved from https://eujournal.org/index.php/esj/article/view/6212

Hamdan, N., McKnight, P., McKnight, K., & Arfstrom, K. M. (2013). *The flipped learning model: A white paper based on the literature review titled "A review of flipped learning."* Arlington, VA: Flipped Learning Network.

Hamilton, M. (1999). The Business Charter for Sustainable Development. International Chamber of Commerce. Retrieved from https://iccwbo.org/content/uploads/sites/3/2015/09/ICC-Business-Charter-for-Sustainable-Development-Business-contributions-to-the-UN-Sustainable-Development-Goals.pdf

Hamilton, K., & Langhorne, P. (2011). *The Practice of Diplomacy*. London: Routledge; doi:10.4324/9780203841891

Hanratty, B., Milton, B., Ashton, M., & Whitehead, M. (2012). McDonalds and KFC, it's never going to happen: The challenges of working with food outlets to tackle the obesogenic environment. *Journal of Public Health, 34*(4), 548–554. doi:10.1093/pubmed/fds036 PMID:22611262

Hansen, K. (2014). When French fries go viral: Mobile media and the transformation of public space in McDonald's Japan. Center for Asian and Pacific Studies. San Diego State University, 14(2).

Harris, R. (2002). *Psihologiya massovyh kommunikacij*. Retrieved from https://uchebnikfree.com/svyazi-obschestvennostyu-upravlenie/sravnenie-razlichnyih-mass-media-mentalnyie-34500.html

Harrison, K. (2013). Multilingual Education. In F. V. Tochon (Ed.), *Language Education Policy Studies*. Madison, WI: University of Wisconsin. Retrieved from http://www.languageeducationpolicy.org

Hawking, S. W. (1988). *A brief history of time*. New York, NY: Bantam Books. doi:10.1063/1.2811637

Hayek, F. (2011). The Constitution of Liberty (Definitive ed.). Chicago: University of Chicago Press.

Heaney, T. W. (2000). Adult education and society. In A. L. Wilson & A. R. Hayes, A. R. (Eds.), Handbook of adult and continuing education (pp. 559-572). San Francisco, CA: Jossey-Bass.

Heugh, K. (2014). Turbulence and dilemma: Implications of diversity and multilingualism in Australian education. *International Journal of Multilingualism, 11*(3), 347–363. doi:10.1080/14790718.2014.921180

Hewitt, H. (2005). *Blog: Understanding the information reformation that's changing your world*. Nashville, TN: Thomas Nelson.

Hill, C. L., & Jones, G. (2009). *Essentials of Strategic Management* (3rd ed.). South-Western Cengage Learning, Nelson Education LTD.

Himesh, S. (2018). Digital revolution and Big Data: A new revolution in agriculture. *Perspectives in Agriculture, Veterinary Science, Nutrition and Natural Resources, 13*(021). doi:10.1079/PAVSNNR201813021

Hofstede, G. (2001). *Culture's consequences: comparing values, behaviors, institutions, and organizationa across nations*. Thousand Oaks, CA: Sage.

Huang, D. (2015). Exploring and assessing effectiveness of English as a medium of instruction courses: The students' perspectives. *Procedia, 173*, 71–78. doi:10.1016/j.sbspro.2015.02.033

Huawei. (2019). 2019 Huawei ICT Sustainable Development Goals Benchmark. Retrieved from https://www.huawei.com/en/about-huawei/sustainability/sdg

Hu, X., Ren, H., Tansey, K., Zheng, Y., Ghent, D., Liu, X., & Yan, L. (2019). Agricultural drought monitoring using European Space Agency Sentinel 3A land surface temperature and normalized difference vegetation index imageries. *Agricultural and Forest Meteorology*, *279*, 107707. doi:10.1016/j.agrformet.2019.107707

Hwang, J. W. (2017). *The effects of mathematics learning using flipped classroom on underachieved students' mathematics learning attitude and academic achievement - Focusing on Operations on Real Numbers, Third Grade, Middle School* [Master's thesis]. Seoul, Korea University.

Hyland, T. (2007). Lifelong learning and vocational education and training: values, social capital and caring in work-based learning provision. doi:10.1007/978-1-4020-6193-6_3

Ibraeva, A. (2018). How is the e-government portal of Kazakhstan developing? Retrieved from https://kursiv.kz/

Ignatyuk, N. A. (2006). Public-private partnership in Russia. *Law and Economics*, *8*, 3–7.

Illeris, K. (2004). A comprehensive understanding of human learning. In K. Illeris (Ed.), *Contemporary theories of learning: learning theorists...in their own words* (pp. 7–20). New York, NY: Routledge.

Illeris, K. (2015). The development of a comprehensive and coherent theory of learning. *European Journal of Education*, *50*(1), 29–40. doi:10.1111/ejed.12103

Imasheva, A. (2019). *Professionally Oriented Foreign Language/English for the specialty "Agrarian Technologies". Kazakh S.* Astana: Seifullin Agritechnical University. Retrieved from http://agr.cskz.kz/

Inganäs, O., & Sundström, V. (2016). Solar energy for electricity and fuels. *Ambio*, *45*(1), 15–23. doi:10.100713280-015-0729-6 PMID:26667056

Internet World Stats. (n.d.). Asia. Retrieved from https://www.internetworldstats.com/asia.htm

Isachenko, A. (1991) Landscape and physical-geographical zoning. Moscow, Russia: Higher School.

Isachenko, A. (1965). *Fundamentals of landscape science and physical-geographical zoning*. Moscow, Russia: Higher School.

Islam, M. F., & Knezevic, R. (2019). The role of MOOCs in achieving the Sustainable Development Goal Four. In *Proceedings of the Western Balkan Information and Media Literacy Conference* (pp. 53-66). Academic Press.

Issabayev, G., & Issabayeva, A. (2013). Emerging Countries for the World: Bio-Food Security through Technologies. *Proceedings of International Conference on Business Management & IS, 1*(1). Retrieved from http://ojs.ijacp.org/index.php/ICBMIS/article/view/59

Issabayeva, A., & Issabayev, G. (2013). Bio-Food Security for Future Generations. *Proceedings QUAESTI, 1*(1), 55-57. Retrieved from https://www.quaesti.com/archive/?vid=1&aid=1&kid=160101

Issabayev, G. A. (2019). *Sovremennyi urbanizm: osnovnyie innovacii i perspectivy razvitiya* [Contemporary urbanism: major innovations and development prospects]. Almaty: Lantar Trade.

Jacovec, J. V. (2004). *Epochal Innovations of the 21st Century*. Moscow, Russia: Economics.

Jannoura, R., Joergensen, R., & Bruns, C. (2014). Organic fertilizer effects on growth, crop yield, and soil microbial biomass indices in sole and intercropped peas and oats under organic farming conditions. *European Journal of Agronomy*, *52*(B), 259-270. doi:10.1016/j.eja.2013.09.001

Jarvis, P. (1985). Thinking critically in an information society: A sociological Analysis. *Lifelong Learning,* 11-14.

Jarvis, P. (2007). *Globalization, lifelong learning and the learning society: Sociological perspectives.* London: Routledge. doi:10.4324/9780203964408

Jarvis, P. (2009). Learning to be a person in society: Learning to be me. In K. Illeris (Ed.), *Contemporary theories of learning: learning theorists...in their own words* (pp. 21–34). New York, NY: Routledge.

Jean-Francois, E. (2015). *Building global education with a local perspective. An introduction to glocal higher education.* New York: Palgrave-Macmillan.

Jin, H. K. (2016). *Application Method of Flipped Learning in Korean Language Instruction* [Master's thesis]. Seoul, Dongguk University.

Joanne, J. W. H. (2012). 'Challenge' or 'collaboration' social interaction and recontextualization: McDonald's CSR report. *Critical Discourse Studies, 9*(2).

John, S. P. (2015). The integration of information technology in higher education: A study of faculty's attitude towards IT adoption in the teaching process. *Contaduría y Administración, 60*, 230–252. doi:10.1016/j.cya.2015.08.004

Johnson, H., & Taylor, K. (2017, October). We visited the 'McDonald's of Russia' that's trying to take over America — here's what it was like. *Business Insider*. Retrieved from https://www.businessinsider.com/teremok-menu-price-taste-test-review-2017-10

Jones, D., & Smith, M. (2015, September). Return to reason: Reviving political realism in western foreign policy. *International Affairs, 91*(5), 933–952. doi:10.1111/1468-2346.12391

Jones, J. W., Antle, J. M., Basso, B., Boote, K. J., Conant, R. T., Foster, I., ... Wheeler, T. R. (2017). Brief history of agricultural systems modeling. *Agricultural Systems, 155*, 240–254. doi:10.1016/j.agsy.2016.05.014 PMID:28701816

Junco, R. G., Heiberger, G., & Loken, E. (2011). The effect of Twitter on college student engagement and grades. *Journal of Computer Assisted Learning, 27*(2), 119–132. doi:10.1111/j.1365-2729.2010.00387.x

Jung, M. (2014). *The Effects of Flipped Classroom on Elementary Learner's Mathematics Academic Achievement and Attitude* [Master's thesis]. Korea National University of Education, Seoul.

Jung, J. A., Bae, J. H., & So, K. H. (2015). Biology Education: The Effect of Flipped Learning of Elementary Science Class on Learning Motivation and Academic Achievement of Elementary Students. *Biology Education, 43*(4), 333–343. doi:10.15717/bioedu.2015.43.4.333

Juvova, A., Chudy, S., Neumeister, P., Plischke, J., & Kvintovaet, J. (2015). Reflection of constructivist theories in current educational practice. *Universal Journal of Educational Research, 3*(5), 345–349. doi:10.13189/ujer.2015.030506

Kahl, J., Alborzi, F., Beck, A., Bügel, S. G., Busscher, N., Geier, U. A., ... Załęcka, A. (2014). Organic food processing: A framework for concept, starting definitions and evaluation. *Journal of the Science of Food and Agriculture, 94*(13), 82–94. doi:10.1002/jsfa.6542 PMID:24375441

Kaitlyn, E. M., & Anastasia, D. E. (2018). *Efficient, helpful, or distracting? A literature review of media multitasking in relation to academic performance.* International Journal of Educational Technology in Higher Education. doi:10.118641239-018-0096-z

Kamble, P. S., & Ovhal, V. V. (2016). Analysis of green economy of India. *North Asian International Research Journal of Social Science & Humanities, 2*(8), 41-66. Retrieved from http://www.nairjc.com/?re=paper&value=social-science-hu manities&month=08&val=NAIRJC&year=2016

Kamneva, K. (2018, September 13). McDonald's in Russia: 30 years of investment in the future. Food familiar to everyone. *Russian newspaper RGRU*, *203*(7666). Retrieved from https://rg.ru/2018/09/13/makdonalds-v-rossii-30-let-investicij-v-budushchee.html

Kant, I. (1785). Fundamental Principles of the Metaphysic of Morals (T.K. Abbott, Ed.). Project Gutenberg.

Kariyeva, J., & Leeuwen, V. (2011). Environmental Drivers of NDVI-Based Vegetation Phenology in Central Asia. *Remote Sensing*, *3*(2), 203–246. doi:10.3390/rs3020203

Kasworm, C. E., Rose, A. D., & Ross-Gordon, J. M. (2010). *Handbook of adult and continuing education*. Thousand Oaks, CA: Sage Publications.

Kasworm, C., & Londoner, C. A. (2000). Adult learning and technology. In A. L. Wilson & E. Hayes (Eds.), *Handbook of adult and continuing education* (pp. 224–242). San Francisco, CA: John Wiley & Sons.

Kasworm, C., Rose, A. D., & Ross-Gordon, J. M. (2010). Adult and continuing education as an intellectual commons. In C. E. Kasworm, A. D. Rose, & J. M. Ross-Gordon (Eds.), *Handbook of adult and continuing education* (pp. 1–12). Thousand Oaks, CA: Sage.

Kates, A. W., Wu, H., & Coryn, C. L. S. (2018). (2018). *The effects of mobile phone use on academic performance: A meta-analysis. Computers & Education*, *127*, 107–112. doi:10.1016/j.compedu.2018.08.012

Kayikci, Y. (2018). Sustainability impact of digitization in logistics. *Procedia Manufacturing*, *21*, 782–789. doi:10.1016/j.promfg.2018.02.184

Kazakhstan Education Act. (2007). Law of the Republic of Kazakhstan about education. Retrieved from https://cis-legislation.com/document.fwx?rgn=18150

Kazakhstan Public-Private Partnership Center. (2016). Official Web page. Retrieved from https://kzppp.kz/

Kazantsev, A. K., & Rubvalter, D. A. (2010). *Public-private partnership in science and innovation*. Moscow, Russia: INFRA-M.

Kazi, A., & Chalgimbaeva, S. (2016). Formation and development of "Electronic government. Retrieved from https://zerde.gov.kz/

KBS. (2014). KBS Panorama. Retrieved from www.kbs.co.kr

Kegan, R. (1994). *In over our heads: The mental demands of modern life*. Cambridge, MA: Harvard University Press.

Keio Research Center for Foreign Language Education. (n.d.). *What is the Problem of English Education Japan?* Retrieved from http://www.flang.keio.ac.jp/en/support/event/contest2007.html

Kelly, K. (2010). From print to pixel. *Smithsonian*, *41*(4), 122–128.

Kenenbaev, S., Iorgansky, A., & Borangaziev, B. (2009). Improved crop production in agricultural landscapes of the erosion of southeastern Kazakhstan. In *Proceedings of the International Conference on Soil Erosion: Problems and ways to improve crop production* (pp. 10-16). Academic Press.

Kenenbaev, S. (2006). *The concept of Adaptive - landscape systems of agriculture to the south-east of Kazakhstan for the period till 2010*. Almaty: Almalybak.

Ketari, L. M., & Khanum, M. A. (2013). Impact of Facebook usage on the academic grades: A case study. *Journal of Computers*, *5*(1), 44–48.

Khalikova, A.A. (2019). Methods of boosting vocabulary skills of elementary level students in the process of foreign language education.

Khalitova, M. M. (2010). *Economic interaction of the state and business in the context of strengthening the social orientation of the economy of Kazakhstan: theory, methodology, mechanism* [Doctorial dissertation]. Institute of Economy, Almaty, Kazakhstan.

Khan Academy. (2016). Retrieved from https://www.khanacademy.org/

Khan, M., & Sarwar, M. (2011). Needs assessment of university teachers for professional enhancement. *International Journal of Business and Management*, *6*(2), 208–212. doi:10.5539/ijbm.v6n2p208

Khasbulatov, K. (2010, January 26). McDonald's in Russia on the eve of its 20th anniversary. Interview. *Echo of Moscow*.

Khati, A. R. (2016). English as a medium of instruction: My Experience from a Nepali Hinterland. *Journal of NELTA*, *21*(1-2), 23–29. doi:10.3126/nelta.v21i1-2.20198

Kheyfets, B., & Chernova, V. II. (2018). Adaptation of market strategies of TNCs in Russia in the context of import substitution policy. *European Research Studies Journal*, *21*(3), 192–205. doi:10.35808/ersj/1053

Kholodnaya, E. V. (2018). On some prospects for the development of electronic governance in the conditions of digital transformation. Retrieved from www.cyberleninka.ru

Kholodnaya, N. D. (2009). Public-private partnership - a new type of relationship in the Russian economy. *State and Municipal Administration Issues*, *2*, 42–49.

Kim, B. (2013). Impacts of S&T Investment as an Innovation Tool in Korea. In *Symposium on Global Perspectives and Issues – Measurement of Economic and Social Impacts of S&T Investments, AAAS 2013 Annual Meeting*. Academic Press.

Kim, J. S. (2018). *A Study of instructional procedures and material development for flipped classroom according to science instructional models* [Master's thesis]. Korea National University of Education.

Kim, B., & Oh, S. H. (2010). *7 Knowledge-Based Elements for Strategic Science and Technology Planning*. Seoul, Korea: Ad Fly.

Kirby, J. R., Knapper, C., Lamon, P., & Egnatoff, W. J. (2010). Development of a scale to measure lifelong learning. *International Journal of Lifelong Education*, *29*(3), 291–302. doi:10.1080/02601371003700584

Kiryushin, V. (1996). *Ecological bases of agriculture*. Moscow, Russia: Kolos.

Kiryushin, V., & Ivanov, A. (2005). *Methodological guiding on agro-ecological assessment of land, design of adaptive landscapes, farming systems and agricultural technology*. Moscow, Russia: FGU Rasinformagroteh.

Kļaviņš, M., Azizov, A., & Zaļoksnis, J. (2014). Environment, pollution, development: The case of Uzbekistan. Riga: UL Press. Retrieved from https://uzwater.ktu.lt/index.php/download-files/compendia-and-textbooks/module-a-environmental-science/129-environment-pollution-development/file

Klimat Zailiyskogo Alatau [Climate of Zailiyskiy Alatau]. (2019). *Silk Road Adventures*. Retrieved from https://silkadv.com/ru/node/6153

Kling, R., & Courtright, C. (2004). Group behavior and learning in electronic forums. In S. Barab, R. Kling, & J. Gray (Eds.), *Designing for virtual communities in the service of learning* (pp. 91–119). Cambridge, UK: Cambridge University Press. doi:10.1017/CBO9780511805080.008

Knizhnikov, Y. (2003). *Fundamentals of aerospace research methods*. Moscow, Russia: Moscow State University.

Knowles, M. (1989). *The making of an adult educator*. San Francisco, CA: Jossey-Bass.

Knowles, M., Holton, E., & Swanson, R. (2005). *The adult learner*. Burlington, MA: Elsevier. doi:10.4324/9780080481913

Kobrin, S. (2008). *Globalization, Transnational Corporations and the Future of Global Governance. Handbook of Research on Global Corporate Citizenship. Cheltenham, UK and Northampton*. MA: Edward Elgar Publishing.

Komorowska, H. (2011). *Issues in Promoting Multilingualism. Teaching – Learning – Assessment*. Warsaw: Foundation for the Development of the Education System.

Kondratiev, N. D. (2002). *Large conjuncture cycles and prediction theories*. Moscow, Russia: Economics.

Kongolo, M. (2010). Job creation versus job shedding and the role of SMEs in economic development. *African Journal of Business Management*, *4*(11), 2288–2295. Retrieved from http://www.academicjournals.org/AJBM

Korea U learning Association. (2014). *Flipped Learning*. Seoul: Contents Media, 201p.

Koroleva, K., & Polivanova, D. (2017). How smartphones help study. Retrieved from https://iq.hse.ru/en/news/201806836.html

Kosarlukov, A. V. (2012). Public-private partnership as a form of interaction between the state and business. In *Proceedings of the VIII International Scientific and practical Conference "Science days – 2012"* (pp. 8-11). Prague, Czech Republic: Publishing House.

Krasnova, G. A., & Belous, V. V. (2016). Network universities: international experience and trends. *Bulletin of Russian Peoples' Friendship University (RUDN)*, *4*, 22-30. Retrieved from https://cyberleninka.ru/article/n/setevye-universitety-zarubezhnyy-opyt-i-mezhdunarodnye-tendentsii

Kravtsova, V. (2005). *Space research methods soils: Proc. handbook for university students*. Moscow, Russia: Aspect Press.

Kudaykulova, H. S. (2007). Electronic government in the Republic of Kazakhstan. Retrieved from https://cyberleninka.ru/

Kuiken, F., & Linden, E. (2013). *Language policy and language education in the Netherlands and Romania*. Amsterdam Center for Language and Communication. doi:10.1075/dujal.2.2.06kui

Kukulska-Hulme, A., & Shield, L. (2008). An overview of mobile assisted language learning: From content delivery to supported collaboration and interaction. Retrieved from https://goo.gl/kgcsrC

Kumar, S., Malav, L., Malav, M., & Khan, Sh. (2015). Biogas Slurry: Source of Nutrients for Eco-friendly Agriculture. *International Journal of Extension Research*, *2*, 42–46. Retrieved from http://www.journalijer.com

Labutina, I. (2004). *Interpretation of satellite pictures*. Moscow, Russia: Aspect Press.

Laliberte, T. R. (2010). *Mixed method study: Exploring the use of educational technology tools in K-12 classrooms* [Doctoral Dissertation]. University of Phoenix.

Latchem, C. (2017). Using ICTs and blended learning in transforming TVET. UNESCO and Commonwealth of learning. Retrieved from https://unesdoc.unesco.org/ark:/48223/pf0000247495

Latova, N.V. & Latov, Y.V. (2007). Peculiarities of "Westernization" of the Students' mentality in modernizing nations. *Sociological researches,* (11), 90-98.

Lavin, T. (2017, April). A Russian Fast-Food Chain Tries Its Luck in America. *The New Yorker*. Retrieved from https://www.newyorker.com/culture/on-and-off-the-avenue/a-russian-fast-food-chain-tries-its-luck-in-america

Lavrik, N.V. (2017). E-democracy: world experience. Retrieved from: https://cyberleninka.ru/

Law of the Republic of Kazakhstan of October 31, 2015 No. 379-V *"On Public-Private Partnership"* (with changes and amendments as of 04.03.2019). (2019). Retrieved from https://online.zakon.kz/document/?doc_id=37704720

Law of the Republic of Tajikistan on the State Protection and Support of Entrepreneurship (2017). Republic of Tajikistan.

Lawrence, M., & Friel, S. (2019). *Healthy and Sustainable Food Systems*. Routledge. doi:10.4324/9781351189033

Lee, B. H., & Lee, H. C. (2016). The Effects of Science Lesson with the Application of Flipped Learning on Science Academic Achievement and Scientific Attitude. *KESES*, *35*(1), 78–88.

Lee, D. Y. (2013). Research on Developing Instructional Design Models for Flipped Learning. *The Journal of Digital Policy & Management*, *11*(12), 83–92.

Lee, H. S., & Kim, C. S. (2015). A study on the Effect of Flipped Learning on Learning Motivation and Academic Achievement. *Korean Computer Education*, *19*(1), 143–147.

Lee, J. (2014). Why Students Don't Participate in English as a medium of instruction Classes in a Korean University: A Case Study. *English Teaching*, *69*(1), 91–117. doi:10.15858/engtea.69.1.201403.91

Lee, J. Y., Kim, Y. H., & Kim, Y. B. (2014). A Study on Application of Learner-Centered Flipped Learning Model. *Educational Technology*, *30*(2), 163–191. doi:10.17232/KSET.30.2.163

Lee, J., & Rim, H. (2018). Evolution of Corporate Social Responsibility: A Content Analysis of United States Magazine Advertising, 1980–2009. *Journal of Promotion Management*, *24*(4), 555–577. doi:10.1080/10496491.2017.1380111

Lee, M. K. (2014). Case Study on Effects and Signification of Flipped Classroom. *Korean Educational Development Institute*, *41*(1), 87–116.

Lesgold, A. (2000). What are the tools for? Revolutionary change does not follow the usual norms. In S. Lajoie (Ed.), *Computers as cognitive tools* (pp. 399–408). Manwah, NH: Lawrence Erlbaum Associates.

Li, T. (2005, June 17). McDonald's new ad depicting customers begging on their knees for discounts offends customers. *Chengdu Commercial Daily*.

Li, T. (2005, June 22). Chinese kneeling for discount in McDonald's ad. *China Daily*. Retrieved from https://sloanreview.mit.edu/article/the-challenge-for-multinational-corporations-in-china-think-local-act-global/

Librando, G. (1959). *Diplomazia commerciale: memorie di carriera* [*Commercial Diplomacy: Memoirs of a Career*]. Roma: G. Pastena.

Limonov, L. E., & Oding, N. U. (2015). *Actual problems of the development of PPP projects in the social sphere in the regions of Russia. International Centre for Social and Economic Research "Leontief Centre". The project "PPP in the social sector - the dissemination of the experience of the UK and St. Petersburg*". St. Petersburg, Russia. Retrieved from http://www.leontief-centre.ru/?lang=l2

Linnik, V. (1990). *Construction of GIS in physical geography: Proc. Allowance*. Moscow, Russia: Moscow State University. University Press.

Li, S., Li, J., Zhang, B., Li, D., Li, G., & Li, Y. (2017). Effect of different organic fertilizers application on growth and environmental risk of nitrate under a vegetable field. *Scientific Reports*, *7*(1), 17020. doi:10.103841598-017-17219-y PMID:29209063

Liu, J. (2008). McDonald's growing in China. *China Daily*.

Loader, B. (1998). Cyberspace divide. In B. Loader (Ed.), *Cyberspace divide*. New York, NY: Routledge. doi:10.4324/9780203169537_chapter_1

Lojeski, K., & Reilly, R. (2008). *Transforming Leadership and Innovation in the Globally Integrated Enterprise*. Hoboken, NJ: John Wiley & Sons.

Lopatova, N. (2019). *International experience in the formation of digital government*. Moscow: Economics and Law.

Losavio, J. (2014, April 2). Crimean crisis and International Law: What Laws are Broken? *Foreign Policy News Journal*.

Lukashova, S., Omirzhanov, Y., & Chongarov, Y. (2015). Prospects and realia of establishing international universities in Kazakhstan. *Concorde*, *4*, 68–74.

Lukovitz, K. (2014, January 21). McDonald's Launches Olympics Social Campaign. *MediaPost* Retrieved from https://www.mediapost.com/publications/article/217783/McDonald's-launches-olympics-social-campaign.html

Macaro, E. (2015). English as a medium of instruction: Time to start asking some difficult questions. *Modern. English Teaching*, *24*(2), 4–7. Retrieved from https://www.modernenglishteacher.com/

Makoveeva, V. V. (2012). Network interaction: The key factor of education, science and business integration. *Bulletin of Tomsk State University*, *354*(1), 163–166.

Malhorta, M., Chen, Y., Criscuolo, A., Qimiao, F., Illieva, I., & Savchenko, Y. (2006). *Expanding access to finance: Good practices and policies for micro, small and medium enterprises*. Washington, DC: World Bank.

Markelov, K., Golovin, V., & Brumshteyn, Yu. (2019). Informatization of Astrakhan agriculture under conditions of Caspian states international relations development In *Proceedings of the International Scientific and Practical Conference "Digital agriculture - development strategy" (ISPC 2019)*. Academic Press. 10.2991/ispc-19.2019.51

Martinez, R. (2016). English as Medium of Instruction (EMI) in Brazilian Higher Education: Challenges and Opportunities. *English in Brazil: Views Policies and Programs, 2*(81), 191-228. Retrieved from https://www.researchgate.net/

Matlack, C. (2014, October 21). Putin's Latest Target: More Than 200 Russian McDonald's. *Bloomberg Business for the week*. Retrieved from https://www.bloomberg.com/news/articles/2014-10-20/putins-latest-target-more-than-200-russian-McDonald's

Matlack, C. (2014, October). Putin's Latest Target: More than 200 Russian McDonald's. *Bloomberg Businessweek*. Retrieved from https://www.bloomberg.com/news/articles/2014-10-20/putins-latest-target-more-than-200-russian-mcdonalds

Matlack, C. (2014, August 20). Can McDonald's be the last victim of Russian retaliation? *Bloomberg Business Week*.

Mazarr, M. (1999). *Global trends 2005: An owner's manual for the next decade*. New York, NY: St. Martin's Press.

Mazhitaeva, S., Smagulova, G., & Tuleuova, B. (2012). Multilingual Education as One of Priority Directions of Educational System Development in the Republic of Kazakhstan. *European Researcher*, *33*(11), 1.

Mazorenko, D. (2016, March 11). How will McDonald's work in Kazakhstan? *Internet Journal Vlast*. Retrieved from https://vlast.kz/biznes/16203-kak-budet-rabotat-McDonald's-v-kazahstane.html

McDonald's accused of food violations in China. (2012). *The Wall Street Journal Digital Network*.

McDonald's in Russia 25 Years of Success. (2015). Russian Newspaper Delovaya Moscow Retrieved from http://www.delmoscow.ru/news/?cid=3fe6b80e&nid=e57fdc2a

McDonald's Kazakhstan official site. (n.d.). History. Retrieved from https://McDonald's.kz/about#tab-2

McDonald's Russia official site. (n.d.). Facts and Numbers. Retrieved from https://mcdonalds.ru/page/mcdonalds_in_russia/

Medeuova, K. (2019). Epistemological breaking and random anthropology. In L. Turarbekova et al. (Eds.), Materials of the second cycle of international scientific events—"The economic role of international educational projects in the global world"—within the framework of the project [regarding the] "Multidimensional study of the history, problems and prospects of the introduction of international educational projects in the Republic of Kazakhstan." Almaty: Ulagat.

Mediterranean Universities Union. (2019, August). Retrieved from http://www.uni-med.net

Medvedeva, S. M. (2014). From scientific creativity to popularization: A theoretical model of scientific communication. *Bulletin of MGIMO-University*, *4*(37), 278–284.

Merriam, S. B. (2008). *Adult learning theory for the twenty-first century in New Directions for adult and continuing education* (pp. 93–98). San Francisco, CA: Jossey-Bass.

Merriam, S. B., Caffarella, R. S., & Baumgartner, L. M. (2006). *Learning in adulthood: A comprehensive guide* (3rd ed.). San Francisco: Jossey-Bass.

Merriam, S., Caffarella, R., & Baumgartner, L. (2006). *Learning in adulthood: a comprehensive guide*. San Francisco, CA: John Wiley & sons.

Message from the Head of the State Kassym-Zhomart Tokayev to the people of Kazakhstan. (2019). Retrieved from http://www.akorda.kz/en/addresses/addresses_of_president/poslanie-glavy-gosudarstva-kasym-zhomarta-tokaeva-narodu-kazahstana

Message to the People of Kazakhstan. (2012). Sotsial'no-ekonomicheskaya modernizatsiya – glavnyi vector razitiya Kazakhstana [Socioeconomic modernisation is a main direction of development of Kazakhstan]. (in Russian)

Meyer, P. (2019). McDonald's Mission Statement & Vision Statement (An Analysis). Retrieved from http://panmore.com/McDonald's-vision-statement-mission-statement-analysis

Mezirow, J., & ... (2000). *Learning as transformation*. San Francisco, CA: Jossey-Bass.

Milovanović, S. (2014). The role and potential of information technology in agricultural improvement. *Economics of Agriculture*, *61*(2), 471–485. doi:10.5937/ekoPolj1402471M

Ministry of Economic Affairs of the Republic of Kazakhstan. (2014). Economic Diplomacy of the Republic of Kazakhstan. Retrieved from http://mfa.gov.kz/en/content-view/ekonomicheskaya-diplomatiya

Ministry of Economic Affairs of the Republic of Kazakhstan. (2014). Investment climate of the Republic of Kazakhstan. Retrieved from http://mfa.gov.kz/en/content-view/ob-investitsionnom-klimate-rk

Mischel, W. (2014). *The Marshmallow Test: Mastering self-control*. New York, NY: Little, Brown.

Moe, M. (2000). *The knowledge web*. Beverly Hills, CA: Knowledge Enterprises Group.

Molch, D., & Verlag, G. (2009). *McDonald's Russia: Managing a crisis. Case Study.*

Molchanova, O. P., & Livshin, A. J. (2009). *Public-private partnership in education*. Moscow, Russia: KDU.

Möllerström, E., Gipe, P., Beurskens, J., & Ottermo, F. (2019). A historical review of vertical axis wind turbines rated 100 kW and above. *Renewable & Sustainable Energy Reviews*, *105*, 1–13. doi:10.1016/j.rser.2018.12.022

Moomaw, W., Bhandary, R., & Kuhl, L. (2016). Sustainable Development Diplomacy: Diagnostics for the Negotiation and Implementation of Sustainable Development. *Global Policy*.

Morgenthau, H. (1946). *Scientific Man versus Power Politics*. IL: University of Chicago Press.

Mousumi, M., & Kusakabe, T. (2017). Proliferating English-Medium Schools in Bangladesh and Their Educational Significance among the "Clientele". *Journal of International Development and Cooperation*, *23*(1), 1–13. Retrieved from https://ir.lib.hiroshimau.ac.jp/

Muangprathub, J., Boonnam, N., Kajornkasirat, S., Lekbangpong, N., Wanichsombat, A., & Nillaor, P. (2019). IoT and agriculture data analysis for smart farm. *Computers and Electronics in Agriculture*, *156*, 467–474. doi:10.1016/j.compag.2018.12.011

Mukovnikova, E. V. (2008). Effective use of digital educational resources in English lessons.

Murray, B. (2019). *UN Sees U.S.-China Trade War Hurting Both Nations' Economies.*

Murugesan, S. (2015). Does Medium of Instruction matter? A propensity score analysis of the effect of English Medium Education on students learning outcomes in India. Retrieved from https://pdfs.semanticscholar.org/b874/647eb6bfb6073f90d86b8a1fae9a72cffc1f.pdf

Naray, O. (2008). *Commercial Diplomacy: A Conceptual Overview.* 7th World Conference of TPOs. The Hague. The Netherlands.

Nastyukova, O. (2019, April 02) Prosto kosmos: Kazakhstanec otkryl startup dlya fermerov, ispolzuya dannye NASA. [Just space: a Kazakhstani opened a startup for farmers using NASA data]. *Forbes Kazakhstan*. Retrieved from https://forbes.kz/made_in_kz/prosto_kosmos_kazahstanets_otkryil_starap_dlya_fermerov_ispolzuya_dannyie_nasa/

Nazarbayev, N. A. (2012) *Kazakhstan 2050*. Retrieved from http://adilet.zan.kz/rus/docs/K1200002050

Nefedova, T. (1990). Problems of nature: Methodological approaches to studying, mapping, zoning. *Bulletin USSR, Geographical Series*, *6*, 37–38.

Nelson J. (2015). The Multilingual App Toolkit Version 3.0.

Nelson, R. (2015). U.S. Sanctions on Russia: Economic implications. *Congressional Research Service*. Retrieved from https://digital.library.unt.edu/ark:/67531/metadc501885/

Network University of the CIS. (2019, July). Retrieved from http://www.ido.rudn.ru/su_sng/

Nieto, S. (2008). *Affirming Diversity: The Sociopolitical Context of Multicultural Education*. Boston, MA: Pearson/Allyn and Bacon.

Nikolaev, V. (1999). *Landscapes of the Asian steppes*. Moscow: Moscow State University Press.

Nilson, L. B. (2003). *Teaching at its best*. San Francisco, CA: Anker Publishing.

Nusche, D., Braun, H., Halasz, G., & Santiago, P. (2014). *OECD Reviews of Evaluation and Assessment in Education: Netherlands*. Retrieved from www.oecd.org/edu/school/OECD-Evaluation-Assessment-Review-Netherlands. pdf

Oderesa, (2015). *Math Class Method of Students Participation through Flipped Classroom Practice* [Master's Thesis]. Busan University.

OECD. (2015). Enhancing excess to finance for SME development in Tajikistan.

Oostendorp, M. (2012). Bilingualism versus multilingualism in the Netherlands. *Language Problems and Language Planning*, *36*(3), 252–272. doi:10.1075/lplp.36.3.04van

Osborne, S. P. (2010). *Public private partnerships: theory and practice in international perspective*. London: Routledge.

Pain, E. A., & Volkogonova, O. D. (Eds.). (2008). Russian modernization: Reflecting on identity. Inst. Kennana. Moscow: Three Squares.

Pais, A. (1982). *Subtle is the Lord: The science and the life of Albert Einstein*. New York, NY: Oxford University Press.

Palande, V., Zaheer, Z., & George, K. (2018). Fully Automated Hydroponic System for Indoor Plant Growth. *Procedia Computer Science*, *129*, 482–488. doi:10.1016/j.procs.2018.03.028

Palloff, R., & Pratt, K. (1999). *Building learning communities in cyberspace*. San Francisco, CA: Jossey-Bass.

Park, S., & Vanhonacker, W. (2007, July). The Challenge for Multinational Corporations in China: Think Local, Act Global. Retrieved from https://www.researchgate.net/publication/271199219_The_Challenge_for_Multinational_Corporations_in_China_Think_Global_Act_Local

Parker, J., & Tazhina, G. (2012). Improving the Workforce in Kazakhstan through Distance Learning Technologies. In Handbook of Research on Technologies for Improving the 21st Century Workforce: Tools for Lifelong Learning. Academic Press. doi:10.4018/978-1-4666-2181-7.ch023

Parker, J. (2009). Adult learning and CTE: A shared history influenced by technology. In V. Wang (Ed.), *Definitive readings in the history, philosophy, practice and theories of career and technical education*. Hershey, PA: IGI Global.

Parker, J. (2012). *Engaging traditional learning and adult learning via information technologies. Pedagogical and andragogical teaching and learning with information communication technologies*. Hershey, PA: IGI Global.

Park, K. B. (2014). Exploration of the possibility of Flipped Learning in social studies. *Social Studies Education*, *53*(3), 107–120.

Patil, A., Chake, A., Helonde, M., & Gupta, P. (2015). Vertical Axis Wind Turbine with Maglev Technology. *International Journal for Scientific Research & Development*, *2*(12). Retrieved from http://www.ijsrd.com/articles/IJSRDV2I12180.pdf

Patrício, D. I., & Rieder, R. (2018). Computer vision and artificial intelligence in precision agriculture for grain crops: A systematic review. *Computers and Electronics in Agriculture*, *153*, 69–81. doi:10.1016/j.compag.2018.08.001

Pavlyutenkova, M. Y. (2016). Electronic government as a vector of innovative state transformations. Retrieved from www.cyberleninka.ru

Pfeil, A. (2015). Digitale und analoge Lernwelten im Deutsch als Fremdsprache-Unterricht Informelles Lernen. *Fremdsprache Deutsch*, *53*.

Piskurich, G. (2006). *Rapid instructional design*. San Francisco, CA: John Wiley & Sons.

Pivoto, D., Waquil, P. D., Talamini, E., Finocchio, C., Corte, V., & Mores, G. (2018). Scientific development of smart farming technologies and their application in Brazil. *Information Processing in Agriculture*, *5*(1), 21–32. doi:10.1016/j.inpa.2017.12.002

Pivovarov, Y. S. (2013). *Russian political tradition and modernity*. Brewers Y.S. Moscow. INION RAS.

Pomfret, R. (2006). *The Central Asian Economies*. Oxford University Press.

Prahalad, C., & Doz, Y. (1986). *The Multinational Mission: Balancing Local Demands and Global Vision*. New York: The Free Press.

Prasad, S. B., Rathore, D., & Singh, A. K. (2017). Recent Advances in Biogas Production. *Chemical Engineering & Process Techniques, 3*(2): 1038. Retrieved from https://www.semanticscholar.org/paper/Recent-Advances-in-Biogas-Production-Prasad-Rathore/b080344c36fd6a08041c92a5b6ac1b64fc943bae

Prensky, M. (2001). Digital natives, digital immigrants. *On the Horizon*, *9*(5), 1–6. doi:10.1108/10748120110424816

Preparing TVET for the digital age: Explainer. (2019, August). *Development Asia*. Retrieved from https://development.asia/explainer/preparing-tvet-digital-age

Prins, N. (n.d.). *An Analysis of the Russian Social Media Landscape in 2019*. Retrieved from https://www.linkfluence.com/blog/russian-social-media-landscape

Public-private partnerships in the US: The state of the market and the road ahead. (2016). Price Waterhouse Coopers. Retrieved from pwc.com/us/infrastructure-ppp

Raja, N., & Masresha, G. (2015). Plant Based Biopesticides: Safer Alternative for Organic Food Production. *Journal of Fertilizers and Pesticides*, *6*(02), e128. doi:10.4172/2471-2728.1000e128

Rakhimov, Z. (2003). *The development of the banking system of Tajikistan in a transitional economy* [doctoral dissertation]. Russian Economic Academy, Moscow, Russia.

Räsänen, A., & Virtanen, T. (2019). Data and resolution requirements in mapping vegetation in spatially heterogeneous landscapes. *Remote Sensing of Environment: Elsevier*, *230*, 111207. doi:10.1016/j.rse.2019.05.026

Rasul, A. (2019, June 5). Central Asia: problems and solutions. *Express K. Part ten*. Retrieved from https://expressk.kz/news/politekonomiya/tsentralnaya_aziya_problemy_i_resheniya_chast_desyataya-142135

Report of the UNCTAD Secretariat. (2003, August). Retrieved from https://unctad.org/en/docs/c2isard3.en.pdf

Report, H. (2014). *Higher education edition:* New media consortium. Retrieved from http://global.oup.com/uk/orc/learnvle/

Report: *Overview of the Higher Education System Kazakhstan*. (2017, February). Education, Audiovisual and Culture Executive Agency (EACEA). doi:10.2797/985596

Rezaeiha, A., Montazeri, H., & Blocken B. (2018). Towards optimal aerodynamic design of vertical axis wind turbines: Impact of solidity and number of blades. *Energy, 165*(B), 1129-1148. Doi:10.1016/j.energy.2018.09.192

Reznichenko, N. V. (2010). Models of public-private partnership. *Bulletin of St. Petersburg University. Management Services*, *4*, 59–83.

Rhoades, E., Friedel, C., & Morgan, A. (2009). Can Web 2.0 improve our collaboration? *Techniques*, *83*(9), 24–27.

Rhys, L. (2019, April 15). 1955: McDonald's opens its first franchise restaurant in Illinois. Business Times. Retrieved from https://home.bt.com/news/on-this-day/april-15-1955-McDonald's-opens-its-first-franchise-restaurant-in-illinois-11363975590701

Robert, I.V. (2014). *Theory and methodology of education informatization (psycho-pedagogical and technological aspects)*. Moscow: BINOM - Laboratoriya znaniy.

Roberts, W. (1991). *Diplomacy in the Information Age. World Today*. Royal Institute of International Relations.

Romaine, S. (1995). *Bilingualism*. Oxford: Blackwell.

Rorty, R. (1982). *Consequences of pragmatism: Essays, 1972–1980*. Minneapolis, MN: University of Minnesota Press.

RT. (2017, December). Russia shouldn't grovel to 'McDonald's bas***ds' – local restaurateur. Retrieved from https://www.rt.com/business/412957-mcdonalds-russia-unfair-benefits/

Ruddick, K. W. (2012). *Improving chemical education from high school to college using a more hands on approach*. Unpublished doctoral dissertation, University of Memphis.

Safarov, E. R. (2010). *Banking and real sectors of economy of Tajikistan* [PhD dissertation].

Salim, S. F. M. Y. S., Mahmood, M. F., & Ahmad, A. B. (2018). The importance of information literacy to support lifelong learning in convergence era. *Development*, *7*(3), 353–362. Retrieved from http://hrmars.com/hrmars_papers/The_Importance_of_Information_Literacy_to_Support_Lifelong_Learning_in_Convergence_Era.pdf

Samuelson, B. L., & Freedman, S. W. (2010). Language policy, multilingual education, and power in Rwanda. *Language Policy*, *9*(3), 191–215. doi:10.100710993-010-9170-7

Saner, R., & Yiu, L. (2003, January). International Economic Diplomacy: Mutations in Post-Modern Times. Netherlands Institute of International Relations. Clingendael.

Sárvári Horváth, I., Tabatabaei, M., Karimi, K., & Kumar, R. (2016). Recent updates on biogas production - a review. *Biofuel Research Journal*, *3*(2), 394–402. doi:10.18331/BRJ2016.3.2.4

Schaffer, S. P., & Richardson, J. C. (2004). Supporting technology integration within a teacher education system. *Educational computing research*, *3*(4), 423-435. Retrieved from https://eric.ed.gov/?id=EJ683701

Schein, E. (2010). *Organizational culture and leadership* (4th ed.). San Francisco, CA: Jossey-Bass.

Scherbenko, E., & Asmus, V. (1990). *The method of digital processing of aerospace information for creating soil maps: Study Earth from space*. Moscow, Russia: Nauka.

Schlitz, S. A. (2009). Developing a culture of assessment through a faculty learning community: a case study. *International journal of teaching and learning in higher education, 21*(1), 133-147. Retrieved from http://www.isetl.org/ijtlhe/

Schmidtlein, S., Feilhauera, H., Thonfeld, F., Faudec, U., Hed, K., & Rocchinie, D. (2013). Assessing floristic composition with multispectral sensors— A comparison based on monotemporal and multiseasonal field spectra. *International Journal of Applied Earth Observation and Geoinformation*, *21*, 218–229. doi:10.1016/j.jag.2012.09.002

Schneider, D. K. (n.d.). *Educational technology.* EduTech Wiki. Retrieved from http://edutechwiki.unige.ch/en/Educational_technology

Schultz, L., & Viczko, M. (2016). Assembling and governing the higher education institution. democracy, social justice and leadership in global higher education. London: Palgrave-Macmillan.

Schumpeter, J. (1942). *Capitalism, socialism and democracy*. New York: Harper & Brothers.

Schwinge, D. (2011). *Bilingual Learning*. Garden City, NY: Adelphi University.

Scilly, M. (2016). Five Dimensions of Corporate Social Responsibility. Retrieved from https://smallbusiness.chron.com/five-dimensions-corporate-social-responsibility-54700.html

Scott, A.J. (2011). In-class versus online video lectures: similar learning outcomes, but a preference for in-class. *Society for the teaching of psychology, 38*(4), 298-302.

Segizbayev, O. A. (1996). *Kazakh philosophy of the 15th–early 20th century*. Almaty: Gylym.

Seleznyeva, M. (2018, February 15). Less fat and sugar. McDonald's will make Happy Mil more useful. Retrieved from https://life.ru/t/новости/1089472/mienshie_zhira_i_sakhara_makdonalds_sdielaiet_khieppi_mil_bolieie_polieznym

Selyanskaya, G. N. (2014). Distributed university: from the university branch network to the electronic network universities. *Modern problems of science and education*, *5*, 1-14. doi:10.17513pno.119-14862

Sergeieva, L. (2018). Modern professional education and educational services market. *Fundamental and applied researches in practice of leading scientific schools*, *28*(4), 122-126. Retrieved from https://www.farplss.org/index.php/journal/article/download/518/481

Serikov, R. S. (2013). Systematization of the main forms of public-private partnership. *Actual Problems of Economics.*, *9*(147), 492–496.

Shabir, G., Hameed, Y. M. Y., Safdar, G., & Gilani, S. M. F. S. (2014). The impact of social media on youth: A case study of bahawalpur city. *Asian Journal of Social Sciences & Humanities*, *3*(4), 132–151.

Shamkhalov, F. I. (2002). *Theory of Public Administration*. Moscow, Russia: Economics.

Shanghai Cooperation Organisation (SCO) University. (2019, June). Retrieved from http://uni-sco.com/?lang=EN

Sharonin, Yu. V. (2019, January 29). Digital technologies in higher and professional education: from personally oriented smart didactics to blockchain in purpose training of specialists. *Modern problems of science and education*, *1*. Retrieved from http://science-education.ru/ru/article/view?id=28507

Shaukenova, Z. K. (2018). "Kazakhstan and Central Asian countries: Tomorrow will be lain today." Kazakhstan Institute for Strategic Studies, under the President of the Republic of Kazakhstan. Retrieved from http://www.kisi.kz/index.php/ru/publikatsii/25-shaukenova-zarema-kaukenovna/35-kazakhstan-i-strany-tsentralnoj-azii-zavtra-zakladyvaetsya-segodnya

Shea-Schultz, H., & Fogarty, J. (2002). *Online learning today: Strategies that work*. San Francisco, CA: Berrett-Koehler Publishers.

Sheluho, M. V. (2012). Vliyanie socialnyh media na sferu obrazovaniya. In *Pedagogicheskoe masterstvo: materialy II Mezhdunar. nauch. konf.* (pp. 26-32). Moscow: Buki-Vedi. Retrieved from https://moluch.ru/conf/ped/archive/65/3189/

Shibkikh, A. (2002). Landscape mapping of the Altai region using GIS technologies to address environmental problems. In *INTERCARTO8: GIS for sustainable Territorial Development: Proceedings of the international conference*. (pp. 205-207) Russia, St. Petersburg: JSC "Map".

Shima, M. (2005). Role and influence of transnational corporations in the global shift at the turn of the twentieth-XXI centuries. *Problems of the theory and practice of management, 3*.

Sibomana, E. (2015). Postcolonial language-in-education policies in Africa: The case of Kenya. *Rwandan Journal of Education, 3*, 37-47. Retrieved from https://www.ajol.info/

Sidorenko, E. L., & Bartsits, I. N. (2019). The effectiveness of digital public administration: theoretical and applied aspects.

Siemens, G. (2008). About: Description of connectivism. *Connectivism: A learning theory for today's learner, website*. Retrieved from http://www.connectivism.ca/about.html

Silberman, M. (2006). *Active training*. San Francisco, CA: John Wiley & Sons.

Smirnov, V. V. (2005). *An open state: ways to achieve it.*

Smokotin, V. M. (2010). Novyi etap v razvitiyi printsipa mnogoyazychiya v Evrope: Postroyeniye mnogoyazychnogo i politkul'turnogo obschestva. Vestnik Tomskogo gosudarstvennogo universiteta [New stage in development of multilingualism principles in Europe: establishment of multilingual, political and cultural society]. *Herald of Tomsk State University*, *333*, 61–66. (in Russian)

Smotritskaya, I. I., & Chernykh, S. I. (2018). Modern Trends in the Digital Transformation of Public Administration. Retrieved from: https://cyberleninka.ru/

Snytko, V., Batuev, A., Whale, A., Konovalova, T., Kuznetsova, T., & Shekhovtsov, A. (2002). Using the experience of the system mapping in the development of regional GIS. In *Proceedings of the VII Scientific Conference on thematic cartography: "Ordnance Survey and GIS support management of regional development* (pp. 57-60). Russia, Irkutsk: Institute of Geography SB RAS.

Soghomonov, A.Y. (2016). Sustainable university (mission, meanings, programs, cases). *Journal of applied ethics*, *49*, 151-170.

Song, E. J., Lee, C.H. (2016). Effect of flipped learning STEAM applied to science and sound chapter on academic achievement and motivation of elementary school student. *The Korean Association of Practical Arts education, 2*, 297-301.

Song, Y., & Kapur, M. (2017). How to flip the classroom- "Productive failure or traditional flipped classroom" pedagogical design? *Journal of Educational Technology & Society*, *20*(1), 292.

Soros J. (1997). A new look at open society. Moscow. Master.

Sosna, S. A. (2003). Concession agreement - a new type of contract in Russian law. *Journal of Russian Law, 2.* Retrieved from http://uristy.ucoz.ru/publ/12-1-0-616

Spanov, M.U., & Zhaleleva, S.Z. (2017). Mechanisms of public and private partnerships for the effective development of self-employment in Kazakhstan. *Bulletin of Kazakh National University, 4*(122), 208-216.

Springett, D. (2015). Education for sustainable development. Challenges of a critical pedagogy. In M. Redclift & D. Springett (Eds.), *Routledge international handbook of sustainable development.* London, New York: Routledge.

State of the Nation Address by the President of the Republic of Kazakhstan Nursultan Nazarbayev. (2018, January 10).

Steffens, K. (2015). Competences, learning theories and MOOCs: Recent developments in lifelong learning. *European Journal of Education*, *50*(1), 41–59. doi:10.1111/ejed.12102

Stout, C., Islam, Sh., White, A., Arnott, S., Kollovozi, E., Shaw, M., ... Bird, B. (2017). Efficiency Improvement of Vertical Axis Wind Turbines with an Upstream Deflector. *Energy Procedia*, *118*, 141–148. doi:10.1016/j.egypro.2017.07.032

Strayer, J. F. (2007). *The effect of the classroom flip on the learning environment: A comparison of learning activity in a traditional classroom and a flip classroom that uses an intelligent tutoring system* [Doctoral thesis]. The Ohio State University.

Styrin, E. M. (2013). *On some prospects for the development of e-government in the context of digital transformation.* Moscow: Pravo.

Styrin, E. M. (2013). *The movement towards open government: global experience*. Moscow: Publishing House of the Higher School of Economics.

Sugden, A. (2001). Organic farming. *Science*, *293*(5527), 17. doi:10.1126cience.293.5527.17a PMID:11995386

Szumowska, E., Popławska-Boruc, A., Kuś, J., Osowiecka, M., & Kramarczyk, J. (2018). When frequent media multitaskers perform worse and when they do not: The role of self-regulation ability and strategy manipulation. *Computers in Human Behavior*, *83*, 184–193.

Taeho, L. (2016). The status of corporate social responsibility research in public relations: A content analysis of published articles in eleven scholarly journals from 1980 to 2015. *Public Relations Review*, *43*(1), 211–218. doi:10.1016/j.pubrev.2016.10.001

Tarafdar, A., Shahi, N., Singh, A., & Sirohi, R. (2017). Optimization of Freeze-Drying Process Parameters for Qualitative Evaluation of Button Mushroom (Agaricus bisporus) Using Response. *Journal of Food Quality*. doi:10.1155/2017/5043612

Tariq, W., Mehboob, M., Khan, M. A., & Ullah, F. (2012). The impact of social media and social networks on education and students of Pakistan. *International Journal of Computer Science Issues*, *9*, 407–411.

Tazhina, G. (2010). Applied psychology in Kazakhstan. *Paper presented at the Kazakhstan in Globe: Socio-Economic and Cultural Aspects, Scientific congress*. Academic Press.

Tazhina, G. (2012). Kazakhstani e-learning experience in higher education. *International journal of multidisciplinary thought*, *2*(2), 435-441.

Teaching practices survey 2016: Compiled U21 results. (2019). Universitas 21. Retrieved from https://universitas21.com/sites/default/files/2019-2/TPS%20compiled%20results%20logo.pdf

Tenizbayeva, M. (2018). 27 schools of Kazakhstan started to learn subjects in English in Almaty. Retrieved from https://www.inform.kz/ru/

Terekhov, A., Tsychuyeva, N., & Muratova, N. (2007). The principles of agro landscapes zoning of arable lands in steppe zone of Northern Kazakhstan using MODIS and IRS LISS. *Modern problems of remote sensing of the earth from space*, *4*(2), 390–397.

Teryakova, A. S., & Bobrova, I. I. (2014) *Vliyanie socialnyh setej na molodyozh* // Portal nauchno-prakticheskih publikacij. Retrieved from http://portalnp.ru/2014/12/2243

The Entrepreneur Code of the Republic of Kazakhstan (as amended and supplemented, as of July 26, 2016). (2016). Retrieved from http://online.zakon.kz/Document/?doc_id = 38259854

The Global Risks Report 2019 (14th ed.). (2019). *World Economic Forum.*

The law of the Republic of Tajikistan "On banking activities ." (2009). Government of Tajikistan.

The law of the Republic of Tajikistan "On microfinance organizations ." (2012). Government of Tajikistan. Retrieved from https://nbt.tj/tj/laws/

The law of the Republic of Tajikistan "On the National Bank of Tajikistan ." (2011). Government of Tajikistan.

The Law on Higher Education. (1992, October 8). *Wet op Hoger Onderwijs en Wetenschappelijk Onderzoek.*

The New York Times. (2002, March). McDonald's to settle suits on beef tallow in French fries. Retrieved from www.nytimes.com/2002/03/09/us/mcdonald-s-to-settle-suits-on-beef-tallow-in-french-fries.html

The OECD and Eurasia. (2019). Supporting Eurasia countries in their reform efforts. Retrieved from https://www.oecd.org/eurasia/countries/

The portal eGov.kz. (2018). Retrieved from https://egov.kz/cms/kk US Open Government Directive

The President of Kazakhstan Nursultan Nazarbayev's Address to the Nation of Kazakhstan. (2017). Retrieved from http://www.akorda.kz/en/

The State Program for Promotion of Employment in the Republic of Tajikistan for 2018-2019] (2017), No 499, Dushanbe, Tajikistan. Available at http://www.adlia.tj/show_doc.fwx?rgn=130357

The State Program of Development and Functioning of Languages of Kazakhstan for 2011- 2020. (2010). Government of Kazakhstan. Retrieved from http://www.primeminister.kz/page/article_item-86

The state program of industrial and innovative development of the Republic of Kazakhstan for 2015–2019. (n.d.). Retrieved from http://www.mid.gov.kz/ru/pages/gosudarstvennaya-programma-industrialno-innovacionnogo-razvitiya-respubliki-kazahstan-na-2015

The Strategy for Development of the Republic of Kazakhstan until 2030. (n.d.). Akorda. Retrieved from http://www.akorda.kz/ru/category/gos_programmi_razvitiya

Theodore, H., & Karl, F. (2000). *International Business Diplomacy. School of Foreign Service*. Washington, D.C.: Georgetown University.

Tikhonova, A. D. (2018). *Social media and youth: the risk of radicalization. Psychology and law, 8*(4), 55-64.

Tinsley, T. (2011). The importance of languages for business. In Towards a language rich Europe. Multilingual essays on language policies and practices (pp. 58-61). Academic Press.

Tonkonog, V. (2017). Topical issues of application of distance learning technologies in the system of development of the Russian Federation. *Editura Universităţii Naţionale de Apărare, 1*(1), 544-549. doi:10.12753/2066-026X-17-080

Tony, R. (2000). *Working for McDonald's in Europe: The unequal struggle*. Psychology Press.

Training needs analysis of Sofia University staff. (2014, November). Retrieved from http://e-center.uni-sofia.bg/TNA_vocational_trainers_en.pdf

Traxler, J. (2009). *Mobile Learning: Transforming the Delivery of Education and Training*. Retrieved from http://www.aupress.ca/index.php/books/120155

Trilling, D. (2014, April 15). Tajikistan: Migrant remittances now exceed half of GDP. *Eurasia Net*. Retrieved from http://www.eurasianet.org/node/68272

Trofimov, A., & Panasyuk, M. (1984). *Geographic information systems and management problems environment*. Kazan, Russia: Kazan University Press.

Trubetskoy, N. S. (1920). *Europe and humanity*. Sofia: Russian-Bulgarian Book Publishing.

Trubetskoy, N. S. (1925). About the Turanian element in Russian culture. In P. N. Savitsky, P. P. Suvchinsky, & N. S. Trubetskoy (Eds.), *Eurasian Temporary* (pp. 351–377). Berlin.

Trubetskoy, N. S. (2000). *The legacy of Genghis Khan*. Moscow: Agraf. (Original work published 1926)

Trubetskoy, N. S. (2015). *A look at Russian history not from the West, but from the East*. Moscow: Direct Media.

Tsukayama, E., Duckworth, A. L., & Kim, B. E. (2013). Domain specific impulsivity in school-age children. *Developmental Science, 16*(6), 879–893. PMID:24118714

Tsychuyeva, N. (2010). GIS-technology application for agrolandscape zoning of arable land in Northern Kazakhstan. *Bulletin of Al-Farabi KazNU, Geographic series., 1*(28), 140–144.

Tucker, G. R. (1999). *A Global Perspective on Bilingualism and Bilingual Education*. Carnegie Mellon University Press.

Tyson, N., Liu, C., & Irion, R. (2000). *The universe: at home in the cosmos*. Washington, D.C.: Joseph Henry Press.

Umarov, K., & Zarifiva, Z. (2005). *Monetary and credit problems of development of the national economy*. Dushanbe, Tajikistan: Irfon.

UNESCO IITE. (2012). *Promotion of the Use of ICTs in TVET in CIS Countries*. Special Report on the Activities Implemented within the joint IFESCCO/UNESCO IITE project. Retrieved from https://iite.unesco.org/publications/3214702/

UNESCO. (2008). *2008-Education for All by 2015 –Will we make it?* Background papers for the Education for All global monitoring report.

UNESCO. (2015). [*Incheon Declaration and Framework for Action.* Retrieved from http://unesdoc.unesco.org/images/0024/002456/245656e.pdf

United Nations Educational, Scientific and Cultural Organisation [UNESCO]. (2003). Education in a Multilingual World.

University of British Columbia. (2017, March 10). Organic is only one ingredient in recipe for sustainable food future: Many shades of gray: The context-dependent performance of organic agriculture. *ScienceDaily.* Retrieved from www.sciencedaily.com/releases/2017/03/170310142337.htm

University of Oxford. *International trends in higher education: Report 2016-17.* (2018, June). Retrieved from http://www.ox.ac.uk/sites/files/oxford/trends%20in%20globalisation_WEB.pdf

Uzun, A. M., & Kilis, S. (2019). Does persistent involvement in media and technology lead to lower academic performance? Evaluating media and technology use in relation to multitasking, self-regulation and academic performance. *Computers in Human Behavior, 90*, 196–203. doi:10.1016/j.chb.2018.08.045

Valmont, W. (2003). *Technology for literacy teaching and learning.* New York, NY: Houghton Mifflin.

Van Eyk, S. (2010). *The OECD Declaration and Decisions Concerning Multinational Enterprises: an Attempt to Tame the Shrew.* Nijmegen: Ars Aequi Libri.

Varnavskiy, V. G. (2005). *Partnership between the government and the private sector: forms, projects, risks.* Moscow, Russia: Science.

Veldstra, M., Alexander, C., & Marshall, M. (2014). To certify or not to certify? Separating the organic production and certification decisions. *Food Policy, 49*(2), 429–436. doi:10.1016/j.foodpol.2014.05.010

Velegol, S. B., & Zappe, S. E. (2016). How does a flipped classroom impact classroom climate? In *Proceedings of the ASEE 123rd Annual Conference & exposition.* Academic Press. 10.18260/p.25479

Velten, S., Leventon, J., Jager, N., & Newig, J. (2015). What Is Sustainable Agriculture? A Systematic Review. *Sustainability, 7*(6), 7833–7865. doi:10.3390u7067833

Vezirov, G. (2017). Pedagogical conditions of informational competence development of pedagogical workers in the advanced training system. *Scientific support of the system of advanced training of personnel, 2*(31), 44-50.

Vincent-Caboud, L., Peigné, J., Casagrande, M., & Silva, E. M. (2017). Overview of Organic Cover Crop-Based No-Tillage Technique in Europe: Farmers' Practices and Research Challenges. *Agriculture, 7*(5), 42–58. doi:10.3390/agriculture7050042

Vinokurov, Y., Rotanova, I., Khlebovich, I., & Shibkikh, A. (2000). News to regional health-ecological mapping / GIS sustainable development of territories. In *Proceedings of the International Conference* (Vol. 1, pp. 84-96). Russia, Moscow: Kola Scientific Center.

Vladimirova, T. N., & Zhilavskaya, I. V. (2011). *Molodezh i media. Celi i cennosti. In materialov I Vserossijskoj nauchno-prakticheskoj konferencii.* Moscow: RIC.

Vladimir, S. (2018). *Business & Economics, International Journal of Business and Economic Sciences Applied Research.* IJBESAR.

Voicu, G., Dincă, M., Paraschiv, G., & Moiceanu, G. (2015). A Review Regarding the Biogas Production Through Anaerobic Digestion of Organic Waste. *Advanced Engineering Forum, 13*, 185-193. doi:10.4028/www.scientific.net/AEF.13.185

Voitko, S. A. (2005). On the use of information and communication technologies in English lessons. *Festival of pedagogical ideas.* Retrieved from http://scientificjournal.ru/a/114-fil/1036-the-use-and.html

Volles, N. (2014, July 18). Lifelong learning in the EU: Changing conceptualisations, actors, and policies. *Studies in Higher Education*, 1–21. doi:10.1080/03075079.2014.927852

Wachter, B. (2015). Teaching in English on the Rise in European Higher Education. *International Higher Education,* (52), 3-4. Retrieved from https://ejournals.bc.edu/ojs/index.php/ihe/article/viewFile/8028/7179

Walikhanov, S. (1835–1865). Collected writings.

Walikhanov, S. (1985). Judicial reform note. In S. Walikhanov (1985), Collected works in five volumes—Volume 4—Alma-Ata: The main edition of the Kazakh Soviet Encyclopedia (pp. 77–104). Academic PRess.

Waston, J. (2006). *Golden Arches East: McDonald's in East Asia*. California: Stanford University Press.

Watty, K., McKay, J., & Ngo, L. (2016). Innovators or inhibitors? Accounting faculty resistance to new educational technologies in higher education. *Journal of Accounting Education*, *36*(C), 1–15. doi:10.1016/j.jaccedu.2016.03.003

Weaver, C. (2014, August 21). Consumer agency takes McDonald's off Moscow's menu. *Financial Times*. Retrieved from https://www.ft.com/content/bfdfe12c-288a-11e4-8bda-00144feabdc0?siteedition=intl#comments-anchor

Wen, C., & Mu, Y. (2015). Power and Performance Management in Nonlinear Virtualized Computing Systems via Predictive Control. *PLoS One*, *10*(7), e0134017. doi:10.1371/journal.pone.0134017 PMID:26225769

Wheatley, M. (1999). *Leadership and the new science: Discovering order in a chaotic world*. San Francisco, CA: Berrett-Koehler Publishers.

White, B. A., & Bridwell, C. (2004). Distance learning techniques. In M. Galbraith (Ed.), *Adult learning methods: A guide for effective instruction* (pp. 273–288). Malabar, FL: Krieger.

Wikipedia. (2019). Rhizome. Retrieved from https://en.wikipedia.org/wiki/Rhizome

Wikipedia. (2019). The Soviet famine of 1932–33. Retrieved from https://en.wikipedia.org/wiki/Soviet_famine_of_1932%E2%80%9333

Wohl, J. (2014, December). Most McDonald's in Russia Reopen. *Chicago Tribune*. Retrieved from https://www.chicagotribune.com/business/ct-mcdonalds-russia-1120-biz-20141119-story.html

Wolff, E. (2000). Language and Society. In B. Heine & D. Nurse (Eds.), *African Languages - An Introduction, 317*. Cambridge University Press.

Woolcock, S. (2014). Globalization, versatility. In M. Teló (Ed.), Europe on the way to better global governance (pp. 203-214). Academic Press.

Worland, J. (2014, August). McDonald's Objects to Russia Restaurant Closures. *Time*.

World Bank Group. (2015, April). *Report on Russian Economy*. Retrieved from https://www.worldbank.org/content/dam/Worldbank/document/eca/russia/rer33-rus.pdf

World Bank. (2014). *Doing Business: Going Beyond Efficiency*. Washington, DC: World Bank Group.

World Economic Forum report: Shaping the future of education, gender and work. (2019, June). Retrieved from http://reports.weforum.org

World Wildfire Fund. McDonald's. Retrieved from https://wwf.ru/business/partners/McDonald's/

Wu, J. Y., & Xie, C. (2018). Using Time Pressure and Note-Taking to Prevent Digital Distraction Behavior and Enhance Online Search Performance: Perspectives from the Load Theory of Attention and Cognitive Control. *Computers in Human Behavior, 88, 244-254.* doi:10.1016/j.chb.2018.07.008

WUN. (2019, June). Worldwide Universities Network Annual Report. Retrieved from https://wun.ac.uk/files/annual_reports/wun_report-final_(medium-res).pdf

Xu, Y. (2014). Understanding CSR from the perspective of Chinese diners: The case of McDonald's. *International Journal of Contemporary Hospitality Management, 26*(6), 1002–1020. doi:10.1108/IJCHM-01-2013-0051

Yandex. (n.d.). Retrieved from https://zen.yandex.ru/media/id/5abb502655876be3093d2ea4/-sovremennye-media-i-rol-molodeji-v-jizni-obscestva-5abd2c05d7bf214e3a1ff6bd

Yatimov, Kh. M. (2004). Development of banking services of the national economy (the case of Tajikistan). Unpublished PhD dissertation, Tajik State University of Commerce, Dushanbe, Tajikistan.

Yermish, I. (2000). A case for case studies via video-conferencing. In L. Lau (Ed.), *Distance learning technologies: issues, trends and opportunities*. Hershey, PA: IGI Global. doi:10.4018/978-1-878289-80-3.ch015

Young, A., & Peterson, J. (2011). The EU and the new trade politics. *Journal of European Public Policy, 13*(6), 795–814. doi:10.1080/13501760600837104

Yurdakul, C. (2017, January 1). An investigation of the relationship between autonomous learning and lifelong learning. *International journal of educational research review, 2*(1), 15-20. Retrieved from https://dergipark.org.tr/download/article-file/298782

Zhaleleva, S. Z. (2012). Features of modern transformations of economic systems. In *Proceedings of the VIII International Scientific and practical Conference "Science days – 2012"* (Vol. 21, pp. 32-35). Prague, Czech Republic: Publishing House.

Zhaleleva, S.Z. (2010b). Model of interaction of government and small business in the Republic of Kazakhstan. *Economy: strategy and practice, 2*(14), 82-86.

Zhaleleva, S.Z. (2016). *Management of Partnership Relations in Kazakhstan.* Almaty, Kazakhstan: Nur-print.

Zhaleleva, R. Z., Gabdullin, R. B., & Zavalishina, A. A. (2013). Factor-targeted approach in the implementation of innovative industrialization of the economy of Kazakhstan. *Actual Problems of Economics, 7*, 323–332.

Zhaleleva, S. Z. (2010 a). Development of public-private partnership in the Republic of Kazakhstan. *KIEM Science Journal, 2*(11), 161–164.

Zhaleleva, S. Z. (2013). Constructing the model for public-private partnership in the Republic of Kazakhstan. *Actual Problems of Economics., 7*(145), 315–322.

Zhetpisbayeva, B. (2009). Teoretiko-metodologicheskiye osnovy poliyazychnogo obrazovaniya [Theoretical and methodological principles of multilingual education]. Academic Press. (in Russian)

Zhilavskaya I. V., Avgustevich S. I. (2012). M. Ekologiya mediaprostranstva. In *materialov II Mezhdunarodnoj nauchno-prakticheskoj konferencii*. Academic Press.

Zhu, L., Anagondahalli, D., & Zhang, A. (2017). Social media and culture in crisis communication: McDonald's and KFC crises management in China. *Public Relations Review, 43*(3), 487–492. doi:10.1016/j.pubrev.2017.03.006

Zhvirblis, A. (2015). Elektronnaya demokratiya. Retrieved from https://www.opendemocracy.net/en/elektronnaya-demokratiya

Ziegler, G. (2013). Multilingualism and the language education landscape: Challenges for teacher training in Europe. *Multilingual Education*, *3*(1), 1. doi:10.1186/2191-5059-3-1

Zinets, N. (2014). McDonald's Closes Restaurants In Crimea. *Business Insider.* Retrieved from https://www.businessinsider.com/r-mcdonalds-quits-crimea-as-fears-of-trade-clash-grow-2014-04

Zudin, A.J. (1996). Russia: business and politics (business and government interaction strategies). *World economy and international relations, 4*, 17-27.

About the Contributors

Gainiya Tazhina is a Director of the Center for Social Research at the University of International Business, Kazakhstan. Her research interests focus on the issues of leadership, professional and career development, youth identity, and nationwide blended/e-learning initiatives. Alongside the research activity, she teaches graduate courses online/classroom on Leadership, Management Psychology, etc. The professional achievements include Erasmus Mundus Lectures on Leadership delivered at the Kozminsky University in Warsaw (2017), the OSF FDFP at Columbia University in NYC (2009-2012), and so on. Her collaboration with IGI Global publisher is a long-standing one and, in the past, has resulted in chapters in "Encyclopedia of E-Leadership, Counseling, and Training" (2011), "Handbook of Research on Technologies for Improving the 21st Century Workforce: Tools for Lifelong Learning" (2012), "Encyclopedia of Information Science and Technology" (4th ed., 2017). Her current work with the publisher is co-editing the book titled "Toward Sustainability Through Digital Technologies and Practices in the Eurasian Region" (to be released in March 2020).

* * *

Aigul Adibayeva graduated from Abay State University. Specialist in international relations, master of economic sciences, candidate of political sciences. University of Kentucky USA, Kentucky, Lexington (1995-1996), student exchange program of Kazakh-American center, undergraduate program exchange with Major in Political Science. Presidential Program Bolashak (1996-1998), USA, San Francisco, San-Francisco State University (SFSU), Undergraduate program, with Major in Political Science. Current work at KIMEP University. Associate dean of the School of Social Sciences. Research interests are in international relations, regional studies, international business and world history. Position held: Full-time Assistant Professor and Associate Dean of the college of social sciences (CSS). Selected articles: Cultural Learnings From America: Kazakhstan Looks At The Trump Administration. In Trump's First 100 Days as President of the United States: International Perspectives and Responses Edited by John Dixon and Max Skidmore; Westphalia Press, Washington, DC (2018). Nation-building and Cultural Policy in Kazakhstan. European Scientific Journal, ISSN: 1857 – 7431, December 2013, special edition, vol. 2, pp. 265-279. A Post-Crisis World: The Chinese Factor in the Transformation of Kazakhstan. Journal of South Asian and Middle Eastern Studies, Villanova University, Villanova PA, issue XXXVII no. 2., 2013. "H. Mackinder's Legacy Today: New Challenges for Kazakhstan and Central Asia", a chapter in the edited book: H. Mackinder and the International Relations in Central Asia (Editor: Nick Megoran) published by: C. Hurst & Co Publishers Ltd., London, ISBN-13: 978-1849042437/ December 2012. "Kazakhstan and OSCE", - a chapter to the electronic manual for Foreign Policy of Kazakhstan Readings / Editor K. White, - KIMEP, 2012-2013; Dictionary of Political Science for Beginners in Transition Countries, electronic resource, KIMEP University, 2013.

Askhatova Ainur was born in 1993 in Almaty, Kazakhstan. A bachelor's degree diploma was obtained on specialty of translation studies in 2015. During the period from 2013-2019 has worked as a translator for the numbers of translation agencies. In 2018 entered the University of International Business to obtain a master's degree on specialty of Teacher of English language.

Aizhan Assylbekova is an Acting Associate Professor in the Department of Cartography and Geoinformatics at Al-Farabi Kazakh National University. Her studies relate to the Application of Geoinformation System (GIS) and Remote Sensing data in geospatial environmental studies, and sustainable development. Aizhan Assylbekova has about 20 academic publications resulted from her consistent research interest in new perspectives of Physical Geography and Remote Sensing methods. She is a grantee of the international scholarships Erasmus Mundus GSmart - Spatial ICT Infrastructures for Smart Places (2015) and EURASIA-PACIFIC UNINET Technology (2013).

Uldana Baizyldayeva is an assistant professor at KIMEP University, PhD in IT, Kazakhstan. The author's research areas: decision support methods system, big data analysis, business intelligence systems, learning management systems, and statistics.

Aizhan Daukenova was born in 1993 in Ust-Kamenogorsk, East Kazakhstan. In 2015, she graduated from S. Amanzholov East Kazakhstan State University, the faculty of Philology. In 2014-2015 she participated in the Erasmus exchange program at University of Wroclaw in Poland. Aizhan has worked as a teacher of English for more than 6 years. Currently, she is a master's degree student at University of International Business, and an English teacher there. Research focus of her master's thesis is the usage of English as a medium of instruction in higher educational institutions.

Galym Issabayev, Honorary Architect of Kazakhstan, is a Head of the Architectural Bureau and an Associate Professor of the Kazakh Leading Academy of Architecture and Civil Engineering, Kazakhstan. He has also 30-year experience in managing design and construction companies. The author of many projects of residential and public buildings. Participated in the development of new regulatory requirements for the content of urban development projects in Kazakhstan. Has more than 50 published scientific papers and articles, as well as international diplomas, and certificates of honor by the governmental agencies. His research interests are in the sphere of regional architecture, energy efficient architecture, sustainable territory planning, and eco-urbanism. Author of the Digital Agropolis concept. Participated in the international forums and conferences in many countries. In 2016, published an e-textbook "Energy-efficient technologies and modern architecture". His monograph "The Features of the Style of Architecture of Kazakhstan: the Second Half of XIX - Beginning of XX Century" (2017), and his textbook "Modern Urbanism: main innovations and development prospects" (2019) were awarded by the first-degree diplomas of Interregional Public Organization for the Promotion of Architectural Education.

Alma Issabayeva is an Associate Professor in Management at the University of International Business (UIB), Kazakhstan. Has 20-year experience in the international development agencies such as EU Tacis, UNDP, and Islamic Development Bank. Participated in development of strategic documents, technical assistance programs and investment projects for Kazakhstan and other Central Asia countries in the sphere of public service, energy, agriculture, small and medium enterprise development, higher education, gender in development, etc. Now is teaching Strategic Management, HR Management, Business Communication, and other courses. Her research interests: food security, socio-economic territory planning, social infrastructure development. Developed a concept of Bio-Food Security, participated in the international scientific conferences, and published several articles developed together with her spouse Dr. Galym Issabayev: Emerging Countries for the World: Bio-Food Security through Technologies (2012), Bio-Food Security for Future Generations (2013), Bio-Food Security: Challenge for Central Asia (2016). Awarded by the certificate of honor of the Ministry of Education and Science of the Republic of Kazakhstan (2018).

Zhibek Kaisar was born on February 26, 1993 in Taraz. From 2010 to 2014 studied at Kazakh Ablai Khan University of International Relations and World Languages. From 2014 to 2016 worked in the linguistic center "Zharkyn bolashak". From 2017 to the present, Zhibek has been working as a teacher of English in a private school. In 2018 entered UIB, to get a master's degree. At the moment she is an English teacher and a master's student at UIB.

Anastassiya A. Khalikova received her MS in two foreign languages (English and Chinese) from the University of International Business in 2019. In 2018 she was hired as an English teacher by the University of International Business and is currently working there. She writes about teaching and learning the English Language.

Meruyert Koshegulova is currently a Ph.D. candidate majoring in Educational Technologies in Seoul, Dongguk University, South Korea. Interested in teaching with digital technologies, especially online education, Massive Open Online Courses, its development and implementation in CIS Countries.

Shokirjon Mahmadov received his MA in International Area Studies from the University of Tsukuba, Japan in 2012 and his second MA in Finance and Credit from the Russian Tajik Slavic University, Tajikistan in 2019. He has extensive working experience with World Bank Tajikistan Office, the University of Central Asia. Currently he is a Senior Program Officer in Japan International Cooperation Agency (Tajikistan Office). He is also a part-time lecturer at the Faculty of International Marketing and Management of the Technological University of Tajikistan. He is one of the developers of a new cross-debate format in Central Asia.

Yerkhan Mindetbay, PhD in Education, Southampton Education School, University of Southampton. PEGasus group member at the University of Southampton. CAS (Computing at School) Research Group member in the UK. Bachelor and Master degree in Computer Science and Engineering. 10 years of work experience as a teacher of Computer Science at high schools in Kazakhstan, during these years had positions as a vice-principal and a project coordinator.

Judith Parker is an adjunct Assistant Professor in the Organization and Leadership Department at Teachers College/Columbia University in New York teaching graduate courses that are totally on-line, totally classroom and blended delivery formats. She has earned an Ed.D. degree from Teachers College/ Columbia University and an M.S. degree in physics from Purdue University in Indiana. Judith is co-author of the book "Pedagogical and Andragogical Teaching and Learning with Information Communication Technologies" and has authored numerous chapters and articles on cross-cultural workplace training and the practice and theories of adult learning and effective technology integration. She has participated in conferences globally, most recently in India and Greece. Judith has over 20 years experience in leadership positions within global business organizations working extensively with technical managers and technical employees throughout Asia and Europe in leadership and technical training skill development. She has received the American Association of Physics Teachers Innovative Teaching Award, the 3M Community Volunteer Award and has been elected a Fellow of the American Association for the Advancement of Science.

Alexandr Pasternak is an Associate Professor of the "Finance and Accounting" department, University of International Business, Kazakhstan, PhD (Economics specialty). Author of 30 publications, among which are scientific journals, monographs, brochures, conference proceedings. Participant of scientific projects in Kazakhstan. Scientific interests are Economy, Electric Power Complex, Metallurgical Complex, Environment, Competitiveness, Strategic Management.

Danial Saari graduated from Abay State University. Specialist in international relations, master of economic sciences. Currently works at Almaty Management University. Head of the Center of political research of the School of Public policy and Law. Research interests are in international relations, regional studies, international business and world history. Coauthor of the "Tales with tails. Bed-time stories" ISBN: 9781477132524, New Jersey, USA 2012. Author of the novel "The lover of blue eyes" published by the Association of the Ecology of Kazakhstani Culture "Golden Age". Almaty, 2017. Coauthor of the "Economic theory: textbook" (in Kazakh, English and Russian). Almaty: AlmaU, 2018. Coauthor of the monograph "International business in the frameworks of multilateral diplomacy" (in English). Almaty: AlmaU, 2018. Appreciation letter from the Association of Higher Education Institutions of Kazakhstan for a contribution into development of country's higher education and productive work in the preparation of specialists of a new generation, Almaty 2016. Appreciation letters from the Akim of the Almaty city and Ministry of Education and Science of the Republic of Kazakhstan for a valued contribution into development of the higher education of the Republic of Kazakhstan, Almaty 2019.

Svetlana A. Silkina got her MS in two foreign languages (English and Chinese) from the University of International Business in 2019. Since 2018 she has been working as an English teacher at the University of International Business.

Natalya Tsychuyeva is an Acting Associate Professor at the Department of Cartography and Geoinformatics at Al-Farabi Kazakh National University and leader researcher in National Center of Space Research and Technologies. Her professional interest is Remote Sensing and Geoinformation System (GIS) for application of land cover/land use changes. Natalya Tsychuyeva has about 30 academic publications resulted from her consistent researches in perspectives of Remote Sensing methods for different uses.

Laura Turarbekova, PhD in Philosophy (Jean Moulin Lyon 3), Assistant Professor at the Faculty of Philosophy and Political Science at the Al-Farabi Kazakh National University, Head of the Project "Multidimensional Research on History, Problems and Perspectives for the Implementation of International Education Projects in the Republic of Kazakhstan" 2018-2020. Postdoctoral fellow (15/03/2018

- 15/06/2018) - FMSH "Atlas - Central Asia - France" in Centre Gilles Gaston Granger of Aix-Marseille University with the project entitled "Children of Postmodernism: The Peculiarities of Reception and Implementation of the Postmodernist Epistemological Programme in France and the Post-Soviet Space Countries"

Raziya Zhaleleva is the Chief Scientific Officer of the Institute of Economics, Committee of Science, the Ministry of Education and Science, Kazakhstan, doctor of economic sciences ("Regional Economy" specialty). Author of more than 100 publications, among which are scientific journals, monographs, brochures, conference proceedings. Coordinator and participant of scientific projects in Kazakhstan. Scientific interests are National Economy, Regional Economy, Competitiveness, Metallurgical Complex, Innovative Industrialization, Factor-Targeted Management, Strategic Management, Public-Private Partnership, Government.

Sofiya Zhaleleva is an Associate Professor of the "Management and Business" department, University of International Business, PhD ("Management" specialty). Author of 40 publications, among which are scientific journals, monographs, brochures, conference proceedings. Coordinator and participant of scientific projects in Kazakhstan and Europe. Scientific interests are Management, Strategic Management, Public-Private Partnership, Competitiveness, Metallurgical Complex, National Economy.

Index

G

H

I

J

K

L

M

N

O

P

R

S

T

U

V

W

Purchase Print, E-Book, or Print + E-Book

IGI Global books are available in three unique pricing formats:
Print Only, E-Book Only, or Print + E-Book. Shipping fees apply.

www.igi-global.com

Recommended Reference Books

ISBN: 978-1-5225-1955-3
© 2017; 397 pp.
List Price: $205

ISBN: 978-1-5225-8217-5
© 2019; 102 pp.
List Price: $135

ISBN: 978-1-5225-8163-5
© 2019; 393 pp.
List Price: $185

ISBN: 978-1-5225-6061-6
© 2019; 396 pp.
List Price: $265

ISBN: 978-1-5225-7195-7
© 2019; 310 pp.
List Price: $195

ISBN: 978-1-5225-8194-9
© 2019; 328 pp.
List Price: $145

Do you want to stay current on the latest research trends, product announcements, news and special offers?
Join IGI Global's mailing list today and start enjoying exclusive perks sent only to IGI Global members.
Add your name to the list at **www.igi-global.com/newsletters.**

Publisher of Peer-Reviewed, Timely, and Innovative Academic Research

IGI Global
DISSEMINATOR OF KNOWLEDGE

www.igi-global.com Sign up at www.igi-global.com/newsletters facebook.com/igiglobal twitter.com/igiglobal linkedin.com/igiglobal

www.ingramcontent.com/pod-product-compliance
Lightning Source LLC
LaVergne TN
LVHW081252011026
849162LV00006BA/1529